MIC

To the memory of Hans J. Dernburg, 1901-1966

MACROECONOMIC ANALYSIS

An Introduction to
Comparative Statics and Dynamics

THOMAS FREDERICK DERNBURG
and JUDITH DUKLER DERNBURG
Oberlin College

ADDISON-WESLEY PUBLISHING COMPANY
Reading, Massachusetts • Menlo Park, California • London • Don Mills, Ontario

Preface

The present volume has several purposes, all of which it attempts to pursue more or less simultaneously. It assumes that the reader is an undergraduate economics or mathematics major or a beginning graduate student who has had the benefit of a fairly rigorous and comprehensive first course in macroeconomic theory and who has been exposed to college mathematics through integral calculus. It also assumes that the undergraduate reader is the type of person who is contemplating graduate work in economics and that he therefore is concerned with finding out how economists think and how they approach some of the analytical problems that interest them.

For such students—and we have been fortunate to have had a large number of them in our classes at Oberlin College—it has always seemed to us that a second course in macroeconomics should attempt to provide them with a taste of graduate work and to emphasize such matters as model building and the techniques and methods of analysis. A student who wishes to specialize in monetary theory, or fiscal economics, or business cycle analysis, can pursue these specialties in graduate school where he will probably receive better instruction in these specialties than we are able to provide. On the other hand, the emphasis on analytical technique not only provides basic knowledge— knowledge that is pertinent to nearly all areas of economic analysis—but also helps to motivate the student by showing him how to move from the passive role of the learner to the active role of the analyst.

The book attempts to put into writing some of the topics that are normally considered in the second course in macroeconomics at Oberlin. In this course we attempt primarily to push our knowledge of macroeconomic theory beyond the first-course level. We attempt, secondly, to study these macroeconomic problems by resort to the model-building approach. Third, and in order to accomplish the first two aims, we attempt to develop those mathematical tools with which most of the students who take the course are not likely to have had extensive previous contact.

Our endeavor, therefore, is to wear three hats at the same time. Such an endeavor, even if it is possible to crowd one hat on top of another, must at times appear clumsy and a bit tortured. The need to develop the mathematics in a coherent fashion sometimes leads to a curious juxtaposition of economic topics. The desire to develop the economics in a systematic manner, without leaving too many intervening gaps, sometimes causes a complicated mathematical topic to be treated prior to a simpler one. The emphasis on methods of analysis, finally, causes some more or less trivial economic problems to be considered while more important ones are left in abeyance. Nevertheless, we are persuaded that the enterprise is worth a try. Former students affirm that they found this way of doing things both interesting and stimulating. Moreover, many of them report that the experience gave them a significant advantage when they entered graduate school, and that it provided them with a more solid background than they would have obtained in a more conventional course in macroeconomic theory.

We wish to make it clear that this volume is not intended to be a book on mathematics or a cookbook of mathematical economics. Any reputable mathematician would shudder at the superficial treatment of many topics, and he would be altogether appalled at our failure to attempt the proof of theorems. But what the mathematician would perhaps regard as a decisive deficiency we hope to convert into an advantage. Many of us, and we freely admit that we ourselves are among the most chronic of such cases, have great difficulty understanding mathematics when it is removed from the context of practical applications whose dimensions we are able to comprehend. Consequently, what we wish to do here is to discuss concrete economic problems and to introduce mathematical tools as they are needed to solve these problems. No mathematical topic is introduced for its own sake or without its being applied to some problem of economic theory.

To get down to specifics: The book is divided into three parts. The first part is devoted to comparative-static macroeconomic analysis. This involves the mechanics of fiscal policy, the theory of economic policy, the comparative statics of the Keynesian system, and some elements of interindustry economics. The main mathematical tool is the differential calculus, with which we assume the student to be familiar. However, interindustry analysis requires matrix algebra, and since this is usually not taught in beginning college math courses, we spend a good deal of time on the elements of this body of mathematics.

Part II, which is devoted to single-equation dynamics, takes up such subjects as the dynamic multiplier, the growth of income and debt, business cycle theory, and neoclassical growth economics. A good deal of time is necessarily spent in this part of the book in helping the student to understand and to work with difference and differential equations.

In Part III we turn to a discussion of multisectoral static and dynamic models. The chief topics covered here are the general principles of stability analysis in simultaneous equation systems, the stability of the Keynesian system and the correspondence principle, multicountry trade, and the stability of the Leontief system. An attempt is made in this part of the book to bring together the tools of analysis that we have attempted to introduce to the reader in earlier chapters.

As for credits: We must first thank present and past students in Economics 328 at Oberlin College for their willingness to serve as guinea pigs and for their many valuable insights and suggestions.   Second, Professor W. H. Locke Anderson of the University of Michigan and Mr. Robert Engle of Cornell University both worked over the manuscript with great care, and both attempted valiantly to impose order upon the reigning chaos. Third, we thank Vera Alferio for typing the manuscript with her characteristic competence and speed. Finally, we regard it as appropriate to thank the staff of Addison-Wesley for seeing so carefully and diligently to the production and publication of the book.

As usual, we acknowledge that we have no one to blame but ourselves for remaining errors, omissions, and other shortcomings.

Oberlin, Ohio   T. F. D.
March 1969   J. D. D.

Contents

PART II: SINGLE EQUATION DYNAMICS

Part I
COMPARATIVE-STATIC
MACROECONOMIC ANALYSIS

CHAPTER 1

Comparative Statics, Dynamics, and the Concept of Equilibrium

Economic analysis has long profited from attempts to analyze the complicated interactions of the economic system by means of mathematical *models*. *Microeconomic* models focus attention upon the behavior of individual economic agents —the individual consumer, the individual producer, the individual market. *Macroeconomic* models, by contrast, abstract from the interrelation between individual agents and describe overall economic behavior in terms of such broad aggregates as total consumption, total investment, government expenditures, and the like.

In the main, this book deals with macroeconomic models. Among the topics to be considered are such familiar ones as the theory of income and employment, the modern theory of economic growth, contemporary approaches to business-cycle theory, and the analysis of the stability of equilibrium.

Beyond the strictly macroeconomic models are those that move in the micro direction by *disaggregating* the macro variables to the extent that they treat entire industries, sectors, regions, or countries as separate entities in the same way that the microeconomist treats the household and the firm.

As a prerequisite for the study of many of the topics dealt with in this volume, it is necessary to have a fairly firm and comprehensive grasp of the modern theory of income and employment. While the reader will undoubtedly already have had a first course in macroeconomics before he moves on to this book, it is nevertheless useful to begin with a quick overall survey. The provision of such a survey, together with a discussion of some more advanced topics, is the purpose of Part I of the book. In general, Part II deals with strictly macroeconomic models, while Part III moves in the direction of microeconomics and focuses attention upon particular industries and regions.

In technical terms, the analysis of Part I is known as *comparative-static* analysis, while the work of Parts II and III resides primarily in the realm of *dynamics*. It is important, at the outset, to understand just exactly what these modes of analysis mean. The remainder of this introductory chapter is therefore devoted to a discussion of the nature of comparative statics and dynamics and to the concept of equilibrium.

The models which the economist constructs to illustrate a process or the effect of a policy generally consist of a set of *behavioral relations* and a set of *equilibrium conditions*. The models, moreover, may be *comparative static* or they may be *dynamic*. As an example of a comparative-static model, consider the simple market model,

$$D = a + bP, \tag{1.1}$$

$$S = u + vP, \tag{1.2}$$

$$D = S, \tag{1.3}$$

where D stands for quantity demanded, S for quantity supplied, and P for market price, while a, b, u, and v are *parameters* which have the characteristic that their values remain unaffected when the variables D, S, and P change. The first equation of the system is the demand equation; the second is the supply equation. Both equations are behavioral relations: They say that quantity demanded by buyers and quantity supplied by sellers both are functions of price. The third equation is the equilibrium condition, which states that price must adjust in such a way as to *clear the market*, i.e., to equate quantity demanded with quantity supplied.

There being three equations and three unknowns, the system may be solved for the equilibrium values of price and quantity. Substituting 1.1 and 1.2 into the equilibrium condition 1.3 yields

$$a + bP = u + vP,$$

which implies that

$$\bar{P} = \frac{a - u}{v - b} \tag{1.4}$$

is the equilibrium price. The bar over P indicates that the calculated value of P is the equilibrium value. If we wish to calculate the equilibrium quantity, we need merely substitute $\bar{P}$ into either the demand or the supply equation to obtain

$$\bar{Q} = \frac{av - bu}{v - b}. \tag{1.5}$$

The situation is depicted in Fig. 1.1. The vertical axis is the quantity axis, while the horizontal axis is the price axis. The vertical intercepts of the demand and supply equations are the parameters a and u, respectively, while b and v are the respective slopes. The intersection defines the equilibrium values $\bar{P}$, and $\bar{Q}$ as previously calculated.

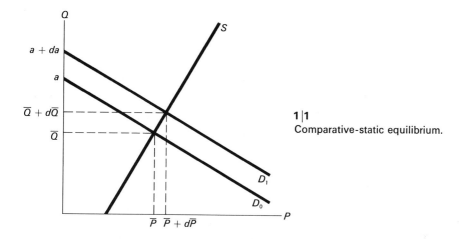

1|1
Comparative-static equilibrium.

The next question that might be asked in comparative-static analysis is: By how much will the equilibrium values of the variables change if there is a shift in one of the parameters? For example, suppose that consumer tastes change in such a way as to make them wish to buy an additional amount da (da stands for "change in a") at all prices. As a consequence of this change in tastes the demand curve shifts up by an amount da, and a new intersection of the demand and supply curves, together with a new equilibrium price and quantity, result. Analytically, we may take Eqs. 1.4 and 1.5 and differentiate them both with respect to a. This yields

$$d\bar{P} = \left(\frac{1}{v - b}\right) da$$

and

$$d\bar{Q} = \left(\frac{v}{v - b}\right) da$$

as the respective changes in the equilibrium values of price and quantity.

It is important to note that the equilibrium values of variables in comparative-static analysis merely represent the solutions to a set of simultaneous equations. There is no indication in a model of this sort about the time path by which the system moves from one equilibrium to another, or, indeed, *whether the new equilibrium will in fact be reached.*

To illustrate the difficulty, let us again consider the same market model as before but let us now date the variables. We assume that quantity demanded during time period t depends on the market price that prevails during that period. We therefore write

$$D_t = a + bP_t \tag{1.6}$$

as the demand equation. Let us next assume, as is often the case in agricultural

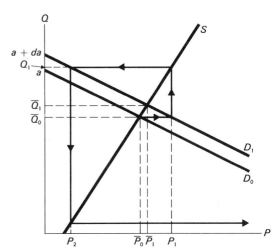

1|2
Unstable equilibrium.

markets, that it takes producers one period to adapt output to changes in price. The supply equation may therefore be written

$$S_t = u + vP_{t-1}. \tag{1.7}$$

Finally, we assume that price adjusts in such a way as to clear the market. Therefore we have the equilibrium condition

$$D_t = S_t. \tag{1.8}$$

If we combine these equations we obtain the expression

$$P_t = \frac{u-a}{b} + \left(\frac{v}{b}\right)P_{t-1}. \tag{1.9}$$

Earlier, when we combined Eqs. 1.1, 1.2, and 1.3, we were able to solve for the equilibrium price. Now, however, we obtain a *difference equation* that expresses price at any time as a function of the price that prevailed in the preceding period. The model has now become a *dynamic* one. Time is included explicitly, and the model specifies how price will react when it is away from its equilibrium value. As can be seen from Eq. 1.9, if we know the price in any period, the equation permits us to calculate it for the subsequent period and, by continuous replacement of P_{t-1} with P_t, for all subsequent periods.

Difference equations such as Eq. 1.9 will be examined in detail in Part II. For our present purpose it is sufficient to explore the behavior of price in this model by means of a diagram. The demand and supply equations in Fig. 1.2 look just exactly the same as those of Fig. 1.1. The equilibrium price, moreover, is the same. Equation 1.9 does not reveal at a glance what the equilibrium price is. However, when we recognize that we could be in equilibrium only if the period-by-period price remains the same, we may let $P_t = P_{t-1} = \bar{P}$. Upon replacing P_t and P_{t-1} by $\bar{P}$ in Eq. 1.9, we obtain

$$\bar{P} = \frac{a - u}{v - b},$$

which, not surprisingly, is exactly the same equilibrium price that we obtained with the static model.

Consider Fig. 1.2 and assume that the market is in equilibrium at $\bar{P}_0$ and $\bar{Q}_0$. As before, assume that consumer demand increases and that the demand curve shifts up by an amount da. The new equilibrium solution is at $\bar{P}_1$ and $\bar{Q}_1$. But by the assumptions of the present model, output cannot be adjusted to changes in price immediately. Consequently, if the market is to be cleared with only output level $\bar{Q}_0$ available, the price must rise to P_1. Producers now react to this higher price by producing output Q_1. However, since consumers only wish to purchase $\bar{Q}_0$ at price P_1, there is excess supply on the market and price now falls to P_2. This will give rise to a subsequent reduction in output, and when this supply restriction occurs, market price again rises.

What we have attempted to trace out above is the well-known *cobweb* type of market behavior which is characterized by period-by-period oscillations in price and quantity. In the particular case we have illustrated the behavior of price is *explosive*, or *antidamped*, which means that once we depart from equilibrium, the oscillations grow ever larger. Therefore, even though the intersection of the demand with the supply function defines an equilibrium point, such a point is *unstable*, by which we mean that once we depart from the equilibrium point, we tend to move farther and farther away as time goes on.

The possibility of unstable equilibria implies that the comparative-static solutions may be wholly misleading. If we begin at $\bar{Q}_0$ and $\bar{P}_0$, and the demand curve shifts by da, comparative-static analysis predicts that we will move to a new equilibrium at $\bar{Q}_1$, $\bar{P}_1$. However, we have seen that this solution will not necessarily be relevant, because the system may behave in such a way as to produce a progressive divergence from equilibrium. We did not, however, know this until we examined the underlying dynamics of the market. Thus comparative-static analysis, while exceedingly useful, must be supplemented by dynamic analysis. It is not enough to know the equilibrium solutions, we must also know if the equilibria are stable—i.e., if the system will actually return to equilibrium following a disturbance—before we can regard the comparative-static solutions as correct.

The proposition that comparative-static analysis must be supplemented by dynamic analysis before the results can be trusted is an extremely important principle of economic analysis. The idea was developed by Professor Samuelson,*

---

* Paul A. Samuelson, *Foundations of Economic Analysis* (Cambridge, Mass.: Harvard University Press, 1947,) Chapter 11.

who called it the "correspondence principle." Its importance to economic analysis is so great that we shall devote practically all of Part III to the exploration of its implications. In the meantime, we conclude this introductory chapter by adding a few notes to the discussion of the concept of equilibrium.

As we have seen, the equilibrium values of a set of variables are those values that result from the solution of a set of simultaneous equations. The equilibrium may be stable; it may be unstable; or it may be neutral. If it is stable, the variable in question will return to equilibrium following a disturbance. If it is unstable, the variable will exhibit progressive divergence from equilibrium as time passes. If the equilibrium is neutral, the variable will tend to remain wherever the disturbance puts it.

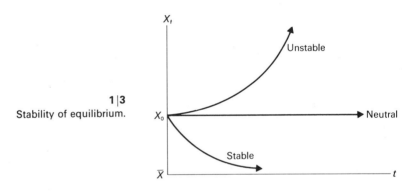

1|3
Stability of equilibrium.

The three cases are illustrated in Fig. 1.3. The variable X_t is plotted on the vertical axis, while time is measured horizontally. The equilibrium value is $\bar{X}$. It is assumed that at time $t = 0$, a disturbance takes place of a sort that makes $X_t = X_0$. In the stable case, X_t approaches $\bar{X}$; in the unstable case, X_t diverges progressively; and in the neutral case, X_t remains at X_0.

The time paths sketched out in Fig. 1.3 are *monotonic*, by which we roughly mean that X_t always keeps moving in the same direction. However, it is also possible for the system to exhibit oscillating behavior, as in the cobweb example, and it is further possible that these oscillations may proceed in a set of discrete period-by-period jumps (again as in the cobweb case) or in a set of smooth continuous waves. However, in all these cases the same concept of stability of equilibrium holds. If the oscillations grow larger in amplitude, the equilibrium about which the oscillations take place is unstable. If the oscillations grow smaller, the equilibrium is stable. And if the oscillations are of uniform amplitude, the equilibrium is neutral.

CHAPTER 2

Income Determination, Fiscal Policy, and the Theory of Economic Policy

2.1 INTRODUCTION

The present chapter begins with a review of the simple theory of income determination. The purpose of the review is to make sure that we begin further work
at the same starting point. We then turn to some questions of fiscal policy: What
are the effects on the level of income of changes in the level of government purchases and in the rate of income taxation? Under what conditions, and why, are
changes in government purchases usually expected to have a more high-powered
effect on the level of income than an equivalent change in tax yield? What is the
nature of automatic or "built-in" stability, and so on? Finally, we shall turn to
the macroeconomic counterpart of welfare economics. This fascinating subject,
which is variously known as "public economics" or "the theory of economic
policy," raises questions such as how a given set of economic targets can best be
achieved through the manipulation of the available policy instruments. The only
bit of mathematics with which the reader will have to be familiar in order to
follow the argument of this chapter is the differential calculus. Moreover, the
examples are so simple that no preliminary review of calculus ought to be
required.

2.2 A REVIEW OF THE SIMPLE THEORY OF INCOME AND EMPLOYMENT *

The theory of income and employment is an aggregative theory which groups all
markets for goods and services into a single *product market*, all financial markets into
a *money market*, and all markets for factor services into a *labor market*. Customarily,

---

* The material in this section is adapted from my paper, "Income and Employment Theory,"
International Encyclopedia of the Social Sciences, Vol. 7, pp. 122–131. For a more detailed discussion
the reader may wish to refer to Dernburg and McDougall, *Macroeconomics*, 3d edition (New
York: McGraw-Hill, 1967), Part II.

the analysis proceeds with a description of the properties of the individual markets and then links them together to achieve a simultaneous equilibrium solution. In this chapter we shall be concerned exclusively with the product market and we shall assume that developments in the financial and the factor markets have no bearing on the outcome.

The sum total of the production of final goods and services (defined as output that is not resold in any form during the accounting period) when valued at market prices is the *gross national product*. The deduction of a *capital consumption allowance* for the replacement of capital equipment that was used up during the course of producing current output reduces this total to the *net national product*, or NNP. When NNP is "deflated" by an index of prices in order to obtain constant dollar values, we call the resultant figure *real NNP*, which henceforth we denote simply as *income*, and to which we give the symbol Y.

The level of income may be broken down into several components. Typically, we divide the economy into sectors and examine the determinants of spending and the income receipts of each sector. A complete analysis would include a household sector, a business sector, a government sector, and a foreign sector. However, for the moment we assume the presence only of a household and a business sector, reserving the addition of the government sector to the next section.

The portion of production that is purchased by households is denoted as consumption, C. The remainder of the nation's output accrues to the business sector in the form of capital goods (new plant and equipment) and as additions to the stocks of finished and unfinished goods. Denoting the product that is retained by the business sector as net realized investment, I_r, we have the basic definition

$$Y \equiv C + I_r.$$

Provided that the business sector retains no earnings, each dollar of expenditure will be received by households as income. Since households are free either to consume or to save their incomes we also have

$$Y \equiv C + S,$$

where S is the level of saving. When we equate the two expressions, we obtain the fundamental accounting identity

$$I_r = S.$$

Having now taken care of some definitional matters, we may proceed with the theory. Let us consider consumption first. Although aggregate consumption spending is related to many variables, we confine ourselves here to the original Keynesian proposition that consumption is an increasing function of the level of income. In Fig. 2.2.1 the curve labeled C represents an illustrative aggregate consumption function. Consumption rises as income rises but not by as much. In the situation depicted in Fig. 2.2.1 a rise in income of 200 units from an initial level of 200 is accompanied by an increase in consumption of 150 to a level of 350.

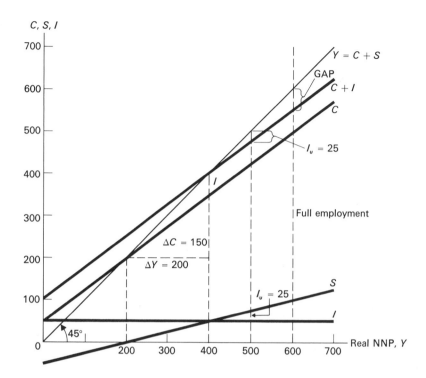

2|2|1
Simple income determination.

The slope of the consumption function $(\partial C/\partial Y)$ is the marginal propensity to consume, which, in this example, has a value of $\frac{3}{4}$.

Because saving is the difference between income and consumption, the level of saving can be measured as the vertical distance between the 45° line and the consumption function, or, as the separate S-schedule of Fig. 2.2.1. The ratio of the change in saving to the corresponding change in income (the slope of the savings function, $\partial S/\partial Y$), is the marginal propensity to save. Since an extra dollar of income must either be spent or saved, the sum of the marginal propensity to consume and the marginal propensity to save must be one.

The consumption function is a schedule of intentions. It indicates what the level of consumption spending will be at different levels of income. To the consumption function we now add a schedule of business intended-investment spending. This schedule may be plotted separately (as the I-curve of Fig. 2.2.1) or it may be added to the consumption function in order to obtain the *aggregate-demand*, $C + I$, schedule. The aggregate-demand schedule shows the level of total spending that will be forthcoming at different levels of income. In the present example it is assumed that intended investment is 50 at all levels of income.

Care must now be taken to distinguish between intended investment, I, and realized investment, I_r. Realized investment consists of all output that is retained by the business sector. Intended investment is only that portion of output that the business sector actually intended to retain when production plans were formulated. Realized investment will exceed intended investment if business overestimates the level of potential sales and it will fall short of intended investment if potential sales are underestimated. The amount of this discrepancy is unintended investment, I_u, so that by definition, $I_r \equiv I + I_u$.

The presence of unintended investment implies that sales forecasts have been mistaken. In order to reduce unintended inventory accumulation output will be cut back; or, in order to offset unintended-inventory depletion (negative unintended investment), production will be increased. Intentions and realizations, then, will be equal only when unintended investment is absent. Since by definition,

$$I_r \equiv I + I_u \equiv S,$$

and since equilibrium requires I_u to be zero, we infer that equilibrium in the market for final goods and services requires intended investment to equal saving. Although realized investment must always equal saving, intended investment will equal saving only when the product market is in equilibrium.

A glance at Fig. 2.2.1 confirms that $I = S$ at an income level of 400. This income level must necessarily also be where the aggregate-demand schedule cuts the 45° line. Any other income level would be characterized by the presence of unintended investment. For example, if business produces 500 billion worth of output, consumption will be 425 and intended investment will be 50. Total demand of 475 therefore falls short of production of 500, with the consequence that unintended investment is 25. Realized investment is 75 and this does, to be sure, equal the level of saving. But undesired inventories will pile up so long as production is maintained at 500, and this means that business must revise its sales estimates and reduce the level of output.

Thus the equilibrium condition may be stated in terms of the equality of intended investment and saving or, and what amounts to the same thing, in terms of equality of aggregate demand and aggregate output. The equilibrium condition may therefore be written either as

$$I = S \quad \text{or as} \quad Y = C + I.$$

Any change that raises the aggregate-demand schedule will raise the level of income. Moreover, the rise in the level of income will exceed the size of the shift in aggregate demand that brings it about. Referring again to Fig. 2.2.1, we may suppose, for a moment, that intended investment is zero and observe that the equilibrium level of income would be 200, since that is where saving is zero. Assume next that intended investment rises from zero to 50 and remains there. The equilibrium level of income jumps to 400—an increase not of 50 but of 200. This multiplied increase in income comes about because the increase in investment spending raises income, which then induces additional consumption spending. It can be seen in Fig. 2.2.1 that the rise in income from 200 to 400 is composed of the investment rise of 50 plus a consumption increase of 150.

The ratio of the change in income to the change in investment is the *multiplier*, and its numerical value is the reciprocal of the marginal propensity to save. If intended investment rises by one dollar, equilibrium will not be restored until saving has also risen by one dollar. If the marginal propensity to save has a value of x, it will require an income increase of $1/x$ dollars to raise saving by one dollar. In the present example, when income rises by one dollar, saving rises by 25 cents. Since saving must rise by one dollar, the required increase in income must be four, and the value of the multiplier is therefore four.

The multiplier permits us to calculate the effect on the level of income of an upward shift in the aggregate-demand schedule. The multiplier also tells us by how much aggregate demand must be raised to reach an income level which will bring full employment. In Fig. 2.2.1, if the equilibrium level of income is 400 and the full-employment level of income is 600, the required increase in income is 200. Since the multiplier is 4, a policy that shifts the aggregate-demand schedule up by 50 will raise income to the full-employment level. The required shift in aggregate demand can also be found by measuring the deflationary gap, which is defined as the deficiency of aggregate demand at full-employment production. Inspection of Fig. 2.2.1 confirms that the magnitude of this gap is 50.

Let us now put this analysis into algebraic form. The consumption function in our example is linear and may therefore be written as

$$C = a + bY = 50 + 0.75Y,$$

where a is the intercept of the consumption function and can be identified at the point of intersection of the function with the vertical axis in Fig. 2.2.1. Parameter b is the marginal propensity to consume. The saving function must be

$$S = Y - C = -a + (1 - b)Y = -50 + 0.25Y,$$

where $1 - b$ is the marginal propensity to save. Since the equilibrium condition is $I = S$, we may insert the saving function and write

$$I = -a + (1 - b)Y, \qquad 50 = -50 + 0.25Y;$$

and by rearranging these expressions, we can solve for the equilibrium level of income,

$$Y = \frac{a + I}{1 - b} = \frac{50 + 50}{1 - 0.75} = 400. \tag{2.2.1}$$

The multiplier may now be calculated by differentiating Eq. 2.2.1 with respect to I. Consequently,

$$\frac{dY}{dI} = \frac{1}{1 - b} = \frac{1}{1 - 0.75} = 4$$

is the investment multiplier. Finally, if we let Y^* stand for the full-employment level of income, and subtract aggregate demand at full employment from Y^*, we obtain the deflationary gap. This calculation yields

$$\text{Gap} = Y^* - (C^* + I) = (1 - b)Y^* - a - I = 0.25(600) - 50 - 50 = 50.$$

2.3 FISCAL POLICY†

The addition of the government sector to the simple model of income and employment requires that we maintain a clear distinction between income before and after taxes. The symbol Y stands for real net national product (income) before taxes. The amount of income that households actually receive is called disposable income, Y_d. Disposable income may differ from Y because business firms choose to retain some part of their earnings, because government takes away a fraction in the form of taxes, and because government makes direct income transfers, such as unemployment compensation payments, to individuals. For our present purposes we shall assume that business retains no earnings and we shall consolidate tax receipts and government transfer payments into an overall sum that we call net tax yield. Thus by definition we have $Y_d = Y - T$, where T is the level of net tax yield of government transfer payments.

The receipts from national economic activity are now split between households and government. Moreover, since disposable income may either be spent or saved, we have $Y \equiv C + S + T$. The national output may be purchased by consumers, by government, or retained by business. Consequently, it must also be true by definition that $Y \equiv C + I_r + G$, where I_r, as previously defined, is the level of realized investment. When we equate the two expressions, we obtain the fundamental accounting identity,

$$I_r + G \equiv S + T.$$

Finally, if income is to be in equilibrium, unintended investment must be zero, so that the equilibrium condition becomes $I + G = S + T$, which states that the "injections" into the income stream $(I + G)$ must equal the "leakages" $(S + T)$ out of it. Alternatively, equilibrium requires that aggregate demand, which now includes government purchases, must equal output. Therefore, $Y = C + I + G$ is an alternative way of stating the equilibrium condition.

Consumption depends upon income after taxes, rather than on income before taxes. This explains how taxes affect the level of consumption spending and therefore also the level of aggregate demand. By varying the amount taken in the form of taxes, the government may vary the disposable income level that is associated with a particular level of income, and it thereby varies the level of consumption associated with that level of income.

---

† The analysis of this section relies heavily upon R. A. Musgrave, *The Theory of Public Finance* (New York: McGraw-Hill, 1959), Chapter 18, and W. A. Salant, "Taxes, Income Determination, and the Balanced Budget Theorem," *Review of Economics and Statistics* (May, 1957).

Consumption, C

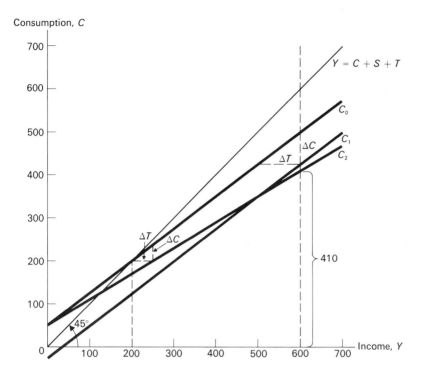

2|3|1
The effect of alternative taxes on the consumption function.

The effect of taxation may be illustrated with the assistance of Fig. 2.3.1. The consumption function C_0 is identical to the consumption function that was illustrated in Fig. 2.2.1. At an income level of 600, the level of consumption is 500. If a poll tax—i.e., a tax that is independent of the level of income—of 100 were imposed, the level of disposable income would be reduced by 100 at all levels of income. Since the marginal propensity to consume disposable income is 0.75, consumption would be 75 less at all levels of income than it was previously. Consequently, the consumption function would become the curve C_1, which is parallel to C_0 but lies below it by a vertical distance of 75, and to the right of C_0 by a horizontal distance, equal to the tax, of 100. It is important to note that the imposition of the tax of 100 would reduce consumption at all levels of income not by 100 but rather by 75; the remaining 25 of the reduction in disposable income would have been saved rather than spent on consumption.

Alternatively, suppose that a proportional income tax of 20% were imposed. At an income level of 600, the tax yield would be 120, and this means that disposable income would fall to 480. Since the marginal propensity to consume disposable income is 0.75, the fall in disposable income of 120 causes consumption to fall by 90, and this means that the level of consumption at an income level of

600 now becomes 410. At lower income levels the rise in tax yield would be less and disposable income and consumption would therefore drop by less. In the case of the income tax, therefore, the consumption function rotates (rather than shifts), and we thus have the new consumption function C_2. Here again, the vertical distance between C_0 and C_2 represents the drop in consumption at the different income levels, while the horizontal difference between the two functions measures the amount of the tax yield.

Algebraically, the three situations may be described as follows. In general, the consumption function is

$$C = 50 + 0.75Y_d = 50 + 0.75(Y - T).$$

Consumption function C_0 is drawn on the assumption that $T = 0$. Consequently, $C_0 = 50 + 0.75Y$. Consumption function C_1 is drawn on the assumption that a poll tax of 100 has been imposed. Therefore, since $T = 100$, we have

$$C_1 = 50 + 0.75(Y - 100) = -25 + 0.75Y,$$

which lies below C_0 by 75 at all levels of income. Finally, in the case of C_2 we have assumed the tax function, $T = 0.2Y$, which implies that

$$C_2 = 50 + 0.75(Y - 0.2Y) = 50 + 0.6Y.$$

We now proceed to the construction of a simple linear model that illustrates the role of fiscal policy in income determination. We know that

$$Y = C + I + G \tag{2.3.1}$$

defines equilibrium in the market for goods and services. Consumption is a linear function of disposable income. Therefore

$$C = a + bY_d = a + b(Y - T). \tag{2.3.2}$$

In addition, we assume that investment, government purchases, and the level of net taxes are all independent of the level of income. The variables G and I are therefore termed "exogenous" or "autonomous" and may be thought of as being of the same character as the parameters a and b. On the other hand, the variables C and Y, whose values depend upon the values of the parameters of the model, are said to be "endogenous" or "induced."

We now substitute Eq. 2.3.2 into Eq. 2.3.1 and solve for the equilibrium level of income. This substitution yields

$$Y = \frac{a - bT + I + G}{1 - b}. \tag{2.3.3}$$

The multiplier with respect to investment is obtained by differentiating Eq. 2.3.3 with respect to I while holding all other variables constant. Consequently,

$$\frac{dY}{dI} = \frac{1}{1 - b}$$

is the investment multiplier. Similarly, the multiplier for an increase in government purchases is obtained by differentiating with respect to G while holding all
other independent variables constant. Therefore

$$\frac{dY}{dG} = \frac{1}{1-b}$$

is the government-purchase multiplier. Similarly,

$$\frac{dY}{dT} = \frac{-b}{1-b}$$

is the tax multiplier. Observe that the tax multiplier is less than the government-
purchase multiplier. This is because a rise in taxes reduces consumption by only
a fraction of the rise in taxes. The remaining drop in disposable income comes at
the expense of saving.

When the government purchase and tax multipliers are added together, we
obtain

$$\frac{dY}{dG} + \frac{dY}{dT} = \frac{1}{1-b} - \frac{b}{1-b} = \frac{1-b}{1-b} = 1.$$

Thus the government-purchase multiplier exceeds the tax multiplier by one,
regardless of the value of the marginal propensity to consume. Put differently, we
may say that a change in government purchases which is balanced by an equal
increase in tax yield will raise the level of income by an amount equal to the
change in government purchases. It is for this reason that the above result is
known as the "unit" or "balanced-budget" multiplier.

Our next step is to incorporate income taxation into the model. Assume now
that the tax function is

$$T = u + vY, \tag{2.3.4}$$

where v is the marginal rate of income taxation and u is the level of net taxes
associated with a zero level of income. When this tax function is substituted into
the consumption function, we obtain

$$C = a - bu + b(1 - v)Y, \tag{2.3.5}$$

and when we substitute this consumption function into the equilibrium condition
and solve for Y, we have

$$Y = \frac{a - bu + I + G}{1 - b(1 - v)}. \tag{2.3.6}$$

Differentiation with respect to I and G provides the multipliers

$$\frac{dY}{dI} = \frac{dY}{dG} = \frac{1}{1 - b(1 - v)}, \tag{2.3.7}$$

which can readily be seen to be less than the multipliers $1/(1 - b)$ that were obtained in the absence of income taxation. To recall why this is so, note that now when Y rises by one dollar, tax collections automatically rise by v, so that disposable income rises by only $(1 - v)$. Consumption accordingly rises by $b(1 - v)$ rather than by b. As a consequence, there is less respending on consumption in response to some dG or dI than there would have been had there been no income taxation.

We have seen that income taxation reduces the value of the multiplier. In the absence of income taxation a fall in income of one dollar would reduce disposable income by a dollar, and consumption, assuming that $b = 0.75$, by 75 cents. However, if the marginal income tax rate is 0.20, there would be a fall in disposable income of only 80 cents, and a fall in consumption of only 60 (0.75×0.80) cents. Similar stabilizing effects come about because of the presence of other "built-in" or "automatic" stabilizers, such as unemployment compensation, reductions in social security tax, and corporate income-tax yield, and farm price-support programs.* What all of these devices have in common is that they break the one-for-one link between changes in income and changes in disposable income, and they thereby serve to stabilize the level of consumption spending.

To return to the model, let us shift the whole tax structure up by some amount du. Differentiation with respect to u yields the multiplier

$$\frac{dY}{du} = \frac{-b}{1 - b(1 - v)}. \tag{2.3.8}$$

Addition of this multiplier to the government-purchase multiplier gives

$$\frac{dY}{dG} + \frac{dY}{du} = \frac{1}{1 - b(1 - v)} - \frac{b}{1 - b(1 - v)},$$

which definitely does not total unity as long as v exceeds zero. The unit multiplier seems therefore not to apply under conditions of income taxation.

The foregoing conclusion is incorrect because induced effects have not been taken into account. Consider Fig. 2.3.2 in which the tax function is diagrammed. Assume that Y_0 is the original equilibrium level of income and T_0 is the level of tax collections. Then increase G by dG and, in order to offset the resultant deficit, shift the tax function up by an amount $du = dG$. The change in tax collections would equal du and therefore dG if the level of income were to remain at Y_0. However, since government purchases and taxes do not have symmetrical effects, there will be some change in income and therefore some induced change in tax collections equal to the change in income times the marginal tax rate. In Fig.

---

* For a detailed discussion of the various automatic stabilizers of the American economy and their quantitative impact, see Wilfred Lewis, Jr., *Federal Fiscal Policy in the Postwar Recessions* (Washington, D.C.: Brookings, 1962), especially Chapters 1–3.

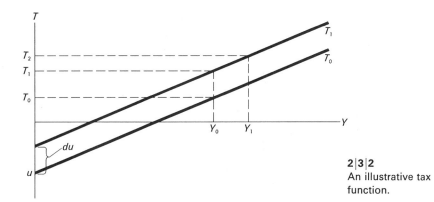

2|3|2
An illustrative tax
function.

2.3.2 we assume that income rises to Y_1 so that tax collections rise from T_0 to T_2 rather than to T_1. Thus even though we attempt to raise G and T by the same amount, we actually find that tax collections rise by more than dG, and it is for this reason that the net multiplier effect is less than one.

Let us now see if we can find some du (shift in the tax function) that will satisfy the unit multiplier condition. From the tax function we have $dT = du + v(dY)$. However, if government purchases rise by the same amount as tax yield, then $dG = dT$, so that $dG = du + v(dY)$ or

$$du = dG - v(dY). \qquad (2.3.9)$$

Differentiating 2.3.6 with respect to both G and u gives

$$dY = \frac{-b(du) + dG}{1 - b(1 - v)},$$

from which it follows that upon substitution of 2.3.9,

$$dY = dG.$$

Evidently the unit multiplier holds, provided induced effects are taken into account. If a change in the tax structure can be found, such as one which will just generate additional revenue equal to some change in government purchases, then the level of income will rise by exactly the amount of the change in G and T.

Finally, let us examine the effect of a change in the tax rate, v. Differentiation of 2.3.6 with respect to v yields

$$\frac{dY}{dv} = \frac{-(a - bu + I + G)b}{[1 - b(1 - v)]^2} = \frac{-bY}{1 - b(1 - v)}. \qquad (2.3.10)$$

In contrast with other multipliers, the multiplier with respect to the marginal tax rate is a function of the level of income. This is because the amount of the change in tax collections, and hence the change in disposable income and consumption, will depend upon the original level of income. If, to cite an extreme example, the level of income is zero, a change in the tax rate can have no effect and the multiplier will therefore be zero.

The change in tax yield resulting from a change in the marginal tax rate is

$$dT = v(dY) + Y(dv),$$

and if this is associated with an equal change in government purchases, then

$$dG = v(dY) + Y(dv),$$

so that

$$dv = \frac{dG - v(dY)}{Y}. \tag{2.3.11}$$

Differentiation of 2.3.6 with respect to G and v yields

$$[1 - b(1 - v)]\, dY = dG - bY(dv),$$

from which it follows that upon substitution of 2.3.11,

$$dY = dG,$$

and the unit multiplier therefore holds again.

The main results of this analysis may be summarized as follows:

1   Changes in government purchases have a more high-powered effect on the level of income than do equal changes in the level of tax yield. Therefore, as a corollary, the fiscal impact of government spending and taxation depends not only upon whether there is a deficit or a surplus but also upon the absolute levels of G and T.

2   Income taxation and automatically induced government transfer-payment schemes reduce the value of the multiplier and therefore have an automatically stabilizing effect upon the level of income.

3   If a change in government purchases is matched by an equal change in tax yield, the level of income will change by the amount of the change in G and T.

While there can be little doubt that the effect on aggregate demand and the level of income of equal changes in G and T will not usually cancel, the proposition that the multiplier of such equal changes is one is generally regarded as a special case rather than as a general rule. The magnitude of the balanced-budget multiplier will depend on such factors as the differential marginal propensities to consume of taxpayers and the recipients of government spending, on the types of taxes that are imposed, and on the presence or absence of money illusion. To cite an extreme example of the latter possibility, suppose that consumers are subject to money illusion and that a sales tax is imposed. The effect of the tax is to raise prices of consumer goods. However, since consumers are assumed not to notice the change in prices and since their incomes remain the same, they spend the same amount on consumption as before. Consequently, their level of real consumption spending falls by the full amount of the sales tax rather than by a fraction. If government then spends the proceeds on goods and services, aggregate demand will be exactly the same as before, and there will be no change in income at all.*

2.4 THE THEORY OF ECONOMIC POLICY

An exceedingly fruitful way of organizing one's thinking about policy problems is to proceed along lines sketched out by Tinbergen† and others, and to classify economic magnitudes into "target" variables and policy "instruments" or "policy parameters." The unemployment rate, for example, might be regarded as a target variable, and a particular value for that rate—say three percent—might be chosen as the target. Macroeconomic planning then involves the adjustment of the instruments—government purchases, various tax rates, etc.—in such a way as to achieve the target values of the variables in question.

The theory of economic policy represents the inverse of conventional economic analysis. For example, we previously considered the effect of an increase in government purchases on the level of income without bothering to inquire if the change was in some sense "good" or "desirable." This mode of analysis is one of cause and effect and therefore resides in the domain of so-called "positive" economics. In the theory of economic policy we proceed in the opposite direction. First we establish some targets that we choose to regard as desirable and we then ask what must be done by way of manipulating the various means (instruments) at our disposal if the desired targets are to be reached. Thus the theory of economic policy resides in the realm of "normative" economics and may, indeed, be thought of as the macroeconomic counterpart of microeconomic welfare theory.

One of the first principles of the theory of economic policy is that given n specific variables to each of which we wish to assign a definite target value, we will usually have to have at our disposal at least n policy instruments if the desired result is to be achieved. Although the presence of n instruments is neither a necessary nor a sufficient condition for the achievement of n targets, we may for the moment suppose that it is and examine a few simple examples that will help us to understand this basic proposition.

Consider first the linear national income model of the previous section,

$$Y = C + I + G,$$
$$C = a + bY,$$

---

* For an analysis of the effect of sales taxes on the level of income, see E. Carey Brown, "Analysis of Consumption Taxes in Terms of the Theory of Income Determination," *American Economic Review* (March, 1950).

† Jan Tinbergen, *On the Theory of Economic Policy* (Amsterdam: North-Holland, 1952) and *Economic Policy: Principles and Design* (Amsterdam: North-Holland, 1956) are among the classic works. Bent Hansen, *The Economic Theory of Fiscal Policy* (Cambridge, Mass.: Harvard University Press, 1958), and Leif Johansen, *Public Economics* (Chicago: Rand McNally, 1965) are characterized by a similar orientation.

where all magnitudes are in real terms. Investment is assumed to be autonomous and cannot be influenced by policy. Income and consumption are endogenous; government purchases is the lone policy instrument. A change in G will yield

$$\frac{dY}{dG} = \frac{1}{1 - b}$$

and

$$\frac{dC}{dG} = \frac{b}{1 - b}$$

for the changes in income and consumption, respectively. Obviously, by manipulating G, we can change either Y or C in the way we like, but we cannot, with only the one instrument, get them both (except by chance) to reach their target levels simultaneously.

If we desire to make both Y and C conform to particular target levels, we shall have to have at our disposal a second instrument. Suppose then that we introduce lump-sum taxation. The model now becomes

$$Y = C + I + G,$$
$$C = a + b(Y - T).$$

Again investment is autonomous and cannot be affected by policy. However, since we now have two target variables, Y and C, and two instruments, G and T, we ought to be able to achieve both targets. Since

$$Y = \frac{a - bT + I + G}{1 - b},$$

it follows that

$$dY = \frac{-b(dT) + dG}{1 - b} \quad \text{and} \quad dC = b(dY - dT).$$

If the desired (target) changes in income and consumption are dY^* and dC^*, respectively, we may insert these target changes into the preceding two expressions to obtain

$$dY^* = \frac{-b(dT) + dG}{1 - b} \tag{2.4.1}$$

$$dC^* = b(dY^* - dT). \tag{2.4.2}$$

Now from 2.4.2 we can calculate that the required change in T is

$$dT^* = dY^* - \frac{dC^*}{b},$$

and by substituting this value into 2.4.1, we find that the required change in G is

$$dG^* = (1 - b)(dY^*) + b(dT^*) = dY^* - dC^*,$$

which, of course, is the self-evident result that the change in government purchases must fill the gap between the target changes in income and consumption.

If we add income taxation to the model, we have

$$Y = C + I + G,$$
$$T = u + vY,$$
$$C = a + b(Y - T) = a - bu + b(1 - v)Y.$$

By combining these equations, we obtain the familiar solution for the equilibrium
level of income,

$$Y = \frac{a - bu + I + G}{1 - b(1 - v)}. \tag{2.4.3}$$

The number of policy instruments has now been increased to three: the level of
government purchases, G, the marginal income tax rate, v, and the exemption
level, u. By differentiating the consumption function with respect to u, v, and Y,
we see that all possible policy-induced changes in consumption are given by

$$dC = -b(du) - bY(dv) + b(1 - v)(dY),$$

which indicates that $dC*$ can be achieved either by varying u or v, and that this
can be made consistent with any $dY*$ that we wish to choose. The addition of
another instrument apparently provides an added degree of flexibility.

If we shift the exemption level, we have

$$dC* = -b(du) + b(1 - v)(dY*),$$

so that

$$du* = (1 - v)(dY*) - \frac{dC*}{b}.$$

The required change in government purchases may now be calculated by differentiating 2.4.3 with respect to u and G and setting $dY = dY*$ and $du = du*$.
This gives

$$dY* = \frac{-b(du*) + dG}{1 - b(1 - v)},$$

so that upon rearranging terms, we find that

$$dG* = [1 - b(1 - v)](dY*) + b(du*) = dY* - dC*,$$

where again it appears that so long as investment remains unaffected by policy,
government purchases must be changed by the amount of the difference between
the target change in consumption and the target change in income.†

_____

† As an exercise, the reader may wish to calculate the target changes in G and in the marginal
tax rate v that would be required to achieve the target changes $dY*$ and $dC*$.

The discussion so far suggests that the attainment of n targets will usually require that we have n instruments of control at our disposable. To generalize more than we have done previously, suppose that the economic system can be described by the following two linear equations,

$$a_{11}x_1 + a_{12}x_2 = y_1,$$
$$a_{21}x_1 + a_{22}x_2 = y_2,$$

where the a_{ij}'s are the parameters of the system, x_1 and x_2 are the target variables, and y_1 and y_2 are the policy parameters. When we assign target values to the variables we, in effect, add equations to the system. Thus, if we assign the target values x_1^* and x_2^* to x_1 and x_2, we add the equations

$$x_1 = x_1^*,$$
$$x_2 = x_2^*.$$

Now when we substituted these target values into the original equations, it becomes obvious that there are only two possible values of the policy parameters, y_1 and y_2, that can be found which will be consistent with all four equations.

This way of looking at the matter illustrates not only the familiar proposition that n targets usually require n policy instruments, but also that policy must be coordinated; i.e., the values of the instrument parameters must be chosen simultaneously. By way of illustration, suppose that x_1 is the level of income, x_2 is the level of prices, and y_1 and y_2 represent the levels of government purchases and the money supply, respectively. Suppose next that we start out at some time with x_1 and x_2 away from their target values, and that the monetary authority acts first to bring the price level to the desired target value (reach its x_2 target by manipulating y_2). If the monetary authority does this, it will change the money supply by a different amount than would be called for if both the monetary and fiscal authorities had coordinated their activities and sought a simultaneous solution to their problem. Reacting to this change, the fiscal authority may overshoot and in its effort to reach the target level of income (x_1^*) cause the price level to depart from its target level. The monetary authority then reacts and in an effort to reach its target of stable prices, it destabilizes the level of income, and so on, back and forth. It is indeed possible that such back and forth uncoordinated action could cause prices and employment to fluctuate about their targets with increasing amplitude, much as price moved farther away from equilibrium in our cobweb-market model in the first chapter. As a general rule, coordination of policies is vital. It is nonsense to say, as we often do, that it is the job of the monetary authority to maintain price stability, while the achievement of full employment is the responsibility of fiscal policy.

We have seen that it is generally necessary to have n instruments to achieve n targets and that the proper value of each instrument parameter depends upon all of the target values simultaneously. Consequently, policy should be fully coordinated; however, there are exceptions to these simple rules.

The equality of instruments and targets is not a necessary condition for the attainment of all targets. Some targets may be achieved quite by accident or as a by-product of the attainment of some other target. Full employment and full capacity, for example, may go hand in hand. It is also possible that some targets may be attained automatically without the assistance of policy. In the classical theory of employment, competition on the labor market guarantees that full employment will be achieved automatically, a circumstance that implies that the n desired ends can be achieved with no more than $n - 1$ instruments. Alternatively, we may say that an automatically achieved target is superfluous and that we therefore have only $n - 1$ targets about which we need to be concerned and for which we require instruments of control.

To illustrate the classical theory, let us go back to the simple model,

$$a_{11}x_1 + a_{12}x_2 = y_1,$$
$$a_{21}x_1 + a_{22}x_2 = y_2,$$

and again imagine that x_1 and x_2 are the levels of income and prices, respectively, and that y_1 and y_2 represent the levels of government purchases and the supply of money. Classical theory would imply that $x_1 = x_1^*$ automatically, and that the parameters a_{11}, a_{12}, and a_{21} are zero. This implies first that y_1 is an irrelevant instrument; i.e., the level of income and the level of prices are independent of the level of government purchases. Second, the fact that a_{21} is zero implies that the price level is directly proportional to the quantity of money. The entire system therefore boils down to

$$x_1 = x_1^*,$$
$$x_2 = x_2^*,$$
$$a_{22}x_2 = y_2.$$

Consequently, in the classical system the level of government purchases is a gratuitous variable; the coordination of policies does not matter, since the price level depends only upon the action of the monetary authority with neither authority able to destabilize the level of income; and the target of stable prices may be achieved through the exercise of only the instrument of monetary control.

The equality of targets and instruments is also not a sufficient condition. Some targets may be plainly out of reach. If we want income to double in a year, we are likely to find that this is not possible because we do not have sufficient resources to achieve such an expansion of output. In other cases targets may be inconsistent with each other. While it may be possible to reduce unemployment to two percent of the labor force, the resultant tightness in the labor market may be so great that there is no acceptable way to maintain stability of wages and prices. If we want consumers to have output of C^*, investors to have I^*, and the government to obtain G^*, and if the sum of these is more than we can produce or borrow from abroad, we are obviously defeated regardless of the number of policy instruments that we have at our disposal.

The problem of inconsistent targets is often unnecessarily exacerbated by an unfortunate tendency to pick irrelevant targets and thereby to confuse means with ends—to treat instruments as though they themselves had target values that are desirable for their own sakes. Although there are numerous examples of this kind of error in the history of economic policy, one in particular has been particularly damaging, that is, the desire to maintain balance in the Federal budget.

To illustrate the effect of a balanced-budget policy, consider again the basic model with which we have been working, namely,

$$Y = C + I + G,$$
$$T = u + vY,$$
$$C = a + b(Y - T) = a - bu + b(1 - v)Y,$$

where the solution for the equilibrium level of income is the familiar expression

$$Y = \frac{a - bu + I + G}{1 - b(1 - v)}.$$

We assume initially that income is at its target value and that the budget is balanced. This means that $Y = Y^*$ and that $D = G - T = 0$, where D is the budgetary deficit. If investment declines by some amount dI, the level of income falls by

$$dY = \frac{dI}{1 - b(1 - v)}, \qquad dI < 0, \tag{2.4.4}$$

and there would result an induced budgetary deficit equal to the induced decline in tax receipts of

$$dT = v(dY) = \frac{v(dI)}{1 - b(1 - v)}.$$

If government purchases were increased to offset the fall in private demand, the required increase in G would equal the fall in investment. Since income would then revert to its original level, there would be no decline in tax receipts, and the deficit would then be equal to the increase in government purchases.

However, if we insist on a balanced budget as our target, and if we utilize changes in G to effect this result, we will have quite a different state of affairs. The balanced budget target requires

$$dD^* = dG - dT = 0.$$

Since a fall in income due to the decline in investment will cause tax collections to fall, government purchases will have to be lowered if the balanced budget target is to be maintained. Consequently, income will change both because of a decline in investment and a decline in government purchases. Thus, in general, the change in income will be

$$dY = \frac{dI + dG}{1 - b(1 - v)} .$$
(2.4.5)

This fall in income implies that there will be an induced change in tax receipts of

$$dT = v(dY) = \frac{v(dI + dG)}{1 - b(1 - v)} ,$$
(2.4.6)

and since the balanced budget target requires that $dT = dG$, we may replace dT by dG in 2.4.6 and solve for the required change in G. This implies that

$$dG = \frac{v(dI)}{(1 - b)(1 - v)} .$$

Since dI is negative, we see that dG must also be negative and this means that fiscal policy now accentuates rather than offsets the fall in private demand.

Returning to 2.4.5 and substituting the calculated change in G into the expression, we find that

$$dY = \left[\frac{dI}{1 - b(1 - v)}\right]\left[1 + \frac{v}{(1 - b)(1 - v)}\right] .$$

Since the expression $dI/[1 - b(1 - v)]$ is the amount by which income would have changed had there been no change in government purchases, and since the term $\{1 + [v/(1 - b)(1 - v)]\}$ is greater than unity, we see that the fall in income now exceeds the decline that would have materialized in the absence of a change in G and that the policy of budgetary balance therefore accentuates the decline in income.

To summarize: The theory of economic policy represents an inversion of the normal mode of economic analysis inasmuch as a given set of desirable ends or targets are posited and it is then asked how these ends can be achieved. As a general rule, n targets require that n instruments of control be available and that the values of all n of the instrument parameters be simultaneously determined. However, the equality of instruments and targets is neither a necessary nor a sufficient condition for the achievement of the n targets, and it need not always be true that each policy-making agency must be aware of the targets and the actions of the other agencies. The confusion of means and ends is a serious problem for economic policy. However, as long as the ends remain a matter to be determined by the values of the community, there is little that the economist can do except to point out the consequence of treating potentially useful policy instruments as though certain values of these instruments were themselves desirable targets.

REFERENCES

E. Cary Brown, "Analysis of Consumption Taxes in Terms of the Theory of Income Determination," *American Economic Review* (March, 1950).

T. F. Dernburg and D. M. McDougall, *Macroeconomics* (New York: McGraw-Hill, 1962), Chapters 5, 6.

Bent Hansen, *The Economic Theory of Fiscal Policy* (Cambridge, Mass.: Harvard University Press, 1958), Part I.

Leif Johansen, *Public Economics* (Chicago: Rand McNally, 1965), Chapters 1–3.

Wilfred Lewis, Jr., *Federal Fiscal Policy in the Post-War Recessions* (Washington, D.C.: Brookings, 1962), Chapters 1–3.

Richard A. Musgrave, *The Theory of Public Finance* (New York: McGraw-Hill, 1959), Chapter 18.

William A. Salant, "Taxes, Income Determination, and the Balanced Budget," *Review of Economics and Statistics* (May, 1957).

Paul A. Samuelson, "The Simple Mathematics of Income Determination," *Income, Employment, and Public Policy: Essays in Honor of Alvin Hansen* (New York: Norton, 1948), pp. 133–155.

Jan Tinbergen, *On the Theory of Economic Policy* (Amsterdam: North-Holland, 1952).

Jan Tinbergen, *Economic Policy: Principles and Design* (Amsterdam: North-Holland, 1956).

CHAPTER 3

The Comparative Statics
of the Keynesian System

3.1 THE KEYNESIAN SYSTEM

Our main purpose in this chapter is to add the monetary sector to the model of income determination. Having accomplished this, we will be able to use the techniques of comparative-static analysis to examine the effectiveness of monetary and fiscal policies in changing the level of income.

Beginning with the consumption function, we assume for present purposes that there is no taxation and that there are no retained earnings. Disposable income therefore equals the real national product, Y, and we therefore write the consumption function as

$$C = C(Y), \qquad 0 < C_y < 1. \tag{3.1.1}$$

This notation simply states that consumption is a function of the level of income and that the marginal propensity to consume—the partial derivative of consumption with respect to income, $\partial C/\partial Y = C_y$—lies between zero and one.

Previously, it was assumed that intended investment is autonomous. Now, however, we adopt the traditional hypothesis that investment is a decreasing function of the rate of interest, i.e.,

$$I = I(i), \qquad I_i < 0. \tag{3.1.2}$$

The theory that underlies this hypothesis is simple and well known. Consider the owner of a sum of money who is trying to decide what to do with his idle balances. Will he lend the money to someone else (i.e., purchase an existing asset, such as a bond) and earn the going rate of return (the market rate of interest, i), or will he purchase a new capital asset such as a new machine or a new building? The answer would appear to depend on whether the expected rate of return on new

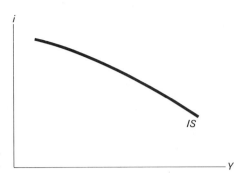

3|1|1
Illustration of product market equilibrium,
$I(i) + G = Y - C(Y)$.

investment exceeds the return on existing assets. Since a fall in the rate of interest implies that the relative preference of new over existing assets increases, a fall in the rate of interest is associated with a rise in intended investment.

Alternatively, if the prospective investor does not have money at his disposal, he must make a decision whether to borrow the funds needed to make the investment. Here again the decision to borrow and to invest depends upon whether the expected rate of return on the new investment project exceeds the cost of borrowing. Consequently, a rise in the rate of interest would reduce the amount of borrowing and the level of intended investment.

Since taxes have been eliminated from the model, the equilibrium condition in the market for goods and services (product market) is $I + G = S$. Since $I = I(i)$ and $C = C(Y)$, we may substitute these equations into the equilibrium condition and obtain

$$I(i) + G = Y - C(Y), \qquad (3.1.3)$$

where $Y - C(Y)$ is the level of saving.

On the basis of the information at hand, the equilibrium level of income is indeterminate. If the interest rate is known, the income level will be known and conversely. Mathematically, there exists one equation with two unknowns, and another equation is therefore needed in order to find the equilibrium values of i and Y.

The relationship between the rate of interest and the equilibrium level of income, as represented by Eq. 3.1.3 is diagramed in Fig. 3.1.1. This relationship is known to economists as the "IS-curve," and it represents the combination of interest rates and associated income levels that imply equilibrium in the market for goods and services.

The slope of the IS-curve must be negative. Since $I_i\, di = (1 - C_y)\, dY$, and $I_i < 0$ and $0 < (1 - C_y) < 1$,

$$\left(\frac{di}{dY}\right)_{IS} = \frac{(1 - C_y)}{I_i} < 0. \qquad (3.1.4)$$

Because a fall in the rate of interest implies a higher level of intended investment and income, a fall in the rate of interest is associated with a rise in the level of income.

Once it is recognized that investment is a function of the rate of interest, it becomes necessary to analyze the determinants of the rate of interest. The discussion to follow, which attempts such an analysis, is considerably more detailed and involved than the discussion of the other components of the Keynesian model. This is because the analysis of the demand for money provides a convenient illustration of how microeconomic propositions can form the basis for macroeconomic inferences. Similar analyses could be performed for the other components of the Keynesian system; however, a single example is sufficient for our purpose.

The rate of interest will be constant and in equilibrium if the price of bonds and other securities are at their equilibrium values. Elementary economics teaches that there is an inverse association between bond prices and the rate of interest. In the case of a perpetual bond the formula

$$V = \frac{R}{i}$$

applies, where R is the annual money return on the bond, i is the rate of interest, and V is the present (market) value of the bond.

There will be no tendency for bond prices, and therefore interest rates, to change if there is no excess demand or excess supply of bonds. This, in turn, means that the portfolios of wealth holders are arranged in such a fashion that no one is inclined to convert bonds into money or conversely. Since an excess demand for bonds implies an excess supply of money (i.e., wealth holders want to divest themselves of money to acquire bonds), equilibrium in the bond market, and therefore equilibrium interest rates, implies that the supply of money must exactly equal the quantity of money balances that wealth holders wish to hold. Consequently, monetary equilibrium can be defined as a situation that is obtained when

$$m_d = m_s,$$

namely, when the demand for money to hold, m_d, just equals the supply of money, m_s.

What are the factors that determine the demand for money, m_d? In traditional theory it is recognized that individuals maintain some average idle balance of cash and deposits because receipts and disbursements are not perfectly synchronized with respect to time. For example, if an individual receives a $10,000 income at the beginning of the year and makes disbursements at a uniform rate throughout the year, ending with a cash balance of zero at the end of the year, his bank account throughout the year would appear as it is depicted in Fig. 3.1.2. The individual's average idle balance is, of course, $5000, and this is what we call his transactions demand for money. The relationship between the demand for

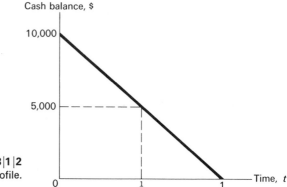

3|1|2
A hypothetical cash balance profile.

money and the level of income in this case is

$$\$5000 = 0.5 \times \$10,000,$$

so that for the economy as a whole we may write,

$$m_d = kY, \qquad\qquad (3.1.5)$$

where m_d is the demand for money in real terms, and k is the length of time the average dollar is held between transactions.

Equation 3.1.5 represents the old-fashioned quantity theory of money in its simplest form. The demand for real money balances is proportional to the level of income. Any excess supply of money would result in an attempt to convert money into bonds, with the consequence that interest rates would fall and investment and income would rise by an amount sufficient to absorb the excess money holdings into transactions holdings and thereby restore monetary equilibrium.

A possible additional demand for money is Keynes' concept of a "speculative" or "liquidity-preference" demand. Keynes considered a model in which long-term bonds and money were the only form of financial asset. After a fall in the interest rate such as would occur when the economy descends into depression, wealth holders would expect the interest rate to rise back to its "normal" higher level. Therefore, anticipating a capital loss on the holding of bonds, wealth holders would demonstrate a liquidity preference and hold money balances as a "speculation." Presumably, the lower the rate of interest relative to its normal level, the greater the probability of capital loss on bond holdings and the greater the speculative demand for money. Thus the Keynesian would replace the classical demand for money function with

$$m_d = L(i, Y), \qquad L_i < 0, \qquad L_y > 0. \qquad (3.1.6)$$

The Keynesian theory of the demand for money has been subjected to numerous criticisms, some warranted and some not. Here it is sufficient to note that as long as money (demand deposits and currency in the hands of the nonbank

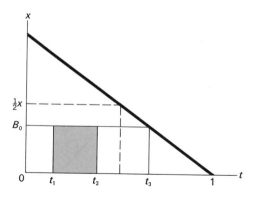

3|1|3
A suboptimal bond-purchase program.

public) can be converted into riskless saving accounts, the proposition that idle balances are held for fear of capital loss becomes difficult to defend. Nevertheless, empirical studies do show a strong inverse association between the rate of interest and the level of average idle balances, and thus as an empirical matter the rate of interest appears to be associated with the demand for money in the way Keynes predicted. Contemporary theorists have suggested that this may be due to the fact that the transactions demand for money may be influenced by the rate of interest. To explore this possibility we follow Tobin's analysis of the transactions demand for money.*

Returning to the case of the individual who receives $10,000 at the beginning of the year and makes disbursements at a constant absolute rate in such a manner as to end the year with a zero balance, it should be noted that one half of the initial balance remains idle for fully one-half of the year. Similarly, two-thirds of the initial balance remains idle for one-third of a year, and one-third remains idle for two-thirds of the year. The individual could therefore take the idle balances and lend them at interest (buy bonds) until he runs out of transactions cash, at which time he may sell the bonds and replenish his transactions balances.

What is an optimal bond purchase program? In Fig. 3.1.3 it is assumed that an individual receives an income of x dollars at time zero, which he spends at a uniform rate so as to reach a zero cash balance at time 1. It is also assumed that he purchases bonds in an amount B_0 at time t_1 and that he sells the bonds at t_2. The shaded area of the diagram therefore represents the time profile of his bond holdings.

Does this assumed behavior provide an optimal schedule? Obviously not: The individual could have increased his interest earnings by buying at the beginning of the period; i.e., he should have made $t_1 = 0$, and he could have increased his earnings by waiting to sell until time t_3, when he runs out of cash. Moreover, the largest shaded rectangle that could be drawn under the curve would be obtained if the initial purchase of bonds equaled one-half of the beginning balance, namely $x/2$

---

* James Tobin, "The Interest Elasticity of the Transactions Demand for Cash," *Review of Economics and Statistics* (August, 1956).

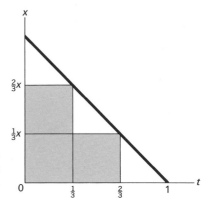

3|1|4
An optimal bond-purchase program involving
three transactions.

dollars. Optimal scheduling therefore suggests the following three rules:

1   Buy bonds at the beginning of the period.

2   Do not sell bonds until you run out of cash.

3   In the case of two transactions (one purchase and one sale) buy $x/2$ bonds.

The wealth holder under consideration could, of course, make three, four, or n transactions. For example, he could put two-thirds of his initial income into bonds. Since he would run out of cash after one-third of the period had elapsed, he could convert half the bond holdings (one-third of his income) into cash at that time. This will permit him to make disbursements until two-thirds of the period has elapsed, at which time he would cash in the remainder of his bond holdings. This program is diagramed in Fig. 3.1.4, in which the shaded area represents the time profile of the individual's bond holdings.

In the case of two transactions the individual should buy $x/2$ bonds at the start of the period. If he makes three transactions, the optimal schedule implies that he should make an initial purchase of $\frac{2}{3}x$. The optimal beginning purchase for four transactions is $\frac{3}{4}x$. And it may therefore be readily inferred that for n transactions the optimal beginning purchase of bonds is

$$B_0 = \frac{(n-1)}{n}\,x.$$

Since the individual holds no bonds at the end of the year, his average bond holdings are

$$\bar{B} = \frac{(n-1)}{2n}\,x,$$

and this means that the revenue which he earns will be

$$R = i\bar{B} = \frac{(n-1)}{2n}\,ix,$$

where i is the rate of interest.

When the revenue function is differentiated with respect to n, we obtain

$$\frac{dR}{dn} = \left[\frac{2n - 2(n-1)}{4n^2}\right] ix = \left[\frac{1}{2n^2}\right] ix,$$

which implies that R will continue to rise as n rises and that maximum revenue is attained when $n \to \infty$. Under these circumstances, the beginning bond purchase becomes $B_0 = x$, the average bond holding is $\bar{B} = x/2$, and revenue is earned on one-half of the initial cash balances in an amount $ix/2$. Revenue is therefore maximized if all initial income is converted into bonds and if bonds are continuously sold off as transactions cash is needed. In such a case, the individual would never hold idle money balances and his transactions demand for money would be zero.

The wealth holder who would always prefer to hold bonds rather than cash—which he could do if he made an infinite number of infinitely small transactions—would soon discover that to do so would be unprofitable because there are transactions costs associated with the conversion of bonds into cash and conversely. These costs may be split into a fixed component per transaction and a variable component that is proportional to the size of the transaction. We begin with a consideration of the case in which the variable cost is zero and the fixed cost is therefore all that requires consideration. Given these assumptions, and assuming that the fixed cost per transaction is a dollars, the total cost of making n transactions must be $C = na$. Referring back to the revenue function, we find that the level of profit is

$$P = R - C = \frac{(n-1)ix}{2n} - na.$$

Differentiation of the profit function with respect to the number of transactions yields

$$\frac{dP}{dn} = \left[\frac{2n - 2(n-1)}{4n^2}\right] ix - a = \left[\frac{1}{2n^2}\right] ix - a,$$

and when we set $dP/dn = 0$, we obtain

$$n = \sqrt{ix/2a} = (ix/2a)^{1/2}, \tag{3.1.7}$$

as the number of transactions that maximizes profits. Taking the second derivative of the profit function, we find that

$$\frac{d^2P}{dn^2} = -\left(\frac{1}{n^3}\right) ix,$$

which is negative and confirms that the solution maximizes, rather than minimizes, profits.

The situation is depicted in Fig. 3.1.5. The cost curve is a straight line, while the revenue function is curved with a diminishing slope that eventually approaches zero at the maximum revenue level of $ix/2$. The slope of the revenue curve—marginal revenue—diminishes as the number of transactions rises, since as we move from three to four transactions the value of the additional bonds that can be

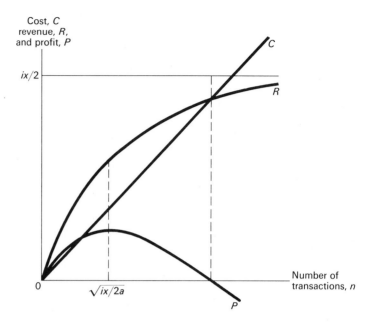

Interest revenue and fixed transactions costs as functions of the number of
transactions.

purchased initially will be less than could be purchased by moving from two to
three transactions. Since

$$\frac{dR}{dn} = \left(\frac{1}{2n^2}\right)ix,$$

marginal revenue obviously diminishes as n increases.

An increase in transactions costs would rotate the cost curve to the left and
would reduce the optimum number of transactions. Similarly, the optimum value
of transactions will rise as the rate of interest rises and as the beginning balance, x,
rises, since both of these changes would raise the revenue curve. These conclusions
are obvious merely from inspection of Eq. 3.1.7. However, it is frequently useful to
prove these conclusions formally by differentiating the equation with respect to
i, x, and a. For example,

$$\frac{dn}{di} = \frac{1}{2}\left(\frac{ix}{2a}\right)^{-1/2}\left(\frac{x}{2a}\right) > 0$$

shows that a rise in the rate of interest would raise the optimum number of transactions.

If there is also a variable cost, b, proportional to the size of the transaction, the problem becomes somewhat more complicated. A round trip of one dollar implies a variable transactions cost of $2b$. Consequently, the time at which the net interest (over and above the variable transactions cost) can begin to be earned is $2b/i$. For example, if $b = 0.02$ and $i = 0.06$, net interest will not be earned until

$$\frac{2b}{i} = \frac{0.04}{0.06} = \frac{2}{3},$$

of the period has past. Therefore the time over which the interest net of variable transactions cost is earned will be $[1 - (2b/i)]$.

If initial bond purchases are in an amount that would require a bond sale prior to time $2b/i$, the transactions cost of the round trip of the bonds that would have to be sold prior to $2b/i$ would exceed the interest that could be earned on these bonds. Therefore the beginning level of bond purchases that could be profitable must be no greater than $x[1 - (2b/i)]$. However, since this amount of bond purchases would leave the wealth holder with no cash at time $2b/i$ and since this means he would have to sell some bonds on which the interest earnings just cover the variable transactions cost, the wealth holder would be better off to purchase

$$B_0 = \frac{x}{2}\left[1 - \frac{2b}{i}\right]$$

bonds if he intends to make only two transactions and

$$B_0 = \frac{(n - 1)}{n} x\left[1 - \frac{2b}{i}\right]$$

bonds if he intends to make n transactions. Therefore the average balance on which the interest net of variable cost is earned is

$$\bar{B} = \frac{(n - 1)}{2n} x\left[1 - \frac{2b}{i}\right].$$

Since net interest is earned only for a period of $[1 - (2b/i)]$ the effective rate of interest on bond holdings is $i[1 - (2b/i)]$, and this means that the level of revenue net of variable transactions costs is

$$R = \frac{(n - 1)}{2n} ix\left[1 - \frac{2b}{i}\right]^2.$$

Finally, when the fixed cost $C = na$ is subtracted from revenue, we obtain the profit function

$$P = \frac{(n - 1)ix}{2n}\left[1 - \frac{2b}{i}\right]^2 - na,$$

which, when differentiated with respect to n yields

$$\frac{dP}{dn} = \frac{ix}{2n^2}\left[1 - \frac{2b}{i}\right]^2 - a.$$

Maximum profit is achieved when this derivative equals zero. Consequently, the optimum number of transactions is

$$n = \sqrt{ix/2a}[1 - (2b/i)].$$

The conclusions regarding changes in i, x, and a are the same as before. In addition, it is now apparent that the number of entrances into the bond market will also decline if the variable cost b rises. In general, therefore, a rise in transactions costs, whether fixed or variable, will reduce the optimum number of transactions, while a rise in the rate of interest or in the beginning cash balance will increase the optimum number of transactions.

The more often, per income-expenditure period, that wealth holders enter the bond market, the smaller will be their ratio of idle cash balances to income. Since a rise in the rate of interest promotes a tendency to economize cash balances in favor of bond holdings, we may conclude that the transactions demand for money is a decreasing function of the rate of interest. One may therefore adopt a demand for money function that is the same as the one implied by Keynes' analysis, namely,

$$m_d = L(i, Y), \qquad L_i < 0, \qquad L_y > 0,$$

without having to agree on the particulars of Keynes' theory of liquidity preference.*

The demand for money is a function of the rate of interest and the level of income. The supply of money, defined as the quantity of currency and deposits in the hands of the nonbank public, is to some extent dependent on commercial bank behavior. However, in the main the money supply is whatever the monetary authority wants it to be.† For present purposes we shall proceed on the assumption that the money supply is fixed until it is changed by central bank action. Therefore

---

* Note that we have specified $L_y > 0$ when, in fact, the inventory model of cash balances predicts that a rise in income will raise the optimal value of n and therefore reduce average cash balances. However, recall that a rise in income is equivalent to a rise in initial cash balances. It is true that a rise in income will raise the optimal n and therefore reduce average cash balances relative to the initial balance. Nevertheless, the absolute level of cash holding will rise as income rises. Moreover, it is doubtful if in the long run a rise in per capita income will reduce the ratio of cash balances to income. This is so because the transactions cost is a labor cost which will rise as per capita income rises. Thus any tendency for n to rise as x rises will be offset by a proportionate increase in transactions costs.

† However, a very persuasive analysis by Robert Mundell, "Capital Mobility and Stabilization Policy Under Fixed and Flexible Exchange Rates," *Canadian Journal of Economics and Political Science* (November, 1963), shows that under conditions of perfect international capital mobility and fixed exchange rates, the monetary authority of a small country may be powerless to affect the size of its domestic money supply.

monetary equilibrium is defined by

$$m_s = L(i, Y), \tag{3.1.8}$$

where m_s, the supply of money in real terms, is assumed to be an exogenous variable.

The components of the model may now be put together and the equilibrium values of the variables may be obtained. In the market for goods and services, equilibrium is attained when

$$I(i) + G = Y - C(Y), \tag{3.1.3}$$

and in the money market we have equilibrium when

$$m_s = L(i, Y). \tag{3.1.8}$$

Thus if G and m_s are known, the unknowns i and Y may be obtained by simultaneous solution of equations 3.1.3 and 3.1.8.

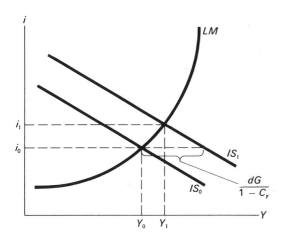

3|1|6
General equilibrium of the product and money markets.

When the rates of interest and associated income levels that provide product market equilibrium are plotted, we obtain the IS-curve which, as we have already seen, has a negative slope. In Fig. 3.1.6 we add to the IS-curve the LM-curve which specifies the interest rates and associated income levels that provide monetary equilibrium. Since by total differentiation of Eq. 3.1.8 with a fixed m_s we obtain

$$0 = L_i\, di + L_y\, dY,$$

we see that

$$\left(\frac{di}{dY}\right)_{LM} = -\frac{L_y}{L_i} > 0, \tag{3.1.9}$$

where the notation $(di/dY)_{LM}$ means "slope of the LM-curve," as distinguished from $(di/dY)_{IS}$, which refers to the slope of the IS-curve. So that we do not forget the economic rationale: We know that a rise in i will lead wealth holders to economize money balances by increasing their bond purchases. This means that additional cash balances are available for transactions, with the consequence that a higher rate of interest would imply monetary equilibrium at a higher level of income.

The general equilibrium solution is diagramed in Fig. 3.1.6. The intersection of the IS- and LM-curves is at i_0 and Y_0 and this accordingly establishes the values of i and Y that satisfy both the conditions for product and monetary equilibrium.

3.2 THE EFFECTIVENESS OF MONETARY AND FISCAL POLICY

It is now possible to examine the effects of monetary and fiscal policies on the level of income and the rate of interest. The effect of fiscal policy (a change in G) may be calculated by differentiating Eqs. 3.1.3 and 3.1.8 totally with respect to G. Following this procedure, we obtain

$$1 = (1 - C_y)\left(\frac{dY}{dG}\right) - I_i\left(\frac{di}{dG}\right), \tag{3.2.1}$$

$$0 = L_y\left(\frac{dY}{dG}\right) + L_i\left(\frac{di}{dG}\right). \tag{3.2.2}$$

These equations may be treated as a set of simultaneous linear equations with variables dY/dG and di/dG and coefficients $(1 - C_y)$, $-I_i$, L_y, and L_i.

The application of Cramer's Rule* for the solution of simultaneous linear equations gives

$$\frac{dY}{dG} = \frac{\begin{vmatrix} 1 & -I_i \\ 0 & L_i \end{vmatrix}}{\begin{vmatrix} 1 - C_y & -I_i \\ L_y & L_i \end{vmatrix}} = \frac{L_i}{L_i(1 - C_y) + L_yI_i} \tag{3.2.3}$$

as the solution for the change in income, and

$$\frac{di}{dG} = \frac{\begin{vmatrix} 1 - C_y & 1 \\ L_y & 0 \end{vmatrix}}{\begin{vmatrix} 1 - C_y & -I_i \\ L_y & L_i \end{vmatrix}} = \frac{-L_y}{L_i(1 - C_y) + L_yI_i} \tag{3.2.4}$$

as the change in the rate of interest. From 3.2.3 it is apparent that the multiplier of income with respect to a change in government purchases is positive, since $(1 - C_y) > 0$, $I_i < 0$, $L_i < 0$, and $L_y > 0$. Similarly, the change in the rate of

---

* The reader who has forgotten or is hazy about Cramer's Rule should consult the appendix to this chapter.

interest is positive, since $L_y > 0$, and the denominator of Eq. 3.2.4, $L_i(1 - C_y) + I_iL_y$, is negative.

The increase in income that results from a rise in G could occur only if additional transactions cash can be found. Given a fixed money supply, this could happen only if wealth holders could be induced to economize cash balances and this, as we have seen, necessitates that the rate of interest rises.

Looked at in terms of the *IS–LM* diagram in Fig. 3.1.6, the increase in G implies a shift to the right of the *IS*-schedule with the consequence that the equilibrium level of income and the rate of interest rise to Y_1 and i_1, respectively. The size of the horizontal shift in the *IS*-curve can be calculated by returning to Eq. 3.1.3 and holding the rate of interest constant while differentiating with respect to G. This gives

$$\frac{dY}{dG} = \frac{1}{1 - C_y},$$

which is nothing other than the simple government purchase multiplier of the last chapter. However, note that the actual income change is less than this shift in the *IS*-curve because of the fact that the rise in the rate of interest causes investment to decline, and that this decline in investment partially offsets the expansionary effect of the increase in G.

If the conditions assumed in the extreme "classical" theory of the demand for money prevail, the offset will be complete and there will be no change in income at all. In the classical theory the demand for money is a function of the level of income but not of the rate of interest. Therefore $L_i = 0$, so that in this case Eq. 3.2.3 would reduce to $dY/dG = 0$.

Thus, if the classical theory of the demand for money is correct, a rise in government purchases would have no effect on the level of income. Each dollar of additional G would merely cause the interest rate to rise by enough to snuff out a dollar of private investment. Government purchase and tax policy in such a world would

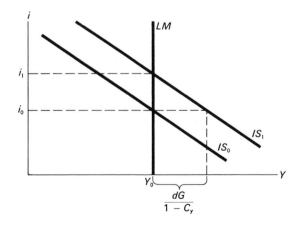

3|2|1
The effect of an increase in government purchases under classical monetary assumptions.

be purely matters of public finance. They would have no effect on the level of income and would therefore serve only to determine how output is distributed between consumption, investment, and government. As can be seen from Eq. 3.1.9, which describes the slope of the LM-curve, the LM-curve in this extreme case would be vertical, so that a shift in the IS-curve could never affect the level of income. This situation is depicted in Fig. 3.2.1, in which it can be seen that despite a shift to the right in the IS-curve from IS_0 to IS_1, the level of income does not change at all.

In an extreme Keynesian world, the demand for money is infinitely elastic with respect to the rate of interest. If the interest rate gets low enough, relative to trans-actions costs, wealth holders will be willing to absorb large additional balances with only a negligible further fall in the rate of interest. Such a situation is the famous Keynesian "liquidity trap" which, if it is obtained, implies that L_i is so large that Eq. 3.2.3 reduces to

$$\frac{dY}{dG} \approx \frac{1}{1 - C_y},$$

while Eq. 3.2.4 reduces to

$$\frac{di}{dG} \approx 0,$$

and the slope of the LM-curve, $-L_y/L_i$, approaches zero.

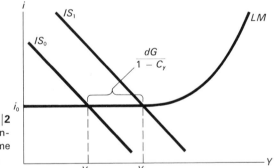

3|2|2
The effect of an increase in govern-ment purchases under extreme Keynesian monetary assumptions.

In the extreme Keynesian case, additional transactions balances can be ob-tained from idle balances without raising the rate of interest. Consequently, the increase in G does not raise the rate of interest, and there is therefore no decline in the level of investment. In this case, therefore, the multiplier becomes identical to the multiplier of Chapter 2, namely, the reciprocal of the marginal propensity to save. As depicted in Fig. 3.2.2, the LM-curve is horizontal in the range in which it is cut by the IS-curve, so that the level of income rises by the full amount of the horizontal shift of the IS-curve.

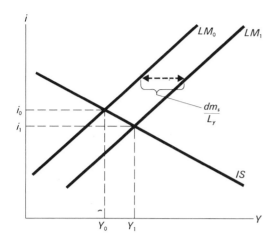

$3|2|3$
The effect of an increase in the money supply.

The effect of monetary policy can be analyzed by differentiating Eq. 3.1.3 and 3.1.8 totally with respect to m_s. We obtain

$$0 = (1 - C_y)\left(\frac{dY}{dm_s}\right) - I_i\left(\frac{di}{dm_s}\right),$$ (3.2.5)

$$1 = L_y\left(\frac{dY}{dm_s}\right) + L_i\left(\frac{di}{dm_s}\right).$$ (3.2.6)

Solving these equations simultaneously, we obtain

$$\frac{dY}{dm_s} = \frac{I_i}{L_i(1 - C_y) + L_y I_i},$$ (3.2.7)

$$\frac{di}{dm_s} = \frac{1 - C_y}{L_i(1 - C_y) + L_y I_i}$$ (3.2.8)

as the changes in the equilibrium levels of income and the rate of interest, respectively.

The first thing to note about these expressions is that the denominator in each case is the same as it was when we changed government purchases. Let us call this denominator Δ and note that since $\Delta < 0$, and $I_i < 0$, an increase in the money supply is associated with an increase in the level of income. Similarly, since $1 - C_y > 0$, the increase in the money supply reduces the rate of interest. These changes are diagramed in Fig. 3.2.3, in which the increase in the money supply causes the LM-curve to shift to the right. The rate of interest falls from i_0 to i_1, and since this causes investment to rise, the level of income rises from Y_0 to Y_1.

In the extreme classical case, $L_i = 0$, which means that the LM-curve is vertical and 3.2.7 reduces to

$$\frac{dY}{dm_s} = \frac{1}{L_y}.$$

The term L_y is the partial derivative of the demand for money with respect to a change in income. If we return to the classical demand function, $m_d = kY$, we see that L_y is nothing other than the k-ratio of classical monetary theory. Since the k-ratio represents the average length of time money is held between transactions, $1/k = 1/L_y$ is the number of times the average dollar turns over each period. Therefore, since each dollar that is added to the money supply can support $1/L_y$ additional transactions, and since on classical assumptions money balances are held purely for transactions purposes, the increase in income will be $1/L_y$ times the increase in the money supply.

By holding the rate of interest constant and differentiating the monetary equilibrium equation, $m_s = L(Y, i)$, with respect to m_s, we can calculate the size of the horizontal shift in the LM-curve. Since $dm_s = L_y \, dY$, if i is held constant, the horizontal shift must be

$$dY = \frac{1}{L_y} \, dm_s,$$

which simply means that since a dollar turns over $1/L_y$ times a year, an increase in the money supply of one dollar will support additional income of $1/L_y$ dollars at a constant rate of interest.

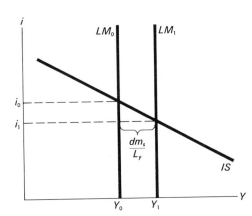

3|2|4

The effect of an increase in the money supply under extreme classical assumptions.

The classical case is illustrated in Fig. 3.2.4. The LM-curve is vertical and the level of income increases by the full amount of the shift in the LM-curve. Returning to Fig. 3.2.3, in which the LM-curve is assumed to have a positive slope, we observe that the income change is less than the full amount of the horizontal shift in the LM-curve. The reason is simple: When the monetary authority increases the money supply, the market rate of interest must fall if monetary equilibrium is to obtain at the preexisting level of income. However, a fall in the rate of interest implies that interest revenues fall relative to transactions costs. Therefore, individuals will increase the level of cash balances that they hold per dollar of

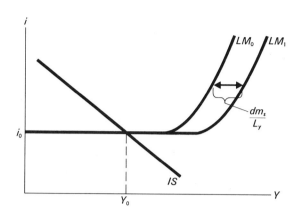

3|2|5
The effect of an increase in the money supply under extreme Keynesian assumptions.

transaction. The income velocity of money therefore decreases, and this implies that the increase in income will be less than in proportion to the increase in the money supply.

In the Keynesian extreme, $L_i \rightarrow \infty$, so that the multipliers given in 3.2.7 and 3.2.8 reduce to

$$\frac{di}{dm_s} = 0, \quad \text{and} \quad \frac{dY}{dm_s} = 0,$$

respectively. In this Keynesian case, which is illustrated in Fig. 3.2.5, the increase in the money supply shifts the LM-curve from LM_0 to LM_1. But this shift in LM has no effect on the rate of interest or on the level of investment, and this, in turn, means that the level of income must remain unchanged. The extreme Keynesian assumptions imply that wealth holders are willing to accept the additional money balances in exchange for bonds with no change in bond prices. If bond prices remain the same, so will the rate of interest.

3.3 THE LIMITATIONS OF COMPARATIVE-STATIC ANALYSIS

The models we have discussed thus far are comparative-static models. The equations yield equilibrium solutions for the variables, but they say nothing at all about the process by which adjustments to equilibrium are made. Analysis of the effect on the equilibrium values of the variables in these models of changes in the parameters of the system is comparative-static analysis. Although the text did include some discussion of the various adjustment processes, the formal models themselves did not provide any clues about these processes.

As pointed out in Chapter 1, the results of comparative-static analysis will sometimes be ambiguous or even misleading and incorrect. In order to find out for sure if comparative-static results are correct, it is necessary to introduce dynamic assumptions and to analyze how the system reacts to disequilibrium.

An illustration of this difficulty in the case of the Keynesian system can be provided by changing the investment demand function to

$$I = I(i, Y), \qquad I_y > 0.$$

Thus it is now assumed that a rise in income will lead to a positive induced change in the level of investment. The parameter I_y is known as the "marginal propensity to invest." Since business firms tend to increase their investment spending when high profits generate high levels of internal funds, and since profits are highly correlated with the level of income, the hypothesis that investment rises as income rises is certainly a reasonable one.

The product and monetary equilibrium equations now become

$$I(i, Y) + G = Y - C(Y),$$
$$m_s = L(i, Y).$$

Total differentiation of these equations with respect to m_s yields

$$0 = (1 - C_y - I_y)\left(\frac{dY}{dm_s}\right) - I_i\left(\frac{di}{dm_s}\right),$$

$$1 = L_y\left(\frac{dY}{dm_s}\right) + L_i\left(\frac{di}{dm_s}\right).$$

When these equations are solved simultaneously, we obtain

$$\frac{dY}{dm_s} = \frac{I_i}{\Delta'},$$

where $\Delta' = L_i(1 - C_y - I_y) + I_i L_y$.

In the model discussed in Sections 3.1 and 3.2, we had

$$\Delta = L_i(1 - C_y) + I_i L_y,$$

which is always negative. However, when allowance is made for the possibility that changes in investment might be induced by changes in income, it becomes apparent that Δ' may be either positive or negative, depending upon the value of the marginal propensity to invest, I_y. Consequently, it cannot be definitely ascertained from comparative statics whether an increase in the money supply will raise the level of income unless the actual values of the parameters (partial derivatives) are known. If Δ' turns out to be positive, dY/dm_s would be negative, and the static model would predict that an increase in the money supply would lower the level of income. Since such a conclusion does not make sense, it is likely that there is something seriously wrong with the comparative-static solution.

Analysis of the adjustment process is required to clear up these difficulties. In subsequent chapters we shall attempt to develop tools of analysis that will permit us to handle such ambiguous cases, and, in Chapter 13, we will take up the dynamics of the Keynesian system explicitly and show that an increase in the money supply can *never* cause the level of income to fall.

REFERENCES

T. F. Dernburg and D. M. McDougall, *Macroeconomics*, 3rd edition (New York: McGraw-Hill, 1968), Chapters 7–10 and appendixes.

J. R. Hicks, "Mr. Keynes and the Classics: A Suggested Interpretation," *Econometrica* (April, 1937).

J. M. Keynes, *The General Theory of Employment, Interest, and Money* (New York: Harcourt-Brace, 1936).

W. L. Smith, "A Graphical Exposition of the Complete Keynesian System," *Southern Economic Journal* (October, 1956).

James Tobin, "Liquidity Preference and Monetary Policy," *Review of Economics and Statistics* (May, 1947).

James Tobin, "The Interest Elasticity of the Transactions Demand for Cash," *Review of Economics and Statistics* (August, 1956).

Appendix to Chapter 3: Determinants

This appendix is designed to provide a quick review of the rules governing determinants. The student who is familiar with such matters as determinants, minors, cofactors, and Cramer's Rule may skip on to Chapter 4.

A determinant is a square array of quantities (elements) that are so related to each other that when the determinant is evaluated, the result is a scalar quantity. The determinant $|A|$ might be written

$$|A| = \begin{vmatrix} a_{11} & a_{12} \\ a_{21} & a_{22} \end{vmatrix}.$$

This 2×2 determinant is evaluated by multiplying the northwest element, a_{11}, by the southeast element, a_{22}, and adding this product to the product of the northeast element, a_{12}, and the southwest element, a_{21}, with its sign changed. Therefore

$$|A| = a_{11}a_{22} - a_{12}a_{21}.$$

In the case of the 3×3 determinant,

$$|A| = \begin{vmatrix} a_{11} & a_{12} & a_{13} \\ a_{21} & a_{22} & a_{23} \\ a_{31} & a_{32} & a_{33} \end{vmatrix},$$

the determinant may be evaluated by summing the product of three northwest-southeast multiplications, namely,

$$a_{11}a_{22}a_{33} + a_{13}a_{21}a_{32} + a_{12}a_{23}a_{31},$$

and then performing the corresponding southwest-northeast multiplications, changing their signs, and adding them to the above sum. Since the southwest-northeast multiplications, with their signs changed, yield

$$- a_{13}a_{22}a_{31} - a_{12}a_{21}a_{33} - a_{11}a_{23}a_{32},$$

the value of the determinant is

$$|A| = a_{11}a_{22}a_{33} + a_{13}a_{21}a_{32} + a_{12}a_{23}a_{31} - a_{13}a_{22}a_{31} - a_{12}a_{21}a_{33} - a_{11}a_{23}a_{32}.$$

It should be noted that each of these products contains one and only one element from each row and column of the determinant.

If the determinant is of an order greater than 3×3, evaluation of the determinants necessitates that it be split into *minors* and *cofactors*. The minor of an element of a determinant is formed by suppressing both the row and the column in which the element appears, and forming a determinant from the remaining elements. For example, in the 3×3 determinant, the minor of the element a_{11} is the determinant

$$\min a_{11} = \begin{vmatrix} a_{22} & a_{23} \\ a_{32} & a_{33} \end{vmatrix},$$

while the minor of a_{13} is,

$$\min a_{13} = \begin{vmatrix} a_{21} & a_{22} \\ a_{31} & a_{32} \end{vmatrix},$$

and the minor of a_{22} is,

$$\min a_{22} = \begin{vmatrix} a_{11} & a_{13} \\ a_{31} & a_{33} \end{vmatrix}.$$

A *cofactor* of an element is the minor of the element with the appropriate sign attached; a cofactor is therefore sometimes referred to as a signed minor. The appropriate sign can be ascertained from the subscripts of the element. If the sum of the subscripts is even, the sign of the cofactor is positive, whereas if the subscripts add up to an odd number, the cofactor is negative. Using the notation A_{ij} to represent the cofactor of the element a_{ij} in the determinant $|A|$, we have

$$A_{11} = \begin{vmatrix} a_{22} & a_{23} \\ a_{32} & a_{33} \end{vmatrix},$$

but

$$A_{12} = -\begin{vmatrix} a_{21} & a_{23} \\ a_{31} & a_{33} \end{vmatrix}$$

and

$$A_{13} = \begin{vmatrix} a_{21} & a_{22} \\ a_{31} & a_{32} \end{vmatrix}.$$

With these rules in mind, we can now evaluate higher-order determinants. In general, the value of a determinant may be found by adding together the product of the elements of any row or column of the determinant with their respective cofactors. If we arbitrarily pick the first column of the 3×3 determinant of $|A|$, we have

$$|A| = a_{11} \begin{vmatrix} a_{22} & a_{23} \\ a_{32} & a_{33} \end{vmatrix} - a_{21} \begin{vmatrix} a_{12} & a_{13} \\ a_{32} & a_{33} \end{vmatrix} + a_{31} \begin{vmatrix} a_{12} & a_{13} \\ a_{22} & a_{23} \end{vmatrix},$$

or, if we pick the first row,

$$|A| = a_{11} \begin{vmatrix} a_{22} & a_{23} \\ a_{32} & a_{33} \end{vmatrix} - a_{12} \begin{vmatrix} a_{21} & a_{23} \\ a_{31} & a_{33} \end{vmatrix} + a_{13} \begin{vmatrix} a_{21} & a_{22} \\ a_{31} & a_{32} \end{vmatrix},$$

which in either case confirms the earlier result obtained for the value of $|A|$.

We are now in a position to make use of a most important concept known as *Cramer's Rule.* The rule states that the solution to a set of simultaneous linear equations, for example,

$$a_{11}x_1 + a_{12}x_2 = y_1,$$

$$a_{21}x_1 + a_{22}x_2 = y_2,$$

where the x's are unknown, can be obtained by forming the ratio of two determinants. The denominator is the determinant formed by the a_{ij} coefficients. Let this denominator be denoted by $|A|$. Then

$$|A| = \begin{vmatrix} a_{11} & a_{12} \\ a_{21} & a_{22} \end{vmatrix} = a_{11}a_{22} - a_{12}a_{21}.$$

The numerator is formed by taking the determinant $|A|$ and replacing the co-efficients in the column associated with the variable for which a solution is sought, by the right-hand terms y_1 and y_2. Thus the solution for x_1 is

$$x_1 = \frac{\begin{vmatrix} y_1 & a_{12} \\ y_2 & a_{22} \end{vmatrix}}{|A|} = \frac{a_{22}y_1}{|A|} - \frac{a_{12}y_2}{|A|},$$

and the solution for x_2 is

$$x_2 = \frac{\begin{vmatrix} a_{11} & y_1 \\ a_{21} & y_2 \end{vmatrix}}{|A|} = \frac{a_{11}y_2}{|A|} - \frac{a_{21}y_1}{|A|}.$$

We now set down some rules governing determinants. These rules are illustrated here for the 2×2 case, however, the student is urged to verify them for the 3×3 case.

Proposition I. If two rows or columns of a determinant are interchanged, the sign of the determinant is changed. For example, if

$$|A| = \begin{vmatrix} a_{11} & a_{12} \\ a_{21} & a_{22} \end{vmatrix} = a_{11}a_{22} - a_{12}a_{21},$$

then

$$\begin{vmatrix} a_{12} & a_{11} \\ a_{22} & a_{21} \end{vmatrix} = a_{12}a_{21} - a_{11}a_{22} = -|A|.$$

Proposition II. If two rows or columns of a determinant are identical, the value of the determinant is zero. For example,

$$|A| = \begin{vmatrix} a_{11} & a_{11} \\ a_{21} & a_{21} \end{vmatrix} = a_{11}a_{21} - a_{11}a_{21} = 0.$$

Proposition III. If one row or column of a determinant is multiplied by a scalar, u, the result equals the value of the determinant multiplied by the scalar. For example,

$$\begin{vmatrix} a_{11}u & a_{12} \\ a_{21}u & a_{22} \end{vmatrix} = (a_{11}a_{22} - a_{12}a_{21})u = |A|u.$$

Proposition IV. If all elements of a determinant are multiplied by the scalar, u, the result equals the value of the determinant multiplied by u raised to the power n, where n is the number of rows (columns) in the determinant. For example,

$$\begin{vmatrix} a_{11}u & a_{12}u \\ a_{21}u & a_{22}u \end{vmatrix} = (a_{11}a_{22} - a_{12}a_{21})u^2 = |A|u^2.$$

Proposition V. A constant multiple of any row (column) of a determinant may be added to or subtracted from any other row (column) without changing the value of the determinant. For example,

$$\begin{vmatrix} a_{11} + a_{12}u & a_{12} \\ a_{21} + a_{22}u & a_{22} \end{vmatrix} = a_{11}a_{22} + ua_{12}a_{22} - a_{12}a_{21} - ua_{12}a_{22} = |A|.$$

For the analysis of the stability of equilibrium in multisectoral models, the concept of a *principal* minor is extremely important. Principal minors are the minors of the elements of the diagonal which runs from the northwest to the southeast of a determinant. Since the subscripts of the elements of this *principal* diagonal are always even, the minors and cofactors of an element of the diagonal of the determinant are the same. For the 4×4 determinant,

$$|A| = \begin{vmatrix} a_{11} & a_{12} & a_{13} & a_{14} \\ a_{21} & a_{22} & a_{23} & a_{24} \\ a_{31} & a_{32} & a_{33} & a_{34} \\ a_{41} & a_{42} & a_{43} & a_{44} \end{vmatrix},$$

the *third-order principal minors* are the determinants

$$A_{11} = \begin{vmatrix} a_{22} & a_{23} & a_{24} \\ a_{32} & a_{33} & a_{34} \\ a_{42} & a_{43} & a_{44} \end{vmatrix}, \qquad A_{22} = \begin{vmatrix} a_{11} & a_{13} & a_{14} \\ a_{31} & a_{33} & a_{34} \\ a_{41} & a_{43} & a_{44} \end{vmatrix},$$

$$A_{33} = \begin{vmatrix} a_{11} & a_{12} & a_{14} \\ a_{21} & a_{22} & a_{24} \\ a_{41} & a_{42} & a_{44} \end{vmatrix}, \qquad A_{44} = \begin{vmatrix} a_{11} & a_{12} & a_{13} \\ a_{21} & a_{22} & a_{23} \\ a_{31} & a_{32} & a_{33} \end{vmatrix},$$

where the notation A_{11} means the principal minor of the element a_{11} of the determinant $|A|$.

The principal minors of the determinants A_{11}, A_{22}, A_{33}, and A_{44} are *second-order principal minors of* $|A|$. The principal minors of A_{11}, for example, are the determinants,

$$A_{11,22} = \begin{vmatrix} a_{33} & a_{34} \\ a_{43} & a_{44} \end{vmatrix}, \quad A_{11,33} = \begin{vmatrix} a_{22} & a_{24} \\ a_{42} & a_{44} \end{vmatrix}, \quad A_{11,44} = \begin{vmatrix} a_{22} & a_{23} \\ a_{32} & a_{33} \end{vmatrix}.$$

As the reader can easily verify by writing out the principal minors of A_{22}, A_{33}, and A_{44}, any minor $A_{ii,jj} = A_{jj,ii}$. Consequently, there are only six *distinct* second-order principal minors of A. They are

$$A_{11,22}, \quad A_{11,33}, \quad A_{11,44},$$
$$A_{22,33}, \quad A_{22,44},$$
$$A_{33,44}.$$

Finally, the first-order principal minors of A are the minors of the elements of the principal diagonal of the second-order minors, and these simply are the elements of the principal diagonal of the determinant $|A|$, namely, a_{11}, a_{22}, a_{33}, and a_{44}.

The number of distinct combinations of n items taken k at a time is given by the well-known formula

$$\frac{n!}{k!(n-k)!},$$

where $n!$, known as "n factorial" is defined as $n(n-1)(n-2)\cdots 1$. Thus in a 4×4 ($n = 4$) determinant, the number of distinct third-order principal minors ($k = 3$) is

$$\frac{(4)(3)(2)(1)}{(3)(2)(4-3)!} = \frac{24}{6} = 4.$$

The number of distinct second-order principal minors ($k = 2$) is

$$\frac{24}{2(4-2)!} = 6,$$

and the number of distinct first-order principal minors equals the number of elements in the principal diagonal, so that in the present case, there are

$$\frac{24}{(4-1)!} = 4$$

distinct first-order principal minors.

CHAPTER 4

Elements of Interindustry Economics

4.1 INTRODUCTION

Sooner or later the macroeconomic planner has to abandon such simple artifacts as the models of Chapters 2 and 3 in favor of a less highly aggregative interindustry and intersectoral view of the economy. One of the most useful planning devices—a tool that links individual industries to the functioning of the economy as a whole—is the input-output table. Developed by W. W. Leontief during the 1930's, input-output analysis has been utilized by governmental agencies both here and abroad, and it constitutes a vital tool of planning in advanced and developing economies. It is hardly an exaggeration to say that no self-respecting planner would proceed very far without constructing or consulting an input-output table.

The mathematical foundation for input-output analysis is the algebra of matrices. Although it has been assumed that the reader has thus far been familiar with the requisite mathematics, past experience suggests that matrix algebra is not a familiar topic to many students of economics. We therefore begin this chapter with an outline of some of the rudiments of this body of mathematics. Thereafter we can proceed with a study of input-output economics.

4.2 THE SIMPLE ELEMENTS OF MATRIX ALGEBRA

By the use of Cramer's Rule it is possible to solve systems of simultaneous linear equations of the second, third, and even nth order. However, solution involves several steps and if the system is complicated enough, the sheer labor of writing out the terms will probably serve to exhaust and discourage the analyst before he gets very far. The analyst, moreover, will often need a way of generalizing his results to encompass equation systems of any order he chooses. Thus it would be of enormous assistance if a complicated system of simultaneous equations, such as

$$y_1 = a_{11}x_1 + a_{12}x_2 + \cdots + a_{1n}x_n,$$
$$y_2 = a_{21}x_1 + a_{22}x_2 + \cdots + a_{2n}x_n,$$
$$\vdots \qquad\qquad\qquad\qquad\qquad (4.2.1)$$
$$y_m = a_{m1}x_1 + a_{m2}x_2 + \cdots + a_{mn}x_n,$$

could be compressed into a simple expression of the form

$$Y = AX.$$

If, in addition, algebraic operations on Y, A, and X could be performed in the same way that they could be performed if Y, A, and X were single algebraic quantities (scalars), it would be possible to prove theorems and propositions for cases of any order. Matrix algebra is the body of mathematics that permits the analyst to perform such apparent feats of mathematical magic.

A matrix is simply an array of numbers. For example,

$$A = \begin{bmatrix} a_{11} & a_{12} \\ a_{21} & a_{22} \end{bmatrix}$$

is a 2×2 square matrix. Each of the terms, a_{ij}, is an *element*. The position of an element in the matrix is denoted by the subscripts, i referring to the row and j to the column in which the element is found. The element a_{21}, for example, is to be found in row 2, column 1.

If the matrix were

$$B = \begin{bmatrix} b_{11} & b_{12} & b_{13} \\ b_{21} & b_{22} & b_{23} \end{bmatrix},$$

we would describe this as a matrix of dimension 2×3. Thus the *dimension* of a matrix is given by the number of rows and columns that it contains.

The interchanging of the rows and columns of a matrix is known as *transposition*, and the transposed matrix A would then be denoted as A'. The transposes of the foregoing matrices A and B are

$$A' = \begin{bmatrix} a_{11} & a_{21} \\ a_{12} & a_{22} \end{bmatrix}, \qquad B' = \begin{bmatrix} b_{11} & b_{21} \\ b_{12} & b_{22} \\ b_{13} & b_{23} \end{bmatrix}.$$

When a matrix consists of a single column, such as

$$X = \begin{bmatrix} x_1 \\ x_2 \\ x_3 \end{bmatrix},$$

we denote the array as a *column vector*. Since the transpose of a column vector is a *row vector*, we generally write the row vector as the transpose of a column vector.

For example, the row vector

$$[x_1 \quad x_2 \quad x_3]$$

is the transpose of the column vector X and is therefore written

$$X' = [x_1 \quad x_2 \quad x_3].$$

When a matrix consists of a single element, as in

$$A = [a], \qquad B = [b_1 + b_2], \qquad \text{or,} \qquad C = [c_1 c_2 + c_3 c_4],$$

the matrix is termed a *scalar*.

A matrix that has ones as the elements of the *principal diagonal* and zeros elsewhere is known as an *identity matrix*. Thus the identity matrix is written

$$I = \begin{bmatrix} 1 & 0 & 0 \\ 0 & 1 & 0 \\ 0 & 0 & 1 \end{bmatrix}.$$

When the ones in the principal diagonal are replaced by a scalar, u, we obtain a *scalar matrix*,

$$uI = \begin{bmatrix} u & 0 & 0 \\ 0 & u & 0 \\ 0 & 0 & u \end{bmatrix},$$

and when the elements in the diagonal differ from each other, we have the *diagonal matrix*,

$$A_{ii} = \begin{bmatrix} a_{11} & 0 & 0 \\ 0 & a_{22} & 0 \\ 0 & 0 & a_{33} \end{bmatrix}.$$

If only the elements above or below the principal diagonal are zero, the matrix is said to be *triangular*. For example,

$$A = \begin{bmatrix} a_{11} & a_{12} & a_{13} \\ 0 & a_{22} & a_{23} \\ 0 & 0 & a_{33} \end{bmatrix}, \qquad B = \begin{bmatrix} b_{11} & 0 & 0 \\ b_{21} & b_{22} & 0 \\ b_{31} & b_{32} & b_{33} \end{bmatrix}$$

are both triangular matrices.

Finally, if a transposed matrix is the same as the original matrix, the matrix is *symmetric*. For example,

$$A = A' = \begin{bmatrix} a_{11} & a_{12} & a_{13} \\ a_{12} & a_{22} & a_{23} \\ a_{13} & a_{23} & a_{33} \end{bmatrix}$$

is a symmetric matrix.

Next, consider some of the elementary algebraic operations that may be undertaken with matrices. Corresponding elements of a matrix may be added if the matrices are of the same dimension. For example, if

$$A = \begin{bmatrix} a_{11} & a_{12} \\ a_{21} & a_{22} \end{bmatrix}, \qquad B = \begin{bmatrix} b_{11} & b_{12} \\ b_{21} & b_{22} \end{bmatrix},$$

then

$$A + B = \begin{bmatrix} a_{11} + b_{11} & a_{12} + b_{12} \\ a_{21} + b_{21} & a_{22} + b_{22} \end{bmatrix}.$$

The order of addition is immaterial. Thus the first rule of matrix addition is that the commutative rule of scalar addition holds, namely, $A + B = B + A$.

Provided again that A and B have the same dimensions, the elements of one may be subtracted from the corresponding elements of the other to form a new matrix. For example,

$$A - B = \begin{bmatrix} a_{11} - b_{11} & a_{12} - b_{12} \\ a_{21} - b_{21} & a_{22} - b_{22} \end{bmatrix},$$

and

$$B - A = \begin{bmatrix} b_{11} - a_{11} & b_{12} - a_{12} \\ b_{21} - a_{21} & b_{22} - a_{22} \end{bmatrix}.$$

The order of subtraction is obviously important. In scalar algebra $a - b$ is not generally equal to $b - a$ and the same is, of course, true for matrix subtraction. Thus it is generally the case that $A - B \neq B - A$.

Two or more matrices may be multiplied to form a new matrix. When we write $C = AB$, we say that C is the result of "premultiplying" B by A, or that C is the result of "postmultiplying" A by B. When we premultiply B by A, we have

$$AB = \begin{bmatrix} a_{11} & a_{12} \\ a_{21} & a_{22} \end{bmatrix} \begin{bmatrix} b_{11} & b_{12} \\ b_{21} & b_{22} \end{bmatrix} = \begin{bmatrix} a_{11}b_{11} + a_{12}b_{21} & a_{11}b_{12} + a_{12}b_{22} \\ a_{21}b_{11} + a_{22}b_{21} & a_{21}b_{12} + a_{22}b_{22} \end{bmatrix}.$$

Let the product AB be denoted as the C-matrix. The element $c_{11} = a_{11}b_{11} + a_{12}b_{21}$ is formed by multiplying the successive elements of the first row of the A-matrix by the successive elements of the first column of the B-matrix and summing the results. Similarly, element c_{12} is formed by multiplying the successive elements of the first row of the A-matrix by the successive elements of the second column of the B-matrix and summing these products. The element c_{21} is formed by multiplying the successive elements of the second row of the A-matrix by their first column B-matrix counterparts and summing these products. Finally, c_{22} is formed by multiplying the successive elements in the second row of the A-matrix by the successive elements in the second column of the B-matrix and summing these products.

It is apparent that A and B need not be of the same dimension for matrix multiplication to be feasible. All that is necessary is that the matrices be *conformable*. This means that if A is postmultiplied by B, A must have as many elements in each row as B has elements in each column. For example, if

$$A = \begin{bmatrix} a_{11} & a_{12} \\ a_{21} & a_{22} \end{bmatrix}, \qquad B = \begin{bmatrix} b_1 \\ b_2 \end{bmatrix},$$

A and B are conformable and AB becomes the column vector,

$$AB = \begin{bmatrix} a_{11}b_1 + a_{12}b_2 \\ a_{21}b_1 + a_{22}b_2 \end{bmatrix}.$$

On the other hand,

$$BA = \begin{bmatrix} b_1 \\ b_2 \end{bmatrix} \begin{bmatrix} a_{11} & a_{12} \\ a_{21} & a_{22} \end{bmatrix},$$

are not conformable and cannot be multiplied, since B has only one column while A has two rows.

As is apparent from these illustrations, the order of multiplication is extremely important; AB turned out to be a column vector, but BA was not conformable with respect to multiplication. Similarly, if a column vector is premultiplied by its transpose, we obtain a sum of squares which, of course, is a scalar. For example,

$$X'X = \begin{bmatrix} x_1 & x_2 & x_3 \end{bmatrix} \begin{bmatrix} x_1 \\ x_2 \\ x_3 \end{bmatrix} = x_1^2 + x_2^2 + x_3^2.$$

However, when we reverse the order of multiplication, we obtain

$$XX' = \begin{bmatrix} x_1 \\ x_2 \\ x_3 \end{bmatrix} \begin{bmatrix} x_1 & x_2 & x_3 \end{bmatrix} = \begin{bmatrix} x_1^2 & x_1x_2 & x_1x_3 \\ x_1x_2 & x_2^2 & x_2x_3 \\ x_1x_3 & x_2x_3 & x_3^2 \end{bmatrix},$$

which is a symmetric matrix. Note, parenthetically, that the sum of the elements of the principal diagonal of $X'X$ and XX' is the same. This sum is known as the *trace* of the matrix and we see from this example that

$$\text{tr } X'X = \text{tr } XX'.$$

Whenever a matrix is pre- or postmultiplied by its transpose, the result is a symmetric matrix. The transpose of a scalar, of course, equals itself and is therefore a trivial case of symmetry. Nevertheless, both of the foregoing multiplications generate symmetric matrices. It is important to bear in mind that while XX' and $X'X$ (and for that matter AA' and $A'A$, etc.) result in symmetric matrices, the resultant matrices will differ, depending upon the order of multiplication.

An extremely important property of matrices is that pre- or postmultiplication of a matrix by the identity matrix leaves the matrix unchanged. For example,

$$\begin{bmatrix} 1 & 0 \\ 0 & 1 \end{bmatrix} \begin{bmatrix} a_{11} & a_{12} \\ a_{21} & a_{22} \end{bmatrix} = \begin{bmatrix} a_{11} & a_{12} \\ a_{21} & a_{22} \end{bmatrix} = \begin{bmatrix} a_{11} & a_{12} \\ a_{21} & a_{22} \end{bmatrix} \begin{bmatrix} 1 & 0 \\ 0 & 1 \end{bmatrix},$$

which implies that $IA = A = AI$.

It can now be seen how, by following the rules of matrix multiplication, the system of Eq. 4.2.1 can be compressed into the expression $Y = AX$. The y_i's form a column vector, while the right-hand terms represent the postmultiplication of the matrix of a_{ij} coefficients by the column vector of x_j's. Thus the system can be written

$$\begin{bmatrix} y_1 \\ y_2 \\ \vdots \\ y_m \end{bmatrix} = \begin{bmatrix} a_{11} & a_{12} & \cdots & a_{1n} \\ a_{21} & a_{22} & \cdots & a_{2n} \\ \vdots & & & \vdots \\ a_{m1} & a_{m2} & \cdots & a_{mn} \end{bmatrix} \begin{bmatrix} x_1 \\ x_2 \\ \vdots \\ x_n \end{bmatrix},$$

or still more simply as $Y = AX$.

The final arithmetic operation that must be considered is the matrix counterpart of division. In the scalar equation $y = ax$ the solution for x is obtained by isolating x on one side of the equation. This is accomplished by dividing both sides of the equation by a or by multiplying both sides of the equation by its reciprocal, $1/a = a^{-1}$. Therefore $x = a^{-1}y$. In matrix algebra we proceed to a solution of an entire vector of unknowns by a process that is in principle similar to multiplying both sides of a matrix equation by the reciprocal of a. If we have the equation $Y = AX$, and we wish to solve for the X-vector, we have to find a new matrix such that when we premultiply both sides of the equation by the new matrix, the result is to isolate the X-vector on one side of the equation. This new matrix is the *inverse matrix*, A^{-1}, and it is defined in such a way that when it is pre- or postmultiplied by the A-matrix, the result is the identity matrix, I. Accordingly,

$$A^{-1}A = I = AA^{-1}$$

defines the inverse matrix.

Having defined the inverse matrix in this fashion, it is now possible to return to the equation

$$Y = AX, \tag{4.2.2}$$

and by following the rules for operating with matrices, we can see how a solution for the X-vector may be obtained. First, premultiply both sides of 4.2.2 by the inverse matrix. This yields $A^{-1}Y = A^{-1}AX$. However, since the inverse is defined in such a way that $A^{-1}A = I$, we have $A^{-1}Y = IX$. Finally, since $IX = X$, we have

$$X = A^{-1}Y. \tag{4.2.3}$$

The formal procedure for inverting a square matrix (no other kind can be inverted) may be outlined in a set of four steps. To illustrate these steps, let us invert the matrix

$$A = \begin{bmatrix} a_{11} & a_{12} \\ a_{21} & a_{22} \end{bmatrix}.$$

Step 1. Form a matrix in which the a_{ij} elements are replaced by their respective cofactors. Therefore form

$$\begin{bmatrix} a_{22} & -a_{21} \\ -a_{12} & a_{11} \end{bmatrix}.$$

Step 2. Transpose the matrix of cofactors. Therefore let

$$A^* = \begin{bmatrix} a_{22} & -a_{12} \\ -a_{21} & a_{11} \end{bmatrix}.$$

Such a transposed matrix of cofactors is known as the adjoint of A, and is usually denoted by A^*.

Step 3. Evaluate the determinant of A. Accordingly,

$$|A| = a_{11}a_{22} - a_{12}a_{21}.$$

Step 4. Form the inverse matrix by dividing each element of the adjoint by $|A|$. Therefore

$$A^{-1} = \begin{bmatrix} \dfrac{a_{22}}{|A|} & \dfrac{-a_{12}}{|A|} \\ \dfrac{-a_{21}}{|A|} & \dfrac{a_{11}}{|A|} \end{bmatrix} = \begin{bmatrix} \dfrac{a_{22}}{a_{11}a_{22} - a_{12}a_{21}} & \dfrac{-a_{12}}{a_{11}a_{22} - a_{12}a_{21}} \\ \dfrac{-a_{21}}{a_{11}a_{22} - a_{12}a_{21}} & \dfrac{a_{11}}{a_{11}a_{22} - a_{12}a_{22}} \end{bmatrix}.$$

Finally, and before doing anything else, check the result by making sure that $AA^{-1} = I$.

The rationale for this procedure follows from a property of determinants that has not as yet been discussed. This is the property that expansions in terms of so-called *alien* cofactors vanish. This means that if the elements of a row or column are multiplied by the cofactors of another row or column, the resultant sum of products will be zero. For example, if we have the determinant

$$|A| = \begin{vmatrix} a_{11} & a_{12} & a_{13} \\ a_{21} & a_{22} & a_{23} \\ a_{31} & a_{32} & a_{33} \end{vmatrix},$$

and we form a matrix of cofactors

$$C = \begin{bmatrix} c_{11} & c_{12} & c_{13} \\ c_{21} & c_{22} & c_{23} \\ c_{31} & c_{32} & c_{33} \end{bmatrix},$$

where, for example,

$$c_{11} = \begin{vmatrix} a_{22} & a_{23} \\ a_{32} & a_{33} \end{vmatrix}, \qquad c_{12} = -\begin{vmatrix} a_{21} & a_{23} \\ a_{31} & a_{33} \end{vmatrix},$$

and so on, then we know that

$$a_{11}c_{11} + a_{12}c_{12} + a_{13}c_{13} = |A|,$$
$$a_{21}c_{21} + a_{22}c_{22} + a_{23}c_{23} = |A|,$$
$$a_{31}c_{31} + a_{32}c_{32} + a_{33}c_{33} = |A|.$$

However, when the elements of a row (column) are multiplied by the corresponding cofactors of a different row (column), the resulting sum is always zero. For example, if we evaluate

$$a_{11}c_{21} + a_{12}c_{22} + a_{13}c_{23},$$

or any such combination, the resulting sum is always zero. The reason for this is simply that expansion of a determinant in terms of alien cofactors is akin to ordinary expansion of a determinant with two identical rows or columns. Such determinants, as we saw before, equal zero.

If we wish to invert the matrix A, and form the transposed matrix of cofactors, namely, the adjoint $A*$, we have

$$A* = C' = \begin{bmatrix} c_{11} & c_{21} & c_{31} \\ c_{12} & c_{22} & c_{32} \\ c_{13} & c_{23} & c_{33} \end{bmatrix}.$$

If we premultiply $A*$ by A, we have

$$AA* = \begin{bmatrix} a_{11} & a_{12} & a_{13} \\ a_{21} & a_{22} & a_{23} \\ a_{31} & a_{32} & a_{33} \end{bmatrix} \begin{bmatrix} c_{11} & c_{21} & c_{31} \\ c_{12} & c_{22} & c_{32} \\ c_{13} & c_{23} & c_{33} \end{bmatrix}.$$

However, since each element not on the principal diagonal of the matrix $AA*$ involves a scalar of the form

$$a_{i1}c_{j1} + a_{i2}c_{j2} + a_{i3}c_{j3} = 0, \qquad i \neq j,$$

and since each term on the principal diagonal consists of an element such as

$$a_{i1}c_{1j} + a_{i2}c_{2j} + a_{i3}c_{3j} = |A|, \qquad i = j,$$

the product $AA*$ is seen to be the matrix

$$AA* = \begin{bmatrix} |A| & 0 & 0 \\ 0 & |A| & 0 \\ 0 & 0 & |A| \end{bmatrix} = |A|I.$$

Consequently, if we have $AA^* = |A|$, and premultiply both sides of this equation by A^{-1}, it follows that $IA^* = A^{-1}|A|$, and that the inverse matrix must therefore be

$$A^{-1} = \frac{A^*}{|A|}.$$

Thus the inverse matrix may be formed by dividing the elements of the adjoint (the transposed matrix of cofactors) by the determinant of A.

We have seen that if $Y = AX$, it will be the case that

$$X = A^{-1}Y. \qquad (4.2.3)$$

The inverse matrix ought therefore to provide the same answer for the solution of simultaneous equations as Cramer's rule. Let the system of equations be

$$a_{11}x_1 + a_{12}x_2 = y_1, \qquad a_{21}x_1 + a_{22}x_2 = y_2,$$

$$\begin{bmatrix} a_{11} & a_{12} \\ a_{21} & a_{12} \end{bmatrix} \begin{bmatrix} x_1 \\ x_2 \end{bmatrix} = \begin{bmatrix} y_1 \\ y_2 \end{bmatrix}.$$

Cramer's rule implies that

$$x_1 = \frac{\begin{vmatrix} y_1 & a_{12} \\ y_2 & a_{22} \end{vmatrix}}{|A|} = \frac{a_{22}}{|A|}y_1 - \frac{a_{12}}{|A|}y_2,$$

$$x_2 = \frac{\begin{vmatrix} a_{11} & y_1 \\ a_{21} & y_2 \end{vmatrix}}{|A|} = \frac{-a_{21}}{|A|}y_1 + \frac{a_{11}}{|A|}y_2. \qquad (4.2.4)$$

Since we have already calculated the inverse of the A-matrix, Eq. 4.2.3 may be written

$$\begin{bmatrix} x_1 \\ x_2 \end{bmatrix} = \begin{bmatrix} \dfrac{a_{22}}{|A|} & \dfrac{-a_{12}}{|A|} \\ \dfrac{-a_{21}}{|A|} & \dfrac{a_{11}}{|A|} \end{bmatrix} \begin{bmatrix} y_1 \\ y_2 \end{bmatrix}.$$

Obtaining the solution for the X-vector is now merely a matter of postmultiplying the inverse matrix by the Y-vector. Therefore

$$x_1 = \frac{a_{22}}{|A|}y_1 - \frac{a_{12}}{|A|}y_2,$$

$$x_2 = \frac{-a_{21}}{|A|}y_1 + \frac{a_{11}}{|A|}y_2,$$

which, of course, is identical to 4.2.4.

We now briefly summarize some of the main rules for operating with matrices, setting them forth without proof or illustration. However, the reader is urged to satisfy himself of their validity by constructing some simple examples along the lines of the Appendix to Chapter 3.

1 $A + B = B + A$. Matrix addition is commutative.

2 $AB \neq BA$. However, $AA^{-1} = A^{-1}A = I$, and tr $(AB) = $ tr (BA).

3 $(A + B) + C = A + (B + C)$. Matrix addition is associative.

4 $(AB)C = A(BC)$. Matrix multiplication is associative.

5 $A(B + C) = AB + AC$. The associative law of multiplication holds.

6 $u(A + B) = uA + uB$, where u is a scalar, and $(u + v)A = uA + vA$, again imply that the distributive law of scalar multiplication holds.

7   Transposition:

a) If $A = A'$, A is a symmetric matrix.

b) If $B = A'A$ and $C = AA'$, B and C are symmetric matrices.

c) $(A')' = A$ implies that the transpose of a transposed matrix equals the original matrix.

d) $(A + B)' = A' + B'$, that is, the transpose of a matrix that represents the sum of two matrices equals the sum of the transposed individual matrices.

e) $(AB)' = B'A'$, that is, if the product AB is transposed, the result equals the transpose of B postmultiplied by the transpose of A. It is vital to note here that the order in which the operations are undertaken is important.

f) $(ABC)' = (C'B'A')$.

g) If A is a scalar, $A = A'$.

8   The Inverse Matrix:

a) $AA^{-1} = A^{-1}A = I$ is the definition of the inverse matrix.

b) $(AB)^{-1} = B^{-1}A^{-1}$, that is, the inverse of the product AB equals the inverse of B, postmultiplied by the inverse of A. Here again the order in which the operations are performed is important.

c) $(B^{-1}A^{-1})AB = I$ (note the order).

d) $(ABC)^{-1} = C^{-1}B^{-1}A^{-1}$.

e) $(A')^{-1} = (A^{-1})'$, that is, the inverse of a transposed matrix equals the transpose of the inverse.

4.3   INPUT-OUTPUT ECONOMICS

The rudiments of matrix algebra that we have learned place us in a position to study the elements of that most important tool of economic analysis, the input-output table. The purpose of input-output analysis is to trace the flow of intermediate production as it makes its way through the structure of industry and to show how production, all along the line, from primary, to intermediate, to finished goods, is affected by a change in the demand for final goods and services.

Table 4.1 represents a hypothetical input-output table. It is assumed in this simple example that the economy does not engage in foreign trade and that the

TABLE 4|1

A Hypothetical Input-Output Table

		Interindustry sales			Final demand	Gross output
		1	2	3		
Interindustry purchases	1	x_{11}	x_{12}	x_{13}	y_1	x_1
	2	x_{21}	x_{22}	x_{23}	y_2	x_2
	3	x_{31}	x_{32}	x_{33}	y_3	x_3
Value added		v_1	v_2	v_3	$\sum y_i = \sum v_j$	
Gross output		x_1	x_2	x_3		$\sum x_i = \sum x_j$

productive sector (the processing sector) of the economy can be divided into three producing industries. Each industry is arrayed both horizontally and vertically in the table. The rows represent the dollar value of industry sales and the columns represent the value of purchases. For example, x_{11} represents the sales of industry 1 to itself (retained production), x_{12} represents the sales of industry 1 to industry 2, and x_{13} represents the sales of industry 1 to industry 3. The sales of the industry to users of final goods and services is the industry's final demand, y_1. In combination, the interindustry sales plus the final demand account for the industry's total production, or gross output, x_1.

Similarly, the gross output of industry 2 is the sum of its interindustry sales $(x_{21} + x_{22} + x_{23})$ plus final demand y_2; and gross output in industry 3 is the sum of interindustry sales $(x_{31} + x_{32} + x_{33})$ plus final demand y_3.

Whereas row i of the table shows the sales of industry i, column j shows the purchases of industry j. Thus x_{11}, x_{21}, and x_{31} represent the interindustry purchases made by industry 1, while x_{12}, x_{22}, x_{32} and x_{13}, x_{23}, x_{33} represent the interindustry purchases of industries 2 and 3, respectively.

The gross output of each industry minus its interindustry purchases must equal the value added by the industry. This value added, in turn, equals the wage, interest and rental payments, and the profits of the industry. Total final demand must equal the sum of all value added at each stage of production. Consequently, denoting value added by v_j, it must be the case that

$$\sum y_i = \sum v_j.$$

The input-output table is perfectly consistent with national accounting concepts. The sum of all gross outputs minus interindustry sales must equal gross output for all industries minus interindustry purchases. The respective differences represent the value of final goods and services and the sum total of factor payments. These differences must, of course, be equal. In the familiar terminology of national accounting, the column entries represent the "sources" of national product, while the rows represent its "uses."

Assuming that we have determined upon a rational basis for classifying industries and that we have been able to collect the requisite data on inter-industry sales and gross output, we can proceed to the construction of an input-output table. We turn now to the procedure for doing this.

Recall that the main purpose of input-output analysis is to calculate the output levels in the various industries that would be required by particular levels of final demands. Given this aim, it is first necessary to establish some functional relationships between industry output levels and the levels of interindustry inputs. The basic assumption made in most input-output analysis is that the purchases of intermediate product of an industry are proportional to the level of gross output of the industry. Consequently, it is assumed that

$$x_{ij} = a_{ij}x_j,$$

which is to say that the sales of industry i to industry j are a constant proportion (a_{ij}) of the output of industry j. Accepting this assumption of constant proportionality between inputs and outputs, we next proceed to the construction of a table of input coefficients. These coefficients are entered in Table 4.2.

TABLE 4|2

Matrix of Technological Coefficients

	1	2	3
1	a_{11}	a_{12}	a_{13}
2	a_{21}	a_{22}	a_{23}
3	a_{31}	a_{32}	a_{33}

The coefficients are obtained by dividing each interindustry sale of Table 4.1 by the gross output level of the purchasing industry. Therefore $a_{ij} = x_{ij}/x_j$ defines the input coefficients; for example, the input coefficient a_{12} of industry 2. This matrix of input coefficients is denoted as the A-matrix.

If we now take the entries of Table 4.1 and replace each x_{ij} by its corresponding $a_{ij}x_j$, we obtain the set of simultaneous linear equations

$$a_{11}x_1 + a_{12}x_2 + a_{13}x_3 + y_1 = x_1,$$
$$a_{21}x_1 + a_{22}x_2 + a_{23}x_3 + y_2 = x_2, \qquad (4.3.1)$$
$$a_{31}x_1 + a_{32}x_2 + a_{33}x_3 + y_3 = x_3.$$

Observe that it makes no difference whether there are three industries or n industries. In either case 4.3.1 could be expressed in matrix notation as $AX + Y = X$.

When the Eqs. 4.3.1 are rearranged with the terms consolidated, we obtain

$$(1 - a_{11})x_1 - a_{12}x_2 - a_{13}x_3 = y_1,$$
$$-a_{21}x_1 + (1 - a_{22})x_2 - a_{23}x_3 = y_2, \qquad (4.3.2)$$
$$-a_{31}x_1 - a_{32}x_2 + (1 - a_{33})x_3 = y_3,$$

which, in matrix form may be written

$$\begin{bmatrix} (1 - a_{11}) & -a_{12} & -a_{13} \\ -a_{21} & (1 - a_{22}) & -a_{23} \\ -a_{31} & -a_{32} & (1 - a_{33}) \end{bmatrix} \begin{bmatrix} x_1 \\ x_2 \\ x_3 \end{bmatrix} = \begin{bmatrix} y_1 \\ y_2 \\ y_3 \end{bmatrix}, \qquad (4.3.3)$$

and therefore compressed to

$$(I - A)X = Y. \qquad (4.3.4)$$

The result given by 4.3.4 could have been derived directly by applying the rules of matrix algebra and the writing out of 4.3.2 and 4.3.3 could have been by-passed. Since $AX + Y = X$, it follows that

$$Y = X - AX, \quad \text{and} \quad Y = IX - AX,$$

so that finally

$$Y = (I - A)X. \qquad (4.3.4)$$

Matrix $I - A$ is known to students of interindustry economics as the "Leontief matrix." As should be clear from 4.3.3, it represents the matrix of input coefficients subtracted from the identity matrix.

We come now to the problem of solving for the X-vector as a function of the Y-vector of final demands. The rules of matrix algebra allow us to see how this can be done. First, premultiply both sides of 4.3.3 by the inverse of the Leontief matrix. This gives

$$(I - A)^{-1}Y = (I - A)^{-1}(I - A)X.$$

However, since $(I - A)^{-1}(I - A) = I$, and $IX = X$, we have

$$X = (I - A)^{-1}Y. \qquad (4.3.5)$$

We therefore conclude that in order to solve for the vector of gross outputs, X, as a function of the vector of final demands, Y, it is necessary to invert the Leontief matrix, $I - A$.

The foregoing represents a simple outline of the main elements of input-output economics. To consolidate our knowledge and to get a better feeling for what is involved, we now turn to a numerical example. Table 4.3 presents the three-industry input-output table as it might appear with some numerical values inserted in place of the x's and y's.

It is assumed in this example that industry 1 retains production valued at 100, that it sells 600 and 250 to industries 2 and 3, respectively, and that its sale of final goods is 50. Gross output of industry 1 is therefore 1000. Similarly, industry 2 retains 400, sells nothing to industry 1, 500 to industry 3, and 1100 to purchasers of final goods and services. The gross output of industry 2 is therefore 2000. Finally, industry 3 makes no sales to other industries. Its gross output of 2500 consists of final goods production of 1750 and retained production of 750.

TABLE 4|3

A Hypothetical Input-Output Table

		Interindustry sales			Final demand	Gross output
		1	2	3		
Interindustry	1	100	600	250	50	1000
purchases	2	0	400	500	1100	2000
	3	0	0	750	1750	2500
Value added		900	1000	1000	2900	
Gross output		1000	2000	2500		5500

Since industry 1 has a gross output of 1000 and its interindustry purchases are only 100, its value added must be 900. Similarly, industry 2's value added must be 1000 $(2000 - 600 - 400)$ and industry 3's value added must be 1000 $(2500 - 250 - 500 - 750)$.

The table of input coefficients may now be derived by dividing each interindustry transaction by the gross output at the bottom of the column in which the transaction appears. Following this procedure, we construct Table 4.4.

TABLE 4|4

Interindustry Input Coefficients

	1	2	3
1	0.1	0.3	0.1
2	0	0.2	0.2
3	0	0	0.3

Table 4.4 reports that an increase in the gross output of one dollar in industry 3 will require output in industries 1, 2, and 3 to increase by 0.1, 0.2, and 0.3 dollars, respectively.

Proceeding to the next step, the Leontief matrix is calculated by subtracting the matrix of input coefficients from the identity matrix. The Leontief matrix is therefore

$$I - A = \begin{bmatrix} 0.9 & -0.3 & -0.1 \\ 0 & 0.8 & -0.2 \\ 0 & 0 & 0.7 \end{bmatrix}.$$

To solve for the output levels associated with particular final demands, we have to invert the Leontief matrix. Following the formal rules, we first form the matrix of cofactors, namely,

$$\text{cof}(I - A) = \begin{bmatrix} 0.56 & 0 & 0 \\ 0.21 & 0.63 & 0 \\ 0.14 & 0.18 & 0.72 \end{bmatrix}.$$

Next, we form the adjoint by transposing the matrix of cofactors. This gives

$$(I - A)^* = \begin{bmatrix} 0.56 & 0.21 & 0.14 \\ 0 & 0.63 & 0.18 \\ 0 & 0 & 0.72 \end{bmatrix}.$$

The inverse matrix is then found by dividing each element of the adjoint by the value of the determinant of $I - A$. Since

$$|I - A| = \begin{vmatrix} 0.9 & -0.3 & -0.1 \\ 0 & 0.8 & -0.2 \\ 0 & 0 & 0.7 \end{vmatrix} = 0.504,$$

the inverse matrix is

$$(I - A)^{-1} = \begin{bmatrix} 1.111 & 0.417 & 0.278 \\ 0 & 1.250 & 0.357 \\ 0 & 0 & 1.429 \end{bmatrix}.$$

To interpret the meaning of the inverse, recall that the solution is of the form $X = (I - A)^{-1}Y$. Consequently, when we multiply out the equations, we have

$$x_1 = 1.111y_1 + 0.417y_2 + 0.278y_3,$$
$$x_2 = (0)y_1 + 1.250y_2 + 0.357y_3,$$
$$x_3 = (0)y_1 + (0)y_2 + 1.429y_3,$$

which means that we have now obtained the solution for each of the gross output levels as functions of the different final demands.

The solution may be used to estimate the effects of a change in one or more final demand levels. For example, a one-dollar increase in final demand for good 3 will increase output in industry 3 by 1.429. In addition, this rise in final demand will, because of interindustry purchases, raise output in industries 1 and 2 by 0.278 and 0.357, respectively. Similarly, a rise in final demand of one dollar for good 2, will raise production in industries 1, 2, and 3 by 0.417, 1.250, and 0, respectively. In general, therefore, any column j of the inverse matrix shows how much output in industry i will rise if the final demand for the product of industry j rises by a dollar. The sum of these column coefficients, moreover, indicates the total increase in output for all industries that results from a one-dollar rise in the final demand for j.

4.4 THE EXISTENCE OF A SOLUTION

The numerical example that we have cooked up for purposes of illustration is "well-behaved," by which, in vague terms, we mean that the results make sense. Formally, we must pose the question: Given a set of positive final demands, will we always be assured of finding a unique set of positive production levels that are consistent with the set of final demands? Or, to put the matter a bit differently, is the final bill of goods producible?

The first requirement, of course, is that the inverse of $I - A$ exists. Since the inverse is formed by dividing each element of the transposed matrix of cofactors by $|I - A|$, it is obvious that $|I - A|$ cannot be zero. In cases where the determinant of a matrix is zero the matrix cannot be inverted, and we describe the matrix as *singular*.

Second, we have to make sure that none of the elements of the inverse are negative. If one or more of the elements of the inverse were negative, we would be faced with the odd result that an increase in final demand would lead to a reduction in output somewhere along the line.

What assumptions do we need to make in order to assure that the results will be well-behaved? We begin with the basic assumption that $0 \leq a_{ij}$. This requirement that each production coefficient be nonnegative simply states that an increase in output cannot lead to a reduction in the demand for inputs.

The second basic assumption is that $1 - a_{ii} > 0$, which states that an industry can never use more of its own output as an input than it can produce. The pig-iron industry, for example, would never produce pig-iron if it had to use one and a half tons of pig-iron just to raise output by a ton.

Given these assumptions, we can get at our problem in the 2×2 case by employing a diagramatic device of Dorfman, Samuelson, and Solow.* Consider the input-output relation

I: $$a_{11}x_1 + a_{12}x_2 + y_1 = x_1,$$
II: $$a_{21}x_1 + a_{22}x_2 + y_2 = x_2.$$

When x_2 and x_1 are measured along the vertical and the horizontal axes, respectively, the two equations emerge as straight lines, such as those depicted in Fig. 4.4.1.

Calculating the slopes of these curves by differentiating the respective functions, we find that in the case of curve I,

$$a_{11}\, dx_1 + a_{12}\, dx_2 = dx_1,$$

which implies that

$$\left(\frac{dx_2}{dx_1}\right)_I = \frac{1 - a_{11}}{a_{12}},$$

---

* R. Dorfman, P. A. Samuelson, and R. M. Solow, *Linear Programming and Economic Analysis* (New York: McGraw-Hill, 1958), pp. 212–215.

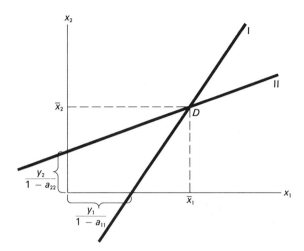

4|4|1
Existence of positive production levels.

and which, by our original assumptions about the coefficients, is positive. Similarly,

$$\left(\frac{dx_2}{dx_1}\right)_{\text{II}} = \frac{a_{21}}{1 - a_{22}},$$

which is also positive.

Next we calculate the x_1-intercept of Eq. I. Setting $x_2 = 0$, we have

$$x_1 = \frac{y_1}{1 - a_{11}},$$

which is positive. Similarly, the x_2-intercept of II is

$$x_2 = \frac{y_2}{1 - a_{22}},$$

which is also positive.

Since the x_1-intercept of I is positive and the x_2-intercept of II is positive, and since both functions have positive slopes, it is apparent from inspection of Fig. 4.4.1 that the slope of I must be greater than the slope of II if a solution in the positive quadrant is to exist. Therefore, since we must have

$$\left(\frac{dx_2}{dx_1}\right)_{\text{I}} > \left(\frac{dx_2}{dx_1}\right)_{\text{II}},$$

it follows that

$$\frac{1 - a_{11}}{a_{12}} > \frac{a_{21}}{1 - a_{22}},$$

which, in turn, implies that

$$(1 - a_{11})(1 - a_{22}) - a_{12}a_{21} = |I - A| > 0.$$

Consequently, we conclude that the determinant of the Leontief matrix must be positive.

To summarize: The condition that positive-equilibrium gross-output levels be associated with any given set of positive final demands requires, assuming that each $1 - a_{ii} > 0$ and each $a_{ij} \geq 0$, that the determinant $|I - A|$ be positive. The discussion above applies to the two-industry case. It implies that the two industries must be capable of supplying their own interindustry demands upon themselves with some surplus left over to satisfy demands that are external to the two industries. Since this would also be required of a three-industry combination and any two-industry subset of the three-industry group, or for n industries and any k industry subset, it appears that all principal minors of the n industry Leontief determinant,

$$|I - A| = \begin{vmatrix} 1 - a_{11} & -a_{12} & \cdots & -a_{1n} \\ -a_{21} & 1 - a_{22} & \cdots & -a_{2n} \\ \vdots & & & \vdots \\ -a_{n1} & -a_{n2} & \cdots & 1 - a_{nn} \end{vmatrix},$$

be positive. These conditions, which we suggest here only intuitively, are known to economists as the Hawkins–Simon conditions.* In Chapter 15 these conditions will be derived and examined with considerable care.

4.5 SOME ALTERNATIVE METHODS FOR INVERTING THE LEONTIEF MATRIX

The numerical example of Section 4.3 was deliberately cooked up in such a fashion as to yield a triangular matrix. In such a case matrix inversion can be accomplished by simple substitution. When it is recognized that many industries do, in fact, sell nothing to many other industries, and when computer assistance is lacking, the triangular matrix may save the day.

If we take Eqs. 4.3.2 and replace the coefficients by their numerical counterparts, we obtain

$$\begin{aligned} 0.9x_1 - 0.3x_2 - 0.1x_3 &= y_1, \\ 0.8x_2 - 0.2x_3 &= y_2, \\ 0.7x_3 &= y_3. \end{aligned} \tag{4.5.1}$$

Beginning with the last equation, we see immediately that

$$x_3 = y_3/0.7 = (0)y_1 + (0)y_2 + 1.429y_3.$$

Thus the elements of the third row of the inverse are immediately established to be 0, 0, and 1.429, respectively. Similarly, since

$$0.8x_2 - 0.2x_3 = y_2 \quad \text{and} \quad x_3 = 1.429y_3,$$

---

* D. Hawkins and H. A. Simon, "Note: Some Conditions of Macroeconomic Stability," *Econometrica* (July–October, 1949).

we have, upon substitution,

$$0.8x_2 - 0.2(1.429)y_3 = y_2$$

or

$$x_2 = (0)y_1 + 1.250y_2 + 0.357y_3,$$

which means that the elements of the second row of the inverse are 0, 1.250, and 0.357, respectively.

Finally, when the calculated values of x_2 and x_3 are substituted into the first equation, we obtain

$$x_1 = 1.111y_1 + 0.417y_2 + 0.278y_3,$$

the respective coefficients of which represent the elements of the first row of the inverse matrix.

A second method of approximating the inverse of the Leontief matrix is known as the power-series method. To illustrate the method, suppose we have the infinite geometric series,

$$y = 1 + a + a^2 + a^3 + a^4 + \cdots + a^{n-1},$$

where all terms are scalar quantities. In order to find the value of y without having to add up all of the individual terms, we multiply both sides of the equation by a. Therefore

$$ay = a + a^2 + a^3 + a^4 + \cdots + a^{n-1} + a^n.$$

The next step is to subtract the second series from the first. This yields $y - ay = 1 - a^n$, so that when we solve for y, we have

$$y = \frac{1 - a^n}{1 - a}.$$

Finally, if a is a fraction and n is very large, $a^n \to 0$, so that in the limit,

$$y = \frac{1}{1 - a}.$$

This result may be used to approximate the inverse of the Leontief matrix. To see this, define a new matrix Z where

$$Z = I + A + A^2 + A^3 + \cdots + A^{n-1}$$

and where A is the matrix of production coefficients. Following the procedure for summing a geometric series, premultiply both sides of the equation by A. This yields the new series,

$$AZ = AI + A^2 + A^3 + \cdots + A^{n-1} + A^n.$$

Next substract the second series from the first to obtain

$$Z - AZ = I - A^n,$$

and since $Z = IZ$, it follows that

$$Z = (I - A)^{-1}(I - A^n).$$

If each element of the matrix A^n becomes smaller as n grows larger, $A^n \to 0$ as $n \to \infty$. Therefore as n gets very large A^n gets very small and may be ignored.* This means that

$$Z = (I - A)^{-1} = I + A + A^2 + A^3 + \cdots + A^{n-1}.$$

It now appears that the inverse of the Leontief matrix may be calculated by a set of successive approximations that involves nothing more than the squaring, cubing, etc., of the matrix of production coefficients. The first approximation is to calculate $I + A$. Then add A^2 and if the result is not satisfactory, add A^3, A^4, and so on, until a reasonable approximation is obtained.

To illustrate this method, we first calculate $I + A$. This gives

$$I + A = \begin{bmatrix} 1 & 0 & 0 \\ 0 & 1 & 0 \\ 0 & 0 & 1 \end{bmatrix} + \begin{bmatrix} 0.1 & 0.3 & 0.1 \\ 0 & 0.2 & 0.2 \\ 0 & 0 & 0.3 \end{bmatrix} = \begin{bmatrix} 1.1 & 0.3 & 0.1 \\ 0 & 1.2 & 0.2 \\ 0 & 0 & 1.3 \end{bmatrix}.$$

Next, since

$$A^2 = \begin{bmatrix} 0.1 & 0.3 & 0.1 \\ 0 & 0.2 & 0.2 \\ 0 & 0 & 0.3 \end{bmatrix} \begin{bmatrix} 0.1 & 0.3 & 0.1 \\ 0 & 0.2 & 0.2 \\ 0 & 0 & 0.3 \end{bmatrix} = \begin{bmatrix} 0.01 & 0.09 & 0.10 \\ 0 & 0.04 & 0.10 \\ 0 & 0 & 0.09 \end{bmatrix},$$

$$I + A + A^2 = \begin{bmatrix} 1.11 & 0.39 & 0.20 \\ 0 & 1.24 & 0.30 \\ 0 & 0 & 1.39 \end{bmatrix}.$$

By comparing this result with the true values of the elements of the inverse, it appears evident that we are already pretty close† to a satisfactory result. To carry the approximation one step further, we next calculate

$$A^3 = AA^2 = \begin{bmatrix} 0.1 & 0.3 & 0.3 \\ 0 & 0.2 & 0.2 \\ 0 & 0 & 0.3 \end{bmatrix} \begin{bmatrix} 0.01 & 0.09 & 0.10 \\ 0 & 0.04 & 0.10 \\ 0 & 0 & 0.09 \end{bmatrix} = \begin{bmatrix} 0.001 & 0.021 & 0.067 \\ 0 & 0.008 & 0.038 \\ 0 & 0 & 0.027 \end{bmatrix}.$$

---

* It can be shown that the series will converge; i.e., $A^n \to 0$ as $n \to \infty$ if the Hawkins-Simon conditions are satisfied.

† To check if we are getting close, we merely have to multiply $I - A$ by our approximation of $(I - A)^{-1}$ and see if the result resembles the I-matrix.

The addition of A^3 to the previous approximation yields

$$I + A + A^2 + A^3 = \begin{bmatrix} 1.111 & 0.411 & 0.267 \\ 0 & 1.248 & 0.338 \\ 0 & 0 & 1.417 \end{bmatrix},$$

at which point it appears that it is scarcely worth the effort of adding A^4.

4.6 SOME EXTENSIONS OF INPUT-OUTPUT ANALYSIS

A. The Demand for Factors of Production

We have seen how final demand can be translated into production levels all along the interindustry network. It is also possible to translate final demand into demands for the various factors of production. The purpose of the extension is to answer questions of the following types. How much labor will be needed to produce a given final bill of goods, or, given a certain supply of labor, what final bill of goods will ensure full utilization of the available labor? How much capital will be required to produce the final bill of goods? How much additional labor and capital will be required in industry i if final demand in industry j rises by one dollar? If excess capacity exists in industry i, how can this excess be absorbed by changes in the level and composition of final demand?

Suppose that production in each sector requires the use of certain quantities of labor, capital, and interindustry inputs. Normally, natural resources would have to be added as a third primary input. However, for the purposes of the following simple illustration, this third input is ignored. We now write

$$\begin{aligned} f_1 &= f_{11} + f_{12} + f_{13}, \\ f_2 &= f_{21} + f_{22} + f_{23}, \end{aligned} \tag{4.6.1}$$

where f_1 and f_2 represent the total use of capital and labor, respectively, $f_{11}, f_{12},$ and f_{13} are the amounts of capital used in industries 1, 2, and 3, respectively, and $f_{21}, f_{22},$ and f_{23} are the amounts of labor used in the respective industries.

To integrate the demand for factors of production into the analysis, we must first define a set of *primary input coefficients*,

$$b_{ij} = \frac{f_{ij}}{x_j}, \tag{4.6.2}$$

and use these coefficients to construct a matrix of primary coefficients,

$$B = \begin{bmatrix} b_{11} & b_{12} & b_{13} \\ b_{21} & b_{22} & b_{23} \end{bmatrix}.$$

The element b_{11} is the amount of capital required to produce one unit of output in industry 1. Similarly, b_{12} and b_{22} are the amounts of capital and labor, respectively, that are required to produce a unit of output in industry 2.

TABLE 4|5

Primary Inputs

		Industry		Total
	1	2	3	
Capital (f_1)	800	4000	2500	7300
Labor (f_2)	500	600	1000	2100
Gross output	1000	2000	2500	5500
Primary 1	0.8	2.0	1.0	
coefficients 2	0.5	0.3	0.4	

When each f_{ij} is replaced by $b_{ij}x_j$, Eqs. 4.6.1 become

$$f_1 = b_{11}x_1 + b_{12}x_2 + b_{13}x_3,$$
$$f_2 = b_{21}x_1 + b_{22}x_2 + b_{23}x_3.$$

In matrix form this set of equations may be written

$$F = BX. \tag{4.6.3}$$

Since we already know that $X = (I - A)^{-1}Y$, it follows that

$$F = B(I - A)^{-1}Y, \tag{4.6.4}$$

and we therefore conclude that the solution for the vector of factor inputs as a function of the vector of final demands merely requires that the matrix of primary input coefficients be postmultiplied by the inverse of the Leontief matrix.

To illustrate this extension of input-output analysis, we shall consider again the basic numerical example and add the information contained in Table 4.5. The table implies that since 800 units of capital and 500 units of labor are used to produce a gross output of 1000 in industry 1, the respective primary input co-efficients are 0.8 and 0.5. Similarly, the capital and labor coefficients are 2.0 and 0.3 in industry 2, and 1.0 and 0.4 in industry 3.

Postmultiplication of the B-matrix by the inverse of the Leontief matrix yields

$$B(I - A)^{-1} = \begin{bmatrix} 0.8 & 2.0 & 1.0 \\ 0.5 & 0.3 & 0.4 \end{bmatrix} \begin{bmatrix} 1.111 & 0.417 & 0.278 \\ 0 & 1.250 & 0.357 \\ 0 & 0 & 1.429 \end{bmatrix}$$

$$= \begin{bmatrix} 0.889 & 2.834 & 2.365 \\ 0.556 & 0.584 & 0.818 \end{bmatrix}.$$

Therefore when we write out the equations which express the demand for factors of production as functions of final demand, we obtain

$$f_1 = 0.889y_1 + 2.834y_2 + 2.365y_3,$$
$$f_2 = 0.556y_1 + 0.584y_2 + 0.818y_3.$$

Let us make sure that we understand these results. According to our calculation it appears that a one-dollar increase in final demand for the product of industry 3 will raise the demand for capital by 2.365 dollars.

From the inverse of the Leontief matrix we know that when final demand in industry 3 rises by one, gross output in industries 1, 2, and 3 will rise by 0.278, 0.357, and 1.429, respectively. Since it requires 0.8, 2.0, and 1.0 dollars of capital to increase output in these respective industries by one dollar, the total increase in the demand for capital must be $0.278(0.8) + 0.357(2.0) + 1.429(1.0) = 2.365$. Note finally that the elements in the first row of the $B(I - A)^{-1}$ matrix represent capital output (capital/final demand) ratios, and that the elements in the second row are the labor-output ratios.

B. Closing the System

In the models that have been considered so far, the levels of final demand have been assumed to be autonomous. However, it should be recognized that if final demand rises as the result of some autonomous change, this will raise not only interindustry outputs, but also, because of the resultant increase in value added (income), induced increases in final demand. Our purpose now is to close the system, i.e., to incorporate induced changes in final demand into the model along with the induced changes in interindustry output that we have already included.

Resort to a numerical example again appears to be the simplest way to illustrate how the model may be closed. Let us now take our basic arithmetic example and amend it in such a way that final demand is split into an induced component and an autonomous component. In particular, assume that

$$y_1 = 0.1y + g_1,$$
$$y_2 = 0.3y + g_2, \qquad\qquad (4.6.5)$$
$$y_3 = 0.4y + g_3,$$

where the g's are the autonomous components of final demand which may be thought of as including investment, government purchases, and that portion of consumption spending that is autonomous. The induced components of consumption spending are $0.1y$, $0.3y$, and $0.4y$, where the coefficients 0.1, 0.3, and 0.4, are the marginal propensities to consume the outputs of industries 1, 2, and 3, respectively. Note that since the sum of these coefficients is 0.8, the aggregate marginal propensity to consume is 0.8. Since this means that the marginal propensity to save is 0.2, we should expect the multiplier to work out to a value of 5.0.

Using our assumed numerical values, our system of interindustry equations now becomes

$$0.9x_1 - 0.3x_2 - 0.1x_3 - 0.1y = g_1,$$
$$(0)x_1 + 0.8x_2 - 0.2x_3 - 0.3y = g_2, \qquad (4.6.6)$$
$$(0)x_1 + (0)x_2 + 0.7x_3 - 0.4y = g_3,$$

where total final demand, y, is now a variable to be determined rather than a quantity whose value is assumed to be given exogenously.

Inspection of this model confirms immediately that the system is under-determined. There are four variables but only three equations. To obtain the fourth equation, note from Table 4.1 that value added in each industry must equal one minus the sum of the input coefficients times industry gross output. Therefore, if v_j stands for value added per unit of final demand in industry j, it can readily be inferred from Table 4.3 that $v_1 = 0.9x_1$, $v_2 = 0.5x_2$, and $v_3 = 0.4x_3$. Since the sum of value added equals the level of income, the final equation becomes

$$0.9x_1 + 0.5x_2 + 0.4x_3 = y.$$

The complete system of equations can now be written as

$$\begin{bmatrix} 0.9 & -0.3 & -0.1 & -0.1 \\ 0 & 0.8 & -0.2 & -0.3 \\ 0 & 0 & 0.7 & -0.4 \\ -0.9 & -0.5 & -0.4 & 1 \end{bmatrix} \begin{bmatrix} x_1 \\ x_2 \\ x_3 \\ y \end{bmatrix} = \begin{bmatrix} g_1 \\ g_2 \\ g_3 \\ 0 \end{bmatrix},$$

or

$$(I - A)X = G,$$

where the matrix of coefficients is a somewhat modified Leontief matrix.

The inverse of the Leontief matrix in this case is

$$(I - A)^{-1} = \begin{bmatrix} 2.847 & 2.153 & 2.014 & 1.736 \\ 2.589 & 3.839 & 2.946 & 2.589 \\ 2.857 & 2.857 & 4.286 & 2.857 \\ 5.000 & 5.000 & 5.000 & 5.000 \end{bmatrix}.$$

Several differences between this result and the inverse of the open model are worth noting. First, as expected, each element of row four of the inverse is the national income multiplier, 5.0. Since $X = (I - A)^{-1}G$, it follows that

$$y = 5g_1 + 5g_2 + 5g_3 = 5(g_1 + g_2 + g_3),$$

which means that the equilibrium level of income is the level of autonomous spending times the multiplier.

The second difference that requires notice is that none of the elements of the inverse in the closed model equal zero. In the open model an increase in final demand in industries 1 or 2 induced no interindustry purchases from industry 3. Consequently, gross output in industry 3 was independent of the final demand in industries 1 and 2, and the corresponding elements in the inverse were therefore equal to zero. However, in the closed model an increase in final demand in industries 1 or 2, even though it gives rise to no interindustry purchases from industry 3, nevertheless raises the level of income and this, in turn, induces an increase in the consumption of the output of industry 3.

Finally, observe that the elements of the inverse in the closed model are much larger than the corresponding elements of the open model. This is because a change in final demand leads not only to induced increases in production to meet the change in final demand but also, because of the resulting income changes, to additional induced changes in production and income.

4.7 REMARKS

We have seen in this chapter how the level of gross output in an industry can be calculated as a function of final demand. Similarly, we have seen how the demand for different factors of production may be derived and how the model may be closed to yield a solution for the level of income. The types of problems that have been discussed here by no means exhaust the list of possible applications of input-output economics. For example, one could apply the principles of input-output analysis to the construction of a multicountry model of international trade or to a multisector interregional model with allowance both for inter- and intraregional transactions.

One failure of models of the kind that have been discussed here is that no recognition is given to the fact that production takes time to adjust to changing demands and that expenditures do not adjust instantaneously to changes in receipts. The models might therefore be extended by incorporating these dynamic elements. Similarly, increased output requires increases in the stock of capital. And these increases affect final demand in subsequent periods. A more sophisticated model might therefore incorporate a dynamic theory of capital stock adjustments. We will look at some of these problems in Part III.

REFERENCES

H. B. Chenery and P. G. Clark, *Interindustry Economics* (New York: Wiley, 1959).

R. Dorfman, P. A. Samuelson, and R. M. Solow, *Linear Programming and Economic Analysis* (New York: McGraw-Hill, 1958), Chapters 9 and 10.

W. D. Evans and M. Hoffenberger, "The Interindustry Relations Study for 1947," *Review of Economics and Statistics* (May, 1952).

D. Hawkins and H. Simon, "Note: Some Conditions of Macroeconomic Stability," *Econometrica* (July–October, 1949).

W. Leontief, *The Structure of the American Economy, 1919–1939* (London: Oxford, 1953).

W. Leontief, *Input-Output Economics* (London: Oxford, 1966).

Part II
SINGLE EQUATION DYNAMICS

CHAPTER 5

Series Summation and Elements
of Multiplier and Investment Analysis

5.1 SUMMING A GEOMETRIC SERIES

The simplest analytical tools are often the most useful. To an economist one such tool is the geometric series. By the use of this device, he is able to tackle and simplify innumerable problems that at first sight appear formidable. Although there are many different types of series, the geometric series is by far the most important. It forms the basis for the multiplier and investment analysis undertaken in this chapter.

A geometric series may be written

$$y = a + ax + ax^2 + ax^3 + \cdots + ax^{n-1}. \tag{5.1.1}$$

To sum the series, first construct a new series by multiplying both sides of 5.1.5 by x. This gives

$$xy = ax + ax^2 + ax^3 + \cdots + ax^{n-1} + ax^n. \tag{5.1.2}$$

Next, subtract 5.1.2 from 5.1.1 to get $y - xy = a - ax^n$, and upon solving for y, to obtain

$$y = \frac{a(1 - x^n)}{1 - x}, \tag{5.1.3}$$

which represents the general formula for the sum of a geometric series of n terms.

5.2 THE DYNAMIC MULTIPLIER

The comparative-static analysis of the first four chapters showed how much of a change in the equilibrium value of a variable takes place under the impact of a change in one of the exogenous variables. However, comparative-static analysis tells nothing about the process of adjustment to the new equilibrium. To study this process, we can frequently obtain assistance from our knowledge of series summation.

Suppose that production adjusts to changes in demand during the quarter in which the change in demand takes place but that consumption responds to changes in income with a lag of one-quarter of a year. If the marginal propensity to consume is the constant b, a rise in income of one dollar in the first quarter will cause consumption to rise by b dollars in the second quarter.

Beginning with an initial equilibrium income level of $\bar{Y}$, suppose that investment rises by some amount ΔI in the first quarter, and let us arbitrarily denote this first quarter as time one ($t = 1$). We assume also that investment thereafter remains above its initial level by the amount ΔI. By the assumption that there is no induced respending during the first quarter, income will rise by the amount of the increase in investment. Therefore $Y_1 = \bar{Y} + \Delta I$. In the second quarter, income will be in excess of the initial level not only because of the fact that investment remains in excess of its initial level, but also because a fraction, b, of the first quarter's income increase will be respent on consumption. Therefore

$$Y_2 = \bar{Y} + \Delta I + b(Y_1 - \bar{Y}) = \bar{Y} + \Delta I + b\Delta I.$$

Similarly, in the third quarter income will exceed the initial level by the ΔI increase in investment spending plus b times the excess of income in the second quarter over the initial level. Therefore

$$Y_3 = \bar{Y} + \Delta I + b(Y_2 - \bar{Y}) = \bar{Y} + \Delta I + b\Delta I + b^2\Delta I.$$

It is evident that if this process is continued and Y_4, Y_5, and so on are calculated, we will be able to infer that for any arbitrary quarter, t, we will have

$$Y_t = \bar{Y} + \Delta I + b\Delta I + b^2\Delta I + b^3\Delta I + \cdots + b^{t-1}\Delta I, \qquad (5.2.1)$$

or by rearranging, we have

$$Y_t - \bar{Y} = \Delta I(1 + b + b^2 + b^3 + \cdots + b^{t-1}), \qquad (5.2.1)$$

where $Y_t - \bar{Y}$ represents the income change over the initial level that will have occurred by quarter t. Since Eq. 5.2.1 is a geometric series, it may be summed by multiplying both sides by b.

Consequently,

$$b(Y_t - \bar{Y}) = \Delta I(b + b^2 + b^3 + \cdots + b^t).$$

When this expression is subtracted from 5.2.1 we get

$$(Y_t - \bar{Y}) - b(Y_t - \bar{Y}) = \Delta I(1 - b^t),$$

so that finally

$$Y_t - \bar{Y} = \frac{\Delta I(1 - b^t)}{1 - b} \qquad (5.2.2)$$

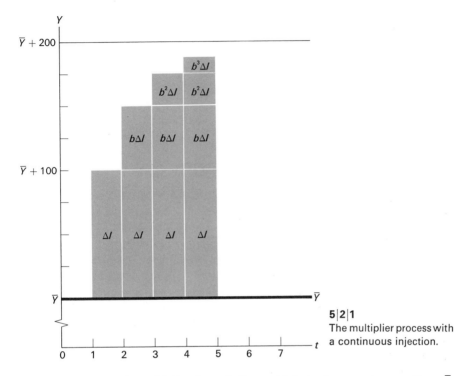

5|2|1
The multiplier process with
a continuous injection.

becomes the dynamic multiplier formula from which the income change, $Y_t - \bar{Y}$, or income level, Y_t, may be calculated for any quarter we like.

If b is a fraction, the term b^t grows smaller as t increases. Therefore, when limit $t \to \infty$, 5.2.2 reduces to

$$Y_t - \bar{Y} = \frac{\Delta I}{1 - b},$$

which exactly corresponds to the comparative-static investment multiplier of Chapter 2. On the other hand, if b exceeds unity, $Y_t - \bar{Y}$ has no limiting value, and the system would then be dynamically unstable.

Equation 5.2.2 traces the time path of income as it adjusts from the old equilibrium level $\bar{Y}$ to the new equilibrium $\bar{Y} + [\Delta I/(1 - b)]$. A hypothetical example of this adjustment process is diagramed in Fig. 5.2.1. It is assumed that $b = 0.5$ and that $\Delta I = 100$. Therefore in the first quarter income rises by 100. In the second quarter ($t = 2$) income exceeds the initial level by $100 + 0.5(100) = 150$. In the third quarter, the excess of income over the original level is $100 + 0.5(150) = 175$, and so on, until finally the new equilibrium is reached at an income level of

$$\frac{\Delta I}{1 - b} = \frac{100}{1 - 0.5} = 200,$$

in excess of the initial equilibrium level.

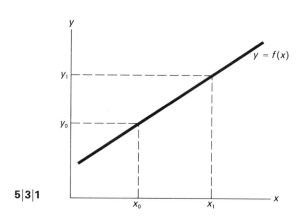

5.3 INVESTMENT AND DISTRIBUTED LAGS

Economists, especially those engaged in forecasting, have noted that the current values of many macroeconomic variables appear to be related to the values of another variable at *several* different times in the past. For example, consumption can best be explained, not by the level of current disposable income alone, or by disposable income one quarter ago, but by current disposable income along with the disposable income levels of several past quarters. Similarly, dividends move sluggishly and appear unrelated to current after-tax profits. However, when dividends are expressed as a function of the after-tax profits of several preceding quarters, the problem of forecasting dividends suddenly becomes very simple.

Although the forecasting of investment spending is much more difficult than the forecasting of consumption, dividends, and other variables, it appears that investment, too, can best be explained by the successive values of income, or profits, at several times in the past rather than the values of these variables at one single time. It takes time to complete investment projects and today's investment spending reflects decisions that were made at different times in the past. If it is true that investment decisions are positively associated with the level of income that prevailed at the time of the decision, and if different projects require different lengths of time to be completed, the current level of investment spending would have to be regarded as a function of income levels throughout the past. In a general linear form the investment function might therefore be written

$$I_t = a + b_0 Y_t + b_1 Y_{t-1} + b_2 Y_{t-2} + \cdots + b_n Y_{t-n}, \qquad (5.3.1)$$

where I_t is the current level of net intended investment spending; Y_{t-2}, for example, is the level of income that prevailed two quarters ago; and n is any number of quarters we like.

As a statistical matter, if we are trying to predict I_t on the basis of Eq. 5.3.1, we would first have to use our knowledge of statistical estimation procedures to find empirical values of the $n + 2$ constants, $a, b_0, b_1, \ldots, b_n$. However, given a limited number of data points (observations), there is a limit to the number of such coefficients that can be estimated. For example, if we have only one data point (point x_0, y_0 in Fig. 5.3.1) and we want to know how y varies when x varies, we will not be able to find out, since it is possible to draw any line at all through the point (x_0, y_0), and it is, provided the relationship between x and y is presumed to be linear, therefore necessary to have at least one more data point (for example, x_1, y_1) to find out how y behaves when x varies. Consequently, it is important, from a statistical point of view, to economize on the number of parameters that we try to estimate within the confines of a limited number of observations.

Moreover, it is difficult to imagine how a cumbersome expression such as Eq. 5.3.1 could be of any use in an analytic model. Nevertheless, the hypothesis that underlies the expression is important, and it is therefore pertinent to inquire how the hypothesis may be preserved and how the expression may be simplified.

The procedure for accomplishing this end, which is due to L. M. Koyck,[*] has had widespread application in econometric and forecasting work. It involves the addition of the reasonable assumption that current investment spending is more heavily dependent upon recent income levels than upon the income levels of the remote past. In other words, it is expected that

$$b_0 > b_1 > b_2 > \cdots > b_n.$$

Moreover, if we assume that the influence of past output levels diminish geometrically with respect to the passage of time, we could replace b_0 by uc^0, b_1 by uc^1, b_2 by uc^2, and could write, in general, $b_i = uc^i$, where u and c are constants and c is a fraction.

When the respective b_i coefficients are replaced by the appropriate uc^i values in Eq. 5.3.1, we obtain

$$I_t = a + uY_t + ucY_{t-1} + uc^2Y_{t-2} + uc^3Y_{t-3} + \cdots + uc^nY_{t-n}. \quad (5.3.2)$$

If Eq. 5.3.2 is true, it must also be the case that

$$I_{t-1} = a + uY_{t-1} + ucY_{t-2} + uc^2Y_{t-3} + \cdots + uc^nY_{t-n-1}. \quad (5.3.3)$$

When both sides of this latter equation are multiplied by c, we obtain

$$cI_{t-1} = ac + ucY_{t-1} + uc^2Y_{t-2} + uc^3Y_{t-3} + \cdots + uc^{n+1}Y_{t-n-1}, \quad (5.3.4)$$

and when 5.3.4 is subtracted from 5.3.2, we find as a result of wholesale cancellation that

$$I_t - cI_{t-1} = a(1 - c) + uY_t - uc^{n+1}Y_{t-n-1}. \quad (5.3.5)$$

Since n can be made as large as we like, and since c is a fraction, the last term can be ignored and the entire distributed lag investment function therefore reduces

---

[*] L. M. Koyck, *Distributed Lags and Investment Analysis* (Amsterdam: North-Holland, 1954).

to the expression

$$I_t = a(1 - c) + uY_t + cI_{t-1}. \qquad (5.3.6)$$

As a result of this bit of series manipulation, it appears that Koyck has shown us how to reduce the distributed-lag investment function into a simple three-variable equation by employing the same sort of simple trick that allows an infinite series to be summed. Such a function is much more manageable from a statistical point of view, and it reflects the hypothesis that investment depends on all past income levels.*

In practice, statistical functions that incorporate distributed-lag hypotheses tend to emerge from the computer in the form of Eq. 5.3.6. If we then wish to know how much investment is currently induced by income, for example, at time $t - 3$, we have to work backwards and convert 5.3.6 into the form of 5.3.2. Note that if 5.3.6 holds it must also be true that

$$I_{t-1} = a(1 - c) + uY_{t-1} + cI_{t-2}, \qquad (5.3.7)$$

$$I_{t-2} = a(1 - c) + uY_{t-2} + cI_{t-3}, \qquad (5.3.8)$$

and so on. Using 5.3.7 to replace I_{t-1} on the right-hand side of 5.3.6, we get

$$I_t = a(1 - c)(1 + c) + uY_t + ucY_{t-1} + c^2 I_{t-2}. \qquad (5.3.9)$$

Similarly, by using 5.3.8, we can replace I_{t-2} in 5.3.9 and obtain

$$I_t = a(1 - c)(1 + c + c^2) + uY_t + ucY_{t-1} + uc^2 Y_{t-2} + c^3 I_{t-3}. \qquad (5.3.10)$$

Evidently, continuous substitution of this sort will yield

$$I_t = a(1 - c)(1 + c + c^2 + \cdots + c^n)$$
$$+ uY_t + ucY_{t-1} + uc^2 Y_{t-2} + \cdots + uc^n Y_{t-n} + c^{n+1} I_{t-n-1}.$$

But since $c < 1$, the series,

$$1 + c + c^2 + \cdots + c^n \to \frac{1}{1 - c}$$

and $c^{n+1} \to 0$, so that, finally, we get

$$I_t = a + uY_t + ucY_{t-1} + \cdots + uc^n Y_{t-n}. \qquad (5.3.6)$$

Consequently, beginning with a statistical procedure that permits us to evaluate the constants $a(1 - c)$, u, and c of Eq. 5.3.6, we can infer that the marginal propensity to invest out of income one period ago is uc, two periods ago it is uc^2, and n periods ago it is uc^n.

---

* For an illustration of an application of the procedure, the reader may wish to examine the papers by Dernburg and Strand, "Cyclical Variation in Civilian Labor Force Participation," *Review of Economics and Statistics* (November, 1964); and "Hidden Unemployment, 1953–1962 · A Quantitative Analysis by Age and Sex," *American Economic Review* (March, 1966).

5.4 DISTRIBUTED LAGS AND MULTIPLIER ANALYSIS

Dynamic multiplier analysis becomes a bit more complicated than the model of Section 5.2 when consumption is assumed to be a function of present, as well as different past income levels. In the last section we looked at some properties of functions that involve distributed lags. Here, let us undertake some multiplier calculations, assuming that the consumption function is the distributed-lag equation

$$C_t = a + b_1 Y_t + b_2 Y_{t-1} + b_3 Y_{t-2} + b_4 Y_{t-3}. \qquad (5.4.1)$$

Assume that the time period is one quarter of a year and suppose that when the parameters are estimated statistically, we get

$$C_t = 50 + 0.40 Y_t + 0.25 Y_{t-1} + 0.12 Y_{t-2} + 0.05 Y_{t-3}. \qquad (5.4.2)$$

Equation 5.4.2 implies that a rise in income in the current quarter of one dollar will raise current consumption by 40 cents. It also implies that there will be a one-quarter delayed increase in consumption of 25 cents, a two-quarter delayed increase of 12 cents, and a three-quarter delayed increase of 5 cents. Each of these consumption increases will generate additional income increases and further consumption increases that, again, are distributed throughout the future. Given this situation of complicated interacting changes, how are we to calculate the dynamic multiplier effects of an increase in exogenous spending?

TABLE 5|1

	Quarter			
	1	2	3	4
1. Marginal propensity Expenditure increase	$b_1 = 0.40$	$b_2 = 0.25$	$b_3 = 0.12$	$b_4 = 0.05$
2. Exogenous	1	0.0	0.0	0.0
3. Induced	0	0.417	0.374	0.323
4. Total	1	0.417	0.374	0.323
5. Income change (multiplier)	1.667	0.695	0.623	0.538

The analysis will be considerably facilitated if we focus attention upon Table 5.1. The first row of the table shows the marginal propensities to consume in quarters 1, 2, 3, and 4 that are associated with a rise in income of one dollar in quarter 1. These propensities are the coefficients of Eq. 5.4.2. The second row of the table shows the exogenous expenditure increases. The third row shows induced expenditure increases. And row four shows the sum of the exogenous and induced expenditure increases. This sum may be thought of as the difference between the initial level of aggregate demand and the level of aggregate demand that actually prevails in the period.

In the present example, we assume that investment rises by one dollar in the first quarter, but that it then slips back to its initial level. Subsequently, we will examine a case in which investment rises permanently to a new higher level. Given this assumption, let us now proceed to a calculation of the income changes (multipliers) that are recorded in row 5.

With investment rising by \$1.00 in the first quarter, we get an immediate rise in income of \$1.00. However, since the first-quarter marginal propensity to consume is $b_1 = 0.40$, this increase in income induces consumption spending of 0.40. But this means that income increases an additional 0.40, so that consumption (again in the first period) rises by $b_1^2 = 0.40(0.40) = 0.16$, and so on. Clearly, the total increase in income in the *first quarter* that results from a \$1.00 rise in exogenous spending must be the series

$$\Delta Y_1 = 1 + b_1 + b_1^2 + b_1^3 + \cdots + b_1^n = \frac{1}{1 - b_1}$$

or

$$\Delta Y_1 = 1 + 0.40 + 0.16 + 0.064 + \cdots + (0.40)^n = \frac{1}{1 - 0.40} = 1.667.$$

This first-quarter income change per dollar of exogenous expenditure increase in the first quarter is known as the *impact* multiplier. Subsequent income increases, again resulting from the initial increase in exogenous spending, are known as *delay* multipliers.

In the second quarter, the first-quarter increase in income of $\Delta Y_1 = 1/(1 - b_1) = 1.667$ raises consumption spending by

$$b_2 \Delta Y_1 = \frac{b_2}{1 - b_1} = 0.25(1.667) = 0.417.$$

Thus aggregate demand in the second quarter is \$0.417 higher than it was initially, just as it was \$1.00 higher than it was initially in the first quarter. The second period entry in row three of Table 5.1 is therefore 0.417.

To calculate the income change in the second quarter, we merely apply the impact multiplier to the expenditure change to get

$$\Delta Y_2 = \frac{1}{1 - b_1} [b_2 \Delta Y_1] = 1.667(0.417) = 0.695.$$

Thus the second-period delay multiplier is 0.695, and this means that a \$1.00 rise in exogenous spending in the first quarter raises income by \$0.695 above the initial level in the second quarter.

In the third quarter aggregate demand rises because the first quarter rise in income induces delayed consumption spending of $b_3 \Delta Y_1$, and because the second-quarter income change induces delayed consumption spending of $b_2 \Delta Y_2$. Applying the impact multiplier to these aggregate-demand increases yields the

TABLE 5|2

		Quarter		
	1	2	3	4
1. Marginal propensity Expenditure increase	0.40	0.25	0.12	0.05
2. Exogenous	1	1	1	1
3. Induced	0	0.417	0.791	1.114
4. Total	1	1.417	1.791	2.114
5. Income change (multiplier)	1.667	2.362	2.985	3.523

third-quarter delay multiplier

$$\Delta Y_3 = \frac{1}{1 - b_1} [b_3 \Delta Y_1 + b_2 \Delta Y_2]$$
$$= 1.667[0.12(1.667) + 0.25(0.695)] = 0.623.$$

In the fourth quarter, there is a three-period-delayed increase in consumption of $b_4 \Delta Y_1$, a two-quarter-delayed increase of $b_3 \Delta Y_2$, and a one-quarter-delayed increase of $b_2 \Delta Y_3$. Consequently, the fourth-quarter delay multiplier is

$$\Delta Y_4 = \frac{1}{1 - b_1} [b_4 \Delta Y_1 + b_3 \Delta Y_2 + b_2 \Delta Y_3]$$
$$= 1.667[0.05(1.667) + 0.12(0.695) + 0.25(0.623)] = 0.538.$$

Of course, we could go on into the fifth, sixth, and subsequent quarters if we are of a mind to do so. However, the four-quarter illustration should be sufficient. The important thing to note is that the calculation of the delay multipliers is merely a matter of counting up the induced aggregate-demand increases and applying the impact multiplier to calculate the income increases that these demand increments create.

Finally, let us consider the case in which investment rises permanently by $1.00. The numerical calculations for this case are entered in Table 5.2. In the first period everything is the same as before; the $1.00 increase in investment raises income by the amount of the impact multiplier. In the second period, there is an induced rise in aggregate demand (over the initial level) of $b_2 \Delta Y_1 = 0.417$. But in addition, there is a new added $1.00 of investment spending. Therefore, the income increase must be

$$\Delta Y_2 = \frac{1}{1 - b_1} [1 + b_2 \Delta Y_1] = 1.667[1 + 0.25(1.667)]$$
$$= 1.667[1 + 0.417] = 2.362.$$

Observe from the fourth rows of Table 5.1 and 5.2 that the expenditure increase in the second quarter of 1.417 is equal to the sum of the first two-quarter expenditure increases that were obtained in the model, in which investment increased by $1.00 in the first quarter, but then dropped to its initial level. Note also that the total income change of $2.362 is nothing other than the sum (1.667 + 0.695) of the first- and second-quarter income changes of Table 5.1. Therefore, and without making any new multiplier calculations, it is evident that the entire process is additive. With investment increasing by $1.00 in the first period and then dropping to its initial level, we get the following income changes:

Quarter	1	2	3	4
	1.667	0.695	0.623	0.538

But if investment rises by $1.00 and remains at the new level, we get

Quarter	1	2	3	4
1	1.667	0.695	0.623	0.538
2		1.667	0.695	0.623
3			1.667	0.695
4				1.667
Total	1.667	2.362	2.985	3.523

Finally, observe that income is in the process of building up to a new equilibrium level. To calculate this level, we need merely note that in equilibrium, $Y_t = Y_{t-1} = \cdots = Y_{t-n}$, so that the consumption function becomes

$$\bar{C} = a + [b_1 + b_2 + b_3 + b_4]\bar{Y},$$

and this implies a static multiplier of

$$\frac{\Delta Y}{\Delta I} = \frac{1}{1 - b_1 - b_2 - b_3 - b_4} = \frac{1}{1 - 0.82} = 5.56.$$

5.5 REPLACEMENT INVESTMENT AND GROWTH

Three theories of investment behavior have been encountered thus far: Investment is a function of the rate of interest; investment is a function of the level of income; and investment is a function of past income levels. A fourth hypothesis which appears prominently in modern business-cycle theory is the notion, often referred to as the acceleration principle, that investment is a function of *changes* in the level of income. The idea derives its rationale from the circumstance that because capital goods are durable, net additions to the stock of capital need to be undertaken only if output increases.

The discussion of the present section follows Robert Eisner's* analysis of the relationship of the growth of income to the rate of capital-goods replacement and

---

* Robert Eisner, "Technological Change, Obsolescence, and Aggregate Demand," *American Economic Review* (March, 1956); and "Technological Change, Obsolescence, and Aggregate Demand: A Reformulation," *American Economic Review* (September, 1956).

to net and gross investment. The analysis provides an interesting application of series summation as well as some insights into the oft-neglected subject of the determination of replacement investment.

Let Y_t and I_t denote the levels of real income and net intended investment, respectively, and let R_t be the level of replacement investment. Consequently, $V_t = R_t + I_t$ defines the level of gross investment, and $v_t = V_t/Y_t$ is the ratio of gross investment to income. It is the determination of the ratio v_t that is the object of Eisner's analysis.

If income grows at the annual percentage rate, g, the increment to income must be gY_t. Further, if it requires k dollars worth of additional capital to produce one dollar's worth of additional output, the additional output of gY_t would require that the capital stock be increased by an amount equal to kgY_t. This reasoning leads to the acceleration-principle type of hypothesis that net investment is

$$I_t = kgY_t, \tag{5.5.1}$$

where k is usually denoted the "acceleration coefficient."

In Eisner's original paper the level of replacement investment was described by the expression

$$R_t = \frac{kY_t(1 + g)^{-a}}{a},$$

where a represents the average life of equipment. The idea behind this formulation seems to be that, since income a years ago was $Y_t(1 + g)^{-a}$, and the capital stock must therefore have been $kY_t(1 + g)^{-a}$, then $1/a$ percent would wear out currently and have to be replaced.

This formulation, as Eisner subsequently recognized, is incorrect and could be correct only if there were no income growth. In that event, there would be no net investment and $1/a$ percent of a constant capital stock would wear out and have to be replaced every year. On the other hand, a correct formulation would recognize that if capital wears out in a years, today's replacement would have to equal all of the capital stock that was built a years ago. Therefore current replacement must equal the net investment that took place a years ago plus the amount of replacement investment that took place at that time. This implies that replacement today must equal the gross investment that took place in year $t - a$. Symbolically, $R_t = I_{t-a} + R_{t-a}$. Similarly, replacement at $t - a$ must equal the level of gross investment at time $t - 2a$. Consequently, $R_{t-a} = I_{t-2a} + R_{t-2a}$, which implies that

$$R_t = I_{t-a} + I_{t-2a} + R_{t-2a}.$$

Since $R_{t-2a} = I_{t-3a} + R_{t-3a}$, etc., it becomes apparent that

$$R_t = I_{t-a} + I_{t-2a} + I_{t-3a} + \cdots + I_{t-(n-1)a} + R_{t-(n-1)a}. \tag{5.5.2}$$

Replacement investment at time t must apparently be the sum of all the net investment that took place $a, 2a, 3a, \ldots, (n-1)a$ years ago.

From Eq. 5.5.1 we have

$$I_{t-a} = kgY_{t-a},$$
$$I_{t-2a} = kgY_{t-2a},$$
$$\vdots$$
$$I_{t-(n-1)a} = kgY_{t-(n-1)a}.$$

Using these expressions to make substitutions in 5.5.2, and adding current net investment, we obtain the relation

$$V_t = I_t + R_t = kg[Y_t + Y_{t-a} + Y_{t-2a} + \cdots + Y_{t-(n-1)a}], \qquad (5.5.3)$$

where, as n gets large, $R_{t-(n-1)a}$ approaches zero. Moreover, since

$$Y_{t-a} = Y_t(1+g)^{-a},$$
$$Y_{t-2a} = Y_t(1+g)^{-2a},$$
$$\vdots$$
$$Y_{t-(n-1)a} = Y_t(1+g)^{-(n-1)a},$$

Eq. 5.5.3 may be converted into the geometric series,

$$V_t = kgY_t[1 + (1+g)^{-a} + (1+g)^{-2a} + \cdots + (1+g)^{-(n-1)a}]. \quad (5.5.4)$$

The next step is obvious. Multiply all terms of the series by $(1+g)^{-a}$ and substract the resulting series from 5.5.4. This yields

$$V_t = \frac{kgY_t[1 - (1+g)^{-na}]}{1 - (1+g)^{-a}},$$

When n is permitted to be very large and when the expression is divided through by Y_t we obtain the result

$$v_t = V_t/Y_t = \frac{kg}{1 - (1+g)^{-a}}, \qquad (5.5.5)$$

wherein the ratio of gross investment to income is seen to be a function of the length of life of equipment, the rate of income growth, and the technological relationship between output and capital requirements.

It remains only to differentiate this function with respect to k, a, and g to show that the ratio of gross investment to income rises as the desired capital output ratio rises, that v falls when the length of capital life increases, and that a rise in the growth rate may either raise or lower the ratio of gross investment to income.

REFERENCES

Robert Eisner, "Technological Change, Obsolescence and Aggregate Demand," *American Economic Review* (March, 1956); and "Technological Change, Obsolescence and Aggregate Demand: A Reformulation," *American Economic Review* (September, 1956).

Alvin H. Hansen, *A Guide to Keynes* (New York: McGraw-Hill, 1953), Chapter 4.

J. R. Hicks, *A Contribution to the Theory of The Trade Cycle* (London: Oxford, 1950), Chapters 2 and 3.

L. M. Koyck, *Distributed Lags and Investment Analysis* (Amsterdam: North-Holland, 1954).

CHAPTER 6

First-Order Difference Equations, the Dynamic Multiplier, the Cobweb Theorem, and Problems of Public Prediction

6.1 DIFFERENCE EQUATIONS, COMPOUND INTEREST, AND THE MULTIPLIER

Economic analysis is replete with cases in which some variables lag or lead other variables by discrete time intervals. The mathematics that deals with problems of this sort is the calculus of finite differences. The basic problem encountered is to determine the value of a variable at some time t when we know the value of that same variable at some time in the past. The equation that expresses the relation between the present value of the variable and its value in the past is a difference equation. For example, the equation $y_t = by_{t-1}$ is said to be a linear first-order homogeneous difference equation. If a constant term is present in the equation, as, for example, in $y_t = by_{t-1} + a$, the equation would be described as a linear first-order *non*homogeneous difference equation. Similarly,

$$y_t = b_1 y_{t-1} + b_2 y_{t-2}$$

is a second-order linear homogeneous difference equation, as is $y_t = by_{t-2}$. Finally,

$$y_t = b_1 y_{t-1} + b_n y_{t-n} + a,$$

is a linear nth order nonhomogeneous difference equation.

A difference equation is nonhomogeneous if it includes a term which is independent of the value of y at some time. This term need not be constant as in the foregoing examples. For example, if $y_t = b_1 y_{t-1} + c^t$, where the term c^t is independent of y, we would still call this equation a linear first-order nonhomogeneous difference equation.

If we have $y_t = by_{t-1}$, we can calculate the value of y_1 if we know y_0. We can then calculate y_2 by substituting y_1 into the expression. Then, y_2 being known, we can find y_3 and so on. In order to avoid this kind of repetitive procedure, we should attempt to find a formula that gives the value of y at any time we choose merely as a function of time. Such a formula is known as a *solution* to the difference equation.

To see how a solution may be obtained, consider the familiar economic problem of calculating compound interest. If a principal sum P_{t-1} is lent out at interest for a year, the value of this sum at the end of the year will be

$$P_t = (1 + i)P_{t-1},\qquad(6.1.1)$$

where i is the rate of interest. This is a linear first-order homogeneous difference equation. We now wish to arrange this equation in such a way that we can tell the value of P_t at any time t without having to know P_{t-1}, P_{t-2}, and so on back to the beginning.

If P_0 is lent out at interest, the value of the funds lent out will equal

$$P_1 = P_0(1 + i)$$

after one year. If P_1 is then lent out for the second year, the value of the principal rises to

$$P_2 = P_1(1 + i)$$

by the end of the second year. However, since

$$P_1 = P_0(1 + i),$$

it follows that

$$P_2 = P_0(1 + i)(1 + i) = P_0(1 + i)^2.$$

Similarly,

$$P_3 = P_2(1 + i) = P_0(1 + i)^3$$

and

$$P_4 = P_0(1 + i)^4.$$

We can easily infer from this procedure that at any time t,

$$P_t = P_0(1 + i)^t,\qquad(6.1.2)$$

which therefore becomes the solution to difference Eq. 6.1.1.

Observe that the solution consists of a constant (P_0) multiplied by another constant $(1 + i)$ raised to the power t. Therefore, instead of proceeding by successive substitution, we may attempt a trial solution which possesses the properties that we expect the final solution to have. Consequently, assume that

$$P_t = mx^t,\qquad(6.1.3)$$

where m and x are constants whose values are to be determined. Substitution of the trial values into Eq. 6.1.1 gives $mx^t = (1 + i)mx^{t-1}$, and when mx^{t-1} is factored from both sides, we obtain the *characteristic* equation,

$$x = 1 + i,$$

where $1 + i$ is known as the *root* of the characteristic equation.

Since we now know the value of x, the trial solution becomes

$$P_t = m(1 + i)^t, \tag{6.1.4}$$

so that it now remains only to find the value of m. In order to accomplish this, some *initial condition* must be specified. This means that we have to know the value of the principal sum at least one time in the past if we are to ascertain its present value. Since P_0 was lent out at time $t = 0$, it follows from 6.1.4 that

$$P_0 = m(1 + i)^0 = m.$$

Therefore, since $m = P_0$, we have the complete solution,

$$P_t = P_0(1 + i)^t, \tag{6.1.2}$$

which satisfies both the difference equation and the initial condition.

When the difference equation is nonhomogeneous, the process of finding a solution is generally undertaken in two steps. To continue with economic examples, let us return to the dynamic multiplier and specify the following linear national income model,

$$Y_t = C_t + I_t, \tag{6.1.5}$$

$$C_t = bY_{t-1} + a, \tag{6.1.6}$$

$$I_t = I_0, \tag{6.1.7}$$

where income at time t equals consumption plus investment, consumption is assumed to lag one period behind income receipts, and investment is autonomous and constant. Substitution of 6.1.6 and 6.1.7 into 6.1.5 yields the linear first-order nonhomogeneous difference equation,

$$Y_t = bY_{t-1} + a + I_0. \tag{6.1.8}$$

To find the solution, we first calculate the stationary equilibrium value of Y. This *stationary* or *particular* solution is the value of Y that we would obtain if $Y_t = Y_{t-1}$. Therefore replace Y_t and Y_{t-1} by $\bar{Y}$ and solve for $\bar{Y}$. This gives

$$\bar{Y} = \frac{a + I_0}{1 - b},$$

which, of course, is nothing other than the level of exogenous spending times the static national-income multiplier and it therefore represents the equilibrium level of income.

The next step is to obtain the *transient* solution. This can be accomplished by splitting income into its equilibrium value plus the displacement of actual income from the equilibrium level. Therefore let

$$Y_t = u_t + \bar{Y}, \tag{6.1.9}$$

where u_t represents the displacement of the actual value of Y_t from the equilibrium value. Using 6.1.9 to make substitutions in 6.1.8, we obtain

$$u_t + \bar{Y} = b(u_{t-1} + \bar{Y}) + a + I_0.$$

When we rearrange the terms of this expression in order to get all the u's over to one side, we obtain

$$u_t - bu_{t-1} = -(1 - b)\bar{Y} + a + I_0. \tag{6.1.10}$$

However, since $\bar{Y} = (a + I_0)/(1 - b)$, the right-hand side of the equation becomes

$$\frac{-(1 - b)(a + I_0)}{1 - b} + a + I_0 = 0.$$

Consequently, it appears that when Y_t and Y_{t-1} are replaced by $u_t + \bar{Y}$ and $u_{t-1} + \bar{Y}$, respectively, the nonhomogeneous difference equation in Y becomes a homogeneous difference equation in the displacement u—namely, Eq. 6.1.10 reduces to

$$u_t = bu_{t-1}. \tag{6.1.11}$$

We now follow our earlier procedure in order to obtain a solution for 6.1.11. Accordingly, assume that

$$u_t = u_0(x)^t, \tag{6.1.12}$$

and substitute this into 6.1.11. This yields

$$u_0(x)^t = bu_0(x)^{t-1},$$

and implies that $x = b$. The transient solution therefore becomes

$$u_t = u_0(b)^t. \tag{6.1.13}$$

To obtain a complete solution, we now substitute Eq. 6.1.13 into 6.1.9 and obtain

$$Y_t = u_0(b)^t + \bar{Y}, \tag{6.1.14}$$

where the value of $\bar{Y}$ is now, of course, known.

If the value of Y at $t = 0$ is Y_0, Eq. 6.1.14 implies that

$$Y_0 = u_0(b)^0 + \bar{Y},$$

$$u_0 = Y_0 - \bar{Y}.$$

Finally, this means that when we return to 6.1.14, we obtain the complete solution,*

$$Y_t = (Y_0 - \bar{Y})b^t + \bar{Y}. \tag{6.1.15}$$

The time path of Y_t is sketched out in Fig. 6.1.1. If there is an initial upward displacement so that income at time zero is $(Y_0 - \bar{Y})$ in excess of $\bar{Y}$, this excess will lead to additional consumption spending at $t = 1$ of $b(Y_0 - \bar{Y})$, and since $b < 1$, the excess of income over $\bar{Y}$ will be less than at time zero. Similarly, at $t = 2$, there will be an excess of consumption spending over the equilibrium level of $b^2(Y_0 - \bar{Y})$, and so forth in succeeding periods. Again, since $b < 1$, $(Y_0 - \bar{Y})b^t$ becomes smaller as t grows, and the system tends therefore to approach equilibrium from above. Of course, if the initial displacement is such that $(Y_0 - \bar{Y}) < 0$, equilibrium will, in steps, be approached from below.

This example illustrates a simple dynamic multiplier with a one-shot injection at $t = 0$ such that it makes income at that time exceed or fall short of its equilibrium value. The result therefore differs from the example of Section 5.2, where it was assumed that investment rises permanently by an amount which will raise the equilibrium level of income to $\bar{Y} + \Delta I/(1 - b)$, where ΔI is the permanent increase in investment.

---

* We have seen above that the solution to a nonhomogeneous first-order difference equation can be obtained by reducing the equation to homogeneous form. This procedure is not actually necessary; however, it is a good deal simpler than straightforward solution. In the multiplier model we have the difference equation,

$$Y_t = bY_{t-1} + a + I_0.$$

It follows from this difference equation that $Y_1 = bY_0 + a + I_0$, and that

$$Y_2 = bY_1 + a + I_0 = b^2Y_0 + (a + I_0)(1 + b).$$

Similarly,

$$Y_3 = bY_2 + a + I_0 = b^3Y_0 + (a + I_0)(1 + b + b^2)$$

and

$$Y_4 = bY_3 + a + I_0 = b^4Y_0 + (a + I_0)(1 + b + b^2 + b^3).$$

We may therefore infer that

$$Y_t = b^tY_0 + (a + I_0)(1 + b + b^2 + b^3 + \cdots + b^{t-1}).$$

Since

$$(1 + b + b^2 + b^3 + \cdots + b^{t-1}) = \frac{1 - b^t}{1 - b},$$

the solution becomes

$$Y_t = Y_0b^t + \frac{(a + I_0)(1 - b^t)}{1 - b}.$$

However, since

$$\bar{Y} = \frac{a + I_0}{1 - b},$$

this reduces to $Y_t = Y_0b^t + \bar{Y}(1 - b^t)$ or, finally, $Y_t = (Y_0 - \bar{Y})b^t + \bar{Y}$.

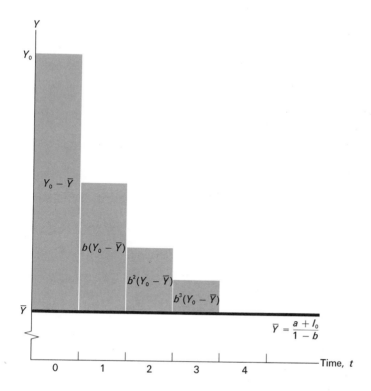

6|1|1
The multiplier process with a single injection.

The solution to the problem when investment rises permanently by some fixed amount, ΔI, is not difficult to determine. We proceed exactly as we did above except that the equilibrium level of income now becomes the original level $\bar{Y}$ plus $\Delta I/(1 - b)$, while the initial condition now is that income equals $\bar{Y}$ at time zero. Replacing the original Y_0 in the equation for the solution (Eq. 6.1.15) by $\bar{Y}$, and the original $\bar{Y}$ by $\bar{Y} + [\Delta I/(1 - b)]$ yields

$$Y_t = \bar{Y} + \frac{\Delta I}{1 - b}\,(1 - b^t),$$

which is the same multiplier formula as the one calculated in the last chapter.

The case of the approach to a new equilibrium under the impact of a permanent displacement (increase in the level of investment) was illustrated in Fig. 5.2.1, where it was shown how successive respending of increments of the increase in investment gradually caused the level of income to rise to the new equilibrium value of $\bar{Y} + [\Delta I/(1 - b)]$.

6.2 THE COBWEB THEOREM

As we saw in Chapter 1, the cobweb theorem provides an example of a first-order difference equation model that exhibits oscillating behavior. The model applies to individual markets that are characterized by the presence of lags in the reaction of supply to changes in price. Even though the cobweb theorem may appear to have no immediate connections with macroeconomics, it is important to study the model, since the question of whether public forecasting tends to be stabilizing or destabilizing—an obviously important macroeconomic question—has generally been analyzed within the framework of the cobweb model.

Consider again the competitive market in which price always adjusts in such a way as to clear the market. Symbolically, this means that

$$D_t = S_t, \tag{6.2.1}$$

where D and S stand for quantities demanded and supplied, respectively. Assume next that the quantity demanded is a function of price in the present period and that the demand curve is linear and has a negative slope. These assumptions imply that

$$D_t = a + bP_t, \qquad b < 0, \tag{6.2.2}$$

where P_t is price in period t. On the supply side, it is assumed that there is a lag of one period between the time price changes and the time it takes for supply to adjust to the change in price. The supply equation is therefore

$$S_t = c + dP_{t-1}, \qquad d > 0. \tag{6.2.3}$$

When Eqs. 6.2.1, 6.2.2, and 6.2.3 are combined into a single equation, the result is the first-order nonhomogeneous difference equation

$$P_t = \frac{c - a}{b} + \frac{d}{b} P_{t-1}. \tag{6.2.4}$$

To get a solution, we proceed as before and first solve for the equilibrium price. We therefore let $P_t = P_{t-1} = \bar{P}$, substitute in 6.2.4, and obtain $\bar{P} = (c - a)/(b - d)$. Next, let

$$P_t = u_t + \bar{P}, \tag{6.2.5}$$

and substitute this expression into 6.2.4. This gives

$$u_t - \frac{d}{b} u_{t-1} = \frac{c - a}{b} - \left(1 - \frac{d}{b}\right)\bar{P},$$

and since $\bar{P} = (c - a)/(b - d)$, the right-hand side equals zero, and we see again that the nonhomogeneous equation in P reduces to a homogeneous equation in the displacement

$$u_t = (d/b)u_{t-1}. \tag{6.2.6}$$

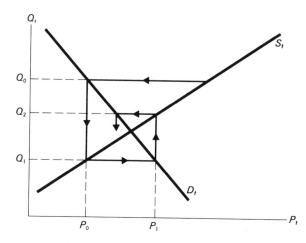

6|2|1
Cobweb market; stable
case.

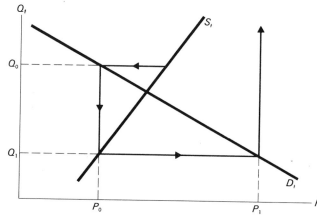

6|2|2
Cobweb market:
unstable case.

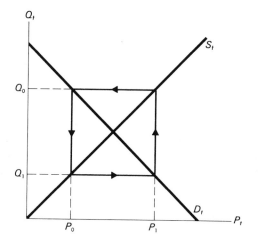

6|2|3
Cobweb market: uniform
oscillations.

The solution to this homogeneous equation is

$$u_t = u_0(d/b)^t, \tag{6.2.7}$$

and this means that 6.2.5 may be written

$$P_t = u_0(d/b)^t + \bar{P}. \tag{6.2.8}$$

It now remains only to evaluate u_0. If at time $t = 0$, price is P_0, Eq. 6.2.8 becomes

$$P_0 = u_0(d/b)^0 + \bar{P},$$

so that $u_0 = P_0 - \bar{P}$, and the complete solution becomes

$$P_t = (P_0 - \bar{P})(d/b)^t + \bar{P}. \tag{6.2.9}$$

Since $d > 0$ and $b < 0$, the root, d/b, is negative. The model therefore exhibits oscillating behavior. If P_0 is greater than $\bar{P}$, price will be above equilibrium when t is even numbered and below equilibrium when t is odd numbered. The opposite would, of course, be the case if P_0 were less than $\bar{P}$.

It is apparent from inspection of Eq. 6.2.9 that the condition for market stability is

$$-1 < d/b < 1. \tag{6.2.10}$$

If the absolute value of d/b is less than unity, $(d/b)^t$ becomes absolutely smaller as t increases. On the other hand, if the absolute value of d/b is greater than unity, $(d/b)^t$ becomes absolutely larger as t increases, and market equilibrium is then *unstable* and the oscillations are *antidamped* or *explosive*.

Whether the market is stable or unstable apparently depends only upon the absolute value of d/b. Since d is the slope of the supply curve—when quantity is measured on the vertical axis and price on the horizontal—and b is the slope of the demand curve, it appears that stability is obtained when the absolute value of the slope of the demand curve exceeds the absolute value of the slope of the supply curve. Similarly, if the slope of the supply curve exceeds the absolute value of the slope of the demand curve, the market is unstable; and if the absolute values of the slopes are equal, the oscillations will be of uniform amplitude.

The three cases are illustrated in Figs. 6.2.1, 6.2.2, and 6.2.3, where the vertical axis is the quantity axis and the horizontal axis measures price. It is assumed in these illustrations that quantity supplied begins at a level of Q_0. In order for output to be sold, price must fall to P_0 and this, in turn, causes output to fall to Q_1, where upon price rises to P_1, and so on, indefinitely.

6.3 ADAPTIVE EXPECTATIONS AND MARKET STABILITY

If producers actually behaved in accordance with the assumptions of the simple cobweb model, we would have to regard them as hopelessly naïve. The anticipated price at marketing time is always assumed to be the price that prevailed in the preceding period even though this would actually happen only when the market is in equilibrium. Therefore if producers really acted in conformity with the assumptions of the simple cobweb, their behavior would imply that they never learn anything from past experience.

One means of eliminating the assumption of naïve behavior is to follow Nerlove[†] and to assume that producers plan their output levels on the basis of a concept of so-called "normal" price. Instead of the supply equation, $S_t = c + dP_{t-1}$, of the naïve cobweb, Nerlove assumes that

$$S_t = c + dP_t^*, \tag{6.3.1}$$

where P_t^* is "normal price," which may conveniently be thought of as anticipated or expected price.

Nerlove's hypothesis with respect to the formation of expected price is

$$P_t^* - P_{t-1}^* = g(P_{t-1} - P_{t-1}^*), \tag{6.3.2}$$

which implies that the change in expected price is proportional to the amount by which expected price one period ago deviated from actual price. The proportionality factor, g, must, as we shall see subsequently, lie between zero and $+1$. If g has a value of zero, then $P_t^* = P_{t-1}^*$, and this implies that producers have a fixed notion of expected price that is not influenced by the behavior of actual price during the most recent marketing period. At the other extreme, if $g = 1$, $P_t^* = P_{t-1}$, in which event we are back to the simple cobweb where expected price equals price one period ago.

The rationale for Nerlove's formulation is not immediately evident. Therefore let us pause to probe behind the scenes to see how price expectations are formed. Let expected price be a weighted average of past prices, namely,

$$P_t^* = v_1 P_{t-1} + v_2 P_{t-2} + \cdots + v_n P_{t-n}.$$

Next, as in Koyck's analysis of investment behavior, assume that the influence of past prices diminishes geometrically as time recedes. Therefore let $v_i = g\lambda^{i-1}$, where λ is a positive fraction. The original expected price formation equation may now be written

$$P_t^* = gP_{t-1} + g\lambda P_{t-2} + g\lambda^2 P_{t-3} + \cdots + g\lambda^{n-1}P_{t-n}. \tag{6.3.3}$$

If 6.3.3 holds, it must also be true that

$$P_{t-1}^* = gP_{t-2} + g\lambda P_{t-3} + g\lambda^2 P_{t-4} + \cdots + g\lambda^{n-1}P_{t-n-1}. \tag{6.3.4}$$

When both sides of 6.3.4 are multiplied by λ, the resulting expression is subtracted from 6.3.3, and the nth order term is dropped, we obtain

$$P_t^* - \lambda P_{t-1}^* = gP_{t-1}. \tag{6.3.5}$$

[†] Mark Nerlove, "Adaptive Expectations and Cobweb Phenomena," *Quarterly Journal of Economics* (May, 1958).

Now consider Eq. 6.3.3 again and imagine that all past prices were equal to the equilibrium price, $\bar{P}$. The equation would then reduce to

$$P_t^* = \bar{P}(g + g\lambda + g\lambda^2 + \cdots + g\lambda^{n-1}).$$

If producers are rational, one would now have to assume that $P_t^* = \bar{P}$, and this implies that

$$1 = g + g\lambda + g\lambda^2 + \cdots + g\lambda^{n-1}.$$

Consequently, $\lambda = g\lambda + g\lambda^2 + g\lambda^3 + \cdots + g\lambda^n$, and this means that

$$1 - \lambda = g - g\lambda^n.$$

Finally, since λ is a fraction, $g\lambda^n \to 0$, and this implies that

$$\lambda = 1 - g. \tag{6.3.6}$$

Using this result to substitute in Eq. 6.3.5, we obtain

$$P_t^* = (1 - g)P_{t-1}^* + gP_{t-1}, \tag{6.3.7}$$

which is equivalent to 6.3.2. We now see how the Nerlove hypothesis may be arrived at. The idea that expected price is a geometrically weighted average of past prices is identical to the statement that the change in expected price $P_t^* - P_{t-1}^*$ is proportional to the deviation between actual and expected price in period $t - 1$.

With these preliminaries out of the way, we may now proceed to an analysis of the behavior of price over time. Since the supply equation implies that

$$P_t^* = (1/d)S_t - c/d,$$

Eq. 6.3.7. may be written as

$$S_t = (1 - g)S_{t-1} + dgP_{t-1} + gc. \tag{6.3.8}$$

The demand equation, $D_t = a + bP_t$, and the market clearing condition, $D_t = S_t$, next permit us to replace S_t and S_{t-1} by $a + bP_t$ and $a + bP_{t-1}$, respectively. Upon making these substitutions and simplifying the resulting expression, Eq. 6.3.8 becomes the first-order linear nonhomogeneous difference equation,

$$P_t = [(1 - g) + dg/b]P_{t-1} + (g/b)(c - a). \tag{6.3.9}$$

Equilibrium price, as usual, is obtained by letting $P_t = P_{t-1} = \bar{P}$. Therefore the equilibrium price is

$$\bar{P} = \frac{c - a}{b - d}, \tag{6.3.10}$$

which, of course, is the expected result. Next let

$$P_t = u_t + \bar{P}, \tag{6.3.11}$$

and substitute this into Eq. 6.3.9. This substitution reduces the difference equation to a homogeneous equation in the displacement, namely,

$$u_t = [(1 - g) + dg/b]u_{t-1}. \tag{6.3.12}$$

The transient solution is

$$u_t = u_0[(1 - g) + dg/b]^t, \tag{6.3.13}$$

and this implies that the complete solution is

$$P_t = (P_0 - \bar{P})[(1 - g) + dg/b]^t + \bar{P}. \tag{6.3.14}$$

Inspection of the solution confirms that the condition for stability of equilibrium in this model is $-1 < 1 - g + dg/b < 1$. Let us rearrange this condition a bit: First subtract 1 from all components of the inequality. Accordingly, $-2 < -g + dg/b < 0$. Next, divide all parts of the inequality by g. This yields $-2/g < -1 + d/b < 0$. Finally, add 1 to all parts. Consequently,

$$1 - 2/g < d/b < 1. \tag{6.3.15}$$

If producer expectations are based purely on the most recent price, $g = 1$, and the stability condition reduces to the naïve cobweb condition,

$$-1 < d/b < 1.$$

However, for values of g less than one (recall that g is bounded by zero and one as limiting values), the quantity $1 - 2/g$ will be less than -1, and this means that the ratio of the slopes of the supply and demand curves, d/b, may now be less than -1, and stability may yet be attained. Observe that the smaller is g (the smaller the weight given to P_{t-1} in forming price expectations), the more stable

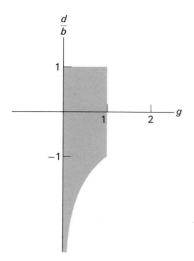

6|3|1
Stability range under adaptive expectations.

the market is likely to become. Finally, note that in the extreme case, as $g \to 0$,

$$1 - 2/g \to -\infty,$$

and this means that the market will be stable so long as $d/b < 1$.

The possibilities are illustrated in Fig. 6.3.1. The values of d/b that provide stability are shown in the shaded area of the diagram. When $g = 1$, d/b must lie between -1 and $+1$. However, as g declines from its maximum value of 1, the lower bound of the stability condition decreases, approaching, in the limit, a value of $-\infty$.

An additional diagram may be helpful for the purpose of interpreting these results. Consider Fig. 6.3.2 where the case of the simple cobweb is contrasted with the model of adaptive expectations. If initial supply is at Q_0, market clearing necessitates a fall in price to P_0. In the naïve cobweb this induces a fall in output to Q_1^n (n for naïve) and a rise in price to P_1^n. This situation is unstable.

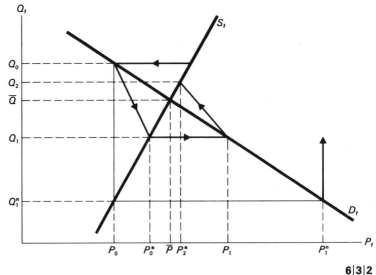

6|3|2
Adaptive expectations and stability.

However, suppose that when output Q_0 causes price to fall to P_0, producers believe instead that price at marketing time will be the more "normal" price P_0^*. They therefore produce quantity Q_1, and thus price rises only to P_1 (as against P_1^n). Further, if it is expected that price in the next period will be between P_0^* and P_1, say at P_2^*, supply will adjust to Q_2, and the price change needed to clear the market will be less than would otherwise have been the case. Adaptive expectations therefore move markets in the direction of greater stability.

6.4 PUBLIC PREDICTION AND THE STABILITY OF EQUILIBRIUM

The problem of the effect of public forecasting or prediction on economic stability is quite obviously of the utmost importance to the macroeconomist. If he predicts inflation, will consumers and business, acting upon the probable validity of the prediction, accelerate the rates at which they purchase goods and services, and thereby behave in such a way as to bring inflation about? If he predicts recession, will business become so pessimistic that investment spending is curtailed with the consequence that deflation will, in fact, be the result?

These are important questions that relate to the effect of public prediction. One might also inquire whether a public forecast, if taken seriously, will not inevitably be wrong. If an agency that attains to perfect knowledge of the behavior of a market correctly predicts price in the future on the assumption that no one acts on the prediction, might not the announcement of the predicted price affect the behavior of economic units in such a way as to render the prediction incorrect? Would this not imply, somewhat paradoxically, that the prediction that is most likely to be correct is the prediction to which no one pays attention?

Some predictions are self-fulfilling and others are self-defeating. If 49 percent of the electorate has determined to vote for the liberal candidate, while 45 percent has decided to vote for the conservative, the outcome will hinge on what the remaining 6 percent of undecided voters decide to do. If an election forecast predicts that the liberal will win and if the 6 percent of undecided voters are subject to bandwagon influences, they will vote for the liberal and the outcome—55 liberal vs. 45 conservative—will prove the prediction correct. On the other hand, if the undecided six percent are given to sympathy for the underdog, they will, after they hear that the conservative is going to lose, cast their votes for the conservative and cause him to be victorious (49 liberal vs. 51 conservative), and thereby cause the prophecy to be self-defeating.

It is fair to say that until recently economists tended to assume that a public agency that engaged in the prediction of economic events would, provided the prediction was taken seriously and acted upon by private economic units, find that its predictions would be rendered incorrect. However, in a path-breaking analysis, Gruenberg and Modigliani,* showed that correct public prediction is quite possible so long as the predicting agency is able to estimate the effects of its predictions on the responses of economic units. Taking a cue from Gruenberg and Modigliani, Devletoglou† undertook to examine the effect of *correct* public prediction upon market stability within the framework of the cobweb model.

---

* Emil Gruenberg and Franco Modigliani, "The Predictability of Social Events," *Journal of Political Economy* (December, 1954).

† E. Devletoglou, "Correct Public Prediction and the Stability of Equilibrium," *Journal of Political Economy* (April, 1961).

The model consists of the following familiar cobweb equations,

$$D_t = S_t,$$
$$D_t = a + bP_t,$$
$$S_t = c + dP_t^*,$$

where P_t^* is the price that producers in period $t - 1$ expect to prevail at time t. Expected price is assumed to be a function of actual price in $t - 1$ and also of the price, F_t, that is predicted by the public forecasting agency. Therefore, expected price is written as

$$P_t^* = kF_t + (1 - k)P_{t-1}, \tag{6.4.1}$$

where k and $1 - k$ are the respective weights that are attached by producers to the forecast price and to the actual price. If $k = 0$, producers have no confidence at all in the forecast so that $P_t^* = P_{t-1}$, and the naïve cobweb behavior prevails. On the other hand, if $k = 1$, producers take the forecast as gospel and $P_t^* = F_t$.

Equating of the demand and supply functions yields

$$a + bP_t = c + dP_t^*. \tag{6.4.2}$$

If the forecast is correct, $P_t = F_t$ and 6.4.1 becomes

$$P_t^* = kP_t + (1 - k)P_{t-1}.$$

When this expression is substituted into 6.4.2 and the terms are rearranged, we obtain

$$P_t = \frac{c - a}{b - dk} + \left[\frac{d(1 - k)}{b - dk}\right]P_{t-1}. \tag{6.4.3}$$

The process of finding the solution need not be repeated in detail. The reader may verify that the solution is

$$P_t = (P_0 - \bar{P})\left[\frac{d(1 - k)}{b - dk}\right]^t + \bar{P}, \tag{6.4.4}$$

where $\bar{P} = (c - a)/(b - d)$.

Inspection of Eq. 6.4.4 confirms that the condition for stability of equilibrium is

$$-1 < \frac{d(1 - k)}{b - dk} < 1.$$

This implies that

$$-b + dk > d(1 - k) > b - dk,$$

where the inequality signs are reversed because $b - dk < 0$. Next, add dk to all parts of the inequality to obtain $-b + 2dk > d > b$, and finally, divide by b, so that

$$-1 + 2dk/b < d/b < 1, \tag{6.4.5}$$

where again the inequalities are reversed because $b < 0$.

When producers have no confidence in the forecast, $k = 0$, and the stability condition reduces to the condition for stability under naïve cobweb assumptions. However, as k increases, i.e., as the weight assigned by producers to the public forecast rises, the term $-1 + 2dk/b$ grows smaller and the range of values of d/b that fall within the stability condition expands.

The analysis of public forecasting and the stability of equilibrium is still in its infancy. For example, one extension might be the following: Devletoglou has assumed that public prediction is correct. But if it is correct, will this not gradually condition producers to believe the prediction, and will this not gradually raise the value of k to 1? Similarly, will not a series of incorrect predictions reduce the degree of confidence that producers have in the forecasting agency? The quantity k ought therefore to be treated, not as a parameter, but rather as a function of the past accuracy of predictions. With the assistance of a high-speed computer, it ought to be possible to trace out cases in which the degree of confidence in the prediction varies as the accuracy of the prediction varies, and to extend the stability condition to include the relative degree of accuracy of the prediction.

6.5 ALTERNATIVE PARTICULAR SOLUTIONS AND THE CONCEPT OF DYNAMIC EQUILIBRIUM

It sometimes occurs that the difference equation is of a type that causes the conventional method of finding a particular solution to fail. For example, when

$$y_t = y_{t-1} + a, \tag{6.5.1}$$

it is obvious merely from inspecting the equation that the solution is going to be $y_t = y_0 + at$, since the period-by-period increment to y is the constant a. Therefore the trial solution $y_t = k(x)^t + \bar{y}$, is bound to fail.

Nevertheless, one can proceed blindly and attempt to find a particular solution by letting $y_t = y_{t-1} = \bar{y}$. Substitution in 6.5.1 now yields $\bar{y} = \bar{y} + a$, which, of course, is nonsense, provided that $a \neq 0$. The trial particular solution therefore fails. In this event we should try

$$\bar{y} = zt, \tag{6.5.2}$$

as a trial solution. Substitution in 6.5.1 now yields

$$zt = z(t - 1) + a,$$

so that $z = a$, and the particular solution is therefore

$$\bar{y} = at. \tag{6.5.3}$$

To get the solution for the transient portion, proceed as before and let $y_t = u_t + \bar{y}$ and substitute this into Eq. 6.5.1. This yields

$$u_t - u_{t-1} = at - at - a + a = 0.$$

Therefore, since $u_t = u_{t-1}$, it follows that $u_t = u_0(1)^t = u_0$, and the complete solution therefore becomes

$$y_t = y_0 + at.$$

Another common occurrence in dynamic economic models is for the non-homogeneous term to exhibit steady growth at a constant percentage rate. As an illustration of this difficulty, consider again the simple multiplier model and suppose that investment grows at a constant percentage rate. Therefore let

$$I_t = I_0 R^t, \tag{6.5.4}$$

where R equals one plus the annual percentage rate of growth of investment. Substitution of the investment function and the consumption function, $C_t = bY_{t-1} + a$, into the definition of income, $Y_t = C_t + I_t$, yields the difference equation,

$$Y_t = bY_{t-1} + a + I_0 R^t. \tag{6.5.5}$$

It is obvious that Eq. 6.5.5 has no stationary particular solution because investment, and therefore the level of income, are growing steadily. In such a case the definition of equilibrium must be expanded to incorporate a concept of *dynamic* or *moving* equilibrium. This dynamic equilibrium is defined as that time path that would reduce the difference equation of the displacements from the equilibrium path to homogeneous form.

Since investment grows at the rate $R - 1$, it is reasonable to suppose as a first approximation that income will grow at the same rate. Therefore we begin by trying a particular solution of the form

$$\bar{Y}_t = ER^t, \tag{6.5.6}$$

where E is a constant to be determined by the requirement that we wish to reduce our basic difference equation to homogeneous form.

Proceeding as before, we define

$$Y_t = u_t + \bar{Y}_t, \tag{6.5.7}$$

where equilibrium income, $\bar{Y}_t$, is now a function of time, rather than a constant. Using 6.5.6 and 6.5.7 to make substitutions, we see that Eq. 6.5.5 becomes

$$u_t + ER^t = b(u_{t-1} + ER^{t-1}) + a + I_0 R^t,$$

and upon rearranging the terms of this expression, we have

$$u_t - bu_{t-1} - a = -ER^t + bER^{t-1} + I_0R^t. \tag{6.5.8}$$

Inspection of Eq. 6.5.8 suggests that it ought to be possible to find a value for E that will cause the entire right-hand side of the equation to vanish. If we are able to accomplish this, we will have found a way to reduce the original difference equation into a new nonhomogeneous difference equation where the non-homogeneous term becomes a constant, rather than the constant a plus the growing term I_0R^t. Accordingly, we set

$$-ER^t + bER^{t-1} + I_0R^t = 0,$$

and solve for the value of E that satisfies this condition. The answer is

$$E = \frac{I_0R}{R - b}. \tag{6.5.9}$$

Using this result to substitute in 6.5.6, we see that the particular solution is

$$\bar{Y}_t = \left[\frac{I_0}{R - b}\right]R^{t+1}. \tag{6.5.10}$$

With the foregoing calculated value of E the right-hand side of Eq. 6.5.8 is zero, and this means that the equation becomes

$$u_t = bu_{t-1} + a, \tag{6.5.11}$$

which is a nonhomogeneous difference equation of the kind that we know how to solve in a straightforward manner. To eliminate the constant term, let $u_t = u_{t-1} = \bar{u}$, and substitute in 6.5.11 to obtain $\bar{u}$. This implies that

$$\bar{u} = \frac{a}{1 - b}. \tag{6.5.12}$$

Next, let

$$u_t = v_t + \bar{u}, \tag{6.5.13}$$

so that upon substitution into 6.5.11, we obtain the homogeneous equation, $v_t = bv_{t-1}$, the solution to which is

$$v_t = v_0(b)^t. \tag{6.5.14}$$

We next work backwards to obtain solutions for u_t and Y_t. Using 6.5.14 to substitute in 6.5.13, we obtain

$$u_t = v_0(b)^t + \bar{u} = v_0(b)^t + \frac{a}{1 - b},$$

and when we substitute this expression into 6.5.7, we get

$$Y_t = v_0(b)^t + \frac{a}{1 - b} + \left[\frac{I_0}{R - b}\right]R^{t+1}. \tag{6.5.15}$$

Finally, when we add the initial condition that $Y = Y_0$ at $t = 0$, Eq. 6.5.15 implies that

$$v_0 = \left[Y_0 - \frac{a}{1 - b} - \frac{I_0 R}{R - b} \right],$$

and this means that the complete solution is

$$Y_t = \left[Y_0 - \frac{a}{1 - b} - \frac{I_0 R}{R - b} \right](b)^t + \frac{a}{1 - b} + \left[\frac{I_0}{R - b} \right] R^{t+1}. \qquad (6.5.16)$$

So long as $b < 1$, Y_t will approach the dynamic equilibrium path which, via our solution, is

$$\bar{Y}_t^* = \frac{a}{1 - b} + \left[\frac{I_0}{R - b} \right] R^{t+1},$$

where the asterisk is to distinguish this solution from our original trial solution,

$$\bar{Y}_t = \left[\frac{I_0}{R - b} \right] R^{t+1}.$$

To summarize: The solution to a difference equation can generally be determined by finding a formula that reduces a nonhomogeneous equation in one variable to a homogeneous equation in some other variable. Usually, this can be done in one step. However, as in the case just illustrated, it can also be done in two steps. The first step was to reduce the equation in Y, which had a constant plus a variable nonhomogeneous term, into an equation in u with a constant nonhomogeneous term. The second step was to reduce this second equation to a homogeneous equation in a second displacement v, and then to work backwards to obtain solutions for u and Y.

If we look at the original equation,

$$Y_t = bY_{t-1} + a + I_0 R^t, \qquad (6.5.5)$$

and the particular solution, it appears that one of the steps could have been by-passed if we had used some common sense and had realized that the particular solution would probably turn out to be of the form

$$\bar{Y}_t = E_0 + E_1 R^t, \qquad (6.5.17)$$

where E_0 and E_1 are constants to be determined by the requirement that when Y_t is replaced by $v_t + \bar{Y}_t$, the resulting difference equation in v is rendered homogeneous. Accordingly, we substitute $v_t + \bar{Y}_t$ into Eq. 6.5.5 and set $v_t = bv_{t-1}$ so that $\bar{Y}_t = b\bar{Y}_{t-1} + a + I_0 R^t$. Using the trial values of 6.5.17, we get

$$E_0 + E_1 R^t = b(E_0 + E_1 R^{t-1}) + a + I_0 R^t.$$

When $t = 0$, this expression becomes

$$E_0 + E_1 = b(E_0 + E_1/R) + a + I_0,$$

and when $t = 1$, it becomes

$$E_0 + E_1 R = b(E_0 + E_1) + a + I_0 R.$$

These two equations may now be solved simultaneously for the required values of E_0 and E_1. Applying Cramer's rule, we obtain

$$E_0 = \frac{a}{1 - b}, \qquad E_1 = \frac{I_0 R}{R - b}.$$

The particular solution is therefore

$$\bar{Y}_t = \frac{a}{1 - b} + \left(\frac{I_0 R}{R - b}\right) R^t,$$

and it is, of course, the same as the solution obtained by the two-step procedure.

REFERENCES

W. J. Baumol, *Economic Dynamics* (New York: Macmillan, 1959), Chapter 14.

E. A. Devletoglou, "Correct Public Prediction and the Stability of Equilibrium," *Journal of Political Economy* (April, 1961).

M. Ezekiel, "The Cobweb Theorem," *Quarterly Journal of Economics* (February, 1938).

E. Gruenberg and F. Modigliani, "The Predictability of Social Events," *Journal of Political Economy* (December, 1954).

J. R. Hicks, *A Contribution to the Theory of the Trade Cycle* (London: Oxford, 1950), Chapters 2 and 3.

M. Nerlove, "Adaptive Expectations and Cobweb Phenomena," *Quarterly Journal of Economics* (May, 1958).

P. A. Samuelson, "Dynamic Process Analysis," Chapter 10 in the American Economic Association's *A Survey of Contemporary Economics*, Vol. I, edited by H. S. Ellis (Philadelphia: Blakiston, 1949).

CHAPTER 7

First-Order Differential Equations
and the Growth of Income and Debt

7.1 FIRST-ORDER DIFFERENTIAL EQUATIONS AND THEIR SOLUTION

An equation in which the value of a variable is a function of its own time derivatives is a differential equation. For example,

$$\frac{dy}{dt} = ay$$

is a first-order linear homogeneous differential equation. Similarly,

$$\frac{dy}{dt} = ay + b$$

is a first-order linear nonhomogeneous differential equation. The expression

$$a_0 \frac{d^2y}{dt^2} + a_1 \frac{dy}{dt} + a_2y = 0$$

is a second-order linear homogeneous differential equation, and

$$a_0 \frac{d^ny}{dt^n} + a_1 \frac{d^{n-1}y}{dt^{n-1}} + \cdots + a_ny = 0,$$

is a linear homogeneous differential equation of order n.

Differential equations, like difference equations, have innumerable uses in macroeconomic dynamics. The process of finding a solution, moreover, is very similar. To see how a solution may be obtained in the first-order case and to study the relationship between difference and differential equations, it is useful to return to the compound interest problem.

When interest is paid once a year, the situation is described by the basic difference equation,

$$P_t = (1 + i)P_{t-1},\tag{7.1.1}$$

which has the solution

$$P_t = P_0(1 + i)^t.\tag{7.1.2}$$

If interest is compounded semiannually, the value of the sum P_0 lent out at the start of the year would be $P_0(1 + i/2)$ after six months. Since this represents the principal upon which interest is figured during the next six months, the value of the loan at the end of the year would be

$$P_0(1 + i/2)(1 + i/2) = P_0(1 + i/2)^2.$$

From this it can readily be inferred that $P_2 = P_0(1 + i/2)^4$, and that at time t

$$P_t = P_0(1 + i/2)^{2t}.\tag{7.1.3}$$

If interest were compounded three times a year, Eq. 7.1.3 would be

$$P_t = P_0(1 + i/3)^{3t},$$

and if compounding takes place n times a year we would have

$$P_t = P_0(1 + i/n)^{nt}.\tag{7.1.4}$$

Now imagine that $n \to \infty$, which means that interest is compounded continuously instead of at discrete intervals. To see the effect of this, first write 7.1.4 as

$$P_t = P_0[(1 + i/n)^{n/i}]^{it}.\tag{7.1.5}$$

The term $(1 + i/n)^{n/i}$ has the property that as n grows larger and larger, the value of the expression approaches a number approximately equal to 2.7183 and is designated by the letter "e," just as 3.1416 is designated as π. Thus Eq. 7.1.5 may be written

$$P = P_0 e^{it},\tag{7.1.6}$$

and it describes the value of the principal at any time t when interest, paid at the rate i, is compounded continuously. If one dollar is lent out initially and the interest rate is 100 percent, Eq. 7.1.6 shows that after one year,

$$P = 1(2.7183)^1 = 2.7183.$$

Thus \$2.72 is the amount that would be received back if a dollar were lent for one year at 100 percent interest if interest is compounded continuously.

The number e has some important properties. First, it is the base of the system of natural logarithms. Therefore, if we take the natural logarithm of Eq. 7.1.6, we would obtain the linear equation,

$$\log_e P = \log_e P_0 + it.$$

Second, e has the characteristic that the derivative of e^t with respect to t equals itself. Consequently,

$$\frac{d}{dt}(e^t) = e^t.$$

Similarly,

$$\frac{d}{dt}(e^{it}) = ie^{it}$$

and

$$\frac{d^2}{dt^2}(e^{it}) = i^2 e^{it}.$$

If we differentiate Eq. 7.1.6 with respect to t, we obtain

$$\frac{dP}{dt} = iP_0 e^{it},$$

and since $P = P_0 e^{it}$, this equation can be written as

$$\frac{dP}{dt} = iP. \qquad (7.1.7)$$

Equation 7.1.7 represents the differential-equation counterpart of the difference equation $P_t = (1 + i)P_{t-1}$. In the case of the latter, interest is compounded at discrete intervals, whereas the differential equation states that the continuous rate of change of the principal is proportional to the principal at that moment of time.

In summary: The difference equation

$$P_t = (1 + i)P_{t-1},$$

which may be written as either

$$P_t - P_{t-1} = iP_{t-1}, \qquad \text{or} \qquad \Delta P_t = iP_{t-1},$$

has the solution $P_t = P_0(1 + i)^t$. Similarly, the solution to the differential equation, $dP/dt = iP$, is

$$P = P_0 e^{it}.$$

In the case of the difference equation, the solution consists of a constant term multiplied by another constant term raised to the power t, and we therefore tried a formula such as $P_t = mx^t$ as a trial solution. In the case of the differential equation, the solution consists of a constant term multiplied by e raised to a power which is a multiple of t. Consequently, if we are trying to solve a differential equation of the form

$$\frac{dP}{dt} = iP, \tag{7.1.7}$$

we should attempt a trial solution of the form

$$P = me^{xt}. \tag{7.1.8}$$

This trial solution implies that

$$\frac{dP}{dt} = xme^{xt}.$$

When the trial values of P and dP/dt are substituted into 7.1.7, we obtain $xme^{xt} = ime^{xt}$, and when me^{xt} is factored from both sides, we see that $x = i$. Consequently, the trial solution now becomes

$$P = me^{it}. \tag{7.1.9}$$

To solve for the value of m, we need an initial condition. Therefore suppose that $P = P_0$ at $t = 0$. Consequently, 7.1.9 implies that

$$P_0 = me^{i(0)} = m,$$

which means that the complete solution is* $P = P_0e^{it}$.

Let us now move to a nonhomogeneous case and analyze the adjustment to equilibrium of the simple macroeconomic model of the first part of Chapter 2. We assume that government purchases and taxes are absent, that investment is autonomous, and that the consumption function is $C = a + bY$. To introduce a dynamic hypothesis, let us now assume that the rate at which income changes equals the difference between intended investment and saving. Accordingly,

$$\frac{dY}{dt} = I - S \tag{7.1.10}$$

is our dynamic hypothesis. When intended investment exceeds saving, aggregate demand exceeds production, and output increases. When intended investment is less than the level of saving, aggregate demand is less than production, and output decreases.

---

* The reader who is up on his integral calculus will have recognized that the equation $dP/dt = iP$ could have been solved by straight-forward integration. Write the equation as $dP/P = i\, dt$, and integrate both sides of the equation. This yields

$$\log_e P = it + b,$$

where b is an arbitrary constant. Next, take the antilog to the base e to obtain $P = ce^{it}$, where $c = \text{antilog}_e b$. And finally, let $P = P_0$ at $t = 0$, so that $P_0 = c$, and the complete solution therefore becomes

$$P = P_0e^{it}.$$

Since the saving function is $S = -a + (1 - b)Y$, Eq. 7.1.10 may be written as the linear first-order nonhomogeneous differential equation,

$$\frac{dY}{dt} = I + a - (1 - b)Y. \qquad (7.1.11)$$

Finding a solution involves essentially the same set of steps as in the case of a nonhomogeneous difference equation. First: Solve for the equilibrium value of Y. Second: Define Y as the sum of the equilibrium value and the displacement from equilibrium. Third: Obtain a solution to the homogeneous differential equation in the displacement. Fourth: Work backwards to get the complete solution.

Beginning with the first step, it is clear that when the system is in a state of equilibrium, dY/dt must be zero and $Y = \bar{Y}$. Accordingly, from 7.1.11 we see that

$$\bar{Y} = \frac{a + I}{1 - b},$$

which confirms that the equilibrium level of income is the level of autonomous spending times the multiplier.

Next, define $Y = u + \bar{Y}$, and observe that

$$\frac{dY}{dt} = \frac{du}{dt},$$

because $d\bar{Y}/dt$ must be zero. Upon making substitutions in 7.1.11, we see that

$$\frac{du}{dt} = I + a - (1 - b)(u + \bar{Y}).$$

However, since $\bar{Y} = (a + I)/(1 - b)$, this reduces to

$$\frac{du}{dt} = -(1 - b)u. \qquad (7.1.12)$$

The solution to 7.1.12 is now obtained by trying a solution of the form

$$u = u_0 e^{xt}, \qquad (7.1.13)$$

from which we derive $du/dt = xu_0 e^{xt}$, which implies that $x = -(1 - b)$. The trial solution (7.1.13) therefore may now be written as

$$u = u_0 e^{-(1-b)t}. \qquad (7.1.14)$$

Since $Y = u + \bar{Y}$, we have from 7.1.14 that

$$Y = u_0 e^{-(1-b)t} + \bar{Y},$$

and if $Y = Y_0$ at $t = 0$, $u_0 = Y_0 - \bar{Y}$, the complete solution becomes

$$Y = (Y_0 - \bar{Y})e^{-(1-b)t} + \bar{Y}. \qquad (7.1.15)$$

Inspection of the solution suggests a number of properties of first-order differential equations of which we should take note. First, we see that the static equilibrium solution, $\bar{Y} = (a + I)/(1 - b)$, is the same regardless of the dynamic properties of the model. Second, we see that unlike difference equation models, a first-order differential equation system cannot produce oscillating behavior. If the root $-(1 - b)$ is negative, the transient portion of the solution merely fades away monotonically and Y will approach $\bar{Y}$. On the other hand, if the root is positive, the transient solution deviates progressively from the equilibrium value $\bar{Y}$. This circumstance implies a third conclusion—namely, that while the condition for stability of equilibrium in a first-order difference equation model is that the root lie between -1 and $+1$, the condition in a first-order differential equation model is that the root be negative. In the present case, the stability condition implies that $-(1 - b) < 0$, and this means that the marginal propensity to consume must be less than unity. If it were greater than unity, an excess of intended investment over saving which would cause income to rise, would induce an increase in consumption greater than the increase in income, and output could never catch up to aggregate demand.

7.2 DOMAR'S MODEL OF ECONOMIC GROWTH

In classical theory, the economic system is assumed automatically to equilibrate at full employment. The rate of growth of per capita output then is determined by how rapidly.society is willing to accumulate capital relative to the growth of labor and how rapidly technical progress succeeds in offsetting diminishing returns.

Keynesian economics emphasized that full employment is not automatically achieved and, with its orientation toward the short-run employment problem, ignored problems of long-run growth and of the role of capital accumulation in the growth process. The economists who first bridged the gap between the Keynesian theory of employment and the dynamics of long-run growth are R. F. Harrod and E. D. Domar.* The models of both these pioneers are quite similar and it will suffice here if we concentrate on Domar's work.

Domar's central proposition is that investment has a dual character. On the one hand, it contributes to aggregate demand and thereby helps to promote full employment and full capacity in the short run. On the other hand, investment involves expansion of the stock of capital and it therefore contributes to the supply of output that the system is capable of producing. The effect of this dual character of investment is illustrated in Fig. 7.2.1. If the full-capacity level of output is Y_0, the level of consumption will be C_0 provided that the full-capacity level of income

---

* R. F. Harrod, "An Essay in Dynamic Theory," *Economic Journal* (March, 1939); and *Towards a Dynamic Economics* (New York: Macmillan, 1952). E. D. Domar, "Capital Expansion, Rate of Growth, and Employment," *Econometrica* (April, 1946); and "Expansion and Employment," *American Economic Review* (March, 1947).

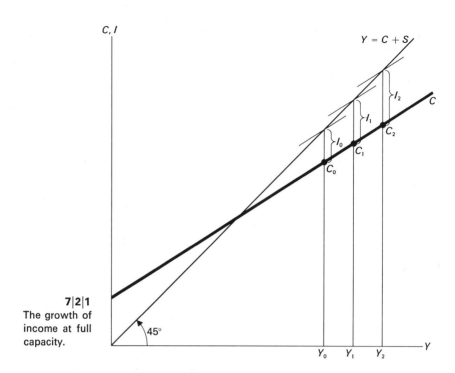

7|2|1
The growth of
income at full
capacity.

is actually attained. To attain Y_0 we must (assuming the absence of government purchases) have forthcoming a level of intended investment of I_0. If we do get this level of investment, the capital stock will increase, and this means that the output level that fully uses the economy's capacity will rise. If the new full-capacity level of income is Y_1, the level of consumption will be C_1, so that intended investment of I_1 will be required to fill the gap between consumption and full-capacity output. However, investment of I_1 further expands the stock of capital so that subsequently Y_2 becomes the full-capacity level of income and intended investment of I_2 will therefore be required to achieve full-capacity utilization. We see therefore that because of the dual nature of investment, the economy must run absolutely faster all the time if it is to remain at full-capacity.

The question that Domar now poses is: How rapidly must investment grow in order for full-capacity output to be maintained? To provide an answer, Domar adds to the simple linear Keynesian model of income determination the assumption that the amount of output that the system is able to produce is proportional to the size of the capital stock. He therefore specifies a linear production function of the form

$$Y = \sigma K, \tag{7.2.1}$$

where K is the stock of capital and σ, the "capital coefficient," can be thought of as representing the average and marginal productivity of capital.

If full-capacity output is to be maintained, the increment to the total demand for goods and services per unit time must just equal the increment to the potential supply that the system can produce. The increment to total demand, of course, is the increase in investment times the multiplier. Thus we write

$$\left(\frac{dY}{dt}\right)_d = \frac{1}{1-b}\left(\frac{dI}{dt}\right),$$

as the increment to demand, where, as usual, b is the marginal propensity to consume. The increment to total supply can be seen from the production function to be

$$\left(\frac{dY}{dt}\right)_s = \sigma\left(\frac{dK}{dt}\right).$$

However, the *change* in the stock of capital is equivalent to the *level* of net investment, $dK/dt = I$, and the supply equation may therefore be written as

$$\left(\frac{dY}{dt}\right)_s = \sigma I.$$

Since the condition for the maintenance of full-capacity output is

$$\left(\frac{dY}{dt}\right)_d = \left(\frac{dY}{dt}\right)_s,$$

it follows from the demand and supply equations that

$$\frac{1}{1-b}\left(\frac{dI}{dt}\right) = \sigma I,$$

and when both sides of the equation are multiplied by $1-b$, it becomes the first-order linear homogeneous differential equation,

$$\frac{dI}{dt} = (1-b)\sigma I. \qquad (7.2.2)$$

The solution to Eq. 7.2.2 is

$$I = I_0 e^{(1-b)\sigma t},$$

which describes the time path of the level of investment that maintains full-capacity output. Moreover, since

$$\frac{1}{I}\frac{dI}{dt} = \sigma(1-b),$$

it is evident that the rate at which investment must grow is the product of the capital coefficient and the marginal propensity to save. If the capital coefficient rises, each dollar of investment adds a greater amount to potential output, and the required level of investment must therefore grow more rapidly. Similarly, if the marginal propensity to save rises, each income level will generate a greater level of saving. Since this means that the required ratio of investment to income rises, the capital stock grows more rapidly, and full-capacity output and investment requirements grow more rapidly.

So far we have solved for the required level of investment. The level of income can now be calculated quite easily. Since

$$Y = C + I, \qquad C = a + bY, \qquad \text{and} \qquad I = I_0 e^{(1-b)\sigma t},$$

we have upon substitution

$$Y = \frac{a}{1-b} + \frac{I_0}{1-b} e^{(1-b)\sigma t},$$

where, evidently, $\bar{Y} = a/(1-b)$ and $I_0/(1-b) = Y_0 - \bar{Y}$.

Finally, as a matter of empirical observation, we find that consumption over the years has remained almost proportional to the level of disposable income. Consequently, it is customary in long-run growth analysis for economists to assume that the intercept, a, of the consumption function is zero. Under these conditions, it is evident that the solution for the level of income reduces to

$$Y = Y_0 e^{(1-b)\sigma t}. \tag{7.2.3}$$

Harrod-Domar type models can be used to illustrate an important source of instability in the economic system. Consider Fig. 7.2.1 again and imagine that when full employment output is Y_1, investment of only I_0 is forthcoming. With this level of investment, the level of income will be Y_0. However, since there is sufficient capacity available to produce Y_1, the result is that business firms find themselves with excess capacity on their hands, and it therefore appears as though they have overinvested when, in fact, a higher level of investment (I_1) would have resulted in the full utilization of capacity. Thus by investing too little, business firms find themselves appearing to have invested too much. Subsequently, with output at Y_0 and capacity at or in excess of what could produce Y_1, the need for additional capacity collapses altogether and investment and income shrink still further.

Alternatively, suppose that full capacity is sufficient only to produce output Y_0, but that intended investment is I_1. Unable to match the demand of Y_1 with output, business finds itself straining against existing capacity, and confronted with a strong incentive to increase investment outlays still further. Overinvestment therefore actually leads to undercapacity and this, in turn, leads to still greater levels of overinvestment.

The chronic instability implied by Harrod-Domar models has caused these models to be described as "razor's edge" models. The economy appears to teeter on a high wire, from which the slightest jolt will cause it to shoot off into chronic depression or hyperinflation. To some extent, this implied instability is the product of a too-rigid view of the technological nature of production, and when we get to neoclassical growth economics, we will see why this is so. Nevertheless, the models point up some important principles of growth and instability that form a solid basis for further study of these subjects.

7.3 THE GROWTH OF INCOME AND DEBT

Keynesian economics implies that the economic system will not automatically regulate itself in such a way as to ensure a return to full employment following a disturbance. In addition, Keynesian analysis implies that monetary policy might not be effective in regulating the level of income. These two circumstances combine to cast federal expenditure and revenue policies in an entirely new light. If the system does not regulate itself automatically, stabilization policy will have to be undertaken. If monetary policy does not work, while fiscal policy is free from the classical objections,* the burden of stabilization policy falls on fiscal policy.

This shifting orientation implies that the goal of budgetary balance must be abandoned and that revenues and expenditures must be adjusted to provide full employment. During the 1930's when continuing mass unemployment led many economists to believe that "underemployment equilibrium"† might be the norm, the attainment of full employment through fiscal policy necessitated that the prospect of more or less perpetual deficits in the federal budget be accepted. Along with this, quite naturally, came a revival of interest in the economics of the national debt.

An extreme Keynesian view of national debt was the position taken by A. P. Lerner.‡ Lerner argued that the size of the debt is essentially irrelevant. Since the nation both owes and owns internally held debt, repayment would merely involve the collection of taxes from the same people who received the payments. Thus the principle of "we owe it to ourselves" implied that the present generation cannot, by creating debt rather than taxing itself, impose a burden on the future generation of taxpayers. Moreover, the debt can never be so large that the interest payments are prohibitive, since the interest payments themselves constitute taxable income. In any case, additional debt can always be issued to pay the interest.

The view of Lerner, though useful as a first approximation, undoubtedly§ oversimplifies the matter and possibly ignores some serious problems. One such

---

* Recall from the discussion in Chapter 3 that fiscal policy will not be effective if the demand for money is inelastic with respect to the rate of interest.

† The doctrine of persistent underemployment or "secular stagnation," as it was called, received its fullest and most persuasive support from A. H. Hansen. See his "Economic Progress and Declining Population Growth," *American Economic Review* (March, 1939).

‡ A. P. Lerner, "Functional Finance and the Federal Debt," *Social Research* (February, 1943); and *The Economics of Control* (New York: Macmillan, 1947), Chapter 24.

§ Some economists take a more serious view of the consequences of national debt. However, since the ins and outs of national-debt economics are not our basic concern here, it suffices to cite J. M. Buchanan, *Public Principles of Public Debt* (Irwin, 1958) as a reference that attempts to provide a contemporary counterweight to views such as Lerner's.

problem is that the bondholders and those who pay the taxes to service (pay the interest on) the debt are not necessarily the same persons. Since there is a strong presumption that the wealthier groups own a disproportionate fraction of the debt, it would appear to follow that an increase in the size of the debt, or a rise in interest rates, would exercise a regressive effect on the distribution of income.

Domar* has constructed a model that is designed to analyze this aspect of the debt-burden question. What he wants to know is whether the redistributive burden of national debt will grow larger or diminish with respect to time. Representation of Domar's model is facilitated by a listing of symbols. It is assumed that the price level remains constant and that the analysis would therefore hold whether the variables are thought of as defined in real or in nominal terms. The symbols are:

D, the value of the national debt;

Y, the level of income;

U, the level of taxable income;

T, the value of interest payments on the national debt;

i, the rate of interest;

v, the tax rate applied to taxable income needed to service the debt; and

α, the proportion of income borrowed annually.

The value of the interest paid on the national debt is $T = iD$. This interest payment is itself a part of taxable income. Therefore $U = Y + T = Y + iD$ defines the level of taxable income. The tax rate (redistributive burden) of the debt is the ratio of tax payments to taxable income. Consequently,

$$v = \frac{T}{U} = \frac{iD}{Y + iD} = \frac{i}{Y/D + i}; \tag{7.3.1}$$

defines the requisite tax rate. From Eq. 7.3.1 we can see that the redistributive burden of the debt depends on the ratio of income to debt and upon the rate of interest. If Y/D rises, the burden falls, and if Y/D falls, the burden rises.

The next step in the analysis is to assume that a constant fraction, α, of the level of income is borrowed each year, and to see what happens to the burden of the debt under alternative assumptions about the growth of income.

First, assume that income does not grow at all. In this case $Y = Y_0$. Since αY_0 is borrowed each year, the debt after t years will be $D = D_0 + \alpha Y_0 t$. When we divide this expression by Y, we have

$$\frac{D}{Y} = \frac{D_0}{Y_0} + \alpha t,$$

---

* E. D. Domar, "The 'Burden of the Debt' and the National Income," *American Economic Review* (December, 1944).

and we therefore conclude that the ratio of debt to income rises continuously. Since as $t \rightarrow \infty$, $D/Y \rightarrow \infty$, it is apparent from 7.3.1 that the tax rate eventually approaches 100 percent, and that the redistributive effect of the interest payments on the debt are likely to become very burdensome indeed.

Next, suppose that income grows by a constant absolute amount each year. This implies that $Y = Y_0 + mt$, where m is the annual absolute increase in income. Each year α percent of this is borrowed. Consequently, the debt at the end of year t is

$$D = D_0 + \alpha(Y_0 + m) + \alpha(Y_0 + 2m) + \alpha(Y_0 + 3m) + \cdots + \alpha(Y_0 + mt).$$

This expression may be rearranged as

$$D = D_0 + \alpha Y_0 t + \alpha m(1 + 2 + 3 + \cdots + t).$$

Since the expression $1 + 2 + 3 + \cdots + t$ is an arithmetic series which has a value of* $t(t + 1)/2$ the equation that expresses the value of the debt becomes

$$D = D_0 + \alpha Y_0 t + \frac{\alpha m t(t + 1)}{2},$$

and the ratio of debt to income must therefore be

$$\frac{D}{Y} = \frac{D_0 + \alpha Y_0 t + [\alpha m t(t + 1)/2]}{Y_0 + mt}.$$

Inspection of this expression indicates that it too approaches infinity as t increases because the term $\alpha m t(t + 1)/2$ contains a squared term, which will dominate the result. Here again, the ratio of debt to income expands indefinitely and the tax rate rises to 100 percent.

Finally, suppose that income grows at a compound exponential rate. In this case we have $Y = Y_0 e^{rt}$, where r is the exponential rate of growth of income. By the assumption that α percent of all income since $t = 0$ is borrowed, the level of debt after t years is

$$D = D_0 + \alpha \int_0^t Y \, dt = D_0 + \alpha Y_0 \int_0^t e^{rt} \, dt.$$

---

* To sum an arithmetic series, note that if the series contains an even number of terms, the first term can be added to the last to get $t + 1$. Similarly, the second term can be added to the next-to-last term and this also yields $t + 1$. Evidently, the series can be arranged to yield $t/2$ terms, each of which has a value of $t + 1$; hence the result $t(t + 1)/2$. This formula also holds when the number of terms is odd. The terms $1 + t$, $2 + (t - 1)$, $3 + (t - 2)$, and so on, each equal twice the value of the middle term, which equals $(1 + t)/2$. The number of such terms is $(t - 1)/2$. Since each has a value of $1 + t$, and the middle term is $(1 + t)/2$, it follows that the sum of the series is

$$\frac{(t - 1)(t + 1)}{2} + \frac{(t + 1)}{2} = \frac{t(t + 1)}{2}.$$

Since the integral of $e^{rt} dt$ is e^{rt}/r, the value of the integral from 0 to t is $(e^{rt} - 1)/r$, and the debt at the end of year t is therefore

$$D = D_0 + \frac{\alpha Y_0}{r} (e^{rt} - 1).$$

Dividing the level of income into this expression gives

$$\frac{D}{Y} = \frac{D_0 + (\alpha Y_0/r)(e^{rt} - 1)}{Y_0 e^{rt}},$$

from which it can readily be inferred that, for limit $t \to \infty$,

$$\frac{D}{Y} = \frac{\alpha}{r}.$$

We now see that when income grows exponentially, the ratio of debt to income approaches a limit given by the ratio of the proportion of income borrowed and the rate of growth of income. The tax rate now becomes

$$v = \frac{i}{(r/\alpha) + i},$$

and it is evident from this that a high rate of income growth relative to the fraction of income borrowed implies a low tax burden, while a high proportion borrowed relative to the growth of income implies the opposite.

The conclusions to be drawn from this analysis are fairly obvious. It is not the absolute size of the debt that is important from the point of view of a changing redistributive burden, it is rather the size of the debt relative to the level of income. If a constant fraction of income is borrowed, the debt will, of course, grow, and if income fails to grow, the debt burden will rise. However, if income grows exponentially, the two magnitudes will tend to grow at the same rate, and the ratio of debt to income, and therefore also the debt burden, will remain constant.

According to Lerner's principles of "functional finance," it is a mistake to think of the purpose of taxation as paying for government spending. Taxation, according to Lerner, should be used to regulate the total level of spending in such a way as to ensure full employment and stable prices. Lerner realized that this view of the role of taxation, if put into practice, might lead to fairly steady increases in the size of the national debt. Although he himself felt that increases in the debt were of little practical importance, he nevertheless tried to assuage the sensibilities of fiscal conservatives by means of an ingenious argument which suggested that deficits and the concomitant creation of debt, if used to combat unemployment, would ultimately lead to a situation where full employment would prevail without the need for further deficits.

Lerner's argument is based on the hypothesis, attributable to A. C. Pigou*
that the level of consumption spending depends upon the level of wealth owned by
consumers as well as upon their disposable income. Pigou's original argument
centered about the effect of a fall in the price level. If the price level declines, the
real value of the public's net claims against the government rises and this increase
in "wealth" causes consumers to increase consumption spending. The consumption function, in other words, shifts up as the price level falls.

The net claims against the government are represented by the stock of currency and the level of public debt held by the private sector of the economy.
Private claims are not counted, because every creditor who benefits from a fall in
the price level is matched by a debtor who loses out. The Pigou argument therefore rests on the presumption of assymetrical behavior between government and
private economic units. While a fall in prices causes private consumption to rise,
it is assumed that the increase in the real value of the claims against the government will not cause public spending to diminish.

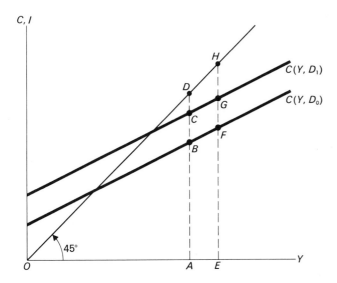

7|3|1
The Lerner effect.

The effect on consumption of a fall in the price level is the "Pigou effect."
Lerner, taking over the general idea, argued that if a deflationary gap is closed
by means of deficit financing, the resulting increase in the public debt held in
private hands will so enrich wealth-holders that the consumption function will
shift up. Moreover, if this process of closing the gap by deficit financing continues,
the consumption function will continue to shift up and eventually the deflationary

---

* A. C. Pigou, "The Classical Stationary State," *Economic Journal* (December, 1943); and
"Economic Progress in a Stable Environment," *Economica* (August, 1947).

gap will be eliminated, and there will be no need for further deficits. Thus the "Lerner effect" provides solace to those who are willing to tolerate temporary deficits but who hope that eventually there will be some "natural" limit to the size of the debt. In Lerner's words,*

> When the national debt has grown so large that people feel themselves so wealthy that they spend enough to provide full employment, there is no need for any further deficits.

Figure 7.3.1, in which real income is measured along the horizontal axis, illustrates the argument. It is assumed that the full-employment level of real income is equal to OA and that the level of consumption associated with this level of income and the national-debt level D_0 is AB. If there are no nonconsumption sources of expenditure, there is a deflationary gap of DB, which implies that government purchases in this amount would have to be made in order to achieve full employment. However, as a result of the deficit, the public debt increases to D_1 and the consumption function shifts up, so that in the next period the gap will be only DC. The required amount of government expenditure therefore declines and will continue to decline progressively until consumption rises to the point where the consumption function intersects the 45° line at point D.

The difficulty with this theory of a natural debt limit is that it takes no note of the possibility that potential output at full employment may increase as a consequence of government spending.† Domar emphasized that investment creates capacity and that this raises the output potential of the economy. Is it not also possible that government purchases might possess investment content and will therefore have the same effect? Since a fraction of total government outlay is for education and training, for the building and improving of transportation and communications facilities, and for the advancement of research and technology, it is obvious that the investment content of government spending is substantial.

Recognition of this circumstance complicates Lerner's simple proposition. We have seen, in Fig. 7.3.1, that if the deflationary gap is DB and government purchases fill this gap, the resulting increase in debt will shift up the consumption function and reduce the size of the gap to DC. However, if the government outlays of DB were made on the construction and improvement of schools, or on the improvement of transportation and communication facilities, their effect will be to raise the full-employment potential output level of the economy. Suppose, in fact, that full employment income rises to OE. In combination with the new consumption function, $C(Y, D_1)$, full-employment output of OE implies the presence of a deflationary gap of GH. This gap may be greater or less than the original gap of DB, depending upon whether the asset effect on consumption of

---

* A. P. Lerner, *The Economics of Employment* (New York: McGraw-Hill, 1951), p. 275.
† The subsequent discussion follows the argument of author's paper, "A Note on Productivity, Wealth, and Fiscal Policy," *National Tax Journal* (September, 1962).

debt creation is stronger than the productivity effect of the increase in government purchases. We therefore see that there is no immediate presumption that the Lerner effect will place a natural limit on the public debt so long as government outlays are not made in wholly unproductive areas.

An answer to the question of whether or not the deflationary gap (and therefore increments to the debt) will diminish can best be sought by recourse to a dynamic model.

For the sake of simplicity, we assume that investment is absent. Consequently,

$$Y = C + G \tag{7.3.2}$$

represents the definition of income. The consumption function is specified as

$$C = aD + bY, \qquad a > 0, \tag{7.3.3}$$

where D is the real value of public debt. This formulation incorporates Lerner's hypothesis that an increase in the debt represents an increase in private wealth and that this will cause consumption to rise. Now suppose, for the remainder of this analysis, that Y represents the full-employment level of income rather than the actual level of income. In the absence of any government purchases, the deflationary gap would be Gap $= Y - C = (1 - b)Y - aD$, and if government purchases were always adjusted in such a way as to eliminate the gap and attain full employment, the level of government purchases would equal the gap, and we would have

$$G = (1 - b)Y - aD. \tag{7.3.4}$$

When we differentiate 7.3.4 with respect to time, we obtain

$$\frac{dG}{dt} = (1 - b)\frac{dY}{dt} - a\frac{dD}{dt}. \tag{7.3.5}$$

Our assumption here is that the deflationary gap is entirely filled by government purchases of goods and services. We further assume that taxes are raised purely for the purpose of servicing the debt. Since interest payments on the debt are recorded as government transfer payments, net taxes are zero and the increment to the debt therefore equals the level of government purchases. Formally, this means that

$$\frac{dD}{dt} = G. \tag{7.3.6}$$

Finally, we assume that each dollar of government outlay on goods and services raises the full-employment output potential of the economy by g percent of the outlay. Consequently, we have

$$\frac{dY}{dt} = gG, \tag{7.3.7}$$

where g may be thought of as the government capital coefficient.

Substituting 7.3.6 and 7.3.7 into 7.3.5 yields the first-order homogeneous differential equation,

$$\frac{dG}{dt} = [(1 - b)g - a]G.$$

The equation has the solution,

$$G = G_0 e^{[(1-b)g-a]t}, \tag{7.3.8}$$

and since this must be consistent with Eq. 7.3.4, it must be the case that

$$G_0 = (1 - b)Y_0 - aD_0.$$

The next task is to solve for the full-employment level of income and for the level of debt. It follows from 7.3.6 that

$$D = D_0 + \int_0^t G\, dt,$$

and since 7.3.8 provides the solution for G, this expression may be written

$$D = D_0 + G_0 \int_0^t e^{[(1-b)g-a]t}\, dt.$$

Evaluation of this integral over the range 0 to t yields

$$D = D_0 + \frac{G_0}{(1 - b)g - a}[e^{[(1-b)g-a]t} - 1] \tag{7.3.9}$$

as the solution for the level of debt.

Similarly, it follows from 7.3.7 that

$$Y = Y_0 + g \int_0^t G\, dt,$$

and this implies that the solution for the level of income is

$$Y = Y_0 + \frac{gG_0}{(1 - b)g - a}[e^{[(1-b)g-a]t} - 1]. \tag{7.3.10}$$

Let us collect the three solutions in order to be better able to analyze the results:

$$G = G_0 e^{[(1-b)g-a]t}, \tag{7.3.8}$$

$$D = D_0 + \frac{G_0}{(1 - b)g - a}[e^{[(1-b)g-a]t} - 1], \tag{7.3.9}$$

$$Y = Y_0 + \frac{gG_0}{(1 - b)g - a}[e^{[(1-b)g-a]t} - 1], \tag{7.3.10}$$

where $G_0 = (1 - b)Y_0 - aD_0$.

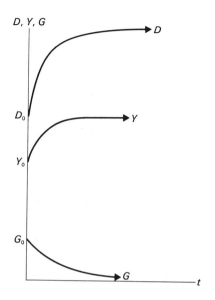

7|3|2
A natural limit to the debt.

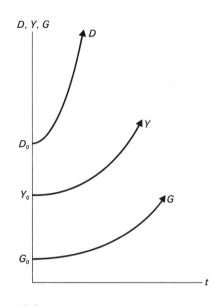

7|3|3
No debt limit.

If $(1 - b)g - a < 0$, we see from 7.3.8 that as $t \to \infty$, $G \to 0$. Similarly, the debt approaches the limit

$$D_0 - \frac{G_0}{(1 - b)g - a},$$

which, of course, is greater than D_0, since $(1 - b)g - a$ is negative. Finally, the level of income approaches the limit

$$Y_0 - \frac{gG_0}{(1 - b)g - a}.$$

Thus we see that if $(1 - b)g - a < 0$, the asset effect on the consumption of rising public debt overcomes the productivity effect with the result that the gap-closing level of government purchases diminishes to zero as time passes, while the levels of debt and income approach "natural" limits. This situation is illustrated in Fig. 7.3.2. Starting with an initial deflationary gap of G_0, the asset effect steadily overcomes the productivity effect so that the gap diminishes and the debt and income levels approach limiting values.

When $(1 - b)g - a > 0$, it is apparent from Eqs. 7.3.8, 7.3.9, and 7.3.10 that all variables grow steadily through time. The productivity effect overcomes the asset effect and this implies that the level of gap-closing, government purchases continues to rise, and so also do the national debt and the level of income. This situation is depicted in Fig. 7.3.3, in which it is obvious that highly productive public investment implies the absence of any natural limit to the debt.

The pure Lerner result would obtain if $g = 0$. In this case Eqs. 7.3.8, 7.3.9, and 7.3.10 become

$$G = G_0 e^{-at}, \qquad Y = Y_0, \qquad D = D_0 + \frac{G_0}{a}(1 - e^{-at}).$$

Here the level of government purchases diminishes steadily; there being no productivity effect, the full-employment level of income remains constant; the debt, finally, approaches the limit $D_0 + G_0/a$.

To consider the opposite extreme, assume next that the asset effect is completely absent. In this case, $a = 0$, and the three solutions reduce to

$$G = G_0 e^{(1-b)gt}, \tag{7.3.11}$$

$$D = D_0 + \frac{G_0}{(1-b)g}[e^{(1-b)gt} - 1], \tag{7.3.12}$$

$$Y = Y_0 + \frac{G_0}{(1-b)}[e^{(1-b)gt} - 1]. \tag{7.3.13}$$

The solution for the level of government purchases looks suspiciously like the Domar result reported in the last section. Indeed, that is almost what it is. The difference simply is that 7.3.11 reports the time path of the level of government purchases that is needed to maintain full employment on the assumption that there is no investment and no asset effect, whereas the Domar result, $I = I_0 e^{(1-b)\sigma t}$, represents the required level of investment if there are no government purchases and no asset effects.

Note finally, that since $a = 0$, then

$$G_0 = (1 - b)Y_0,$$

and this implies that the solution for the level of income (Eq. 7.3.12) reduces to

$$Y = Y_0 e^{(1-b)gt},$$

which, with g replacing σ, is the solution for the level of income in the Domar model when the intercept of the consumption function is zero.

In conclusion: The foregoing considerations suggest that government deficits that are incurred in order to maintain full employment will tend to eliminate themselves in the event that the expenditures are unproductive. However, if the expenditures are productive, their effect will be to raise the full employment level of output and they may therefore increase the magnitude of required future deficits. Paradoxically, this implies that the very kinds of public expenditures that are most frequently deplored by the opponents of deficit financing as an instrument of stabilization policy are those that may ultimately eliminate the need for deficit financing, while the types of productive expenditures that are generally applauded are the very types of expenditures that may necessitate increases in the magnitudes of future deficits.

REFERENCES

W. J. Baumol, *Economic Dynamics*, 2nd ed. (New York: Macmillan, 1959), Chapter 14.

T. F. Dernburg, "A Note on Productivity, Wealth, and Fiscal Policy," *National Tax Journal* (September, 1962).

E. D. Domar, "Capital Expansion, Rate of Growth and Employment," *Econometrica* (April, 1946).

———, "Expansion and Employment," *American Economic Review* (March, 1947).

———, "The 'Burden of the Debt' and the National Income," *American Economic Review* (December, 1944).

R. F. Harrod, "An Essay in Dynamic Theory," *Economic Journal* (March, 1939).

———, *Towards a Dynamic Economics* (New York: Macmillan, 1952).

A. P. Lerner, "Functional Finance and the Federal Debt," *Social Research* (February, 1943).

———, *The Economics of Control* (New York: Macmillan, 1947), Chapter 24.

———, *The Economics of Employment* (New York: McGraw-Hill, 1951).

A. C. Pigou, "The Classical Stationary State," *Economic Journal* (December, 1943).

———, "Economic Progress in a Stable Environment," *Economica* (August, 1947).

Second-Order Difference Equations and Linear Models of the Cycle

8.1 SECOND-ORDER DIFFERENCE EQUATIONS AND THEIR SOLUTION

Difference equations are popular with business-cycle theorists not only because they allow for the fact that certain variables lead or lag other variables with which they are functionally related, but also because even the simplest first- and second-order models yield a rich variety of solutions that help to illustrate important economic processes and phenomena. The second-order difference equation is a particularly favored device of business-cycle analysis because, unlike the first-order difference equation, oscillations are not limited to the period by period variety.

In this chapter we begin with a short discussion of how to solve second-order difference equations and we then apply our knowledge to the Hicks-Samuelson multiplier-accelerator models of the cycle and to Metzler's models of inventory fluctuation.

Consider the second-order linear nonhomogeneous difference equation,

$$ay_t + by_{t-1} + cy_{t-2} = g.$$

The first step in finding a solution to this equation is to calculate the equilibrium value of y. At equilibrium, $y_t = y_{t-1} = y_{t-2} = \bar{y}$, and it therefore follows that

$$\bar{y} = \frac{g}{a + b + c}.$$

The next step is to define $y_t = u_t + \bar{y}$, where u_t is the displacement from equilibrium. Consequently,

$$a(u_t + \bar{y}) + b(u_{t-1} + \bar{y}) + c(u_{t-2} + \bar{y}) = g.$$

When $\bar{y}$ is replaced by its calculated value, this equation reduces to the homogeneous second-order difference equation,

$$au_t + bu_{t-1} + cu_{t-2} = 0. \tag{8.1.1}$$

Proceeding as we did in the first-order case, we attempt the trial solution $u_t = x^t$ and substitute this into 8.1.1 to obtain

$$(ax^2 + bx + c)x^{t-2} = 0,$$

where $ax^2 + bx + c = 0$ is the characteristic equation.

The characteristic roots are found by means of the quadratic formula; they are

$$x_1 = \frac{-b + \sqrt{b^2 - 4ac}}{2a},$$

$$x_2 = \frac{-b - \sqrt{b^2 - 4ac}}{2a}.$$

If $u = x_1^t$ and $u = x_2^t$ are both solutions to the difference equation, then so also is $u_t = m_1 x_1^t + m_2 x_2^t$, and this means that the complete solution is of the form

$$y_t = m_1 x_1^t + m_2 x_2^t + \bar{y}, \tag{8.1.2}$$

where x_1, x_2, and $\bar{y}$ are now known, and where the arbitrary constants, m_1 and m_2, remain to be determined by the initial conditions. If at $t = 0$ and $t = 1$, y has values of y_0 and y_1, respectively, we have from Eq. 8.1.2 that

$$y_0 = m_1 + m_2 + \bar{y},$$
$$y_1 = m_1 x_1 + m_2 x_2 + \bar{y}.$$

These equations may now be solved simultaneously for m_1 and m_2; the resulting values may be substituted into 8.1.2; and the complete solution is thereby obtained.

Barring complications, the solution to the second-order difference equation is of the form

$$y_t = m_1 x_1^t + m_2 x_2^t + \bar{y}.$$

From inspection of this solution it appears that the behavior of the system is eventually dominated by whichever one of the roots has the largest absolute value. If both roots lie between -1 and $+1$, the system is stable and y_t approaches $\bar{y}$ as t increases. In the event that the roots are positive, the period-by-period changes will be in the same direction. However, if one, or both are negative, the system will exhibit period-by-period oscillations, and if one (or both) of the roots is less than -1, the oscillations will grow in amplitude. Whereas stability in a differential equation model requires all roots to be negative,* stability in a difference equation system requires them to lie between -1 and $+1$.

---

* As we shall show subsequently, stability of a differential equation system requires only that the real parts of the roots be negative. The statement in the text is strictly true only if all roots are real.

8.2 THE HICKS-SAMUELSON MULTIPLIER-ACCELERATOR INTERACTION *

According to the acceleration principle, investment in capital goods depends upon changes in the level of output. Because capital goods are durable, it would be possible, provided existing capacity is adequate, to produce a constant level of output without ever undertaking any net investment. However, should demand increase, it will be necessary if the system is operating at full capacity, to add to the stock of capital in order to produce an increase in output. This idea that net investment is a function of *changes* in the level of output, represents the fundamental basis for much of the modern literature of business-cycle theory.

The acceleration principle establishes a causal link between changes in output and the level of investment. However, to construct a complete theory of the cycle, it is necessary, as well, to complete the loop and to explain how changes in investment affect output. This link is provided by the theory of the multiplier. In combination, the theory of the multiplier and the acceleration principle provide a possible explanation of cyclical fluctuations in business activity. For example, one could imagine that a disturbance would cause income to rise, and that this rise in income would induce investment and thereby, via the multiplier, to raise income still further. This rise in income would, in turn, cause further investment to be induced; income would rise again; and so on in a cumulative dynamic process.

Because the marginal propensity to consume is less than unity, it becomes possible to visualize a self-limiting cumulative process that would generate its own turning points without resort to such external factors (nonlinearities) as full employment or limits to the expansion of bank credit. For example, if income rises by an amount Δy, and if this induces additional investment in an amount just sufficient to raise income in the next period by Δy, the same quantity of investment would be induced in each of the two periods. However, once investment reaches a plateau, income no longer rises, and since a constant level of income can be produced with a constant capital stock, net investment would collapse, and the cycle would then start its downward course.

One of the first writers to combine the multiplier and the acceleration principle into a formal income-generation model was P. A. Samuelson.† Using our own symbols rather than his, we write Samuelson's investment function a $I_t = w(C_t - C_{t-1}) + \bar{I}$, where C_t is the level of consumption spending in time period t, w is the "acceleration coefficient," and $\bar{I}$ is the autonomous component of investment. The consumption function is

$$C_t = bY_{t-1} + a,$$

---

* P. A. Samuelson, "Interactions Between the Multiplier Analysis and the Principle of Acceleration," *Review of Economics and Statistics* (May, 1939); J. R. Hicks, *A Contribution to the Theory of the Trade Cycle* (London: Oxford University Press, 1950).
† Samuelson, "Interactions Between the Multiplier Analysis and the Principle of Acceleration," *op. cit.*

from which it can be seen that changes in consumption are assumed to lag one period behind changes in income. When these two equations are combined with the definition of income, $Y_t = C_t + I_t$, we obtain

$$Y_t = w(C_t - C_{t-1}) + bY_{t-1} + a + \bar{I}.$$

Finally, when the consumption function is used to substitute for C_t and C_{t-1}, the result is the second-order difference equation,

$$Y_t - bw(Y_{t-1} - Y_{t-2}) - bY_{t-1} = a + \bar{I}, \tag{8.2.1}$$

which we may rearrange as

$$Y_t - b(1 + w)Y_{t-1} + bwY_{t-2} = a + \bar{I}. \tag{8.2.2}$$

A very similar formulation of the multiplier-accelerator interaction is the model of Professor Hicks. He argues that induced investment should properly be a function not only of changes in consumption but of changes in investment as well. He writes

> The building of houses, for instance, reckons as investment activity; but an increase in the demand for new houses induces investment in brick works, saw mills, and glass works just in the same way as an increase in the demand for cigarettes induces investment in cigarette making machinery.*

In addition to the assumption that induced investment is a function of changes in output as a whole rather than changes in consumption alone, Hicks believes that net investment should be broken up into an induced component and a growing autonomous component. The autonomous component depends upon long-run factors such as the growth of population and the advance of technology, and is assumed to grow at a constant percentage rate. Investment in the Hicks model may therefore be written

$$I_t = v(Y_{t-1} - Y_{t-2}) + I_0 r^t, \tag{8.2.3}$$

where $v(Y_{t-1} - Y_{t-2})$ is induced investment, $I_0 r^t$ is autonomous investment, and v is the acceleration coefficient.

Hicks is concerned with cyclical fluctuations about a long-run trend, and he therefore ignores the constant term in the consumption function and writes

$$C_t = (1 - s)Y_{t-1}, \tag{8.2.4}$$

where s is the marginal propensity to save.†

---

* Hicks, *Trade Cycle*, op. cit., p. 38.
† The subsequent analysis is somewhat facilitated by replacing the marginal propensity to consume, b, by one minus the marginal propensity to save, $1 - s$.

When Eqs. 8.2.3 and 8.2.4 are substituted into the definition of income, we obtain the second-order nonhomogeneous difference equation,

$$Y_t = v(Y_{t-1} - Y_{t-2}) + (1 - s)Y_{t-1} + I_0 r^t \qquad (8.2.5)$$

or

$$Y_t - (1 - s + v)Y_{t-1} + vY_{t-2} = I_0 r^t. \qquad (8.2.6)$$

To obtain a solution, we proceed as we did in Chapter 6 and imagine that dynamic equilibrium implies a growth of income at the rate $r - 1$. Consequently, let

$$Y_t = u_t + \bar{Y}_t, \qquad (8.2.7)$$

and assume that

$$\bar{Y}_t = Er^t, \qquad (8.2.8)$$

where E is a constant to be determined by the requirement that we seek to make the difference equation in the displacement u_t homogeneous. Substituting 8.2.7 and 8.2.8 into 8.2.6 gives

$$u_t + Er^t - (1 - s + v)u_{t-1} - (1 - s + v)Er^{t-1} + vu_{t-2} + vEr^{t-2} = I_0 r^t.$$

Since we wish to make

$$u_t - (1 - s + v)u_{t-1} + vu_{t-2} = 0, \qquad (8.2.9)$$

we should attempt to solve for the value of E that will satisfy the equation

$$Er^t - (1 - s + v)Er^{t-1} + vEr^{t-2} = I_0 r^t.$$

Upon factoring r^{t-2} out of this last expression, we obtain

$$E[r^2 - (1 - s + v)r + v] = I_0 r^2.$$

Therefore the solution for E is

$$E = \frac{I_0 r^2}{r^2 - (1 - s + v)r + v}. \qquad (8.2.10)$$

Substituting this result into 8.2.8, we see that the particular solution is the moving equilibrium,

$$\bar{Y}_t = \frac{I_0 r^{t+2}}{r^2 - (1 - s + v)r + v}. \qquad (8.2.11)$$

Before proceeding to the complete solution, it is instructive to examine the properties of the equilibrium path as given in Eq. 8.2.11, and, particularly, the initial equilibrium income level as specified in Eq. 8.2.10.

Observe first that since the parameter r equals one plus the rate of growth of autonomous investment, the absence of growth in autonomous investment implies that $E = I_0/s$, which is the familiar result that the static equilibrium level of income equals the level of autonomous spending times the multiplier.

Differentiating Eq. 8.2.10 partially with respect to s, we obtain

$$\frac{\partial E}{\partial s} = \frac{-E^2}{I_0 r} < 0,$$

which shows that because a higher marginal propensity to save implies a lower multiplier, a lower equilibrium level of income is associated with a given level of autonomous investment.

Similarly,

$$\frac{\partial E}{\partial v} = \frac{-(1 - r)E^2}{I_0 r^2} > 0,$$

and this shows that so long as there is some growth in autonomous investment $(r > 1)$, a higher acceleration coefficient implies a higher associated level of autonomous investment, and therefore a higher dynamic equilibrium level of income.

The behavior of the system when it is away from equilibrium depends upon the value of the roots of the characteristic equation of Eq. 8.2.9. Utilizing the trial solution $u_t = x^t$, we see immediately that the characteristic equation is

$$x^2 - (1 - s + v)x + v = 0, \qquad (8.2.12)$$

and when we apply the quadratic formula, we see that the roots are

$$x_1 = \frac{(1 - s + v) + \sqrt{(1 - s + v)^2 - 4v}}{2}$$

$$\qquad (8.2.13)$$

$$x_2 = \frac{(1 - s + v) - \sqrt{(1 - s + v)^2 - 4v}}{2}.$$

Finally, the complete solution is of the form

$$Y_t = m_1 x_1^t + m_2 x_2^t + \bar{Y}_t.$$

Depending upon the values of v and s, several modes of behavior are possible. If the roots are real and lie between 0 and $+1$, the system will fall back towards equilibrium following a disturbance much as in the case of the simple multiplier. If the roots are negative, the system will exhibit period-by-period oscillations, and if one or both of the roots is less than -1, the oscillations will be antidamped. If the dominant root is positive and greater than one, the system will tend to move monotonically away from equilibrium. Finally, if the roots are complex, the system will oscillate, but not from one period to the next. Moreover, these oscillations may be either damped or explosive.

We now turn to an examination of the roots of the characteristic equation to see if we can determine the ranges of values for v and s that will produce some of these various modes of behavior. Inspection of the roots indicates that if they are

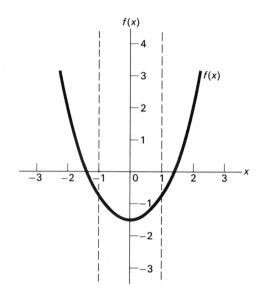

8|2|1

real, it must be the case that $(1 - s + v)^2 > 4v$. From this it follows that

$$(1 - s + v) > 2\sqrt{v}, \quad \text{and that} \quad 1 - 2\sqrt{v} + v > s.$$

Since this must mean either that

$$(1 - \sqrt{v})^2 > s \quad \text{or} \quad (\sqrt{v} - 1)^2 > s,$$

there are two possible cases that yield real roots. It further follows that

$$1 - \sqrt{v} > \sqrt{s} \quad \text{or} \quad \sqrt{v} - 1 > \sqrt{s},$$

so that, finally,

$$v < (1 - \sqrt{s})^2 \quad \text{and} \quad v > (1 + \sqrt{s})^2.$$

To see what is implied by these two cases, we follow a common procedure of the theory of equations and write the characteristic equation as the parabola

$$f(x) = x^2 - (1 - s + v)x + v. \tag{8.2.14}$$

Since the behavior of the system depends upon whether the roots lie between $-\infty$ and -1, -1 and 0, 0 and $+1$, $+1$ and $+\infty$, we evaluate the function at these critical points. The results are reported in the accompanying table, where it can be seen that $f(x)$ is positive at all the critical x-values.

x	$-\infty$	-1	0	$+1$	$+\infty$
$f(x)$	$+$	$2(1 + v) - s$	v	s	$+$

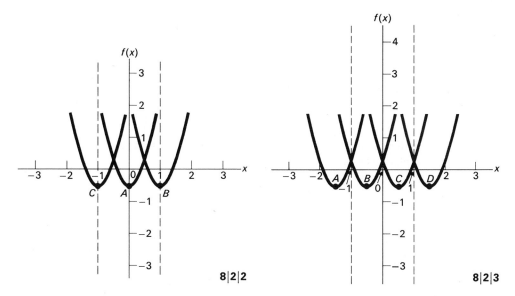

8|2|2

8|2|3

When x is very large, either positively or negatively, the square term of the parabola will dominate the result and both $f(-\infty)$ and $f(+\infty)$ must therefore be positive. Moreover, so long as the roots are real, the parabola must cut the x-axis in two places, and it must therefore reach a minimum below the axis. Thus we can infer that the parabola must have a shape something like the shape of the curve depicted in Fig. 8.2.1.

Since the value of the function is positive at all the critical points and since a parabola changes direction only once, it must be the case that both roots must lie between two consecutive critical values of x. For example, it would be impossible for the actual parabola to appear as it does in Fig. 8.2.1 because in that case $f(-1)$, $f(0)$, and $f(1)$ would all be negative. Nor could it be any of the cases depicted in Fig. 8.2.2. In the case of curve A, $f(-1)$ and $f(1)$ are positive but $f(0)$ is negative. Curve B has $f(-1)$ and $f(0)$ positive but $f(1)$ is negative. Finally, curve C is positive at $x = 0$ and $x = 1$, but is negative at $x = -1$. We can definitely conclude that the true parabola must be similar to one of the curves of Fig. 8.2.3. These curves are characterized by the property that both roots lie inside one of the possible critical ranges.

We are now reduced to four possibilities in the real root case: (1) both roots may be less than -1; (2) both roots may lie between 0 and -1; (3) both roots may lie between 0 and $+1$; and (4) both roots may be greater than $+1$. Can the field be narrowed still further?

By differentiating the function (8.2.14) with respect to x and setting the resulting derivative equal to zero, we can find the minimum point. Let $f'(x) = 2x - (1 - s + v) = 0$, from which it follows that

$$x_{\min} = \frac{(1 - s + v)}{2} > 0.$$

Since x_{min} is positive, curves A and B of Fig. 8.2.3 are ruled out, and it follows that there can be no oscillations if the roots are real.

We now know that both roots must lie either between 0 and $+1$ or they must both be greater than $+1$. To complete our present bit of detective work, we take the critical values that were previously calculated, namely,

$$v < (1 - \sqrt{s})^2, \qquad v > (1 + \sqrt{s})^2,$$

and use these to replace v in the expression for the minimum point of the parabola. If we replace v by $(1 - \sqrt{s})^2$, we have

$$x_{min} = \frac{1 - s + (1 - \sqrt{s})^2}{2} = 1 - \sqrt{s},$$

which is positive and less than $+1$. Hence in this case both roots lie between 0 and $+1$, and we therefore conclude that if $v < (1 - \sqrt{s})^2$, the time path of Y will exhibit damped monotonic behavior, that is, $Y_t \to \bar{Y}_t$ as $t \to \infty$.

Similarly, if we replace v by $(1 + \sqrt{s})^2$, we have

$$x_{min} = \frac{1 - s + (1 + \sqrt{s})^2}{2} = 1 + \sqrt{s},$$

which is greater than $+1$. It must therefore be the case that both roots are greater than $+1$ when $v > (1 + \sqrt{s})^2$. Since both of the roots in this case are positive and greater than $+1$, we conclude that the time path of Y_t is monotonic and antidamped.

To summarize: If $v < (1 - \sqrt{s})^2$, both roots must be positive and less than $+1$, and the system therefore returns monotonically to equilibrium following a disturbance. On the other hand, if $v > (1 + \sqrt{s})^2$, both roots are positive and greater than $+1$ and the system moves monotonically away from equilibrium in an "explosive" manner. Finally, oscillations are not possible if the roots are real, since real roots can never be negative in the multiplier-accelerator model.

The critical ranges are delineated in Fig. 8.2.4. In region I, $v < (1 - \sqrt{s})^2$, and in region IV, $v > (1 + \sqrt{s})^2$. The area in between (regions II and III) is the range of complex roots. Analysis of cases that fall in this range will have to wait while we pause to digress briefly on the subject of complex roots.

8.3 COMPLEX ROOTS

If the roots of the Hicks model are of such a sort that $(1 - s + v)^2 < 4v$, the expression

$$\frac{\sqrt{(1 - s + v)^2 - 4v}}{2}, \tag{8.3.1}$$

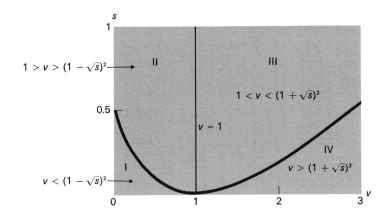

8|2|4
Hicks model: Critical
regions for v and s.

would convey the instruction to take the square root of a negative number even though such a miracle cannot be performed. However, observe that since 8.3.1 could just as well be written

$$\left[\frac{\sqrt{4v - (1 - s + v)^2}}{2}\right](\sqrt{-1}), \tag{8.3.2}$$

the problem becomes one of dealing with the term $\sqrt{-1}$.

As a matter of convention, the character "i" is used to denote $\sqrt{-1}$. Consequently, $i^2 = -1$, $i^3 = -\sqrt{-1}$, and $i^4 = 1$. An expression such as 8.3.2 is known as an *imaginary number* and may be written in shorthand form as βi. If we let α stand for the real part of the roots of the Hicks model, namely $(1 - s+v)/2$, the two roots become the *complex numbers*,

$$x_1 = \alpha + \beta i = \frac{(1 - s + v) + [\sqrt{4v - (1 - s + v)^2}](\sqrt{-1})}{2},$$

$$x_2 = \alpha + \beta i = \frac{(1 - s + v) - [\sqrt{4v - (1 - s + v)^2}](\sqrt{-1})}{2}. \tag{8.3.3}$$

Complex roots always occur in pairs with equal real parts. If one of the roots is $\alpha + \beta i$, there must be one other root equal to $\alpha - \beta i$, and the two roots are referred to as complex conjugates.

To see how the presence of complex roots affects the solution to the difference equation

$$u_t - (1 - s + v)u_{t-1} + vu_{t-2} = 0, \tag{8.2.9}$$

it will help to refer to Fig. 8.3.1 in which the real parts are measured horizontally, and the imaginary parts are diagramed vertically. If a straight line is drawn to connect the origin to the points (α, β) and $(\alpha, -\beta)$, this line, via the Pythagorean

Theorem, will have a distance of

$$M = \sqrt{\alpha^2 + \beta^2}, \tag{8.3.4}$$

where M is referred to as the *modulus* of the complex roots. The modulus generates an angle of θ degrees with respect to the horizontal (real) axis.
Now, note that since

$$\cos \theta = \frac{\alpha}{\sqrt{\alpha^2 + \beta^2}} = \frac{\alpha}{M}$$

and

$$\sin \theta = \frac{\beta}{\sqrt{\alpha^2 + \beta^2}} = \frac{\beta}{M},$$

the roots $\alpha + \beta i$ and $\alpha - \beta i$ may be written

$$\alpha + \beta i = M[\cos \theta + i \sin \theta],$$
$$\alpha - \beta i = M[\cos \theta - i \sin \theta].$$

However, since the solution to Eq. 8.2.9 is of the form

$$u_t = m_1 x_1^t + m_2 x_2^t = m_1(\alpha + \beta i)^t + m_2(\alpha - \beta i)^t,$$

it follows that

$$u_t = m_1[M(\cos \theta + i \sin \theta)]^t + m_2[M(\cos \theta - i \sin \theta)]^t. \tag{8.3.5}$$

Via an important result known as De Moivre's Theorem, it can be proved that $(\cos \theta + i \sin \theta)^t = \cos \theta t + i \sin \theta t$. Consequently, Eq. 8.3.5 may be written as

$$u_t = M^t[m_1(\cos \theta t + i \sin \theta t) + m_2(\cos \theta t - i \sin \theta t)],$$

which obviously equals

$$u_t = M^t[(m_1 + m_2) \cos \theta t + (m_1 - m_2)i \sin \theta t]. \tag{8.3.6}$$

Finally, since $m_1 + m_2$ and $(m_1 - m_2)i$ are arbitrary constants that depend upon the initial conditions, Eq. 8.3.6 may be written as

$$u_t = M^t(n_1 \cos \theta t + n_2 \sin \theta t), \tag{8.3.7}$$

and this therefore constitutes the solution to the second-order homogeneous difference equation when the roots are complex.

Inasmuch as the territory we are attempting to cover here may be a bit unfamiliar, let us resort to a numerical example to see what is involved. Suppose that the roots are

$$x_1 = 2 + 2i, \qquad x_2 = 2 - 2i.$$

If we were to plot these coordinates in a diagram such as Fig. 8.3.1, we would see immediately that the coordinates of the root $2 + 2i$ imply that the angle θ is $45°$.

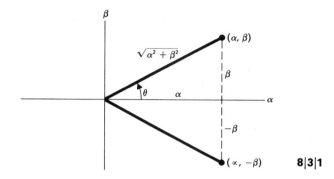

8|3|1

Moreover, it is evident that the modulus has a value of $\sqrt{2^2 + 2^2} = \sqrt{8}$. Consequently, Eq. 8.3.7 may be written as

$$u_t = (\sqrt{8})^t [n_1 \cos (45°t) + n_2 \sin (45°t)]. \tag{8.3.8}$$

Now consider the expression

$$n_1 \cos (45°t) + n_2 \sin (45°t). \tag{8.3.9}$$

When $t = 0$, we have $\cos (45°t) = \cos (0) = 1$, and $\sin (45°t) = \sin (0) = 0$. Consequently, the value of the expression when $t = 0$ is n_1. However, when $t = 8$, we have $\cos (360°) = \cos (0) = 1$, and $\sin (360°) = \sin (0) = 0$, and the value of expression 8.3.9 is therefore again equal to n_1.

Similarly, when $t = 2$, we have $\cos (45°t) = \cos (90°) = 0$, and $\sin (90°) = 1$, so that in this case the value of 8.3.9 is n_2. The same result, however, appears for $t = 10$. In this case we have

$$n_1 \cos (45°t) + n_2 \sin (45°t) = n_1 \cos (450°) + n_2 \sin (450°)$$
$$= n_1 \cos (90°) + n_2 \sin (90°) = n_2.$$

From this example it is evident that the portion of the solution represented by expression 8.3.9 is purely repetitive. It neither grows nor decays but rather produces a set of oscillations of uniform amplitude. In the present case, for example, we end up back where we started from every eight periods, and it is therefore apparent that the period required to complete one full cycle—i.e., to move from the initial position, up through a peak, then back through a trough, and finally back to the initial position—is eight periods. Moreover, it appears that the number of periods involved equals the value of the angle θ divided into 360°. Equation 8.3.9 is diagrammed in Fig. 8.3.2, in which it is assumed that n_1 and n_2 both equal 1.

Now let us take one more look at the complete solution. We have

$$u_t = M^t [n_1 \cos \theta t + n_2 \sin \theta t].$$

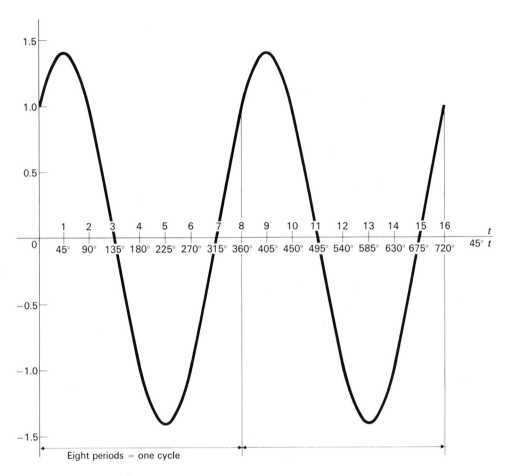

8|3|2
Time path of cos 45°t + sin 45°t.

Since we know that the term in brackets yields a purely repetitive time-path at intervals of $360°/\theta$ periods, it is obvious that whether the oscillations are damped or explosive must depend entirely upon the value of the modulus, M. If $M > 1$, M^t grows larger with the passage of time, and the amplitude of the oscillations increases. If $M < 1$, M^t diminishes as t increases, and the amplitude of the oscillations grows smaller. Oscillations of uniform amplitude apparently occur when $M = 1$.

This analysis permits us to state the stability condition for a difference-equation model in general terms. Given that $y_t = u_t + \bar{y}$, the transient portion, u_t, will decay to zero with the passage of time, and y_t will approach $\bar{y}$ if the *moduli* of all characteristic roots are less than unity in absolute terms. Therefore, it is sometimes said that the moduli of the characteristic roots must lie within the *unit circle* of the complex plane. This condition is general and encompasses real root cases. The angle of a real root is zero, it has no imaginary part, and its modulus,

$$M = \sqrt{\alpha^2 + \beta^2},$$

therefore reduces to $M = |\alpha|$. This, of course, is to say that the modulus of a real root simply equals the absolute value of the root.

We can now complete the analysis of the Hicks-Samuelson model. What we want to find are the critical values of v and s that demark damped from anti-damped oscillations. Since this depends only on the value of the modulus, we set $1 = \sqrt{\alpha^2 + \beta^2}$ and ask what this condition implies about the values of v and s. Since

$$\alpha^2 = \frac{(1 - s + v)^2}{4} \quad \text{and} \quad \beta^2 = \frac{4v - (1 - s + v)^2}{4},$$

we have

$$1 = \frac{(1 - s + v)^2}{4} + \frac{4v - (1 - s + v)^2}{4},$$

and this implies that the critical condition is $v = 1$. Thus when $v > 1$, the oscillations are of increasing amplitude (antidamped) and when $v < 1$, the oscillations are of decreasing amplitude.

Referring to Fig. 8.2.4, we see that there are four types of behavior possible in the multiplier-accelerator model and that each such pattern depends upon the combination of values of v and s that are obtained. When $v < (1 - \sqrt{s})^2$, the system returns monotonically back to equilibrium following a disturbance. This is region I of Fig. 8.2.4 where the accelerator is so weak that it produces no basic change over the simple-multiplier process. In region II, where $(1 - \sqrt{s})^2 < v < 1$, the roots are complex but the modulus is less than one and the system exhibits damped oscillations. When $v = 1$, the oscillations are of uniform amplitude. In region III, where $1 < v < (1 + \sqrt{s})^2$, the oscillations are of increasing amplitude. And, finally, in region IV, where $v > (1 + \sqrt{s})^2$, the accelerator is so powerful that the system proceeds monotonically in an exponential growth path.

Once the behavior of a second-order difference equation model has been examined in detail, it is usually not necessary to repeat the entire process for models that are similar with the exception of a few wrinkles. To see this, let us compare the Hicks model with the Samuelson model. Referring to Eqs. 8.2.1 and 8.2.5, it is evident that in the Hicks case the homogeneous form of the original difference equation may be written

$$u_t - v(u_{t-1} - u_{t-2}) - (1 - s)u_{t-1} = 0.$$

In the Samuelson model, on the other hand, the difference equation, when arranged in the same way, is

$$u_t - bw(u_{t-1} - u_{t-2}) - bu_{t-1} = 0.$$

Consequently, it is evident that the Samuelson counterpart of v is bw, while the counterpart of $(1 - s)$ is b. Making appropriate substitutions in the Hicks critical values for real roots, we replace

$$v < (1 - \sqrt{s})^2$$

by

$$bw < (1 - \sqrt{s})^2,$$

and when we rearrange this expression, we have

$$w < \frac{(1 - \sqrt{s})^2}{1 - s}$$

as the condition for damped monotonic behavior in the Samuelson model.

Similarly, the Hicks condition for anti-damped monotonic behavior is $v > (1 + \sqrt{s})^2$, so that when we replace v by $bw = (1 - s)w$, we have

$$w > \frac{(1 + \sqrt{s})^2}{1 - s}$$

as the critical condition under which the Samuelson model exhibits antidamped monotonic behavior.

Finally, oscillations of uniform amplitude occur in the Hicks model when $v = 1$. Again, replacing v by $wb = w(1 - s)$, we find that oscillations of uniform amplitude occur when* $w = 1/b = 1/(1 - s)$.

The critical regions of the Samuelson model are diagramed in Fig. 8.3.3. It can be seen there that the main difference between the Hicks and the Samuelson

---

* Samuelson writes the critical condition that demarks real from complex roots as $b = 4w/(1 + w)^2$. However, this comes to the same thing as the conditions derived in the text. Replacing b by $1 - s$ we get

$$1 - s = \frac{4w}{(1 + w)^2},$$

which implies that $(1 - s)(1 + 2w + w^2) = 4w$ and $(1 - 2w + w^2) - s(1 + 2w + w^2) = 0$. This means either that $(1 - w)^2 = s(1 + w)^2$, or that $(w - 1)^2 = s(1 + w)^2$. In the former case we have $1 - w = \sqrt{s} + w\sqrt{s}$, so that

$$w = (1 - \sqrt{s})/(1 + \sqrt{s}),$$

and in the latter case,

$$w = (1 + \sqrt{s})/(1 - \sqrt{s}).$$

Taking the first critical condition and multiplying numerator and denominator by $1 - \sqrt{s}$ yields the condition of the text,

$$w = (1 - \sqrt{s})^2/(1 - s).$$

Similarly, when numerator and denominator of the second critical condition are multiplied by $(1 + \sqrt{s})$, we obtain

$$w = (1 + \sqrt{s})^2/(1 - s).$$

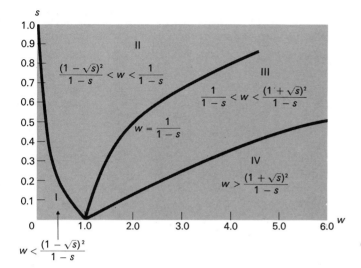

$$w < \frac{(1-\sqrt{s})^2}{1-s}$$

8|3|3
Samuelson model: critical values of w and s.

models is that the critical line that demarks damped from antidamped oscillations in the Samuelson model depends both on the marginal propensity to consume and upon the acceleration coefficient, whereas in the Hicks model the condition depends only on the value of the acceleration coefficient. The Samuelson model, moreover, is less volatile for comparable values of the parameters because it is only changes in consumption that induce investment, whereas in the Hicks model investment is induced by changes in output as a whole.

The acceleration principle, in the simple form in which it has been presented here, is a grossly inadequate explanation of the business cycle. Fully aware of the inadequacies of simple linear models, Professor Hicks went on in his book to construct an elaborate nonlinear theory of the business cycle. In the next chapter, which we devote to nonlinear cycle models, we shall attempt to complete the analysis.

8.4 INVENTORY FLUCTUATIONS

The reactions of business enterprise to the effects upon their inventories of differences between the actual and the anticipated level of sales during some period of time may operate to produce cycles in a manner that is very similar to the fluctuations caused by the acceleration principle. In this section, we shall examine a few of the simpler models of inventory adjustment. The models are the product of the work of L. A. Metzler,* and the interested reader is strongly urged to consult Metzler's famous paper.

---

* L. A. Metzler, "The Nature and Stability of Inventory Cycles," *Review of Economics and Statistics*, **23** (August, 1941).

Metzler assumes that there is no income-expenditure lag and that current consumption is therefore a function of current income. Thus the consumption function may be written as

$$C_t = bY_t. \tag{8.4.1}$$

The level of income is given by

$$Y_t = U_t + V_t + \check{I}, \tag{8.4.2}$$

where U_t represents production to meet anticipated sales, V_t is production for inventory, and $\check{I}$ is noninduced investment.

Production is based on sales expectations and these expectations, in the simplest of the Metzler models, equals sales of the preceding period. Consequently, we write

$$U_t = C_{t-1} = bY_{t-1}. \tag{8.4.3}$$

Metzler begins his analysis with a model that assumes inventory behavior to be purely passive. Orders equal expected sales and any difference between actual and anticipated sales is met by inventory accumulation (or decumulation) and no subsequent effort is made to deplete (or replenish) inventories to some "normal" level. Consequently, $V_t = 0$, and by the use of Eqs. 8.4.3 and 8.4.2 this becomes

$$Y_t = bY_{t-1} + \check{I}, \tag{8.4.4}$$

which has the solution

$$Y_t = (Y_0 - \bar{Y})b^t + \bar{Y}, \tag{8.4.5}$$

where

$$\bar{Y} = \frac{\check{I}}{1 - b}. \tag{8.4.6}$$

As can be seen from inspection of the solution, passive inventory behavior has the effect that a dynamic process identical to the simple multiplier is generated. A disturbance that raises consumption by one dollar causes the increased demand to be met out of inventories. However, since anticipated consumption rises by the amount of the disturbance, production increases by a dollar. However, the induced increase in consumption is b dollars, and thus actual sales fall short of anticipated sales by $1 - b$ dollars. In the next period, expected sales are b dollars in excess of the initial level. Consequently, production is b dollars more than initially. However, since actual sales will now be b^2 dollars over the initial level, the difference between anticipated and actual sales will be $b - b^2$. Apparently, then, passive inventory policy results in a monotonic return to the original equilibrium level of income. Sales in each period and anticipated sales in excess of the equilibrium level compare as follows:

Period	Sales *	Anticipated sales *
0	1	0
1	b	1
2	b^2	b
3	b^3	b^2
. . .	. . .	. . .
n	b^n	b^{n-1}

Since the two column sums will become equal as $t \to \infty$ (provided that $b < 1$), we conclude that the initial inventory loss is exactly offset by subsequent inventory increases due to the overestimation of anticipated sales. Passive inventory policy therefore implies that once the dynamic process works itself out, the situation, with respect to the level of income and with respect to the level of stocks, will be the same as prior to the disturbance.†

The second model we wish to study is constructed on the assumption that entrepreneurs attempt to maintain inventories at some constant "normal" level. If inventories are initially at their normal level and actual and anticipated sales in the preceding period are equal, there will be no orders for purposes of inventory accumulation. However, if actual sales in the preceding period exceed anticipated sales, there will be an attempt to replenish stocks in an amount equal to the discrepancy between actual and anticipated sales. Consequently, in this case we have

$$V_t = \text{actual sales } (t - 1) - \text{anticipated sales } (t - 1).$$

However, since actual sales in $t - 1$ equal bY_{t-1}, while anticipated sales equal bY_{t-2}, we have

$$V_t = b(Y_{t-1} - Y_{t-2}).$$

Using Eqs. 8.4.2 and 8.4.3, it follows that

$$Y_t = 2bY_{t-1} - bY_{t-2} + I. \tag{8.4.7}$$

Evidently, the characteristic equation in this case is $x^2 - 2bx + b = 0$, and it follows that the roots are

$$x_1 = b + \sqrt{b(b - 1)},$$
$$x_2 = b - \sqrt{b(b - 1)}.$$

---

* In excess of the equilibrium level.
† The reader is urged as an exercise to work out the case in which noninduced investment rises *permanently* by some arbitrary amount.

From inspection of the roots, it is evident that so long as the marginal propensity to consume has a value of less than unity, the roots will be complex, and this means that the system will produce oscillating behavior. Moreover, since the modulus of the complex roots is

$$M = \sqrt{\alpha^2 + \beta^2} = \sqrt{b^2 + b(1 - b)} = \sqrt{b} < 1,$$

it is apparent that the oscillations will be damped.

In this model, a disturbance that raises sales above the expected equilibrium level causes orders to increase not only because expected sales rise, but also because merchants wish to replenish inventories by the amount of their mistake in sales forecasting. As a result, income and actual sales rise again and this leads to yet another attempt to increase inventories. The process of expansion comes to a halt and a turning point is reached because, the marginal propensity to consume being less than unity, sales increase less rapidly than output and there therefore develops in each period some surplus of production over sales which is available for inventory adjustment. Consequently, actual inventories eventually catch up to desired inventories, and when this happens, orders to raise inventories fall to zero, and there then occurs an absolute decline in production and income (even though consumption may still be rising) and the cycle enters a phase of contraction. The contraction phase, again, is brought to a halt because, with a marginal propensity to consume of less than unity, consumption falls less rapidly than income and excess stocks are therefore gradually eliminated. If the marginal propensity to consume had a value of unity, sales and income would always change by the same amount and it would never be possible either to accumulate additional inventories or to work off a surplus. Thus it is the marginal propensity to consume of less than unity that gives rise to the possibility of self-limiting inventory cycles.

The third model we wish to consider differs from the preceding case in that we now assume that entrepreneurs desire to maintain inventories in proportion to the level of current sales. Thus, if expected sales equal U_t, the desired level of stocks will be

$$kU_t = kC_{t-1} = kbY_{t-1}.$$

The actual level of stocks at the end of period $t - 1$ equals the desired level for that period, $U_{t-1} = kbY_{t-2}$, plus or minus a discrepancy caused by faulty sales forecasting. Since the expected level of sales was bY_{t-2}, but the actual level of sales was bY_{t-1}, the sales discrepancy was

$$U_{t-1} - U_{t-2} = b(Y_{t-1} - Y_{t-2}).$$

Consequently, the actual level of stocks at the end of $t - 1$ is $kbY_{t-2} - b(Y_{t-1} - Y_{t-2})$, and since the desired level of stocks is kbY_{t-1}, orders to bring inventories to desired levels will be

$$V_t = kbY_{t-1} - kbY_{t-2} + b(Y_{t-1} - Y_{t-2}) = b(k + 1)(Y_{t-1} - Y_{t-2}).$$

When orders to meet expected sales, $U_t = C_{t-1} = bY_{t-1}$, are added to the above inventory adjustment relation, and when noninduced investment is taken into account, we have

$$Y_t = bY_{t-1} + b(k + 1)(Y_{t-1} - Y_{t-2}) + \dot{I} \tag{8.4.8}$$

or

$$Y_t = b(k + 2)Y_{t-1} - b(k + 1)Y_{t-2} + \dot{I}. \tag{8.4.9}$$

It is evident from inspection of 8.4.9 that the characteristic equation is

$$x^2 - b(k + 2)x + b(k + 1) = 0, \tag{8.4.10}$$

and the roots are therefore

$$\begin{aligned} x_1 &= \frac{b(k + 2)}{2} + \frac{\sqrt{b^2(k + 2)^2 - 4b(k + 1)}}{2}, \\ x_2 &= \frac{b(k + 2)}{2} - \frac{\sqrt{b^2(k + 2)^2 - 4b(k + 1)}}{2}. \end{aligned} \tag{8.4.11}$$

Relating 8.4.8 to the Hicks model, where

$$Y_t = (1 - s)Y_{t-1} + v(Y_{t-1} - Y_{t-2}) + I_0 r^t,$$

we see that b corresponds to $1 - s$, and $b(k + 1)$ corresponds to v. In the Hicks model we saw that the conditions under which real roots can be obtained were

$$v < (1 - \sqrt{s})^2 \quad \text{or} \quad v > (1 + \sqrt{s})^2.$$

Consequently, the inventory model implies that

$$b(k + 1) < (1 - \sqrt{s})^2 \quad \text{or} \quad b(k + 1) > (1 + \sqrt{s})^2.$$

Since $b = 1 - s$, this implies that

$$k + 1 < \frac{(1 - \sqrt{s})^2}{1 - s} \quad \text{or} \quad k + 1 > \frac{(1 + \sqrt{s})^2}{1 - s},$$

and it therefore follows that

$$k < \frac{2(s - \sqrt{s})}{1 - s} \quad \text{or} \quad k > \frac{2(s + \sqrt{s})}{1 - s}. \tag{8.4.12}$$

Provided that $0 < s < 1$, $s - \sqrt{s}$ must be negative, and this implies that the condition

$$k < \frac{2(s - \sqrt{s})}{1 - s}$$

cannot be obtained for positive values of k. This means that it is impossible for the system to yield damped monotonic behavior and the real root case can therefore be obtained only when

$$k > \frac{2(s + \sqrt{s})}{1 - s}.$$

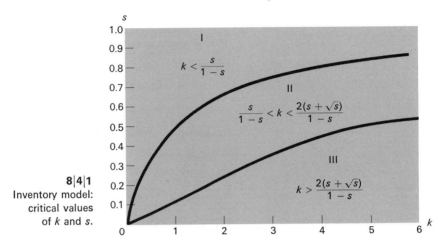

8|4|1
Inventory model:
critical values
of k and s.

Since this corresponds to the Hicks condition, $v > (1 + \sqrt{s})^2$, it follows that the system will exhibit antidamped monotonic behavior if this condition is obtained.

When the roots are complex, we have from 8.4.11 that

$$x_1 = \alpha + \beta i = \frac{b(k + 2)}{2} + \left[\frac{\sqrt{4b(k + 1) - b^2(k + 2)^2}}{2}\right](i) .$$

The modulus of the complex roots is

$$M = \sqrt{\alpha^2 + \beta^2} = \sqrt{\frac{b^2(k + 2)^2}{4} + \frac{4b(k + 1) - b^2(k + 2)^2}{4}},$$

and it therefore follows that $M = \sqrt{b(k + 1)}$.

If the oscillations are antidamped, $M > 1$, so that $b(k + 1) > 1$, which implies that $k + 1 > 1/b$, or, finally,

$$k > \frac{1 - b}{b} = \frac{s}{1 - s}.$$

Antidamped oscillations therefore occur when the desired ratio of stocks to sales exceeds the ratio of the marginal propensity to save to the marginal propensity to consume. The oscillations will be damped if the opposite is the case. The greater the marginal propensity to save, the more likely it is that the system will be stable.

The critical regions for this model are plotted in Fig. 8.4.1. It is apparent that a tendency to adjust inventories to proportionality with the level of sales reduces the likelihood that the dampening effect of saving will make it possible for stocks to adjust to desired levels, and this increases the probability of dynamic instability.

A selected bibliography on the dynamics of business cycles is presented at the end of Chapter 9.

Nonlinear Models of the Cycle

9.1 ANALYSIS OF NONLINEAR MODELS

Linear models possess the virtue of simplicity and of lending themselves to straightforward solution. However, they represent only one class of models and for many purposes they are inadequate. In dealing with nonlinear models, economists have generally followed one of two procedures. One approach is to assume that the functions may be regarded as linear over small ranges. Linear approximations are then derived and stability conditions are obtained on the assumption that the conditions hold only over the small range in question. In this way "local" stability is established and "global" stability* may then sometimes be inferred from additional information. For example, even though a function may be nonlinear, global stability may be inferred from the fact that the sign of the slope of the function is always the same or that it always lies within certain critical ranges. This is the approach that is usually employed in analysis of the stability of equilibrium in multiple-market schemes, and it will be discussed at length in Part III.

The second approach, which we shall concentrate upon in this chapter, is qualitative. It involves the graphic representation of the nonlinear function in a so-called *phase diagram* which permits the time path to be traced and the stability of equilibrium to be inferred.

To illustrate a phase diagram, we shall consider the familiar diagram of income determination in which income is measured horizontally, aggregate demand is measured vertically, and the 45° line serves as a guideline which indicates that at any point on this line vertical and horizontal distances are equal.

---

* Global stability is said to be obtained if the time path of the system is damped, regardless of the magnitude of the initial displacement.

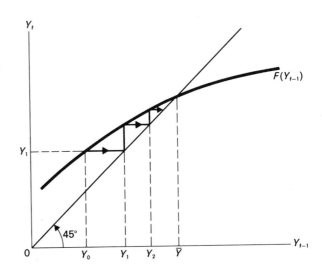

9|1|1
Monotonic convergence.

If there is an expenditure lag of one period, expenditure in period t is a function of income in $t - 1$. If the relationship is linear, the problem is the simple-multiplier problem of Chapters 5 and 6. However, if the relationship is nonlinear, we might write

$$Y_t = F(Y_{t-1}),$$

and we could depict the situation as in Fig. 9.1.1, in which Y_t is measured vertically and Y_{t-1} is measured horizontally.

If the initial level of income is Y_0, aggregate demand (measured vertically) is Y_1, and this means that income rises to Y_1. However, this means that aggregate demand now becomes Y_2 and so will the level of income. The process continues until equilibrium is reached at $\bar{Y}$, where aggregate demand intersects the $45°$ line. From this we can immediately conclude that if the slope of the function $Y_t = F(Y_{t-1})$ is positive but less than one, the system will move monotonically in the direction of equilibrium. Formally, if the slope

$$0 < \frac{dF(Y_{t-1})}{dY_{t-1}} < 1,$$

the time path will be monotonic and Y_t will approach $\bar{Y}$ with the passage of time.

In Fig. 9.1.2 a similar situation is depicted, except that now the slope of the function exceeds $+1$. Beginning at Y_0, the next period finds the value of Y at Y_1, and the second period finds it reduced to Y_2. Similarly, if we begin at Y_0' in excess of the equilibrium level, Y increases to Y_1' in the next period, and to Y_2' in the second period. Thus equilibrium is unstable when

$$\frac{dF(Y_{t-1})}{dY_{t-1}} > 1,$$

in which case the time path exhibits monotonic divergence away from equilibrium.

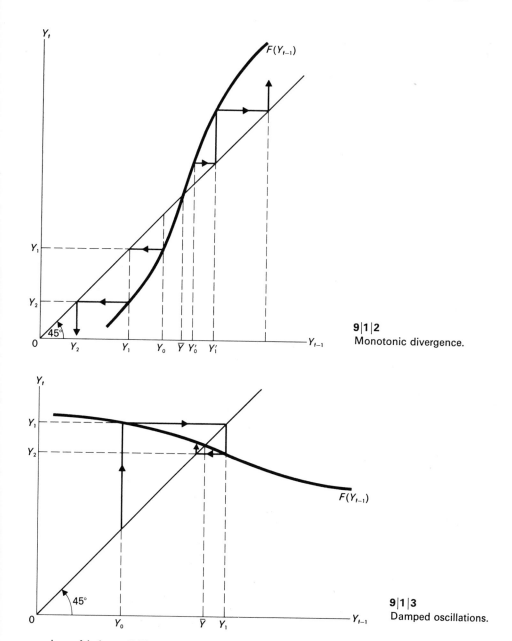

$9|1|2$
Monotonic divergence.

$9|1|3$
Damped oscillations.

As a third possibility, imagine that the slope of the function $Y_t = F(Y_{t-1})$ is negative. Beginning at Y_0 in Fig. 9.1.3, we see that Y will first rise to Y_1, then fall to Y_2, and subsequently alternately rise and fall in even smaller oscillations until equilibrium is reached. Here it is apparent that the system exhibits damped oscillations. On the other hand, in Fig. 9.1.4, where the slope of the phase line is less than -1, the oscillations are antidamped.

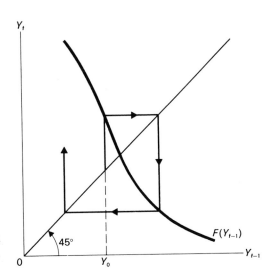

9|1|4
Antidamped oscillations.

From this brief glimpse, we see that there are four possibilities in cases where the slope of the function always lies within certain critical ranges. When

$$0 < \frac{dF(Y_{t-1})}{dY_{t-1}} < 1,$$

the system is stable and approaches equilibrium monotonically. When

$$\frac{dF(Y_{t-1})}{dY_{t-1}} > 1,$$

the system is unstable and departs from equilibrium monotonically. When

$$-1 < \frac{dF(Y_{t-1})}{dY_{t-1}} < 0,$$

the system exhibits damped oscillations, and finally, when

$$\frac{dF(Y_{t-1})}{dY_{t-1}} < -1,$$

the oscillations are explosive.

If the slope of the function falls in different critical regions for different values of Y_{t-1}, the result may be to produce *limit cycles*. To illustrate, consider Fig. 9.1.5, and note that the slope to the left of point A is greater than -1. Between A and B the slope is less than -1, and to the right of B it is again greater than -1. Note that if we start the system off at Y_0, the result is to produce a set of antidamped oscillations, but that these oscillations gradually become uniform in amplitude. Similarly, if we start the system off outside the limit cycle, at Y_0' for example, we will initially have damped oscillations which then develop into oscillations of uniform amplitude, as the limit is approached.

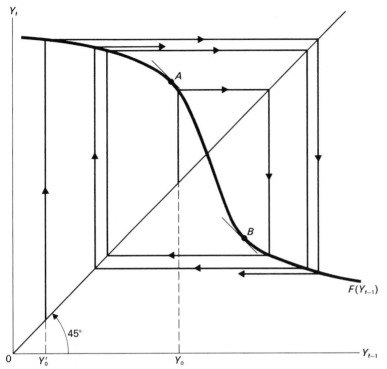

9|1|5
A limit cycle.

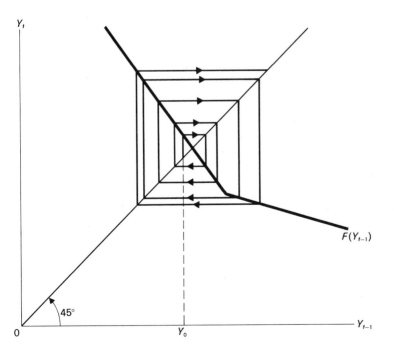

9|1|6
A kinked limit
cycle.

A limit cycle may be generated by the presence of a kink in the phase line. Such a kinked limit cycle is illustrated in Fig. 9.1.6. To the left of the kink the slope is less than -1 and to the right it is greater than -1. Starting off at Y_0, we see that initially we get a set of antidamped oscillations, but that eventually a limit is approached and the oscillations then attain uniform amplitude.

As can be seen from looking at the foregoing phase diagrams, Y_t always increases whenever the phase line is above the 45° line, and it always decreases when the phase line is below the 45° line. When the phase line has a positive slope, the reactions are such that in the next period the phase line will continue to be above (or below) the 45° line depending upon which situation prevailed in the preceding period, and the result therefore is to produce monotonic behavior. On the other hand, when the phase line has a negative slope, the reactions are such that if initially the phase line is below the 45° line, in the next period it will be above it, with the consequence that oscillating behavior materializes. Moreover, if oscillating behavior is to occur, the phase line must have a negative slope where it crosses the 45° line. This is illustrated in Fig. 9.1.7 where, despite the fact that

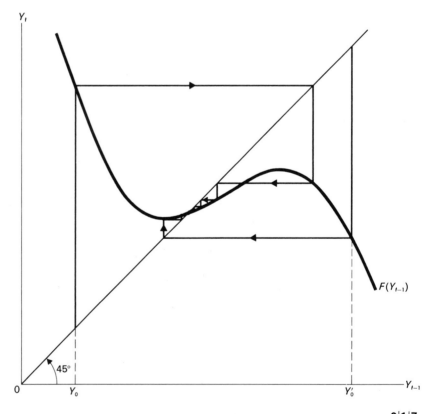

9|1|7

A phase line must have negative slope at the 45° line crossing to produce oscillations.

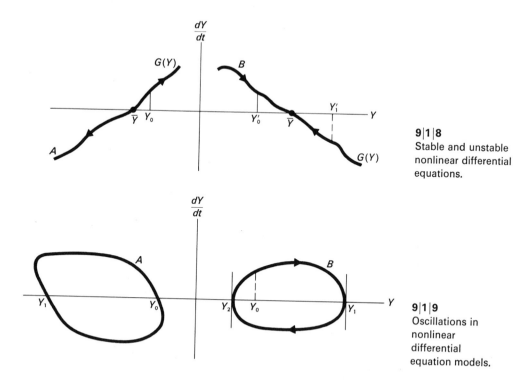

9|1|8
Stable and unstable
nonlinear differential
equations.

9|1|9
Oscillations in
nonlinear
differential
equation models.

the phase line is for the most part negatively sloped, it crosses the 45° line at a place where its slope is positive. Even though an initial oscillation is possible, the result is monotonic behavior.

Phase diagrams may be used to analyze nonlinear differential equation models. For example, let $dY/dt = G(Y)$, and consider Fig. 9.1.8, in which Y is plotted along the horizontal axis, and dY/dt along the vertical axis. Whenever the phase line is above the Y-axis, dY/dt is positive and Y must be increasing. Similarly, whenever the phase line is below the Y-axis, dY/dt is negative and Y must be decreasing. Consequently, stability of equilibrium requires that the phase line be negatively sloped. In Fig. 9.1.8 it can be seen that phase line A represents an unstable situation. At Y_0, dY/dt is positive, Y therefore increases, and the movement is away from equilibrium. Phase line B, however, represents a stable situation. At Y_0', dY/dt is positive and Y tends to increase and move towards equilibrium, while at Y_1', dY/dt is negative, and Y tends to decrease towards equilibrium. Of course, equilibrium is where $dY/dt = 0$, and is therefore to be found at the intersection of the phase line with the Y-axis.

An oscillating system requires that the phase line cut the Y-axis at two points, since we could not otherwise get switching back and forth of dY/dt from positive to negative values and conversely. Oscillating behavior also requires that the slope of the phase line at the point of intersection be infinite. The situation depicted as curve A in Fig. 9.1.9 is untenable because to the right of Y_0, dY/dt is negative and Y cannot therefore continue to increase. Similarly, to the left of Y_1, dY/dt is positive and Y cannot therefore continue to decrease. On the other hand, curve B provides the possibility of oscillation. At Y_0, dY/dt is positive and income increases. When it reaches Y_1, $dY/dt = 0$, and when the phase line goes below the Y-axis, $dY/dt < 0$, and income decreases, until Y_2 is reached, where dY/dt and Y both reverse direction simultaneously. Therefore note that the slope of the phase line must always be infinite at the point of intersection of the line with the Y-axis, because of the fact that both dY/dt and Y must change direction simultaneously.

9.2 PROFESSOR HICKS'S NONLINEAR MODEL OF THE CYCLE*

Although the multiplier-accelerator interaction which we studied in the last chapter is the fundamental driving mechanism of his theory of the cycle, Professor Hicks believes that a purely linear model cannot be an adequate representation of the cyclical process. There is, first, the fact that the accelerator is assymetrical. Disinvestment in capital goods cannot take place in the same way as investment. While an increase in demand will lead to proportional capital expansion, a contraction of demand does not lead to a proportional shrinkage in the stock of capital. Instead, when demand shrinks, excess capacity appears. The process of adjusting the capital stock to the lower level of demand is a slow and gradual process of waiting for depreciation and obsolescence to take its toll. Gross investment can never be negative and this, in turn, puts a limit, equal to the rate of depreciation, on the extent to which net investment can be negative. Thus while the combined interaction of the multiplier and the accelerator explains the expansionary process, contraction represents a situation wherein gross induced investment falls immediately to zero and income then shrinks via the conventional multiplier process.

The practical matter of realistic parameter values also mitigates against the adequacy of representing the business cycle as a purely linear process. Fluctuations in income have tended, relative to the trend of GNP, to be fairly uniform. However, in a linear model uniform oscillations would only occur through the happy accident that the acceleration coefficient happened (in Hicks's model) to equal unity. Any value of v below $+1$ would produce damped oscillations and the interesting question would then be to detect the nature of the shock mechanism that produced a new set of disturbances that kept the cycle going in a fairly uniform pattern. On the other hand, if the acceleration coefficient exceeds unity, fluctuations would be of ever increasing amplitude. In Hicks's view, the true value of the acceleration coefficient is well in excess of the value that would yield uniform oscillations in a linear model. Consequently, Hicks believes that while

* J. R. Hicks, *A Contribution to the Theory of the Trade Cycle* (London: Oxford University Press, 1950). See also, "Mr. Harrod's Dynamic Theory," *Economica* (May, 1949).

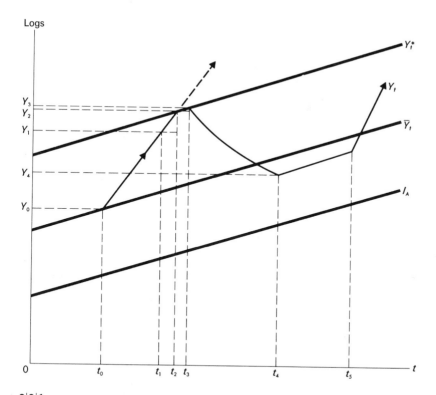

9|2|1
Outline of the cyclical process; the Hicks model.

the system tends to be characterized by an explosive accelerator, this accelerator must be constrained by fairly well-defined "floors" and "ceilings" to contraction and expansion if uniform oscillations are to be explained.

Hicks's complete model can be illustrated with the assistance of Fig. 9.2.1. Time is plotted on the horizontal axis and the logarithms of various magnitudes are plotted vertically. Curve I_a represents the path of autonomous investment. Autonomous investment is assumed to grow at a constant percentage rate so that, when plotted on semilog paper, it emerges as a straight line. The line labeled $\bar{Y}_t$ is the moving equilibrium path of income which, as calculated in the last chapter, is

$$\bar{Y}_t = \frac{I_0 r^{t+2}}{r^2 - (1 - s + v)r + v}.$$

Finally, the curve labeled Y_t^* represents the "ceiling" to expansion imposed by the available supply of resources. Hicks is not explicit about the nature of this ceiling, i.e., is it full employment, full capacity, or both? He merely describes it as a ceiling of "real resources" that is assumed to grow at the same rate as autonomous investment which, in turn, is a function of population growth, technical progress, and the like.

In describing the cyclical process, it is useful to begin at income level Y_0 on the equilibrium path. Continuation along this equilibrium path is not possible, because the growth in autonomous investment causes income to rise and this, via the acceleration principle, induces an increase in investment. The increase in investment raises income still further and this induces a still larger increase in investment. If the value of the acceleration coefficient is assumed to be such as to produce monotonic explosive behavior, output would tend to continue to rise at an exponential rate. However, once the ceiling is reached at Y_2, output can increase only at the rate of growth of the ceiling level, and this means there must be an absolute decline in the increase in output ($Y_3 - Y_2$, as compared with $Y_2 - Y_1$). Recalling that induced investment is given by the function

$$I_t = v(Y_{t-1} - Y_{t-2}),$$

it follows that there will be a fall in the absolute level of investment and that income will therefore fall.

The cycle now enters its phase of contraction. The fall in income means that excess capacity develops. When this happens, induced investment falls to zero. This, in turn, implies an income shrinkage via the multiplier process, which eventually brings the economy to a depression low equal to the level of autonomous spending times the multiplier.

Assume that this depression level of income is Y_4. There now occurs a period during which depreciation and obsolescence wear down the capital stock. When, in combination with rising autonomous investment and income and the elimination of excess capacity due to depreciation and obsolescence, the time comes when excess capacity is eliminated, an increase in output then again sets the accelerator in motion and the cycle once again enters its expansion phase.

The presence of nonlinearities (floors and ceilings) and assymetrical behavior as between expansion and contraction has the effect that oscillations of relatively constant amplitude occur regardless of the values of the parameters of the system. In the present case the explosive accelerator is turned down by the ceiling; the multiplier then takes over, and once the accelerator again comes into play, it does so with a new set of initial conditions. The same sort of thing would happen if the value of the acceleration coefficient were such as to produce damped or anti-damped oscillations in a linear model. In such a case the initial expansion might not be sufficient to drive output to the ceiling.* Thus contraction would commence prior to the "collision" with the ceiling. However, because of the asymmetrical nature of expansion and contraction, a switch to the pure multiplier

---

* Hicks calls an upswing that is halted by collision with the ceiling a "constrained" cycle, whereas an upswing that turns down for lack of sufficient force to reach the ceiling is called a "free" cycle.

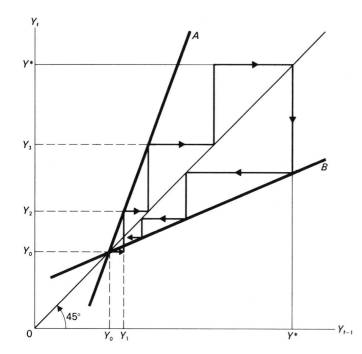

9|2|2
Phase diagram of the
Hicks model.

phase would take place; the system would then move to recession, and, because
the subsequent expansion would be powered by an entirely new set of initial
conditions, an identical cycle could then be generated.

   This example illustrates the basic difficulty with linear models.   In such
models behavior throughout the future is entirely governed by the initial conditions and by the values of the parameters. With the presence of constraints such
as the Hicksian floors and ceilings it is possible to explain uniform oscillations
without resort to the assumption that the value of the acceleration coefficient is,
as if by magic, equal to unity, and without any need to assume that the future is
inexorably governed by some set of initial conditions that put the system in
motion hundreds of years ago.

   Professor Hicks's model can be represented in a phase diagram such as that of
Fig. 9.2.2. Expansion is driven by an explosive accelerator, and phase line A,
with a slope in excess of $+1$, therefore describes expansion. Contraction, however, takes place via the simple multiplier. With a marginal propensity to consume of less than $+1$, the appropriate phase line may be represented as a curve
such as curve B.

   Suppose that income is in equilibrium at Y_0. The growth of autonomous
investment raises income to Y_1, and this sets the accelerator in motion, leading
first to expansion to Y_2, then to Y_3, and so on. Expansion would continue indefinitely were it not for the intervention of the ceiling at Y^*. Output now cannot

increase, so investment collapses and phase line B takes over. There follows a set of period-by-period contractions in output until equilibrium is again reached at the intersection of phase line B with the 45° line. Finally, once excess capacity is worked off, a subsequent increase in output induces investment, and expansion again follows phase line A.

9.3 GOODWIN'S NONLINEAR ACCELERATOR

Professor Goodwin's* nonlinear accelerator model is similar to the model of Professor Hicks and is expressed in terms of differential equations. The equations of the Goodwin model are as follows. First, income is the sum of consumption and investment,

$$Y = C + I, \tag{9.3.1}$$

and the consumption function is

$$C = a + bY. \tag{9.3.2}$$

Second, Goodwin assumes that the desired stock of capital is proportional to the level of output. Consequently,

$$K_d = gY, \tag{9.3.3}$$

where K_d is the desired stock of capital and g is the desired ratio of capital to output. Finally, Goodwin assumes that net investment can take on only three possible values where the particular value which is obtained depends upon whether the actual capital stock, K, is less than, equal to, or greater than, the desired capital stock. When the actual stock of capital is less than the desired level, positive net investment takes place at the rate $(dK/dt)_1$. When the capital stock just equals the desired capital stock, there is no net investment. And when the actual capital stock exceeds the desired level, net investment is negative and equals the rate of depreciation $(dK/dt)_3$. Thus, in summary, we have

$$
\begin{aligned}
(dK/dt)_1 &> 0, & K &< K_d, \\
(dK/dt)_2 &= 0, & K &= K_d, \\
(dK/dt)_3 &< 0, & K &> K_d.
\end{aligned}
\tag{9.3.4}
$$

To understand the workings of Goodwin's model, it is important to bear in mind that no matter how great the excess of desired capital stock over actual capital stock, the level of positive net investment (and therefore the increase in the capital stock per unit time) is fixed at the rate $(dK/dt)_1$. This, according to Goodwin, is because the capacity of the capital goods industries is fixed.

Since there are only three possible levels of net investment, it follows that there are only three possible levels of income which, by combining 9.3.4 and 9.3.2

---

* Richard M. Goodwin, "The Nonlinear Accelerator and the Persistence of Business Cycles," *Econometrica*, **19** (1951).

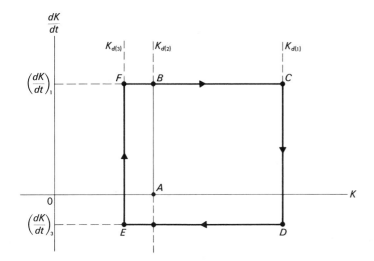

9|3|1
Phase diagram of the
Goodwin model.

with 9.3.1, can be seen to be

$$Y_1 = \left(\frac{1}{1-b}\right)[a + (dK/dt)_1], \qquad K < K_d,$$

$$Y_2 = \left(\frac{1}{1-b}\right)a, \qquad\qquad\qquad K = K_d, \qquad (9.3.5)$$

$$Y_3 = \left(\frac{1}{1-b}\right)[a + (dK/dt)_3], \qquad K > K_d.$$

Finally, via 9.3.3 the respective desired capital stock levels are

$$K_{d(1)} = gY_1,$$
$$K_{d(2)} = gY_2,$$
$$K_{d(3)} = gY_3.$$

The cyclical process can now be traced by means of a phase diagram. In Fig. 9.3.1 the stock of capital is plotted on the horizontal axis and the level of net investment (change in the stock of capital) is plotted vertically. The vertical line, $K_{d(1)}$, represents the desired capital stock when income is at Y_1, and the actual stock of capital is less than the desired level; $K_{d(2)}$ is the desired capital stock when net investment is zero, and income is at Y_2; and $K_{d(3)}$ is the desired capital stock when there is excess capacity, and income is at Y_3.

Because investment when $K < K_d$ is a positive constant, the phase line labeled $(dK/dt)_1$, which represents the behavior of the system during expansion, is a horizontal line parallel to the K-axis. Suppose now that we begin with actual capital stock equal to desired capital stock with zero net investment and the system temporarily in equilibrium at point A. This equilibrium situation cannot persist. The capital stock depreciates with time, and when this happens the actual capital stock falls below the desired level. However, this causes investment to rise to $(dK/dt)_1$; income therefore rises to Y_1, and the desired capital stock jumps to $K_{d(1)} = gY_1$. This puts the system at point B in the diagram.

Next there follows a period of capital accumulation during which the system follows the $(dK/dt)_1$ phase line to the right. However, since the level of income remains constant while the capital stock continues to increase, there comes a time (when the phase line reaches the $K_{d(1)}$ vertical at point C) when actual capital stock catches up to the desired capital stock. When this happens, there is no need for further net investment. Consequently, net investment drops to zero and income shrinks. The shrinkage in income now causes the capital stock to be in excess of the desired stock, and negative net investment then takes place by the depreciation rate $(dK/dt)_3$, and this, finally, means that the desired stock of capital drops to $K_{d(3)}$.

Retracing our steps, we see that when the phase line $(dK/dt)_1$ crosses the $K_{d(1)}$ vertical line, actual capital catches up to desired capital, and investment and income shrink. There then follows a period of capital decumulation along phase line $(dK/dt)_3$ and since the desired level of capital stock is $K_{d(3)}$, this process of decumulation continues until the phase line cuts the $K_{d(3)}$ vertical at point E. When this situation arises, further decumulation of capital causes the desired capital stock to exceed the actual capital stock; a phase change then takes place, and net investment rises to $(dK/dt)_1$ (the system now jumps to point F), and expansion out to point C then again takes place.

To summarize: The key to Goodwin's model is the fact that the actual stock of capital and the desired stock of capital seem unable to dance in step. Expansion is viewed as a period during which actual capital tries to catch up to desired capital. When actual capital succeeds in catching up, the expansion comes to a halt, and this induces income shrinkage and a fall in desired capital. Recession, then, is a process of working off excess capacity, which ultimately comes to a halt as actual capacity again pulls into equality with desired capacity.

9.4 THE CEILING

According to Hicks, the ceiling to output expansion is imposed by a limit upon available "real resources," while in Goodwin's view, actual capacity catches up to desired capacity because the rate of capital accumulation is limited by the capacity of the capital goods industries. Let us see, in this section, if the nature of the ceiling can be pinpointed. In particular, is the ceiling the consequence of a capital-goods scarcity, or is it due to the full employment of labor?* Our approach is to compute the ratio of capital to output as a function of time. If this ratio remains the same or increases, we would have to conclude that capital shortage cannot be responsible for a ceiling to expansion.

---

* The analysis of this section is based on T. F. Dernburg's paper "The Output Ceiling," *Metroeconomica*, **14** (1962).

A more general form of the acceleration principle would let intended investment at time t be a function of past changes in output. Actual additions to the stock of capital would therefore also be a function of past output changes and may be assumed to be a linear combination of such past changes. Consequently, let

$$K_t - K_{t-1} = a_1(Y_{t-1} - Y_{t-2}) + a_2(Y_{t-2} - Y_{t-3}) + \cdots + a_n(Y_{t-n} - Y_{t-n-1}),$$

(9.4.1)

where $K_t - K_{t-1}$ is the change in the stock of capital and the a_i's are a set of constant coefficients.

The ceiling is relevant only when the accelerator is explosive. Consequently, we assume that output grows according to the compound growth formula,

$$Y_t = Y_0(1 + r)^t.$$

(9.4.2)

Substituting this expression for Y_t into 9.4.1, we obtain

$$K_t - K_{t-1} = Y_{t-1}\{a_1[1 - (1 + r)^{-1}] + a_2[(1 + r)^{-1} - (1 + r)^{-2}] + \cdots$$
$$+ a_n[(1 + r)^{-(n+1)} - (1 + r)^{-n}]\}.$$

(9.4.3)

Since the expression in the brackets is a constant, we may replace it by the constant B and write

$$K_t - K_{t-1} = BY_{t-1}.$$

(9.4.4)

This implies that

$$K_1 = BY_0 + K_0,$$
$$K_2 = BY_1 + K_1 = B(Y_0 + Y_1) + K_0,$$
$$K_3 = BY_2 + K_2 = B(Y_0 + Y_1 + Y_2) + K_0,$$
$$\vdots$$
$$K_t = B \sum_{i=0}^{t-1} Y_i + K_0.$$

(9.4.5)

However, using 9.4.2 to replace the Y_i's, we may express this as

$$K_t = \frac{BY_0}{r}[(1 + r)^t - 1] + K_0.$$

(9.4.6)

Using 9.4.6 and 9.4.2, we can now calculate the capital output ratio and the rate of growth of the capital stock. For the capital output ratio we get

$$\frac{K_t}{Y_t} = \frac{B}{r} + \left[\frac{K_0}{Y_0} - \frac{B}{r}\right]\left[\frac{1}{(1 + r)^t}\right],$$

(9.4.7)

and for the rate of growth of the capital stock we get

$$\frac{K_t - K_{t-1}}{K_{t-1}} = r\left\{\frac{BY_0(1 + r)^{t-1}}{BY_0(1 + r)^{t-1} + rY_0[(K_0/Y_0) - (B/r)]}\right\}.$$

(9.4.8)

We are now ready to draw some conclusions about the ceiling. Note first of all that when t approaches infinity,

$$\frac{K_t}{Y_t} \to \frac{B}{r} \quad \text{and} \quad \frac{K_t - K_{t-1}}{K_{t-1}} \to r,$$

from which we see that when t is very large, the capital stock tends to grow at the same rate as the rate of growth of output, and the capital output ratio therefore becomes constant. A capital shortage under condition of steady growth would not be possible because such a shortage would imply that the capital stock was growing less rapidly than the level of output. Thus we may conclude, as a first approximation, that the longer a boom is sustained, the less likely it is to be halted by a capacity ceiling.

Business-cycle analysis is properly concerned with the short run, and the limiting cases should not be taken as more than suggestive. Let us therefore consider three cases which are distinguished from each other by the way in which the initial conditions differ from the limiting values of the capital output ratio. One possibility is that

$$K_0/Y_0 < B/r,$$

in which event the capital output ratio grows larger throughout the expansion phase of the cycle. This case obviously is of no interest, since capital becomes relatively more abundant.

In the second case we assume that

$$K_0/Y_0 = B/r.$$

Here the initial value of the capital output ratio equals its limiting value. As can be seen by substituting B/r in place of K_0/Y_0, Eq. 9.4.7 reduces to

$$K_t/Y_t = B/r.$$

Thus the capital output ratio is always constant and there can be no capital shortage at any one time relative to any other time. Once an expansion gets underway, it is no more retarded by capital drag at one stage of the expansion than it is at any other stage.

A close examination of the acceleration principle suggests that this is the case which is implicit in models of the cycle such as Professor Hicks' model. Recall that Hicks' basic conclusions are derived from a model in which the investment function is

$$I_t = v(Y_{t-1} - Y_{t-2}),$$

where v is the acceleration coefficient and is assumed constant. Investment is undertaken for the purpose of adjusting capacity to changes in the flow of output. If there were excess capacity, there would be no induced investment, and cyclical expansion would not take place. It is only when excess capacity is eliminated that a subsequent change in output induces investment. Thus it is implicit in the Hicks' model that there is never any excess capacity during expansion and that the system produces the required additional capital as it goes along. Since the capital output ratio remains constant, capital shortage cannot be introduced to explain the ceiling.

Goodwin explicitly states that capital shortage is the source of a limit to cyclical expansion. Given a fixed amount of new capital that the system can produce in each period, the expansion level of income is fixed, and since this implies that the actual stock of capital continues to grow while the desired stock remains fixed, actual capital must catch up to desired capital, and a downturn then takes place.

Goodwin is able to get this result only by making a wholly unreasonable assumption about the behavior of the capital-goods industries. He seems to assume that it is the consumer-goods industries that do all the investing, while the capacity of the capital-goods industries remains constant. Professor Norton comments that

> ...this is not...good theory. Capital goods are used to produce capital goods, just as they are used to produce consumer's goods. There is no difference either from the technical side of production or from the standpoint of economic motivation... It is profitable, in general, to produce capital goods for the investment-goods industries, just as it is profitable to produce capital goods for the consumption-goods industries.*

Professor Hicks, who relates investment to changes in output as a whole rather than to changes in consumption, as in the Samuelson model, clearly agrees with this view.

Had the investment-goods industries, in Goodwin's model, produced investment goods for their own use, their ability to produce investment goods would have increased, and the quantity of new capacity available in each period would have increased. Along with this would come growth of income and growth in the desired stock of capital. Since it is assumed that expansion does not get under way until excess capacity is eliminated, and since, as we have shown, the capital output ratio remains constant under these conditions, it follows that there would have been no tendency for the actual capital stock to catch up to the desired capital stock, and there would therefore have been no reason for a downturn to occur due to capital shortage.

The final case to be considered is a situation where

$$K_0/Y_0 > B/r,$$

which implies that the capital-output ratio falls as expansion proceeds. Here there is the possibility of a capacity ceiling developing from the circumstance that

---

* F. E. Norton, "The Accelerator and the Over-Investment and Under-Consumption Models," *Economic Journal,* **66** (March, 1956), p. 57.

output can expand more rapidly while excess capacity is available than it can once the excess is absorbed.

The present case is incompatible with the aggregative acceleration-principle-type models we have studied, because it implies that economic expansion takes place when excess capacity is present. However, we might visualize a case of the sort discussed by Mrs. Robinson.* Imagine an acceleration-type expansion that develops while some industries still operate with excess capacity and others have reached full capacity and must therefore invest in order to meet added capacity requirements. Thus if the consumer-goods industries have run out of excess capacity while capital-goods industries still have ample capacity available, a rapid increase in the rate of investment in the consumer-goods industries will be possible. When the time arrives at which excess capacity is eliminated everywhere, the consumer-goods industries will no longer be able to expand as rapidly unless there is an expansion of investment-goods capacity. Since this can be achieved only by an absolute reduction in investment in consumer-goods industries, new capacity cannot be obtained in the desired amounts.

An upper turning point of this sort may conceivably be encountered. The following two considerations, however, mitigate against this possibility. First, if expansion can get beyond the time at which investment-goods capacity is exhausted and proceed at a new higher rate, it can continue to do so indefinitely because from that day forward, capacity and output will remain proportional to each other. Second, if expansion cannot get past the critical time when investment-goods capacity is exhausted, we would be obliged to conclude that investment-goods capacity can never be expanded. It would be difficult, indeed, to find a case of the present sort in business-cycle history.

The case for a real resource ceiling rests on the assumption that the supply of factors of production cannot indefinitely be expanded as rapidly as the cyclical growth of the demand for these factors. Since the capital stock grows endogenously as the system expands and at a rate that tends to maintain a constant capital output ratio, a resource ceiling resulting from growing relative capital shortage is impossible. Thus, if business cycles are brought to a halt by collision with a ceiling, this ceiling must result from the full employment of the labor force. The essential point to note is that capital equipment holds a unique place as a factor of production because it expands endogenously as output itself expands. The same is not true of the labor force, and it is for this reason that the real resource-ceiling hypothesis may be a plausible one.

REFERENCES

W. J. Baumol, *Economic Dynamics* (New York: Macmillan, 1960), Part IV.

T. F. Dernburg, "The Output Ceiling," *Metroeconomica*, **14** (1962).

---

* Joan Robinson, *The Rate of Interest and Other Essays* (London: Macmillan, 1952), pp. 133–135

R. M. Goodwin, "The Nonlinear Accelerator and the Persistence of Business Cycles," *Econometrica*, **19** (1951).

J. R. Hicks, *A Contribution to the Theory of the Trade Cycle* (London: Oxford University Press, 1950).

J. R. Hicks, "Mr. Harrod's Dynamic Theory," *Economica* (May, 1949).

N. Kaldor, "A Model of the Trade Cycle," *Economic Journal* (March, 1940).

L. A. Metzler, "The Nature and Stability of Inventory Cycles," *Review of Economics and Statistics* (August, 1941).

L. A. Metzler, "Business Cycles and the Modern Theory of Employment," *American Economic Review* (June, 1946).

P. A. Samuelson, "Interactions Between the Multiplier Analysis and the Principle of Acceleration," *Review of Economics and Statistics* (May, 1939).

P. A. Samuelson, "A Synthesis of the Principle of Acceleration and the Multiplier," *Journal of Political Economy* (December, 1939).

CHAPTER 10

Introduction to Neoclassical Growth Economics

10.1 INTRODUCTION

A basic concern of economists has been the long-run growth and development of the economy. During the great depression of the 1930's, interest shifted to the short-run problem of explaining the cause of depression and to devising means for restoring full employment. However, the traditional concern with growth and development has returned. Among the first of the post-Keynesian growth theorists were Harrod and Domar. Their work, in turn, has been superseded by a mushrooming contemporary development known as neoclassical growth economics. The rudiments of this body of analysis are the subject of this and the next chapter. We follow our usual procedure of beginning with the growth counterpart of comparative-static analysis and then proceed to an analysis of the stability of equilibrium.

In attempting to understand neoclassical theory, it is useful to begin with a brief review of Harrod-Domar-type models. To recall the discussion of Chapter 7, potential output in the Domar model is proportional to the stock of capital. However, it is unrealistic to assume that capital is the only factor of production. Thus, to put the technological assumptions of the model into more general terms, we might regard the model as implying that output is produced with fixed factor proportions and that the production function is

$$Q_t = \min(\sigma K_t, \tau L_t) \tag{10.1.1}$$

where L_t is the supply of labor, and Q_t is the level of "potential output," i.e., the maximum level of output that the system is capable of producing at any one time.

Thus, if labor were the limiting factor, the rate of growth of output would equal the rate of growth of the labor force, which we shall denote by the parameter n; whereas if capital is the limiting factor, output grows at the rate $s\sigma$, where

s is the marginal and average propensity to save and σ is the capital coefficient. Steady exponential growth at full capacity and full employment could occur in this model only under the accidental condition that $n = s\sigma$.

The Harrod-Domar models are clearly too rigid to serve as more than a first step in the analysis of growth. Neoclassical theory has attempted to get away from this rigidity by allowing for the possibility of substitution between labor and capital, and for the presence of diminishing returns to the factors of production. The theory further attempts to make explicit allowance for technical change and for such other economic processes as depreciation of the capital stock. Finally, whereas Domar calculated the rate of growth that was necessary to maintain full employment, neoclassical theory takes full employment for granted and attempts to analyze the nature of the growth path in such an idyllic state.

In this and the succeeding chapter we attempt to summarize the essentials of neoclassical growth economics. The present chapter deals with the simplest and most familiar case in which the economy is assumed to be characterized by the presence of diminishing returns and of constant returns to scale. Technical change is assumed to be a function of time and is independent of the level of investment or of the age-composition of the capital stock. Chapter 11 then attempts to relax some of the more unrealistic assumptions that characterize the model of the present chapter.

10.2 INGREDIENTS OF NEOCLASSICAL THEORY

The first assumption of neoclassical growth economics is that full employment prevails at all times. This assumption implies that the level of net investment, dK/dt, must always equal the fraction of full-employment output that is saved, sQ. Consequently, we have

$$\frac{dK}{dt} = sQ, \tag{10.2.1}$$

which defines the level of saving and investment and therefore also the supply of new capital.

The second assumption of neoclassical growth theory is that the supply of labor grows at a constant exponential rate. Consequently,

$$L = L_0 e^{nt} \tag{10.2.2}$$

is the supply function, where n is the rate of growth of the labor force. It is important to note that the labor supply is assumed independent of real wages and other economic magnitudes and is purely a function of time.

The third requirement for the neoclassical growth theorist is that he specify an aggregate production function for the economy that allows for factor substitution and technical change. In its most general form such a function might be written $Q = F(K, L; t)$, where the trend variable t allows for shifts in the production function that result from technical change. In the event that technical change has the property that it raises the efficiency of both K and L in the same proportion, it is said to be "Hicks neutral." In this event the production function can be written $Q = A(t)F(K, L)$, where $A(t)$ is an index of technical change. Calculating marginal products by means of partial differentiation, we obtain

$$\frac{\partial Q}{\partial L} = A(t)\,\frac{\partial F}{\partial L}, \qquad \frac{\partial Q}{\partial K} = A(t)\,\frac{\partial F}{\partial K},$$

and it is therefore evident that an increase in the technical change index would raise both marginal products in the same proportion. Consequently, the marginal rate of substitution, which is the ratio of the marginal products with the sign changed, is independent of the technical change index.

Capital augmenting technical change, sometimes described as "Solow neutral" technical change, implies that the production function should be written

$$Q = F(K, L; t) = G[A(t)K, L],$$

and labor augmenting, or "Harrod neutral," technical change implies that

$$Q = F(K, L; t) = H[K, A(t)L].$$

Consequently, if technical change is capital augmenting, a slowing down of the rate of technical change can be offset by an increase in the rate at which the system supplies new capital. Similarly, the rate of growth of output need not be limited by the rate of growth of the labor supply if labor-augmenting technical change is present. Thus we might say that purely labor-augmenting technical change implies that labor and technical change are perfect substitutes for each other in the production process, but that the same is not true for capital and technical change. The opposite would, of course, be the case if technical change were purely capital augmenting.*

For the purposes of the analysis of the present chapter, we shall assume that the aggregate production function for the economy is the familiar Cobb-Douglas function,

$$Q = Ae^{rt}K^{a}L^{1-a}. \tag{10.2.3}$$

The term Ae^{rt} is the index of technical change, and it grows at the rate r. As before, Q is potential output, i.e., that output which can be produced by full

---

* As we saw above, "Hicks neutral" technical change leaves the marginal rate of substitution unaffected. However, this is not true of capital or of labor-augmenting technical change. As an example, take the case of labor-augmenting technical change. Let the production function be

$$Q = H[K, A(t)L] = H[K, L^*(t)],$$

where $L^*(t)$ is augmented labor. Calculating marginal products, we get

$$\frac{\partial Q}{\partial K} = \frac{\partial H}{\partial K}, \qquad \frac{\partial Q}{\partial L} = \frac{\partial H}{\partial L^*}\frac{\partial L^*}{\partial L} = \frac{\partial H}{\partial L}A(t).$$

The marginal product of labor depends on the shape of $A(t)$, while the marginal product of capital does not. The marginal rate of substitution therefore varies with technical change.

employment of both the stock of capital, K, and the supply of labor, L. The exponents a and $1 - a$ are positive fractions that sum to one.

It is important to understand the properties of the Cobb-Douglas function before we attempt to explore the nature of the growth process. The first thing to note is that the production function is homogeneous of degree one. This means that if capital and labor are both increased by some proportion u, output will rise in the same proportion. That this is so is evident from the fact that

$$Ae^{rt}(Ku)^a(Lu)^{1-a} = Ae^{rt}K^aL^{1-a}u^au^{1-a} = Qu.$$

Consequently, if inputs of labor and capital are both doubled, the level of output will be doubled.

Since the production function is homogeneous, it can be written

$$Q = A[e^{(r/a)t}K]^aL^{1-a} = A[e^{(r/1-a)t}L]^{1-a}K^a = Ae^{rt}K^aL^{1-a},$$

which shows that technical change in the Cobb-Douglas case can be regarded as capital augmenting, as labor augmenting, or as neutral.

Partial differentiation of the production function with respect to K and L yields the respective marginal products,

$$\frac{\partial Q}{\partial K} = aAe^{rt}K^{a-1}L^{1-a} = a\frac{Q}{K}$$

$$\frac{\partial Q}{\partial L} = (1 - a)Ae^{rt}K^aL^{-a} = (1 - a)\frac{Q}{L}. \tag{10.2.4}$$

Inspection of these equations shows that the marginal products of capital and labor diminish as the ratio of potential output to capital and labor, respectively, decreases. The Cobb-Douglas function is therefore characterized by the presence of diminishing returns to the factors of production.

The marginal rate of substitution is the ratio of the marginal products with a negative sign attached. Using 10.2.4, we obtain

$$S(K, L) = \frac{\partial Q/\partial K}{\partial Q/\partial L} = \frac{-a(Q/K)}{(1-a)(Q/L)} = \frac{-a}{1-a}(L/K), \tag{10.2.5}$$

which shows that the production isoquants are convex to the origin. When both sides of 10.2.5 are multiplied by K/L and the left-hand terms are rearranged, we get

$$N(K, L) = \frac{-a}{1-a}, \tag{10.2.6}$$

which defines the elasticity of the production isoquant and shows that given percentage reductions in capital can be compensated by a constant percentage increase in labor inputs, so as to leave output unchanged. For example, if $a = \frac{1}{4}$, then $N(K, L) = -\frac{1}{3}$, which implies that output will be unchanged if a 1% reduction in capital is replaced by a $\frac{1}{3}\%$ increase in the quantity of labor.

Under conditions of competitive equilibrium, the real wage will equal the marginal product of labor and the rate of interest will equal the marginal product of capital. Consequently, the aggregative shares of the national product that accrue to capital and labor, respectively, can, through the use of 10.2.4, be seen to be

$$K\frac{\partial Q}{\partial K} = aQ,$$
$$L\frac{\partial Q}{\partial L} = (1 - a)Q.$$

(10.2.7)

Dividing both expressions through by Q, we get the relative shares,

$$\frac{K}{Q}\frac{\partial Q}{\partial K} = a,$$
$$\frac{L}{Q}\frac{\partial Q}{\partial L} = 1 - a.$$

(10.2.8)

Since the terms on the left-hand side are elasticities, we see that the exponents a and $1 - a$ represent not only the relative shares of capital and labor, respectively, but also the elasticities of output with respect to the stock of capital and the labor supply. Again, using the example of $a = \frac{1}{4}$, a 1% increase in the stock of capital raises output by $\frac{1}{4}\%$, while a 1% increase in the labor force increases output by $\frac{3}{4}\%$.

10.3 EQUILIBRIUM GROWTH IN A NEOCLASSICAL MODEL

As we have seen in previous chapters, the growth counterpart of static equilibrium is a situation in which the variable in question grows at a steady exponential rate. Equilibrium growth in a neoclassical model is consistent with this concept of dynamic equilibrium. It is a situation in which all variables, such as output, the labor supply, the stock of capital, and the level of investment, either grow at constant exponential rates, or they do not change at all. Such a state has been described by Mrs. Robinson as a "golden age" of accumulation. Although this is a "mythical state of affairs not likely to obtain in any actual economy,"[*] it is no more of an abstraction than a situation of stationary equilibrium in an ordinary market. As we have tried to emphasize throughout, equilibrium of whatever variety is an indispensible analytical artifact with which analysis usefully commences.

For an economy in a golden age we must have

$$\bar{Q} = \bar{Q}_0 e^{qt},$$
$$\bar{K} = \bar{K}_0 e^{ht},$$
$$\bar{I} = \bar{I}_0 e^{mt},$$
$$L = L_0 e^{nt},$$

(10.3.1)

---

[*] Joan Robinson, *The Accumulation of Capital* (Homewood, Ill.: Irwin, 1956), p. 99.

where q, h, m, and n are constant growth rates and where the bars over the variables denote golden-age (equilibrium growth) magnitudes.

At full employment, it must be the case that investment equals full-employment saving. Moreover, net investment equals the change in the stock of capital. Consequently,

$$I = \frac{dK}{dt} = sQ,$$

so that on using 10.3.1, we have

$$\bar{I}_0 e^{mt} = h\bar{K}_0 e^{ht} = s\bar{Q}_0 e^{qt}. \tag{10.3.2}$$

Evidently, the only way that 10.3.2 can hold for all values of t is for all the growth rates m, h, and q to equal each other. Thus investment grows at the same rate as the stock of capital, and this common rate must, in turn, equal the rate of output growth. Let us call this rate the golden-age rate of growth and denote it by the symbol g.

To find the value of the golden-age growth rate, we return to the production function,

$$Q = Ae^{rt}K^aL^{1-a}, \tag{10.3.3}$$

and differentiate with respect to time. This yields

$$\frac{dQ}{dt} = rQ + \frac{aAe^{rt}K^aL^{1-a}}{K}\frac{dK}{dt} + \frac{(1-a)Ae^{rt}K^aL^{1-a}}{L}\frac{dL}{dt}.$$

Dividing both sides by Q and simplifying, we get

$$\frac{1}{Q}\frac{dQ}{dt} = r + a\frac{1}{K}\frac{dK}{dt} + (1-a)\frac{1}{L}\frac{dL}{dt}.$$

But $(1/Q)(dQ/dt)$ is the rate of growth of output, q; $(1/K)(dK/dt)$ is the rate of growth of the capital stock, h; and $(1/L)(dL/dt)$ is the rate of growth of the labor force, n. Consequently,

$$q = r + ah + (1-a)n, \tag{10.3.4}$$

but since in a golden age both q and h equal g, it follows that

$$g = \frac{r}{1-a} + n.$$

Apparently, the equilibrium growth rate is a function of the rate of technical progress, the rate of growth of the labor force, and the share of capital. Note that since the rate of growth of output per worker must be $g - n = r/(1-a)$, no growth in per capita output is possible in the absence of technical progress. If r were zero, capital and output would all grow at a rate equal to, and determined by, the rate of growth of the labor force, and output per head would remain unchanged.

If the capital stock and the level of output grow at the same rate, it must be the case that the capital-output ratio remains constant. Therefore the capital-output ratio at any time will equal the initial equilibrium ratio $\bar{K}_0/\bar{Q}_0$. From Eq. 10.3.2 it is evident that

$$\bar{K}/\bar{Q} = \bar{K}_0/\bar{Q}_0 = s/g, \tag{10.3.5}$$

so that the golden age capital-output ratio is equal to the ratio of the saving rate to the growth rate. For example, with $s = 0.20$ and $g = 0.04$, the capital-output ratio would equal 5.

Next, recall from the previous section that the marginal product of capital in the Cobb-Douglas case is $\partial Q/\partial K = a(Q/K)$. Under competitive equilibrium conditions, the marginal product of capital must equal the rate of interest. Consequently, upon using 10.3.5, we have

$$\frac{\partial \bar{Q}}{\partial K} = a\frac{g}{s} = i, \tag{10.3.6}$$

where i stands for the rate of interest. If, in a golden age, $a = 0.25$, $s = 0.20$, and $g = 0.04$, the marginal product of capital and the rate of interest would remain constant at a value of 5%.

The marginal product of labor was calculated in the last section as $\partial Q/dL = (1 - a)(Q/L)$. However, since $\bar{Q} = \bar{Q}_0 e^{gt}$, and $L = L_0 e^{nt}$, this becomes

$$\frac{\partial \bar{Q}}{\partial L} = (1 - a)\frac{\bar{Q}_0}{L_0}e^{(g-n)t} = (1 - a)\frac{\bar{Q}_0}{L_0}e^{[r/(1-a)]t}, \tag{10.3.7}$$

and it is therefore evident that the marginal product of labor, and thus the real wage, grows at the rate of growth of per capita output.

These results imply a further important property of golden-age growth, namely, that the existence of golden-age growth requires technical change to be everywhere labor augmenting. "Hicks neutral" technical change raises both marginal products proportionately; capital-augmenting technical change raises the marginal product of capital, but not the marginal product of labor. Only labor-augmenting technical change conforms to the requirement that both the marginal product of capital and the capital output ratio be constant, while the marginal product of labor rises in proportion to the rate of technical change. Note that if we rewrite the Cobb-Douglas function so as to obtain labor-augmenting technical change, and also use the labor-supply function, we can write

$$Q = AK^a(L_0 e^{gt})^{1-a}, \tag{10.3.8}$$

which shows that augmented labor grows at the golden-age growth rate. Moreover,

$$Q = A\left[\frac{K}{L_0 e^{gt}}\right]^a L_0 e^{gt}, \tag{10.3.9}$$

so that, since Q grows at the rate g, the ratio of capital to augmented labor must be constant if golden-age growth is to exist.

As a common-sense matter, if capital and output grow at the same rate and if per capita output is not to drop steadily, capital and output must grow at least as rapidly as the labor supply. But, given more rapid growth of K and Q relative to L, there would develop a growing relative shortage of labor with the passage of time, unless the more rapid rate of capital growth is exactly matched by proportional growth of augmented labor.

A preliminary summary of results is now in order. In a golden age:

1   Investment, the stock of capital, and the level of output all grow at the rate of growth of augmented labor. In the Cobb-Douglas model this means that $g = r/(1 - a) + n$.

2   It follows as a corollary that per capita output cannot grow in the absence of technical progress. If $r = 0$, $g = n$, and $\bar{I}$, $\bar{K}$, and $\bar{Q}$ all grow at the rate of growth of the labor force.

3   The capital-output ratio is constant and equal to the ratio of the saving rate to the golden-age growth rate, i.e., $\bar{K}/\bar{Q} = s/g$.

4   The marginal product of capital, and therefore the rate of interest, is constant and is given by the expression $i = a(g/s)$, while the marginal product of labor grows at the rate $r/(1 - a)$.

5   It follows that the existence of golden-age growth requires technical change to be everywhere labor augmenting.

One of the most important circumstances to note about golden-age growth is that the growth rate is not a function of the saving rate. This is a surprising outcome that differs from Domar's result that the growth rate is the product of the capital coefficient and the saving rate. The reason for this difference is that an increase in the fraction of income saved will accelerate the growth of capital and output temporarily, but that diminishing returns will eventually restore the original growth rate. If capital grows more rapidly than augmented labor, the marginal product of capital will fall and the rate of growth of output will therefore also tend to fall. Consequently, the growth rate will tend to diminish until capital and output again grow at the rate of growth of augmented labor. An increase in the fraction of income saved cannot therefore permanently raise the growth rate. Ultimately, a new golden age will be approached where all magnitudes again grow at the rate g, and since $\bar{K}/\bar{Q} = s/g$, the effect of the higher saving rate will be to raise the equilibrium capital output ratio but not the growth rate. To emphasize the point again: Unless the capital stock grows at the rate at which augmented labor grows, the marginal product of capital will change and so also will the rate of growth of output. Thus the only condition under which output can grow at a constant rate is if $\bar{K}$, $\bar{I}$, and $\bar{Q}$ all grow at the rate of growth of augmented labor.

Although the equilibrium growth rate is not a function of the saving rate, it is evident from Eq. 10.3.5,

$$\bar{K}/\bar{Q} = s/g,$$

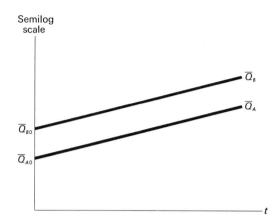

10|3|1
Different golden-age paths are
logarithmically parallel.

that the saving rate determines the capital output ratio. Thus, comparing two
golden ages with equal growth rates, the one which has the higher saving rate
will have the higher capital output ratio, and, with positive marginal products,
the higher level of output. Thus we may say that the fraction of income saved
affects the level at which the economy grows (the initial conditions) but it does
not affect the rate at which it grows.

The situation is illustrated in Fig. 10.3.1. Economies A and B are identical in
all respects except that B saves a larger fraction of its income. Thus although both
grow at the same rate, B has a higher capital-output ratio and therefore a permanently higher level of output. To put it simply, a change in the saving rate
shifts the intercept of the growth curve, but it does not affect its slope.

The circumstance that the saving rate determines the *level* at which golden-
age growth takes place, but not the *rate* of growth, gives rise to a most important
result of neoclassical growth economics—namely, that it is possible to pick a
particular saving rate that will maximize per capita consumption for all time.
We have seen that the higher the saving rate, the greater the level of output at
any one time. On the other hand, a greater level of saving relative to a given
output reduces the consumption of society at that time. If a higher saving rate in
society B were to raise its growth rate permanently above that of A, B would
eventually enjoy both more consumption and saving than A. However, if the
two grow at the same rate, B's higher saving rate may not make it any better off
despite its permanently higher level of output. The reason for this is that B may
save such a large fraction of its higher output, that the amount left for consumption is less than in A's economy, even though A's total output may be lower.

The rule according to which A and B should behave in order to maximize
their per capita consumption is known as the "golden rule of accumulation." It
is a golden rule because it instructs today's generation to do on behalf of the future
as it would have had the past generation do for it.

To derive the golden rule, we should first note that if golden age output in
economy A is given by $\bar{Q}_a = \bar{Q}_{a0}e^{gt}$, and in B by $\bar{Q}_b = \bar{Q}_{b0}e^{gt}$, then the equality

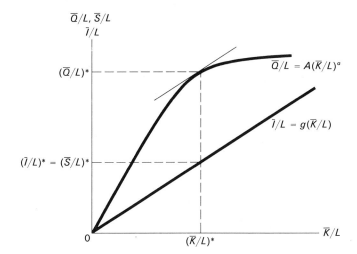

10|3|2
Golden-age growth and the golden rule of accumulation

of the growth rates implies that

$$\frac{\bar{Q}_b}{\bar{Q}_a} = \frac{\bar{Q}_{b0}}{\bar{Q}_{a0}},$$

and it means that the ratios of the output levels at any time will always be the same as they are initially. Thus if we want to know why B's output exceeds A's, it will be sufficient to look only at the factors that make for a difference in the initial conditions in the two economies. The same would, of course, also be true for per capita consumption. This means, and this is the crucial point, that if the saving rate can be found that maximizes per capita consumption at any one time, that same saving rate will do so for *all time*.

The golden rule can easily be derived mathematically, given the results on golden-age growth we already have. However, it is perhaps more instructive to find the rule with the assistance of a diagram. Since we want to maximize per capita consumption, we plot all variables as ratios to the quantity of labor in Fig. 10.3.2. On the horizontal axis we post the capital-to-labor ratio, and on the vertical axis we plot per capita investment (equal to per capita saving) and per capita output.

Since saving equals investment, it must be the case that

$$\bar{I}/L = s(\bar{Q}/L). \tag{10.3.10}$$

Moreover, since investment is the change in the stock of capital, golden-age investment must equal the equilibrium growth rate times the stock of capital, so that

$$\bar{I}/L = g(\bar{K}/L). \tag{10.3.11}$$

On equating the two expressions, we get our earlier result (Eq. 10.3.5),

$$\bar{K}/\bar{Q} = s/g \quad \text{or} \quad g = s(\bar{Q}/\bar{K}). \tag{10.3.12}$$

From Eq. 10.3.11 it is evident that per capita investment (saving) is directly proportional to the capital-labor ratio. Consequently, we may draw the $\bar{I}/L$-curve as a straight line which emanates from the origin. Note that the slope of the curve is the golden-age growth rate, and note also from Eq. 10.3.12 that this is equivalent to $s(\bar{Q}/\bar{K})$.

Next, take the production function, hold t constant at $t = 0$ (any other fixed value would do), and divide both sides by L. This gives

$$\bar{Q}/L = A(\bar{K}/L)^a \tag{10.3.13}$$

which, when plotted in Fig. 10.3.2, yields the $\bar{Q}/L$-curve. The slope of the curve is

$$\frac{d(\bar{Q}/L)}{d(\bar{K}/L)} = a\frac{\bar{Q}}{\bar{K}} \tag{10.3.14}$$

which, as we saw in Section 10.2, equals the marginal product of capital. Observe that the marginal product is positive but that it diminishes as $\bar{K}/L$ increases and that the $\bar{Q}/L$-curve therefore has a positive but decreasing slope.

The $\bar{Q}/L$-curve represents the level of per capita output, while the $\bar{I}/L$-curve specifies the level of per capita investment (saving) associated with different capital-labor ratios. Consequently, per capita consumption is maximized when the vertical difference between the two curves is at a maximum. Thus the optimum golden age is found at that capital labor ratio which equalizes the slopes of the two functions.

The slope of the $\bar{I}/L$-curve (via Eqs. 10.3.11 and 10.3.12) is $s(\bar{Q}/\bar{K})$, and the slope of the $\bar{Q}/L$-curve is the marginal product of capital, $a(\bar{Q}/\bar{K})$, so that on equating the two we find that per capita consumption is maximized when $a = s$. Thus, since a is capital's share of the national product, the golden rule states that per capita consumption will be maximized for all time if society always saves and invests its competitive profits and consumes its labor income.

Observe next that the slope of the $\bar{I}/L$-curve is also equal to the golden-age growth rate, while the marginal product of capital equals the rate of interest, which, therefore equals the slope of the $\bar{Q}/L$-curve. Consequently, an alternative way of stating the golden rule is $g = i$, which means that in an optimal golden age, the rate of interest will just equal the growth rate.[*] Alternatively, we may say that the marginal product of capital must equal the rate of growth of augmented labor. If the rate of interest exceeds the rate of growth of augmented labor, a higher saving rate would add more to per capita consumption due to the higher per capita output this provides, even though a smaller fraction of the higher per capita output would be consumed.

---

[*] Earlier we saw (Eq. 10.3.6) that on any golden-age path, $i = a(g/s)$. However, on the optimal path, $a = s$, so that $g = i$.

The optimal golden age in Fig. 10.3.2 is at capital labor ratio $(\bar{K}/L)^*$ where the vertical distance between $\bar{Q}/L$ and $\bar{I}/L$ is greatest. Society could choose to save less and consume a larger fraction of its output; however, the loss in output due to the lower capital labor ratio exceeds the decline in saving so that per capita consumption drops. Similarly, an increase in saving would yield more output, since the $\bar{K}/L$-ratio would rise, but this increase would not compensate for the loss in consumption due to the higher saving. At the extremes, illustrated by the points of intersection of the curves, a society that saves and invests nothing will have no output and therefore no consumption. Conversely, a compulsively frugal society which saves and invests all its output, will have a very large output, but like the society that saves nothing, it too will have no consumption.

10.4 STABILITY OF THE GOLDEN AGE

Can golden-age growth persist, or will a disturbance cause the time-path of output to diverge progressively from the golden-age path? If the golden-age path is stable, does this mean that foreign aid from economy A to B ultimately leaves the respective economies just as well off as though the aid had never been given, or will the aid make some permanent difference?

To answer these questions, we must attempt a general solution to the time-path of output in the neoclassical model. Once we have such a solution, we can then analyze the stability of the equilibrium growth path. We begin by differentiating the production function with respect to time. This yields

$$\frac{dQ}{dt} = rQ + aAe^{rt}K^{a-1}L^{1-a}\frac{dK}{dt} + (1-a)Ae^{rt}K^aL^{-a}\frac{dL}{dt}. \quad (10.4.1)$$

Substituting the rate of growth of the labor supply, n, in place of $(1/L)(dL/dt)$, and using the full-employment condition to replace dK/dt by sQ, we find that this expression reduces to

$$\frac{dQ}{dt} = [r + n(1-a)]Q + asAe^{rt}K^{a-1}L^{1-a}Q. \quad (10.4.2)$$

To eliminate K from this differential equation, we return to the production function and write

$$K^a = \frac{Q}{Ae^{rt}L^{1-a}}.$$

It follows that

$$K^{a-1} = \left[\frac{Q}{Ae^{rt}L^{1-a}}\right]^{(a-1)/a}. \quad (10.4.3)$$

When this expression is used to replace K^{a-1} in Eq. 10.4.2, and terms are consolidated, we obtain the basic differential equation,

$$\frac{dQ}{dt} = [r + n(1-a)]Q + asA^{(1/a)}L_0^{(1-a)/a}Q^{(2a-1)/a}e^{[r+n(1-a)]t/a}. \quad (10.4.4)$$

To get a better look at the equation, we shorten the expression by defining

$$c_1 = r + n(1 - a),$$
$$c_2 = asA^{(1/a)}L_0^{(1-a)/a},$$
$$c_3 = \frac{2a - 1}{a}, \quad 1 - c_3 = \frac{1 - a}{a}, \tag{10.4.5}$$
$$c_4 = \frac{r + n(1 - a)}{a}.$$

Substituting this short-hand notation, we get

$$\frac{dQ}{dt} = c_1 Q + c_2 Q^{c_3} e^{c_4 t}, \tag{10.4.6}$$

which is a special type of differential equation known to mathematicians as a Bernoulli equation.

Before proceeding further, we should return to the production function and observe that since labor supply and technical progress are predetermined, output can deviate from its equilibrium value only if the capital stock differs from its equilibrium value. Indeed, we could equate saving and investment, and write

$$\frac{dK}{dt} = sQ = sAe^{rt}K^a L^{1-a},$$

and then proceed to solve this differential equation by direct integration. However, since the equation in output (10.4.6) recurs in all the models to be discussed subsequently, it is worth taking some time to see how it can be solved.

The first step in finding a solution for Eq. 10.4.6 is to see if a transformation can be found that puts the equation into a familiar and manageable form. Therefore, define

$$Z = Q^{1-c_3}, \tag{10.4.7}$$

and note that

$$\frac{dZ}{dt} = (1 - c_3)Q^{-c_3}\frac{dQ}{dt},$$

from which it follows that

$$\frac{dQ}{dt} = \frac{1}{(1 - c_3)Q^{-c_3}}\frac{dZ}{dt}. \tag{10.4.8}$$

Using 10.4.8 to make substitutions in 10.4.6, we get

$$\frac{1}{(1 - c_3)Q^{-c_3}}\frac{dZ}{dt} = c_1 Q + c_2 Q^{c_3} e^{c_4 t}.$$

Multiplying both sides of this expression by $(1 - c_3)Q^{-c_3}$ gives

$$\frac{dZ}{dt} = c_1(1 - c_3)Q^{1-c_3} + c_2(1 - c_3)e^{c_4 t},$$

and since $Z = Q^{1-c_3}$, we have

$$\frac{dZ}{dt} = c_1(1 - c_3)Z + c_2(1 - c_3)e^{c_4 t}. \tag{10.4.9}$$

Equation 10.4.9 is a first-order differential equation that can be solved by the methods discussed in Chapter 7. We begin by dividing Z into an equilibrium component $\bar{Z}$ and a displacement v. Consequently, let

$$Z = \bar{Z} + v, \qquad \frac{dZ}{dt} = \frac{d\bar{Z}}{dt} + \frac{dv}{dt}. \tag{10.4.10}$$

Substituting these values into 10.4.9 yields

$$\frac{d\bar{Z}}{dt} + \frac{dv}{dt} = c_1(1 - c_3)(\bar{Z} + v) + c_2(1 - c_3)e^{c_4 t}. \tag{10.4.11}$$

To reduce Eq. 10.4.11 to homogeneous form in the displacement, v, that is, to make

$$\frac{dv}{dt} = c_1(1 - c_3)v, \tag{10.4.12}$$

we would have to find that value of $\bar{Z}$ which makes

$$\frac{d\bar{Z}}{dt} = c_1(1 - c_3)\bar{Z} + c_2(1 - c_3)e^{c_4 t}. \tag{10.4.13}$$

Inspection of Eq. 10.4.13 shows that since the term $c_2(1 - c_3)e^{c_4 t}$ grows exponentially, the nearest approximation to a concept of equilibrium in this model is one that permits $\bar{Z}$ to grow exponentially and at the rate c_4. Accordingly, we assume that

$$\bar{Z} = \bar{Z}_0 e^{c_4 t}, \tag{10.4.14}$$

in which event it follows that

$$\frac{d\bar{Z}}{dt} = c_4 \bar{Z}_0 e^{c_4 t}. \tag{10.4.15}$$

Using these assumed values in 10.4.13, we obtain

$$c_4 \bar{Z}_0 e^{c_4 t} = c_1(1 - c_3)\bar{Z}_0 e^{c_4 t} + c_2(1 - c_3)e^{c_4 t}. \tag{10.4.16}$$

Since $e^{c_4 t}$ can be factored out of the equation, we can write

$$c_4 \bar{Z}_0 = c_1(1 - c_3)\bar{Z}_0 + c_2(1 - c_3), \tag{10.4.17}$$

and it therefore follows that Eq. 10.4.12 can be rendered valid if we can solve for the value of $\bar{Z}_0$ that satisfies Eq. 10.4.17. Evidently,

$$\bar{Z}_0 = \frac{c_2(1 - c_3)}{c_4 - c_1(1 - c_3)}. \tag{10.4.18}$$

Applying this result to Eq. 10.4.14, we get

$$\bar{Z} = \left[\frac{c_2(1 - c_3)}{c_4 - c_1(1 - c_3)}\right]e^{c_4 t}.$$

Further, since $Z = Q^{1-c_3}$, it follows that

$$\bar{Q} = \left[\frac{c_2(1 - c_3)}{c_4 - c_1(1 - c_3)}\right]^{1/(1-c_3)}e^{[c_4/(1-c_3)]t} = \bar{Q}_0 e^{(c_4/1-c_3)t} \quad (10.4.19)$$

defines the equilibrium path of output.*

Having calculated the $\bar{Z}$-values that satisfy Eq. 10.4.13, it now follows that, upon using these values, Eq. 10.4.11 reduces to the homogeneous form,

$$\frac{dv}{dt} = c_1(1 - c_3)v. \quad (10.4.20)$$

The solution to 10.4.20 is

$$v = Me^{c_1(1-c_3)t}, \quad (10.4.21)$$

where M is a constant that depends on the initial conditions. Working back to get the complete solution, it follows from 10.4.10 and 10.4.14 that

$$Z = \bar{Z}_0 e^{c_4 t} + Me^{c_1(1-c_3)t}. \quad (10.4.22)$$

If at $t = 0$, $Z = Z_0$, this equation implies that $M = Z_0 - \bar{Z}_0$, and we therefore have the solution for Z,

$$Z = \bar{Z}_0 e^{c_4 t} + (Z_0 - \bar{Z}_0)e^{c_1(1-c_3)t}. \quad (10.4.23)$$

Finally, applying the original transformation, $Z = Q^{1-c_3}$, to Eq. 10.4.23, we get the solution for the level of output,

$$Q = [\bar{Q}_0^{1-c_3}e^{c_4 t} + (Q_0^{1-c_3} - \bar{Q}_0^{1-c_3})e^{c_1(1-c_3)t}]^{1/(1-c_3)}. \quad (10.4.24)$$

Inspection of Eq. 10.4.24 shows immediately that the system is unstable in the conventional sense that the absolute deviations between actual output and equilibrium output grow larger with the passage of time. Since

$$c_1(1 - c_3) = [r + n(1 - a)]\left(\frac{1 - a}{a}\right) > 0,$$

it is evident that the absolute discrepancy between Q_0 and $\bar{Q}_0$ grows wider at an

---

* If we replace the various c's by the respective values specified in 10.4.5, and if we recall that golden-age growth requires the capital output ratio to equal the ratio of the saving rate to the golden-age growth rate, we can reduce 10.4.19 to $\bar{Q} = [A\bar{K}_0^a L_0^{1-a}]e^{gt}$, which shows that the equilibrium solution as specified in 10.4.19 is identical to the golden-age solution. Note in particular that the equilibrium growth rate is the golden-age growth rate, namely,

$$\frac{c_4}{1 - c_3} = \frac{r}{1 - a} + n = g.$$

exponential rate. This means that if the economy is on a golden-age path, and if it subsequently receives foreign aid in the form of a capital transfer, it will henceforth enjoy ever higher output than would otherwise have been the case. Higher capital stock at time zero means higher output, higher saving, more investment, and therefore permanently higher future capital stock and output levels.

Equilibrium in a dynamic context is defined as a path of steady exponential growth. The criterion for stability of equilibrium ought also to be put in relative terms. We might therefore define a system to be stable if the percentage deviation from the equilibrium path diminishes with the passage of time. According to this criterion we would say that the system is stable if

$$\lim_{t \to \infty} \left(\frac{Q - \bar{Q}}{\bar{Q}} \right) = 0,$$

or, to put the same condition differently, if

$$\lim_{t \to \infty} \left(\frac{Q}{\bar{Q}} \right) = 1.$$

Before proceeding, note that since $Z = Q^{1 - c_3}$, it follows that $(Z/\bar{Z}) = (Q/\bar{Q})^{1 - c_3}$, and that $Q/\bar{Q}$ will approach unity only if $Z/\bar{Z}$ does so.

Now note from Eq. 10.4.23 that

$$\left(\frac{Z}{\bar{Z}} \right) = 1 + \left(\frac{Z_0 - \bar{Z}_0}{\bar{Z}_0} \right) e^{[c_1(1 - c_3) - c_4]t},$$

so that the stability condition is met if $c_1(1 - c_3) - c_4 < 0$. Substituting from 10.4.5, we see that the condition implies that

$$[r + n(1 - a)] \left(\frac{1 - a}{a} \right) - \frac{[r + n(1 - a)]}{a} < 0,$$

so that $a > 0$.

Apparently, it is only necessary for the capital elasticity of output to be positive in order to ensure "relative" stability. Note that since the ratio $Q/\bar{Q}$ approaches unity through time, the respective magnitudes must grow at the same rate in the limit. Since $\bar{Q}$ grows at the golden-age rate, g, it follows that Q will do so also. Consequently, we may say that the golden-age growth rate is stable. Higher initial capital stock implies permanently higher output. However, the long-run growth rate will tend to be the same.

CHAPTER 11

Extensions of Neoclassical Growth Economics

11.1 INTRODUCTION

In the neoclassical model of Chapter 10, capital was implicitly assumed to have an infinite life span. In such an economy spinning jennies and wood-burning locomotives would both still be in use, forty-year-old propeller-driven airplanes would operate alongside modern jet-propelled 727's, and all the Model-T Fords that were ever built would still be on the road. An additional problem with the model of Chapter 10 is that it denigrates the role of investment in growth. In that model technical change was a function of time and had nothing to do with the amount of new (and improved) capital that accrues to the system. Actually, however, technical change mainly affects the economy by being "embodied" in new investment. If there were no new investment, all the technological ingenuity of scientists and engineers would go to waste except for the fraction that improved the efficiency of the labor force (health, education, and other "investment in human capital"), and that fraction that improved the efficiency of existing capital and labor through so-called "organizational" technical changes (time-motion improvements, reorganization of assembly lines, better accounting and administrative techniques, etc.). Evidently, a model that allows technical change to be embodied in new capital would be more realistic.

Third, the model of Chapter 10 assumed continuous substitution between labor and capital in the production process. However, this assumption flies in the face of the typical modern technological relationship. It is reasonable enough to expect that factors can be substituted for one another when investment decisions are being made, since entrepreneurs often have a choice of installing a range of alternative production processes. However, once the chosen process is in place, the factor proportions tend to be rigid and the "soft putty" of the planning stage turns into the "hard clay" of the operating stage.

In this chapter, we shall attempt to modify the model of Chapter 10 along the various lines suggested above. It will be shown that capital depreciation does not alter the results of the simple model. The addition of embodied technical change, similarly, requires a redefinition of the concept of capital, but it does not change the basic results of the golden age. An analysis of "putty-clay" models discloses the surprising result that neoclassical variety golden-age growth can occur with fixed coefficients of production, provided only that factor substitution is possible at the investment planning stage.

11.2 DEPRECIATION IN THE NEOCLASSICAL MODEL

In this section, we undertake the task of integrating depreciation into the neoclassical model. If there is never any depreciation of capital, net national product and gross national product would be identical, and net and gross investment would be the same. However, when the wearing-out of capital stock is taken into account, it becomes important to distinguish between net and gross output and between net and gross saving and investment.

We assume the labor supply and production functions to be the same as before except that Q now stands for gross output, and I stands for gross investment. Gross investment consists of two distinct components: additions to the stock of capital (net investment), and replacement investment. The latter we assumed to be proportional to the size of the capital stock.* Consequently, each year a constant fraction, u, of the capital stock is retired and replaced. Gross investment may therefore be written

$$I = \frac{dK}{dt} + uK, \tag{11.2.1}$$

and since gross investment must equal the level of gross saving at full employment,

$$I = sQ = \frac{dK}{dt} + uK. \tag{11.2.2}$$

As before, a golden age is characterized by exponential growth of all magnitudes, so that again

$$\bar{K} = \bar{K}_0 e^{ht}, \qquad \bar{Q} = \bar{Q}_0 e^{qt}, \qquad L = L_0 e^{nt}. \tag{11.2.3}$$

Golden-age gross investment equals the change in the stock of capital plus depreciation. Therefore

$$\bar{I} = \frac{d\bar{K}}{dt} + u\bar{K} = (h + u)\bar{K} = (h + u)\bar{K}_0 e^{ht}, \tag{11.2.4}$$

and since gross investment equals gross saving, it follows via 11.2.2, 11.2.3, and

---

* The rationale behind this assumption is discussed in the next section.

11.2.4 that

$$s\bar{Q}_0 e^{qt} = (h + u)\bar{K}_0 e^{ht}. \qquad (11.2.5)$$

It follows that $q = h$, and from the relation (10.3.4),

$$q = r + ah + (1 - a)n,$$

which was derived from the production function in the last chapter, that

$$g = h = q = \frac{r}{1 - a} + n,$$

where as before, g is the golden-age growth rate.

Going back to 11.2.5 and replacing h by g it is evident that

$$\frac{\bar{K}_0}{\bar{Q}_0} = \frac{\bar{K}}{\bar{Q}} = \frac{s}{g + u}, \qquad (11.2.6)$$

which implies that the capital-output ratio equals the ratio of the (gross) saving rate to the sum of the golden-age rate of growth plus the rate of depreciation.

The golden rule can be derived without difficulty. First, use Eq. 11.2.6 to eliminate $\bar{K}$ from the production function; set $t = 0$; and rearrange the expression to yield per capita output. These steps give

$$\frac{\bar{Q}_0}{L} = A^{1/(1-a)}\left(\frac{s}{g + u}\right)^{a/(1-a)},$$

and imply that per capita consumption must be

$$\frac{\bar{C}_0}{L} = (1 - s)\frac{\bar{Q}_0}{L} = (1 - s)A^{1/(1-a)}\left(\frac{s}{g + u}\right)^{a/(1-a)}.$$

Now differentiate this function with respect to the saving rate and set the resultant derivative equal to zero in order to obtain a maximum. The outcome is the golden rule, $a = s$, which now states that per capita consumption is maximized if society saves and invests its gross profits and consumes its labor income.

From the production function we can calculate that the gross marginal product of capital is

$$\partial\bar{Q}/\partial\bar{K} = a(\bar{Q}/\bar{K}).$$

The net marginal productivity of capital must equal the rate of interest, which therefore must equal the gross marginal product minus the rate of depreciation. It follows that $i + u = a(\bar{Q}/\bar{K})$. Since we know from Eq. 11.2.6 that $\bar{Q}/\bar{K} = (g + u)/s$, we have the relation

$$i + u = a\frac{(g + u)}{s},$$

which obtains in any golden age. However, since the golden rule requires that $a = s$, this last expression reduces to $i = g$, and we therefore have our earlier result that the net marginal product of capital equals the golden-age growth rate in the optimum golden age.

In Chapter 10 we examined the stability of golden-age equilibrium by differentiating the production function with respect to time and solving the resultant differential equation. Differentiation of the production function yielded

$$\frac{dQ}{dt} = [r + n(1 - a)]Q + aAe^{rt}K^{a-1}L^{1-a}\frac{dK}{dt}. \tag{11.2.7}$$

Ignoring depreciation, we replaced dK/dt by sQ. However, in the present case, we must replace dK/dt by $sQ - uK$, and we therefore write Eq. 11.2.7 as

$$\frac{dQ}{dt} = [r + n(1 - a)]Q + aAe^{rt}K^{a-1}L^{1-a}(sQ - uK). \tag{11.2.8}$$

However, the term $-aAe^{rt}K^{a-1}L^{1-a}uK$ equals $-uaQ$, and Eq. 11.2.8 therefore reduces to

$$\frac{dQ}{dt} = [r + n(1 - a) - ua]Q + asAe^{rt}K^{a-1}L^{1-a}Q. \tag{11.2.9}$$

Comparing Eq. 11.2.9 with the differential equation (10.4.2) of Chapter 10, we see immediately that the two equations are identical except that the coefficient of Q, which we wrote as c_1, now equals $r + n(1 - a) - ua$, instead of $r + n(1 - a)$. Consequently, it is obvious that we need not repeat the entire solution and that it is only necessary to replace the original value of c_1 with its new value wherever the coefficient c_1 appears.

Referring again to the results of Chapter 10, we see that the general solution as given by Eq. 10.4.23 implies that the golden-age growth rate will eventually be approximated if $c_4 > c_1(1 - c_3)$, which, in the case of Chapter 10, simply required a to be positive. Assuming that a is positive, we can substitute our new c_1 value into the stability condition and find that it must now be the case that $g > -u$.

To conclude: One might well suppose that an economy in which capital life was perpetual would differ significantly from the economy in which capital life was finite. As we have seen, this is not the case. If a constant proportion of the capital stock is junked each year, and new capital is constructed at a constant exponential rate, the rate of increase of the capital stock will be constant. If this rate of capital growth equals the rate of output growth, the golden-age conditions set forth in the text will be satisfied and capital and output will grow at the rate of growth of augmented labor.

The golden rule is unaffected by finite capital life. However, the capital-output ratio is reduced by the presence of depreciation, and the gross marginal product of capital is therefore increased. This increase exactly equals the rate of depreciation so that the net marginal productivity of capital, and therefore the competitive rate of interest, continues to equal the golden-age rate of growth.

11.3 EMBODIED TECHNICAL CHANGE

The model of Chapter 10, as well as the amended version of the preceding section, assigns a very meager role to a rise in the rate of growth of capital as a means of raising the growth rate of output in the short-run, and it emphasizes that a rise in the fraction of income saved and invested can have no permanent effect on the rate of growth. Solow, for example, has used an expression such as Eq. 10.3.4, namely,

$$q = r + ah + (1 - a)n,$$

to illustrate that a doubling of the fraction of income saved would, given an initial capital output ratio of 3 to 1, raise the rate of growth of output by roughly one percent in the short-run. Remarking on this circumstance, Solow comments that, "This seems like a meager reward for what is, after all, a revolution in the speed of accumulation of capital."[*]

To deal with this apparent anomaly, Solow has emphasized that technical change is of two fundamentally different kinds. First, there is technical change that may be thought of as essentially organizational and which growth theorists describe as *disembodied* technical change. It consists of such changes as improvements in the efficiency of labor due to better education and training, and improvements in the organization of enterprise that are independent of the type or age of the capital equipment that is employed. Another type of technical change, however, is represented by improvements in the quality of capital goods, and the extent to which the system benefits from such technical changes depends upon the amount of new capital that is introduced and upon the rate at which old capital is replaced.

The latter form of technical change is called *embodied* technical change, and it differs from organizational or disembodied technical change in that new technology gets into the system only because there is new investment that brings improved equipment into the productive process. Because the efficiency of each unit of capital depends upon the age of the capital, if technical change is embodied, growth models that incorporate embodied technical change are usually described as "vintage" models.

The type of technical change assumed by the model of Chapter 10 is obviously purely of a disembodied variety. Our purpose now is to incorporate embodied technical change into the analysis as espoused by theorists who hold the so-called "new view" of investment. At the outset, we shall assume that all technical change is embodied and thereafter we shall allow for both forms of technical change.

---

[*] Robert M. Solow, "Investment and Technical Progress," in Arrow, Karlin, and Suppes, Eds., *Mathematical Methods in the Social Sciences* (Stanford, Calif.: Stanford University Press, 1960). The discussion of this section relies heavily upon this brilliant paper by Solow.

Following Solow, we begin by defining a vintage of capital. Capital of vintage v is defined as all capital v years old that is still in use at time t. Thus $K(t, v)$ stands for the quantity of capital of vintage v that remains in use at time t.* Similarly, $L(t, v)$ is the quantity of labor that is used on capital of vintage v at time t, and $Q(t, v)$ is the current output produced by machines of this vintage.

We next assume that production that results from the use of capital of any single vintage is related to the inputs of labor and capital by the Cobb-Douglas function. Consequently, we write

$$Q(t, v) = L(t, v)^{1-a} B e^{\lambda v} K(t, v)^{a}, \qquad (11.3.1)$$

where $Be^{\lambda v}$ is an index of *embodied* technical change. Earlier vintage capital in this formulation is less productive than later vintage capital, and the rate of improvement is given by the positive parameter λ.

Aggregate output at time t is the sum, over all vintages, of the output of each vintage. Therefore

$$Q(t) = \int_{-\infty}^{t} Q(t, v) \, dv \qquad (11.3.2)$$

is the level of total output. Similarly, the total labor force is the sum of labor employed on all vintages of capital,

$$L(t) = \int_{-\infty}^{t} L(t, v) \, dv = L_0 e^{nt}. \qquad (11.3.3)$$

Capital of vintage v at time v, $K(v, v)$ is gross investment at time v. It equals additions to the capital stock at time v plus replacement at that time. We therefore write

$$K(v, v) = I(v) = \frac{dK}{dv} + D(v), \qquad (11.3.4)$$

where $D(v)$ is the level of replacement investment at time v.

The assumption according to which replacement is governed is different in neoclassical models than in the Eisner model that was examined in Chapter 5. There it was assumed that the life of capital equipment is exactly x years, so that *all* new capital constructed in year v would have to be replaced at intervals of $v + x, v + 2x, \ldots, v + nx$ years. Capital in this view is known as capital of the "one-hoss shay" variety, which is to say that the capital goods remains in perfect running order, with no loss of efficiency for exactly x years, at which time it suddenly disintegrates into a heap of dust.

---

* Our notation throughout the next few pages will differ from our previous notation because of the importance of distinguishing between v and t. In past chapters, we would have designated Q_t as output at time t. However, we now replace this by $Q(t)$, and we write $Q(t, v)$ as output produced at time t by capital of vintage v.

Neoclassical theory, on the other hand, assumes that a vintage of capital begins to suffer attrition from the moment it is installed. Thus it is assumed that so long as a piece of capital is "alive," it produces the same output as it did when it was "born." However, there is a mortality table applicable to capital so that in any given period of time a certain number of machines of each vintage dies. Consequently, of the one-hoss shays that are built at any time, some shays collapse sooner than others.

If we assume that the proportion of machines of a given vintage that collapse at any time is proportional to the number that still operate,

$$D(v) = uK(v),$$

which simply states that the rate of depreciation at time v is proportional to the total physical capital stock in existence at time v. From this it follows that the surviving capital of any vintage is the original investment $I(v)$ depreciated to the present day, namely,*

$$K(t, v) = I(v)e^{-u(t-v)}. \tag{11.3.5}$$

We must now attempt to show that if production for each vintage of capital is Cobb-Douglas, then the production function for all vintages aggregated together will also be Cobb-Douglas. To anticipate the result, we will obtain the function

$$Q(t) = Ae^{rt}L(t)^{1-a}J(t)^a,$$

where r is the rate of disembodied technical change, and $J(t)$ is an efficiency measure of the capital stock which we shall denote as "effective capital."

The first step is to differentiate Eq. 11.3.1 partially with respect to $L(t)$ to obtain the marginal product of labor on capital of vintage v. Therefore

$$\frac{\partial Q(t, v)}{\partial L(t, v)} = (1 - a)L(t, v)^{-a}Be^{\lambda v}K(t, v)^a. \tag{11.3.6}$$

We next assume that firms, in order to maximize profits, equalize the marginal product of labor over all vintages of capital. We therefore replace $\partial Q(t, v)/\partial L(t, v)$

---

* If capital depreciates at the rate u, which is proportional to $K(t, v)$, the rate of change of surviving capital of vintage v must be

$$\frac{dK(t, v)}{dt} = -uK(t, v).$$

If we try the solution, $K(t, v) = Me^{q(t-v)}$, we get $K(t, v) = Me^{-u(t-v)}$. When $t = v$, that is, when the capital of vintage v is originally constructed,

$$K(v, v) = I(v) = M.$$

Consequently, we have the solution given in the text,

$$K(t, v) = I(v)e^{-u(t-v)}.$$

by $F(t)$ and write

$$F(t) = (1 - a)L(t, v)^{-a}Be^{\lambda v}K(t, v)^a, \qquad (11.3.7)$$

where $F(t)$ is independent of the vintage of capital. Third, we use Eq. 11.3.5 to substitute for $K(t, v)^a$. This converts 11.3.7 into

$$F(t) = (1 - a)L(t, v)^{-a}Be^{\lambda v}I(v)^a e^{-au(t-v)}. \qquad (11.3.8)$$

By rearranging this expression, we can solve for the quantity of labor that is applied to capital of vintage v, namely,

$$L(t, v) = [(1 - a)B]^{1/a}F(t)^{(-1/a)}I(v)e^{[-u(t-v)+(\lambda/a)v]}, \qquad (11.3.9)$$

which we rewrite as

$$L(t, v) = G(t)I(v)e^{[u+(\lambda/a)]v}, \qquad (11.3.10)$$

where

$$G(t) = [(1 - a)B]^{(1/a)}F(t)^{(-1/a)}e^{-ut}, \qquad (11.3.11)$$

which, like $F(t)$, is independent of v.

When we integrate Eq. 11.3.10 over all vintages, we get the total supply of labor,

$$L(t) = G(t)\int_{-\infty}^{t} I(v)e^{[u+(\lambda/a)]v}\,dv. \qquad (11.3.12)$$

Similarly, to solve for total output, we first use Eq. 11.3.10 to eliminate $L(t, v)$ from the production function, Eq. 11.3.1. This substitution yields

$$Q(t, v) = G(t)^{1-a}I(v)^{1-a}e^{(1-a)[u+\lambda/a]v}Be^{\lambda v}K(t, v)^a.$$

However, via Eq. 11.3.5 we see that this expression may be reduced to

$$Q(t, v) = G(t)^{1-a}I(v)Be^{-aut}e^{[u+\lambda/a]v}. \qquad (11.3.13)$$

Integration over all vintages to get total output gives

$$Q(t) = G(t)^{1-a}Be^{-uat}\int_{-\infty}^{t} I(v)e^{[u+\lambda/a]v}\,dv. \qquad (11.3.14)$$

When the labor supply Eq. 11.3.12 is compared with the result for total output, as expressed in 11.3.14, it becomes apparent that the term to be integrated is identical in both cases. Let us write this integral as $Z(v)$. We then have

$$L(t) = G(t)Z(v) \qquad (11.3.15)$$

as a short form version of the labor supply equation and

$$Q(t) = G(t)^{1-a}Be^{-aut}Z(v). \qquad (11.3.16)$$

From Eq. 11.3.15 it follows that

$$G(t)^{1-a} = L(t)^{1-a}Z(v)^{a-1}.$$

Substituting in 11.3.16, we now get the Cobb-Douglas result,

$$Q(t) = L(t)^{1-a}[Z(v)B^{(1/a)}e^{-ut}]^a. \tag{11.3.17}$$

Consequently, if we let

$$J(t) = Z(v)B^{(1/a)}e^{-ut} = B^{(1/a)}e^{-ut} \int_{-\infty}^{t} I(v)e^{(u+\lambda/a)v}\,dv, \tag{11.3.18}$$

we can write the Cobb-Douglas function,

$$Q(t) = L(t)^{1-a}J(t)^a, \tag{11.3.19}$$

where, as can be seen from Eq. 11.3.18, $J(t)$ is a measure of the stock of capital adjusted for depreciation and for embodied technical change.

To summarize: If the production function for each vintage of capital is Cobb-Douglas and if labor is allocated so as to equalize marginal labor products over all vintages, the aggregate production function will be Cobb-Douglas, where $K(t)$ is replaced by effective capital $J(t)$, which incorporates the effect of embodied technical change. If we wish also to add disembodied technical change, we can write the production function as

$$Q(t) = Ae^{rt}L(t)^{1-a}J(t)^a, \tag{11.3.20}$$

where r is the rate of disembodied technical change.

We can now incorporate these results into a neoclassical growth model.* Dropping the time subscripts, and proceeding as with our notation of the last chapter, we have the production function,

$$Q = Ae^{rt}L^{1-a}J^a. \tag{11.3.20}$$

To this we add the usual labor supply function,

$$L = L_0 e^{nt}, \tag{11.3.21}$$

and the full-employment condition,

$$I = sQ = \frac{dK}{dt} + uK. \tag{11.3.22}$$

Differentiated with respect to time, Eq. 11.3.20 becomes

$$\frac{dQ}{dt} = [r + n(1-a)]Q + aAe^{rt}L^{1-a}J^{a-1}\frac{dJ}{dt}. \tag{11.3.23}$$

It is necessary next to make the appropriate substitution for dJ/dt. Equation 11.3.18 defined J as

$$J = e^{-ut} \int_{-\infty}^{t} I(v)e^{(u+\lambda/a)v}\,dv, \tag{11.3.24}$$

---

* The subsequent discussion relies heavily on E. M. Phelps, "The New View of Investment: A Neoclassical Analysis," *Quarterly Journal of Economics* (November, 1962).

where the term $B^{1/a}$ is assumed to have been absorbed into the constant A of the production function as it is written in Eq. 11.3.20. Differentiating Eq. 11.3.24 with respect to time gives

$$\frac{dJ}{dt} = -uJ + e^{-ut}\frac{d}{dt}\left[\int_{-\infty}^{t} I(v)e^{(u+\lambda/a)v}\,dv\right]. \qquad (11.3.25)$$

The deriviative of the integral in the above expression, evaluated at time t, is simply $I(t)e^{(u+\lambda/a)t}$, so that the equation becomes

$$dJ/dt = -uJ + I(t)e^{(\lambda/a)t}.$$

Finally, since $I = sQ$, we have

$$dJ/dt = -uJ + sQe^{(\lambda/a)t}. \qquad (11.3.26)$$

When we use Eq. 11.3.26 to substitute in Eq. 11.3.23, we get

$$\frac{dQ}{dt} = [r + n(1-a)]Q - aAe^{rt}L^{1-a}J^{a-1}uJ + asAe^{rt}L^{1-a}J^{a-1}Qe^{(\lambda/a)t}.$$

However, since the term $-aAe^{rt}L^{1-a}J^{a-1}uJ$ equals $-auQ$, we can write this as

$$\frac{dQ}{dt} = [r + n(1-a) - au]Q + asAe^{rt}L^{1-a}J^{a-1}Qe^{(\lambda/a)t}. \qquad (11.3.27)$$

From inspection of Eq. 11.3.27 it is evident that the equation is of the exact same form as Eq. 10.4.2 of the last chapter. Consequently, we can use the production function to eliminate J^{a-1} by writing

$$J^{a-1} = \left[\frac{Q}{Ae^{rt}L^{1-a}}\right]^{(a-1)/a}$$

and substitute this into Eq. 11.3.27. If, in addition, we use the labor supply function to replace L by L_0e^{nt}, Eq. 11.3.27 reduces to the familiar Bernoulli equation,

$$\frac{dQ}{dt} = c_1 Q + c_2 Q^{c_3}e^{c_4 t}, \qquad (11.3.28)$$

where in the present case,

$$c_1 = r + n(1-a) - au;$$
$$c_2 = asA^{(1/a)}L_0^{[(1-a)/a]};$$
$$c_3 = \frac{2a-1}{a}, \qquad 1 - c_3 = \frac{1-a}{a}; \qquad (11.3.29)$$
$$c_4 = \frac{r + \lambda + n(1-a)}{a}.$$

From here on the analysis is simple and becomes a repetition of earlier work. To vary the format slightly, we resort to a somewhat different, though equivalent, procedure for deriving the golden-age growth rate. We know that in the golden age we must have

$$\bar{Q} = \bar{Q}_0 e^{gt}, \qquad \frac{d\bar{Q}}{dt} = g\bar{Q}_0 e^{gt}.$$

Substituting these values into the Bernoulli equation (Eq. 11.3.28), we get

$$g\bar{Q} = c_1\bar{Q} + c_2\bar{Q}^{c_3}e^{c_4 t},$$

and when we solve this equation for $\bar{Q}$, we obtain

$$\bar{Q} = \left[\frac{c_2}{g - c_1}\right]^{1/(1 - c_3)} e^{[c_4/(1 - c_3)]t} = \bar{Q}_0 e^{[c_4/(1 - c_3)]t}. \qquad (11.3.30)$$

Evidently, the equilibrium growth rate must equal $c_4/(1 - c_3)$, so that on using 11.3.29 we have

$$g = \frac{c_4}{1 - c_3} = \frac{r + \lambda}{1 - a} + n.$$

We therefore find that the equilibrium growth rate differs from our earlier result only in that the rate of growth of embodied technical change is added to the rate of growth of disembodied technical change.

Growth of effective capital must also conform to the golden-age requirement of steady growth. Therefore let

$$\bar{J} = \bar{J}_0 e^{jt}, \qquad \frac{d\bar{J}}{dt} = j\bar{J}_0 e^{jt}. \qquad (11.3.31)$$

From Eq. 11.3.26 we know that

$$\frac{dJ}{dt} = -uJ + sQe^{(\lambda/a)t}.$$

On using 11.3.31, and replacing Q by $\bar{Q}_0 e^{gt}$, this expression becomes

$$j\bar{J}_0 e^{jt} = -u\bar{J}_0 e^{jt} + s\bar{Q}_0 e^{(g + \lambda/a)t},$$

from which it follows that

$$(j + u)\bar{J}_0 e^{jt} = s\bar{Q}_0 e^{(g + \lambda/a)t}. \qquad (11.3.32)$$

If this equation is to hold for all values of t, it must be the case that the golden-age rate of growth of effective capital is

$$j = g + \lambda/a,$$

and it therefore follows that effective capital grows more rapidly than physical capital at the rate λ/a.

The reader can now easily verify that the equilibrium physical capital-output ratio is $s/(g + u)$, that the equilibrium effective capital to output ratio is

$$\frac{s}{j + u} e^{(\lambda/a)t} = \frac{s}{g + \lambda/a + u} e^{(\lambda/a)t}$$

that the marginal product of physical capital is $a(g + u)/s$, and that when $a = s$, per capita consumption is at a maximum and the golden-age growth rate equals the net return on capital. Finally, it can easily be shown that golden-age growth is stable by noting that the stability condition

$$c_4 > c_1(1 - c_3) \qquad \text{or} \qquad g > c_1,$$

is met, provided that a, u, and λ are positive.

To conclude the discussion, we can now return to the short-run problem with which Solow was concerned. Since the rate of growth of effective capital exceeds the rate of growth of actual capital, it is evident that an increase in the rate of accumulation of actual capital of, say one percent, will raise the rate of growth of effective capital by more than one percent because this raises the proportion of the capital stock that is new and more productive. From this we can readily infer that a one-percent increase in the rate of growth of actual capital will produce a greater increase in the short-run rate of output growth than the increase that was implied by the model in which technical change was assumed to be purely disembodied.

We have seen, however, that the equilibrium rate of growth remains a function of the rate of technical progress and the rate of growth of the labor supply, and that it remains independent of the saving rate. With purely disembodied technical change, a rise in the saving rate raises the ratio of capital to output for all time, but it does not make capital and output grow any faster in the long-run, since output cannot grow any faster than the rate of growth of augmented labor without causing the marginal product of capital and the growth rate to fall. The effect of an increase in the saving rate in the embodied model is not only to increase the size of the capital stock relative to output but also to modernize it. However, here again there are limits. A completely modern capital stock would require all previous capital to be junked and the system would therefore have to replace all capital each year. Thus there is an equilibrium age of capital that goes along with golden-age growth. If the system is to remain on a steady growth path, the marginal product of physical capital must remain constant, and this means that effective capital must grow at the rate $g + \lambda/a$, while actual capital grows at the rate g.

11.4 FIXED FACTOR PROPORTIONS AND NEOCLASSICAL GROWTH

The model discussed in the last section was constructed on the assumption that after each increment to the capital stock, the labor force is redistributed over all vintages of capital in such a way that the marginal product of labor is equalized. The model we are about to consider does not permit substitution over vintages of capital. In a manner similar to the Domar model, we now assume that once a machine is in place its labor requirement is fixed over its life time. However, unlike the Domar model, factors can be substituted for each other at the time at which capital is constructed. It is because factor proportions are variable in the planning stage but fixed thereafter that models which incorporate these assumptions are called putty-clay models. In the present section we examine one of the simpler of these models.*

The following are the basic assumptions of the model:

1   There are two factors of production, labor and capital, that produce a homogeneous output which may be either consumed or invested.

2   The two factors can be substituted continuously for each other at the planning stage; however, once a particular productive process is chosen, the factor proportions become fixed for the life of the machines.

3   Capital depreciates at a rate that is proportional to the quantity of surviving capital.

The assumption governing depreciation is the same as before, namely, that capital is subject to an exponential decay function. Therefore, if $K(v, v)$ is the capital created at time v, the depreciation of this vintage of capital at time t is $D(t, v) = uK(t, v)$, and the capital of vintage v that survives at time t is

$$K(t, v) = e^{-u(t-v)}K(v, v). \tag{11.4.1}$$

It is convenient again to resort to the notation of the last section where, for example, $Q(t)$ is output at time t, and $Q(t, v)$ is output produced at time t by capital of vintage v. Therefore $Q(t, t)$ is the output produced by newly created capital, $K(t, t)$, and by that part of the labor supply, $L(t, t)$, that is not tied up in production with previously created capital.

Factor substitution is possible when $v = t$, but not otherwise. When $v = t$, we assume that the technology is of the Cobb-Douglas form. Therefore we define the incremental production function,

$$Q(t, t) = Ae^{rt}K(t, t)^a L(t, t)^{1-a}. \tag{11.4.2}$$

If capital decays at the rate u, surviving capital of vintage v at time t is $K(t, v) = e^{-u(t-v)}K(v, v)$. Total surviving capital for all vintages is therefore

$$K(t) = \int_{-\infty}^{t} e^{-u(t-v)}K(v, v)\, dv. \tag{11.4.3}$$

Similarly, by the assumption of fixed-factor proportions, total output must be

$$Q(t) = \int_{-\infty}^{t} e^{-u(t-v)}Q(v, v)\, dv, \tag{11.4.4}$$

---

* The discussion in this section is adapted from Leif Johansen's inventive article, "Substitution vs. Fixed Production Coefficients in the Theory of Economic Growth," *Econometrica* (May, 1959). A similar analysis is provided by Edmund Phelps, "Substitution, Fixed Proportions, Growth, and Distribution," *International Economic Review* (September, 1963).

and the total quantity of labor employed is

$$L(t) = L_0 e^{nt} = \int_{-\infty}^{t} e^{-u(t-v)} L(v, v) \, dv. \qquad (11.4.5)$$

The net addition to the stock of capital at time t is the level of gross investment minus depreciation,

$$dK/dt = K(t, t) - uK(t), \qquad (11.4.6)$$

which, of course, is what we would get if we differentiated Eq. 11.4.3. Moreover, gross investment $K(t, t)$ must equal the level of gross saving and we therefore have

$$K(t, t) = sQ(t). \qquad (11.4.7)$$

Taking stock, we see that the present model consists of six equations in six unknowns, $Q(t, t)$, $L(t, t)$, $K(t, t)$, $Q(t)$, $L(t)$, and $K(t)$. At no point in the development of the model has factor substitution been allowed for, once capital and labor are in place. The model of the last section assumed that the marginal product of labor would be equalized over all vintages of capital. However, we cannot resort to that assumption when factor proportions are fixed. How, then, can aggregate output be described and at what rate will it grow?

We begin by differentiating Eq. 11.4.4 with respect to time to obtain the change in aggregate output,

$$dQ/dt = Q(t, t) - uQ(t). \qquad (11.4.8)$$

Substituting the production function for $Q(t, t)$, we get

$$dQ/dt = Ae^{rt} K(t, t)^a L(t, t)^{1-a} - uQ(t), \qquad (11.4.9)$$

where it is evident that if $K(t, t)$ and $L(t, t)$ can be expressed as functions of $Q(t)$ and of t, we will be able to obtain a differential equation that can be solved to yield the time-path of output.

To eliminate $L(t, t)$, we differentiate Eq. 11.4.5 with respect to time to obtain

$$dL/dt = L(t, t) - uL(t). \qquad (11.4.10)$$

Recalling that $dL/dt = nL_0 e^{nt} = nL(t)$ is the exogenous increase in the supply of labor, we find that $nL(t) = L(t, t) - uL(t)$, so that

$$L(t, t) = (n + u)L(t), \qquad (11.4.11)$$

which means that the labor available to be applied to newly created capital at time t is the exogenous growth of labor supply, plus the labor which is released from currently retired machines.

Using Eq. 11.4.7 to replace $K(t, t)$ by $sQ(t)$ and Eq. 11.4.11 to substitute for $L(t, t)$, we find that Eq. 11.4.9 can now be written

$$dQ/dt = -uQ + Ae^{rt}s^a (n + u)^{1-a} Q(t)^a L(t)^{1-a}. \qquad (11.4.12)$$

When we drop the time subscripts and replace $L(t)$ by $L_0 e^{nt}$, we get the differential equation

$$\frac{dQ}{dt} = -uQ + [As^a(n + u)^{1-a}L_0^{1-a}]Q^a e^{[r + n(1 - a)]t}, \qquad (11.4.13)$$

which is of the familiar Bernoulli form,

$$\frac{dQ}{dt} = c_1 Q + c_2 Q^{c_3} e^{c_4 t},$$

where, in this case,

$$
\begin{aligned}
c_1 &= -u, \\
c_2 &= As^a(n + u)^{1-a}L_0^{1-a}, \\
c_3 &= a, \\
c_4 &= r + n(1 - a).
\end{aligned}
\qquad (11.4.14)
$$

The results are very similar to the results in the other neoclassical models we have examined. The equilibrium rate of growth of capital, investment, and output is

$$\frac{c_4}{1 - c_3} = \frac{r}{1 - a} + n = g. \qquad (11.4.15)$$

Further, the equilibrium capital-output ratio is the same as always $[s/(g + u)]$, the marginal product of capital is $(a/s)(g + u)$, and since the golden rule still requires that $a = s$, it also follows that the equilibrium growth rate equals the net marginal return on capital when the golden rule is observed. Finally, stability of the golden age merely requires that $g > -u$, assuming that a is positive.

In conclusion, the difference between the model of fixed-factor proportions and the Domar model discussed in Chapter 7 is that substitution is possible at the margin in the putty-clay model, whereas factor proportions are fixed at all times in the Domar model. The assumption of overall substitution, which is made in the earlier neoclassical models, turns out to be gratuitous. It is substitution at the planning stage that accounts for the differences between the Domar and the neoclassical results.

There are many additional branches of neoclassical growth theory that we have not explored here. Putty-clay models have been extended to allow for changing wage rates and for economically determined rates of depreciation. Other models have been constructed that attempt to divide the economy into sectors. The possibilities of extending this fascinating field, as is the case with most fields of macroeconomic analysis, appear to be boundless.

REFERENCES

John Fei, "Per Capita Consumption and Growth," *Quarterly Journal of Economics* (February, 1965).

Leif Johansen, "Substitution vs. Fixed Production Coefficients in the Theory of Economic Growth," *Econometrica* (May, 1959).

Edmund S. Phelps, "The Golden Rule of Accumulation: A Fable for Growthmen," *American Economic Review* (September, 1961).

————, "Substitution, Fixed Proportions, Growth, and Distributions," *International Economic Review* (September, 1963).

————, "The New View of Investment: A Neoclassical Analysis," *Quarterly Journal of Economics* (November, 1962).

————, "Second Essay on the Golden Rule of Accumulation," *American Economic Review* (September, 1965).

————, *Golden Rules of Economic Growth* (New York: Norton, 1966).

Robert M. Solow, "A Contribution to the Theory of Economic Growth," *Quarterly Journal of Economics* (February, 1956).

————, "Investment and Technical Progress," in Arrow, Karlin, and Suppes, eds., *Mathematical Methods in the Social Sciences* (Stanford, Calif.: Stanford University Press, 1960).

————, "Technical Change and the Aggregate Production Function," *Review of Economics and Statistics* (August, 1957).

For some of the topics not covered in Chapters 10 and 11 see:

John Conlisk, "Unemployment in a Neoclassical Growth Model: The Effect on Speed of Adjustment," *Economic Journal* (September, 1966).

John Fei and Gustav Ranis, "A Theory of Economic Development," *American Economic Review* (September, 1961).

————, "Innovation, Capital Accumulation, and Economic Development," *American Economic Review* (June, 1963).

Hirofumi Uzawa, "On a Two-Sector Model of Economic Growth," *Review of Economic Studies* (May, 1962).

CHAPTER 12

Stability Analysis in Higher-Order Single-Equation Models

12.1 INTRODUCTION

In this chapter we conclude the analysis of single-equation differential and difference equation models. The main purpose of the chapter is to provide some tools of analysis that serve as the basis for the simultaneous equation models that we wish to discuss in Part III. Unfortunately, we have to cover quite a bit of mathematical territory before we can get to the economic applications and we can only hope that the reader will have the patience to bear with us while we wend our way down this road.

12.2 HIGHER-ORDER DIFFERENTIAL EQUATIONS AND THE STABILITY OF EQUILIBRIUM

The solution to the second-order differential equation

$$a \frac{d^2y}{dt^2} + b \frac{dy}{dt} + cy = g, \qquad (12.2.1)$$

where a, b, c, and g are constants, proceeds along a route quite similar to that taken in finding the solution to a first-order equation. The first step is to find the equilibrium level of y. Since all of the time derivatives must be zero at equilibrium, we see immediately that

$$\bar{y} = g/c. \qquad (12.2.2)$$

The next step is to define y as the sum of the equilibrium value plus a displacement u. Therefore

$$y = u + \bar{y}. \qquad (12.2.3)$$

Since the time derivatives of $\bar{y}$ are zero, we have

$$\frac{dy}{dt} = \frac{du}{dt}, \qquad \frac{d^2y}{dt^2} = \frac{d^2u}{dt^2},$$

so that upon making substitutions in 12.2.1, we obtain the homogeneous equation

$$a\frac{d^2u}{dt^2} + b\frac{du}{dt} + cu = 0. \qquad (12.2.4)$$

which could just as well be written

$$a\frac{d^2y}{dt^2} + b\frac{dy}{dt} + c(y - \bar{y}) = 0.$$

We now attempt a trial solution of the form

$$u = e^{xt}. \qquad (12.2.5)$$

This trial solution implies that

$$\frac{du}{dt} = xe^{xt}, \qquad \frac{d^2u}{dt^2} = x^2e^{xt}.$$

When these trial values are substituted into 12.2.4, we obtain the expression $ax^2e^{xt} + bxe^{xt} + ce^{xt} = 0$, and since e^{xt} appears in each term, we have

$$(ax^2 + bx + c)e^{xt} = (ax^2 + bx + c)u = 0,$$

where the expression

$$ax^2 + bx + c = 0 \qquad (12.2.6)$$

is known as the *characteristic equation*.

Whereas a first-order differential equation had only a single *characteristic root*, we now see that the second-order equation has two such roots. To solve for the values of these roots, we use the quadratic formula according to which

$$x_1 = \frac{-b + \sqrt{b^2 - 4ac}}{2a},$$
$$\qquad (12.2.7)$$
$$x_2 = \frac{-b - \sqrt{b^2 - 4ac}}{2a}.$$

Since the second-order equation has two characteristic roots, there are two possible solutions,

$$u = e^{x_1t}, \qquad u = e^{x_2t}. \qquad (12.2.8)$$

We now state without proof that if both equations in 12.2.8 are solutions, the expression

$$u = m_1e^{x_1t} + m_2e^{x_2t}, \qquad (12.2.9)$$

is also a solution. In this expression the terms m_1 and m_2 are constants whose values are to be determined by the initial conditions.

Since the values of x_1 and x_2 are now known, we can proceed to a complete solution. Via 12.2.3 and 12.2.9 we have

$$y = m_1 e^{x_1 t} + m_2 e^{x_2 t} + \bar{y}. \tag{12.2.10}$$

Since we have two constants, m_1 and m_2, we have to have two initial conditions in order to get the complete solution. Suppose therefore that we know that at $t = 0$,

$$y = k_1, \qquad \frac{dy}{dt} = k_2.$$

Equation 12.2.10 then implies that

$$k_1 = m_1 + m_2 + \bar{y},$$
$$k_2 = x_1 m_1 + x_2 m_2.$$

These two equations may now be solved simultaneously for the values of m_1 and m_2; the results may then be substituted into 12.2.9 and the complete solution is thereby obtained.

If the term $b^2 - 4ac$ of the roots is negative, the roots are complex conjugate. However, if $b^2 - 4ac > 0$, the roots are *real*, and the solution is straightforward. It is apparent from Eq. 12.2.10 that in such a case the time-path of y will approach $\bar{y}$ only if both of the roots are negative. If, for example, $x_1 < 0$, while $x_2 > 0$, the term $e^{x_1 t}$ will decay to zero. However, the term $e^{x_2 t}$ will grow exponentially and y will therefore also grow exponentially away from $\bar{y}$ and, in the limit, at the continuous rate x_2. Thus the condition for stability of equilibrium in a second-order differential equation model, provided that the roots are real, is that both of the characteristic roots be negative.

When $b^2 - 4ac < 0$, the roots are *complex*, and when this is the case, we can write them as

$$x_1 = \frac{-b}{2a} + \frac{\sqrt{4ac - b^2}}{2a} (\sqrt{-1}) = \alpha + \beta i,$$

$$x_2 = \frac{-b}{2a} - \frac{\sqrt{4ac - b^2}}{2a} \sqrt{-1} = \alpha - \beta i, \tag{12.2.11}$$

where the character i is again employed to denote the term $\sqrt{-1}$. The portion $\alpha = -b/2a$ is the *real part* of the complex roots. The *imaginary* parts of the respective roots are βi and $-\beta i$. When the real part, α, is added to the imaginary parts βi and $-\beta i$, we have the *complex conjugate* roots

$$x_1 = \alpha + \beta i,$$
$$x_2 = \alpha - \beta i.$$

We wish now to show the following: Given the differential equation

$$a \frac{d^2 y}{dt^2} + b \frac{dy}{dt} + cy = 0,$$

with characteristic equation $ax^2 + bx + c = 0$ and complex conjugate roots such as 12.2.11, we may express the solution,

$$y = m_1 e^{x_1 t} + m_2 e^{x_2 t} = m_1 e^{(\alpha + \beta i)t} + m_2 e^{(\alpha - \beta i)t}, \qquad (12.2.12)$$

as

$$y = e^{\alpha t}[n_1 \cos (\beta t) + n_2 \sin (\beta t)]. \qquad (12.2.13)$$

The bracketed term in Eq. 12.2.13 is purely repetitive and generates the same values every 360°. For example, $n_1 \cos (0) + n_2 \sin (0) = n_1$; however, $n_1 \cos (360°) + n_2 \sin (360°)$ also equals n_1. Consequently, it appears that whether the value of the function grows or decays depends entirely upon whether the term $e^{\alpha t}$ grows or decays, and this depends upon whether α is positive or negative. However, since $\alpha \ (= -b/2a)$ represents the real part of the two complex conjugate roots, we see that stability of equilibrium is obtained if the real parts of the roots are negative. Thus we can generalize the stability condition to cover both real and complex roots by saying that stability is obtained when the *real parts* of all the characteristic roots are negative.

Let us now see how we can convert a solution such as Eq. 12.2.12 into an expression of the form of 12.2.13. The first thing to observe is that Eq. 12.2.12 can be written as

$$y = e^{\alpha t}[m_1 e^{\beta i t} + m_2 e^{-\beta i t}]. \qquad (12.2.14)$$

Next, and we state this without proof, the function e^x may be written as the polynomial equation

$$e^x = a_0 + a_1 x + a_2 x^2 + a_3 x^3 + \cdots + a_n x^n + \cdots. \qquad (12.2.15)$$

From inspection of this expression, we see that when $x = 0$, the equation reduces to $e^0 = a_0 = 1$. Similarly,

$$\frac{d(e^x)}{dx} = e^x = a_1 + 2a_2 x + 3a_3 x^2 + 4a_4 x^3 + \cdots + na_n x^{n-1} + \cdots,$$

so that when $x = 0$, $e^0 = 1 = a_1$. Taking the next higher derivative, we obtain

$$\frac{d^2(e^x)}{dx^2} = e^x = 2a_2 + 6a_3 x + 12a_4 x^2 + 20a_5 x^3 + \cdots + n(n-1)a_n x^{n-2} + \cdots,$$

so that at $x = 0$, $e^0 = 1 = 2a_2$ and therefore, $a_2 = \frac{1}{2}$. If we try this differentiation process one more time, we obtain

$$\frac{d^3(e^x)}{dx^3} = e^x = 6a_3 + 24a_4 x + 60a_5 x^2 + \cdots + n(n-1)(n-2)a_n x^{n-3},$$

so that when $x = 0$, $e^0 = 1 = 6a_3$, and $a_3 = 1/3!$.

If we march ahead with this procedure, we will find that the respective co-efficients will have the values $a_0 = 1$, $a_1 = 1/1!$, $a_2 = 1/2!$, $a_3 = 1/3!$, $a_4 = 1/4!$,

$\ldots, a_n = 1/n!$. Consequently, we see that Eq. 12.2.15 may be expressed as*

$$e^x = 1 + x + \frac{1}{2!} x^2 + \frac{1}{3!} x^3 + \frac{1}{4!} x^4 + \cdots + \frac{1}{n!} x^n + \cdots. \quad (12.2.16)$$

If Eq. 12.2.16 is valid, it follows that

$$e^{ix} = 1 + ix + \frac{1}{2!} (ix)^2 + \frac{1}{3!} (ix)^3 + \frac{1}{4!} (ix)^4 + \cdots + \frac{1}{n!} (ix)^n \cdots. \quad (12.2.17)$$

However, since $i = \sqrt{-1}$, $i^2 = -1$, $i^3 = -\sqrt{-1} = -i$, $i^4 = 1$, $i^5 = i$, $i^6 = i^2$, and so on, it follows that Eq. 12.2.17 may be written

$$e^{ix} = \left[1 - \frac{1}{2!} x^2 + \frac{1}{4!} x^4 - \frac{1}{6!} x^6 + \frac{1}{8!} x^8 - \cdots \right]$$
$$+ i\left[x - \frac{1}{3!} x^3 + \frac{1}{5!} x^5 - \frac{1}{7!} x^7 + \frac{1}{9!} x^9 - \cdots \right] \quad (12.2.18)$$
$$= Q + iR.$$

Trigonometric functions may also be expressed in the form of polynomials. Consider the functions

$$\cos (x) = b_0 + b_1 x + b_2 x^2 + b_3 x^3 + \cdots + b_n x^n + \cdots, \quad (12.2.19)$$
$$\sin (x) = c_0 + c_1 x + c_2 x^2 + c_3 x^3 + \cdots + c_n x^n + \cdots, \quad (12.2.20)$$

and let us attempt to evaluate the coefficients of these equations by successive differentiation. When we do this, we need to remember that $(d/dx) \sin (x) = \cos (x)$ and that $(d/dx) \cos (x) = -\sin (x)$. Beginning with Eq. 12.2.19, we see that

$$\frac{d \cos (x)}{dx} = -\sin (x) = b_1 + 2b_2 x + 3b_3 x^2 + 4b_4 x^3 + \cdots,$$

$$\frac{d^2 \cos (x)}{dx^2} = -\cos (x) = 2b_2 + 6b_3 x + 12b_4 x^2 + \cdots,$$

$$\frac{d^3 \cos (x)}{dx^3} = \sin (x) = 6b_3 + 24b_4 x + \cdots,$$

$$\frac{d^4 \cos (x)}{dx^4} = \cos (x) = 24b_4 + \cdots,$$

$$\cdots = \cdots = \cdots.$$

---

* In passing it should be observed that if we let $x = 1$ in Eq. 12.2.16, we obtain

$$e = 1 + 1 + \tfrac{1}{2} + \tfrac{1}{6} + \tfrac{1}{24} + \tfrac{1}{120} + \cdots,$$

or in decimal form,

$$e = 1 + 1 + 0.5 + 0.1667 + 0.0417 + 0.0083 + \cdots \approx 2.718.$$

When $x = 0$, the initial equation and the successive derivatives imply that

$$\cos (0) = 1 = b_0, \qquad b_0 = 1,$$
$$-\sin (0) = 0 = b_1, \qquad b_1 = 0,$$
$$-\cos (0) = -1 = 2b_2, \qquad b_2 = -\frac{1}{2!},$$
$$\sin (0) = 0 = 6b_3, \qquad b_3 = 0,$$
$$\cos (0) = 1 = 24b_4, \qquad b_4 = \frac{1}{4!}.$$

Moreover, we may readily infer that $b_5 = 0$, $b_6 = -1/6!$, $b_7 = 0$, $b_8 = 1/8!$, and so forth.

Using these coefficients to substitute in Eq. 12.2.19, we see that the expression may now be written

$$\cos (x) = 1 - \frac{1}{2!} x^2 + \frac{1}{4!} x^4 - \frac{1}{6!} x^6 + \frac{1}{8!} x^8 - \cdots, \qquad (12.2.21)$$

and when we refer to Eq. 12.2.18, we see that this constitutes the real part Q of the expression $e^{ix} = Q + iR$.

The reader may now readily confirm that if we take Eq. 12.2.20 and differentiate the expression successively with respect to x and evaluate the derivatives at $x = 0$, the coefficients will be $c_0 = 0$, $c_1 = 1$, $c_2 = 0$, $c_3 = -1/3!$, $c_4 = 0$, $c_5 = 1/5!$, and so on. Consequently, Eq. 12.2.20 may be written

$$\sin (x) = x - \frac{1}{3!} x^3 + \frac{1}{5!} x^5 - \frac{1}{7!} x^7 + \cdots, \qquad (12.2.22)$$

and this equals the part R of Eq. 12.2.18. Thus we now see that since Eq. 12.2.21 equals the part Q and Eq. 12.2.22 equals the part R, Eq. 12.2.18 may be written quite simply as

$$e^{ix} = Q + iR = \cos (x) + i \sin (x). \qquad (12.2.23)$$

Now let us go back to Eq. 12.2.14, namely ·

$$y = e^{\alpha t}[m_1 e^{\beta it} + m_2 e^{-\beta it}]. \qquad (12.2.14)$$

Using 12.2.23, we see that this may now be written

$$y = e^{\alpha t}\{m_1[\cos (\beta t) + i \sin (\beta t)] + m_2[\cos (-\beta t) + i \sin (-\beta t)]\}.$$

However, since $\cos (-\beta t) = \cos (\beta t)$ and $\sin (-\beta t) = -\sin (\beta t)$ for any angle βt, it follows that

$$y = e^{\alpha t}[(m_1 + m_2) \cos (\beta t) + (m_1 - m_2)i \sin (\beta t)].$$

Finally, since $m_1 + m_2$ and $(m_1 - m_2)i$ are arbitrary constants that depend upon the initial conditions, we assign them the values n_1 and n_2, respectively, and our complete solution therefore becomes Eq. 12.2.13, namely

$$y = e^{\alpha t}[n_1 \cos (\beta t) + n_2 \sin (\beta t)]. \tag{12.2.13}$$

In conclusion: We have seen that the solution to the second-order differential equation with complex conjugate roots may be expressed in the form of Eq. 12.2.13. From this we infer that the growth or decay of the function depends only upon the value of α. Since α is the real part of the roots, we conclude that stability of equilibrium requires that the real parts of all the characteristic roots be negative.

We can now go on to the general nth-order case. To solve the linear homogeneous differential equation

$$a_0 \frac{d^n y}{dt^n} + a_1 \frac{d^{n-1} y}{dt^{n-1}} + \cdots + a_n y = 0, \tag{12.2.24}$$

we attempt the trial solution, $y = e^{qt}$, and upon substitution into 12.2.24, we derive the characteristic equation,

$$a_0 q^n + a_1 q^{n-1} + \cdots + a_n = 0. \tag{12.2.25}$$

Since there are n characteristic roots, we will obtain a solution of the form

$$y = m_1 e^{q_1 t} + m_2 e^{q_2 t} + \cdots + m_n e^{q_n t},$$

and it is therefore evident that stability of equilibrium (the decay of y to zero) requires the real parts of all n roots to be negative.

Evaluation of these characteristic roots is a cumbersome task. However, if the purpose of the analysis is merely to test for stability of equilibrium, evaluation may be bypassed by the application of a few rules and devices.

The first rule of which we should inform ourselves is *Descarte's rule of signs.* The rule works as follows: Consider the polynomial equation

$$x^n + c_1 x^{n-1} + c_2 x^{n-2} + \cdots + c_n = 0, \tag{12.2.26}$$

and note that if all of the c's are positive, this equation could not possibly be satisfied for any nonnegative value of x that we might care to substitute. Consequently, we see that if all the c's are positive, it would be impossible for the equation to have any positive or zero real roots. Moreover, we can count the number of positive roots by counting the number of sign changes that take place between the successive coefficients. To illustrate, assume that there are two negative roots, $x = -a$ and $x = -b$. The characteristic equation would then be

$$(x + a)(x + b) = x^2 + (a + b)x + ab = 0.$$

Here there are no sign changes and there are therefore no positive roots. Suppose next that both roots are positive. Hence $x = a$ and $x = b$, so that

$$(x - a)(x - b) = x^2 - (a + b)x + ab = 0.$$

The signs run $+ - +$ and since there are two sign changes, both roots must be positive. It is obvious from inspection of this equation that it could never be satisfied by any negative value of x that we might care to choose.

Finally, if one of the roots is negative, we have either

$$(x - a)(x + b) = x^2 + (b - a)x - ab = 0$$

or

$$(x + a)(x - b) = x^2 + (a - b)x - ab = 0.$$

In the first case, if a is greater than b, the signs run $+ - -$, and if b is greater than a, the signs run $+ + -$. In the second case, if $a > b$, the signs run $+ + -$, whereas if $a < b$, they run $+ - -$. Consequently, all four cases involve one sign change and there is therefore one positive root and one negative root.

To firm up the rule of signs a bit more, consider a third-degree polynomial with negative roots, $-a$, $-b$, and $-c$. In this event, the characteristic equation is

$$(x + a)(x + b)(x + c) = x^3 + (a + b + c)x^2 + (ab + ac + bc)x + abc.$$

Since there is no sign change, all of the roots are negative. At the opposite extreme, if the roots are all positive and equal to a, b, and c, respectively, we obtain

$$(x - a)(x - b)(x - c) = x^3 - (a + b + c)x^2 + (ab + ac + bc)x - abc,$$

where the signs run $+ - + -$, and since there are three sign changes, all roots are positive.

Finally, suppose that $x = a$, $x = b$, and $x = -c$. In this case,

$$(x - a)(x - b)(x + c) = x^3 - (a + b - c)x^2 + (ab - ac - bc)x + abc.$$

Evidently the signs of the coefficients of x^2 and x are ambiguous. However, this circumstance creates no great difficulty. The signs could run

$$+ - - + \;.$$
$$+ + - +$$
$$+ - + +$$
$$+ + + +.$$

In the first three of these cases there are two sign changes and therefore two positive roots. The only inadmissable combination is the last set because the presence of no sign changes would imply the absence of any positive roots. For the last case to hold, $-(a + b - c)$ would have to be positive and so would $ab - ac - bc$. Now if $-(a + b - c)$ is positive, it would have to be the case that $c > a + b$. However, if this is the case, it would have to follow that

$$ab - ac - bc = ab - c(a + b) < ab - (a + b)(a + b).$$

But since

$$ab - (a + b)(a + b) = -(a^2 + ab + b^2)$$

is necessarily negative, it must be the case that $ab - ac - bc$ is also negative, and we therefore see that the coefficients of both x^2 and x cannot be of the same sign.

If we had had four roots or n roots, the rule of signs would still hold. Suppose that the respective roots are $-a$, $-b$, $-c$, and $-d$. In this case the characteristic equation is

$$x^4 + (a + b + c + d)x^3 + (ab + ac + ad + bc + bd + cd)x^2$$
$$+ (abc + abd + acd + bcd)x + abcd = 0.$$

From inspection of this result, as well as from the preceding two- and three-root cases, we can readily infer that in the general polynomial equation (12.2.26) the coefficient c_1 will always be the sum of the roots with the sign of this sum changed. The coefficient c_2 represents the sum of the product of all the roots taken two at a time. Similarly, c_3 is the sum of the product of the roots taken three at a time with the sign of this sum changed. And, in general, the coefficient c_i ($i \neq 0$) is the sum of the product of the n roots taken i at a time, where the sign attached to this sum is $(-1)^i$. The last coefficient, c_n, must be the product of the n roots taken n at a time, and since there is only one such combination, c_n is the product of the roots. If there is an odd number of roots and if all are negative, their product will be negative; if there is an even number of roots, their product will be positive. Hence the sign attached to the product of the roots is $(-1)^n$.

The number of distinct combinations of n terms taken r at a time is

$$\frac{n!}{r!(n - r)!}.$$

Therefore, since c_2 is the sum of the products of the roots taken two at a time, there are

$$\frac{4 \times 3 \times 2}{2 \times 2} = 6$$

such terms if $n = 4$. Coefficient c_3 is $(-1)^3$ multiplied by the sum of the product of the roots taken three at a time. Consequently, there are

$$\frac{4 \times 3 \times 2}{3 \times 2(4 - 3)} = 4,$$

such products in c_3.

It is evident from this discussion that Descarte's rule of signs permits us to make the important inference that whenever all terms of the characteristic equation (12.2.25) are divided by a_0, and the equation is put in the form

$$q^n + c_1 q^{n-1} + c_2 q^{n-2} + \cdots + c_n = 0, \qquad (12.2.27)$$

the values of all of the c_i coefficients must be positive if all n of the roots are negative. Similarly, if we find that one or more of the coefficients of the characteristic equation are negative, we know that the system possesses positive roots, and the system is therefore dynamically unstable.

Descarte's rule of signs does not constitute a sufficient test for stability of equilibrium because it only covers cases in which all roots are known to be real or cases in which the root with the largest real part is known to be real. It is possible for all the coefficients of the characteristic equation to be positive and yet the real parts of complex roots to be positive at the same time. An example, borrowed from Samuelson,* serves as an illustration. Let the characteristic equation be

$$(x + 1)(x^2 - 0.001x + 1) = x^3 + 0.999x^2 + 0.999x + 1 = 0.$$

In this example all of the coefficients of the characteristic equation are positive despite the fact that the roots of $x^2 - 0.001x + 1$ are

$$\frac{0.001 \pm \sqrt{(-0.001)^2 - 4}}{2},$$

where it is evident that the real parts of the roots are positive. Consequently, if some of the roots of the characteristic equation are complex conjugate, it is possible for the real parts to be positive and for all of the coefficients of the characteristic equation to be positive at the same time.

Taking account of complex roots, the necessary and sufficient condition for stability of equilibrium in a differential equation model is that *all* the n successive determinants,

$$|c_1|, \quad \begin{vmatrix} c_1 & c_3 \\ 1 & c_2 \end{vmatrix}, \quad \begin{vmatrix} c_1 & c_3 & c_5 \\ 1 & c_2 & c_4 \\ 0 & c_1 & c_3 \end{vmatrix}, \quad \begin{vmatrix} c_1 & c_3 & c_5 & c_7 \\ 1 & c_2 & c_4 & c_6 \\ 0 & c_1 & c_3 & c_5 \\ 0 & 1 & c_2 & c_4 \end{vmatrix}, \cdots,$$

where the elements of the determinants are the coefficients of the characteristic equation, be positive. These conditions for stability were derived by the mathematician E. J. Routh, and the determinants are therefore usually referred to as the Routh determinants.†

Because of its great simplicity, it would be a pity if the Descarte rule of signs could never be used as a sufficient test for stability. Fortunately, many of the most important models that we encounter in macroeconomics are of a sort for which it can be proved that the rule of signs is a sufficient condition for stability. In Chapter 15 we will see that this is the case.

12.3 DIFFERENCE EQUATIONS

The discussion of Chapter 8 permits us to complete the analysis of difference equations in short order. We know that stability of equilibrium in a difference-

---

* P. A. Samuelson, *Foundations of Economic Analysis, op. cit.,* p. 432.
† For a proof of the Routh theorem the reader is referred to Samuelson, *Foundations, op. cit.,* pp. 429–435.

equation model requires that the moduli of all the roots lie within the unit circle of the complex plain, and for real roots this means that their absolute values must be less than unity.

In the case of the general nth order nonhomogeneous difference equation,

$$a_0 y_t + a_1 y_{t-1} + a_2 y_{t-2} + \cdots + a_n y_{t-n} = g, \qquad (12.3.1)$$

we first solve for the equilibrium value $\bar{y}$ by setting $\bar{y} = y_t = y_{t-1} = \cdots = y_{t-n}$. Accordingly,

$$\bar{y} = \frac{g}{\sum\limits_{i=0}^{n} a_i}.$$

Next, we define $u_t = y_t - \bar{y}$, and substitute in 12.3.1 to obtain the homogeneous difference equation,

$$a_0 u_t + a_1 u_{t-1} + a_2 u_{t-2} + \cdots + a_n u_{t-n} = 0. \qquad (12.3.2)$$

If we attempt the trial solution, $u_t = \lambda^t$, and make substitutions in 12.3.2, we obtain the characteristic equation

$$a_0 \lambda^t + a_1 \lambda^{t-1} + a_2 \lambda^{t-2} + \cdots + a_n = 0, \qquad (12.2.3)$$

and when we solve for the characteristic roots, we obtain a solution of the form

$$y_t = \bar{y} + m_1 \lambda_1^t + m_2 \lambda_2^t + \cdots + m_n \lambda_n^t.$$

To take account of the possible presence of complex roots, we may write the solution even more generally, as

$$y_t = \bar{y} + M_1^t(k_{11} \cos \theta_1 t + k_{12} \sin \theta_1 t) + M_2^t(k_{21} \cos \theta_2 t + k_{22} \sin \theta_2 t)$$
$$+ \cdots + M_i^t(k_{i1} \cos \theta_i t + k_{i2} \sin \theta_i t),$$

where M_i is the modulus of the ith pair of complex roots, θ_i is its angle, and the k's are constants that depend upon the initial conditions. Stability, evidently, requires that all of the moduli be less than unity. The necessary and sufficient condition that this be the case is that the n successive determinants,

$$\begin{vmatrix} 1 & c_n \\ c_n & 1 \end{vmatrix}, \quad \begin{vmatrix} 1 & 0 & c_n & c_{n-1} \\ c_1 & 1 & 0 & c_n \\ c_n & 0 & 1 & c_1 \\ c_{n-1} & c_n & 0 & 1 \end{vmatrix}, \ldots, \quad \begin{vmatrix} 1 & 0 & \cdots & 0 & c_n & c_{n-1} & \cdots & c_1 \\ c_1 & 1 & \cdots & 0 & 0 & c_n & \cdots & c_2 \\ \vdots & & & & & & & \vdots \\ c_{n-1} & c_{n-2} & \cdots & 1 & 0 & 0 & \cdots & c_n \\ c_n & 0 & \cdots & 0 & 1 & c_1 & \cdots & c_{n-1} \\ c_{n-1} & c_n & \cdots & 0 & 0 & 1 & \cdots & c_{n-2} \\ \vdots & & & & & & & \vdots \\ c_1 & c_2 & \cdots & c_n & 0 & 0 & \cdots & 1 \end{vmatrix},$$

are positive. The elements of these determinants represent the coefficients of the characteristic equation when it is written

$$\lambda^t + c_1\lambda^{t-1} + c_2\lambda^{t-2} + \cdots + c_n = 0,$$

and the dashed lines that appear to partition the determinants are inserted in order to bring out their symmetry. These determinants represent the difference-equation counterparts of the Routhian determinants that we use to test for stability in a differential equation system, and they are known as the Schurr determinants.

Appendix to Chapter 12

SPECIAL PROBLEMS IN THE SOLUTION OF DIFFERENTIAL EQUATIONS

A. When the Particular Solution Fails

Consider the differential equation

$$a \frac{dy^2}{dt^2} + b \frac{dy}{dt} + cy = g. \tag{12.A.1}$$

Ordinarily, when we set all of the time derivatives equal to zero, we obtain the particular solution, $\bar{y} = g/c$. However, if $c = 0$, the usual method of finding the particular solution fails, provided, of course, that $g \neq 0$.

In such a case we should try a particular solution of the form $\bar{y} = zt$, from which it follows that

$$\frac{d\bar{y}}{dt} = z \quad \text{and} \quad \frac{d^2\bar{y}}{dt^2} = 0.$$

Next, let $y = u + \bar{y}$ and make the appropriate substitutions in 12.A.1. Recalling that $c = 0$ by our present assumption, we have

$$a \frac{d^2u}{dt^2} + b \left[\frac{du}{dt} + z \right] = g,$$

and if we wish to reduce this to

$$a \frac{d^2u}{dt^2} + b \frac{du}{dt} = 0, \tag{12.A.2}$$

it must be the case that $z = g/b$, and the particular solution therefore becomes

$$\bar{y} = (g/b)t.$$

Inspection of 12.A.2 confirms that the characteristic equation is $ax^2 + bx = 0$, and since this may be written

$$x(ax + b) = 0,$$

we see that the roots are $x_1 = 0$, $x_2 = -b/a$, respectively. Thus whenever $c = 0$, at least one of the roots of the characteristic equation must be zero.

Having found the roots, we now see that the solution to 12.A.2 is

$$u = m_1 e^{0t} + m_2 e^{(-b/a)t} = m_1 + m_2 e^{(-b/a)t},$$

and the solution for y must therefore be of the form

$$y = m_1 + m_2 e^{(-b/a)t} + (g/b)t.$$

By inspection of the solution, we see that in a case of this sort the system will exhibit exponential growth toward, or away from, a linear trend depending upon whether $(-b/a)$ is negative or positive.

If both b and c in Eq. 12.A.1 are zero, the equation becomes

$$a\frac{d^2y}{dt^2} = g. \tag{12.A.3}$$

If we try the conventional method of finding a particular solution, we will have $g = 0$. Similarly, if we try $\bar{y} = zt$, this will also fail because $d^2\bar{y}/dt^2 = 0$. In this case we therefore ought to try $\bar{y} = zt^2$, from which it follows that

$$\frac{d\bar{y}}{dt} = 2zt, \qquad \frac{d^2\bar{y}}{dt^2} = 2z.$$

Using these trial values along with $y = u + \bar{y}$ to substitute in 12.A.3, we obtain

$$a\left[\frac{d^2u}{dt^2} + 2z\right] = g.$$

Therefore, if

$$a\frac{d^2u}{dt^2} = 0, \tag{12.A.4}$$

it must be the case that $z = g/2a$, and the particular solution therefore becomes

$$\bar{y} = (g/2a)t^2.$$

The characteristic equation of 12.A.4 is $ax^2 = 0$, and both characteristic roots therefore equal zero. The solution to the transient portion now becomes

$$u = m_1 e^{0t} + m_2 e^{0t} = m_1 + m_2,$$

and the complete solution therefore appears to be

$$y = m_1 + m_2 + (g/2a)t^2. \tag{12.A.5}$$

However, there is a difficulty here. If we have the initial conditions $y = k_1$ and $dy/dt = k_2$ at $t = 0$, we find from 12.A.5 that

$$k_1 = m_1 + m_2,$$
$$k_2 = 0,$$

and the solution cannot therefore be made consistent with the arbitrary intial conditions. This is a difficulty that is generally encountered when the roots are identical. Coping with this difficulty is the next problem of this appendix.

B. Identical Characteristic Roots

Suppose we have the differential equation

$$\frac{d^2y}{dt^2} - 2a\frac{dy}{dt} + a^2 = 0,$$

with initial conditions,

$$k_1 = y, \qquad k_2 = \frac{dy}{dt},$$

at $t = 0$. The characteristic equation here is $x^2 - 2ax + a^2 = 0$, and it is obvious that the roots are $x_1 = x_2 = a$. Following ordinary procedures, we have the solution,

$$y = m_1 e^{at} + m_2 e^{at} = (m_1 + m_2) e^{at}.$$

The difficulty with this solution is that it may not be consistent with the two initial conditions. Since the solution implies that

$$k_1 = m_1 + m_2,$$
$$k_2 = a(m_1 + m_2),$$

our solution could be valid only if $k_2 = ak_1$.

In such a case we resort to the proposition that if a differential equation has identical roots $(x_1 = x_2)$, so that $y = e^{x_1 t}$ is a solution, it will also be the case that $te^{x_1 t}$ is a solution. Accordingly, our solution may be written

$$y = m_1 e^{at} + m_2 t e^{at} = (m_1 + m_2 t) e^{at}.$$

At $t = 0$ we have from this,

$$k_1 = m_1,$$
$$k_2 = am_1 + m_2.$$

Consequently, $m_2 = k_2 - ak_1$ and the complete solution is therefore

$$y = k_1 + (k_2 - ak_1) te^{at}.$$

We now see that we ought to have written Eq. 12.A.5 as

$$y = m_1 + m_2 t + (g/2a) t^2.$$

With $y = k_1$ and $dy/dt = k_2$ at $t = 0$. this implies that

$$k_1 = m_1, \qquad k_2 = m_2,$$

so that the complete solution is the parabola

$$y = k_1 + k_2 t + (g/2a) t^2.$$

C. Moving Equilibrium

The nonhomogeneous portion of the differential equation may be practically anything at all. It could be a constant: it could be of the form me^{nt}; it could be a repetitive oscillating term such as cos (xt), or it could be just about anything else.

One of the most frequent occurrences in macroeconomic differential equation models is the case of a nonhomogeneous term that grows at a constant exponential rate. This, indeed, is a case that we have already met in our discussion of neo-classical growth economics.

Suppose we begin with the familiar dynamic hypothesis that the rate at which income changes equals the difference between intended investment and saving,

$$\frac{dY}{dt} = I - S, \tag{12.C.1}$$

and that we assume investment to grow at the compound exponential rate r. Consequently, we assume that $I = I_0 e^{rt}$, and if we let the saving function be $S = (1 - b)Y$, 12.C.1 becomes the differential equation,

$$\frac{dY}{dt} = -(1 - b)Y + I_0 e^{rt}. \tag{12.C.2}$$

Our criterion for a particular solution is that if we replace Y by $u + \bar{Y}$, where u is the displacement from the particular solution, the resulting differential equation in u will be homogeneous. Consequently, let

$$Y = u + \bar{Y}, \tag{12.C.3}$$

and assume that

$$\bar{Y} = E e^{rt}, \tag{12.C.4}$$

where E is to be chosen in such a way as to make

$$\frac{du}{dt} + (1 - b)u = 0. \tag{12.C.5}$$

Substitution of 12.C.3, and 12.C.4 into 12.C.2 gives

$$\frac{du}{dt} + rE e^{rt} + (1 - b)(u + E e^{rt}) = I_0 e^{rt}.$$

If 12.C.5 holds, it must be the case that

$$rE^{rt} + (1 - b)E e^{rt} = I_0 e^{rt}$$

or

$$rE + (1 - b)E = I_0.$$

Solving for E, we have

$$E = \frac{I_0}{r + (1 - b)},$$

and the particular solution therefore becomes

$$\bar{Y} = \frac{I_0}{r + (1 - b)} e^{rt}.$$

Finally, the solution to 12.C.5 is

$$u = u_0 e^{-(1-b)t},$$

and the solution for Y is therefore of the form,

$$Y = u_0 e^{-(1-b)t} + \frac{I_0}{r + (1 - b)} e^{rt}.$$

As may readily be ascertained from inspection of this solution, the level of income in this case will move toward or away from the exponential equilibrium growth path depending upon whether $-(1 - b)$ is negative or positive.

Part III
MULTIPLE-COMPARTMENT
MACRODYNAMIC MODELS

CHAPTER 13

Stability Analysis of the Keynesian System and the Correspondence Principle

13.1 INTRODUCTION TO PART III

We have already found that the dynamic properties of a market could render the results of comparative-static analysis erroneous. We found further that in order to distinguish correct from erroneous comparative-static results, it was necessary to supplement comparative statics with an examination of the underlying dynamics of the system. This circumstance holds true not only for a single market but for systems of multiple compartments—sectors, countries, markets, industries —as well. Professor Samuelson, who is responsible for the first complete integration of comparative-static and dynamic analysis puts the matter as follows:

> Simply to know that there are efficacious 'laws' determining equilibrium tells us nothing of the character of these laws. In order for the analysis to be useful it must provide information concerning *the way* in which our equilibrium quantities will change as the result of changes in the parameters ...*

In a similar vein, Professor Hicks, whose seminal work paved the way for many subsequent advances tells us that

> The laws of change of the price-system, like the laws of change of individual demand, have to be derived from stability conditions. We first examine what changes are necessary in order that a given equilibrium system should be stable; then we make an assumption of regularity, that positions in the

---

* Paul A. Samuelson, *Foundations of Economic Analysis* (Cambridge, Mass.: Harvard University Press, 1947), p. 257. The italics in the above quote are mine. The analysis of this chapter relies heavily on Chapter 9 of Samuelson's book. That chapter is similar to Samuelson's earlier paper, "The Stability of Equilibrium: Comparative Statics and Dynamics," *Econometrica*, April 1941.

neighborhood of the equilibrium position will be stable also; and thence we deduce rules about the way in which the price-system will react to changes in tastes and resources.*

In Part II of this book we learned how to test for the stability of dynamic systems that could be expressed as a difference or a differential equation in a single variable. Our purpose in Part III is to extend our discussion to systems consisting of multiple compartments and to deduce stability conditions for the simultaneous equations that describe such multicompartment systems. Once we learn how to do this, we will have acquired a most important set of analytical tools, since we will then know how to distinguish correct from erroneous comparative-static results in models of n sectors, where n is any number we like.

The territory to be covered is considerable and the steps, from start to finish, are many. It therefore seems appropriate to follow a somewhat unorthodox procedure and to begin with a familiar example that permits us to illustrate the importance of the method of analysis without getting bogged down in its technical details. In this way it will be possible to set our sights firmly on the importance of the analytical procedures that follow. In subsequent chapters we shall discuss the general principles of stability analysis in simultaneous equation models and we shall then put the tools to work to analyze several multisectoral models.

13.2 THE KEYNESIAN SYSTEM

Consider the Keynesian model,

$$I(Y, i) = Y - C(Y), \tag{13.2.1}$$

$$m_s = L(Y, i), \tag{13.2.2}$$

where all of the variables are defined as they were in Chapter 3, and where the partial derivatives have the signs

$$I_y > 0, \qquad I_i < 0, \qquad 0 < C_y < 1, \qquad L_y > 0, \qquad L_i < 0.$$

The model differs from the model of Chapter 3 only in that investment is now assumed to be a function of the level of income as well as the rate of interest. The slope of the LM-curve is

$$\left(\frac{di}{dY}\right)_{LM} = -\frac{L_y}{L_i}. \tag{13.2.3}$$

and the slope of the IS-curve is

$$\left(\frac{di}{dY}\right)_{IS} = \frac{1 - C_y - I_y}{I_i} \tag{13.2.4}$$

---

* J. R. Hicks, *Value and Capital* (London: Oxford University Press, 1939), p. 62.

and its sign may now be either positive or negative whereas when $I_y = 0$, it could only have been negative.

If the marginal propensity to save, $1 - C_y$, is greater than the marginal propensity to invest, the slope of the IS-curve will be negative. If the opposite is the case, the slope will be positive. When $1 - C_y < I_y$, an increase in income of one dollar will induce additional consumption and investment spending in excess of a dollar, and equilibrium in the market for goods and services could therefore not be restored unless the rate of interest rises and dampens the increase in intended investment. Consequently, when the "marginal propensity to spend," $C_y + I_y$, exceeds unity, product market equilibrium cannot be achieved unless a rise in income is associated with a rise in the rate of interest, and this means that the IS-curve must be positively sloped.

Total differentiation of Eqs. 13.2.1 and 13.2.2 with respect to m_s permits us to estimate the effect of an increase in the money supply. This implies that

$$0 = (1 - C_y - I_y)\left(\frac{dY}{dm_s}\right) - I_i\left(\frac{di}{dm_s}\right),$$

$$1 = L_y\left(\frac{dY}{dm_s}\right) + L_i\left(\frac{di}{dm_s}\right).$$

Using Cramer's Rule to solve for the change in income gives

$$\frac{dY}{dm_s} = \frac{\begin{vmatrix} 0 & -I_i \\ 1 & L_i \end{vmatrix}}{\Delta} = \frac{I_i}{\Delta}$$

where

$$\Delta = \begin{vmatrix} (1 - C_y - I_y) & -I_i \\ L_y & L_i \end{vmatrix} = L_i(1 - C_y - I_y) + L_y I_i. \qquad (13.2.5)$$

In the model of Chapter 3, investment was assumed to be a function only of the rate of interest. That model may now be thought of as a special case of the present model—namely, when $I_y = 0$. If this were the case, Δ would equal $L_i(1 - C_y) + L_y I_i$, and since this is definitely negative, we could conclude that an increase in the money supply (except in the extreme Keynesian case where $L_i \to \infty$) would always imply the expected result of an increase in income. However, with $I_y > 0$, the sign of Δ is ambiguous, and comparative-static analysis could easily predict that an increase in the money supply would cause the level of income to fall.

Stability analysis can help to avoid nonsense results that sometimes appear in comparative-static analysis. Assume that the rate of income change equals the difference between intended investment and saving and that money-market adjustments take place so rapidly relative to income adjustments that they may

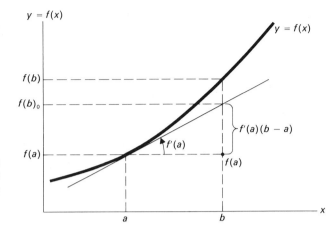

13|2|1
Linear approximation
of the value of a
function

be considered instantaneous. These assumptions imply the dynamic model,

$$\frac{dY}{dt} = I(Y, i) + C(Y) - Y, \tag{13.2.6}$$

$$0 = L(Y, i) - m_s. \tag{13.2.7}$$

Analysis of this dynamic model is complicated by the fact that the equations are not in linear form. Although we know how to deal with linear equations, non-linear ones tend to defy analysis, and we ought therefore to find a way to seek linear approximations. Accomplishing this end requires that we embark on a short digression.

Consider the function $y = f(x)$, which is depicted in Fig. 13.2.1, and suppose that we are trying to find the value of the function when $x = b$, in terms of what we know about it when $x = a$. If the value of the function at $x = a$ is $f(a)$ and we knew nothing else about it, our best guess as to the value of the function at $x = b$ would be that it had the same value as at $x = a$, namely, $f(b) = f(a)$ and, indeed, if the function turned out to be a straight line with zero slope, the approximation would be perfect.

The function depicted in Fig. 13.2.1 is not, however, a straight line with zero slope. Nevertheless, we can make headway if we know the slope (derivative) of the function at $x = a$, and the x-distance between points a and b. We could then improve the approximation by adding to the original approximation the product of the derivative of the function at $x = a$ times the distance, $b - a$. Thus the second approximation is

$$f(b) = f(a) + f'(a)(b - a), \tag{13.2.8}$$

where $f'(a)$ is the derivative with respect to x of the function at point $x = a$. This point is represented in Fig. 13.2.1 by the vertical coordinate $f(b)_0$.

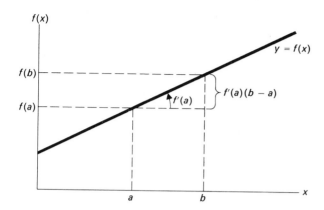

13|2|2
The value of a linear function at $x=b$.

Note that if the function had been a straight line, such as is depicted in Fig. 13.2.2, this second approximation would have been perfect. In the case of a straight line, it must always be the case that $f(b)$ exactly equals $f(a) + f'(a)(b - a)$.

In a nonlinear case expression 13.2.8 only represents an approximation. However, and this is the important point, if the distance between b and a is very small, the linear approximation will be a very good one, and this is the all-important circumstance from the point of view of stability analysis.*

Returning to the dynamic Keynesian model as expressed in Eqs. 13.2.6 and 13.2.7, we now attempt to put the equations in linear homogeneous form. To do this we liken the equilibrium values of income and the rate of interest to the point a of Fig. 13.2.1 and the actual values of Y and i to the point b. Consequently, the linear approximation for $I(Y, i)$ is

$$I(\bar{Y}, i) + I_y(Y - \bar{Y}) + I_i(i - i).$$

Similarly, the linear approximation for $C(Y)$ is

$$C(\bar{Y}) + C_y(Y - \bar{Y}).$$

Consequently, Eq. 13.2.6 may be replaced by the approximation

$$\frac{dY}{dt} = I(\bar{Y}, i) + C(\bar{Y}) + I_y(Y - \bar{Y}) + C_y(Y - \bar{Y}) + I_i(i - i) - \bar{Y} - (Y - \bar{Y}).$$

$$(13.2.9)$$

However, since

$$I(\bar{Y}, i) + C(\bar{Y}) = \bar{Y},$$

---

* Expression 13.2.8 represents an approximation of $f(b)$ which formally represents the linear terms of a Taylor expansion. The reader who wishes to see how the approximation may be improved and who is not familiar with Taylor's expansion should consult the appendix to this chapter.

Eq. 13.2.9 reduces to the linear homogeneous form,

$$\frac{dY}{dt} = [I_y + C_y - 1](Y - \bar{Y}) + I_i(i - \bar{i}). \tag{13.2.10}$$

The identical procedure may now be applied to Eq. 13.2.7 to obtain

$$0 = L_y(Y - \bar{Y}) + L_i(i - \bar{i}), \tag{13.2.11}$$

and we therefore see that the complete simultaneous equation system can be expressed in linear homogeneous form.

By inspection of Eqs. 13.2.10 and 13.2.11, we see immediately that we will have a solution of the form

$$Y = \bar{Y} + Me^{qt}, \tag{13.2.12}$$

where q is the characteristic root of the equation. This equation implies that

$$\frac{dY}{dt} = qMe^{qt}$$

and that

$$\frac{dY}{dt} = q(Y - \bar{Y}). \tag{13.2.13}$$

Utilizing 13.2.13 to replace the left-hand side of 13.2.10 with $q(Y - \bar{Y})$, and consolidating terms, we have

$$\begin{aligned} 0 &= [q + (1 - C_y - I_y)](Y - \bar{Y}) - I_i(i - \bar{i}) \\ 0 &= \qquad\qquad L_y(Y - \bar{Y}) + L_i(i - \bar{i}). \end{aligned} \tag{13.2.14}$$

If this set of equations is to be generally valid for all values of Y and i, it must be the case that the determinant formed by the coefficients equal zero.* Accordingly, the *characteristic determinant* is

$$\begin{vmatrix} q + (1 - C_y - I_y) & -I_i \\ L_y & L_i \end{vmatrix} = 0.$$

When we evaluate the determinant, we obtain the *characteristic equation*,

$$L_i q + L_i(1 - C_y - I_y) + I_i L_y = 0. \tag{13.2.15}$$

---

* As an illustration of this proposition, consider the simultaneous equations

$$a_{11}x_1 + a_{12}x_2 = 0,$$
$$a_{21}x_1 + a_{22}x_2 = 0.$$

If both of these equations are to hold regardless of the values of x_1 and x_2, it must be the case that $x_1 = -(a_{12}/a_{11})x_2$ and $x_1 = -(a_{22}/a_{21})x_2$. This means that $a_{11}a_{22} = a_{12}a_{21}$ and it therefore follows that the value of the determinant of coefficients,

$$\begin{vmatrix} a_{11} & a_{12} \\ a_{21} & a_{22} \end{vmatrix} = a_{11}a_{22} - a_{12}a_{21} = 0.$$

The expression $L_i(1 - C_y - I_y) + I_i L_y$ is simply the term Δ that represents the denominator of the comparative-static solution and it is sometimes called the *determinant of coefficients*. Since Eq. 13.2.15 may be written $L_i q + \Delta = 0$, we have

$$q = -\frac{\Delta}{L_i}.$$

Since q is the characteristic root of the differential equation (13.2.12) and since this root must be negative if the system is stable, it follows that the stability condition is

$$q = -\frac{\Delta}{L_i} < 0.$$

Since we also know that $L_i < 0$, stability clearly requires that Δ be negative, and the stability condition may therefore be written

$$\Delta = L_i(1 - C_y - I_y) + I_i L_y < 0.$$

When the stability condition is rearranged as

$$\left(\frac{1 - C_y - I_y}{I_i}\right) + \left(\frac{L_y}{L_i}\right) < 0,$$

we see from Eqs. 13.2.3 and 13.2.4 that the condition may be expressed in terms of the slopes of the *IS*- and *LM*-curves, namely, as

$$\left(\frac{di}{dY}\right)_{IS} - \left(\frac{di}{dY}\right)_{LM} < 0.$$

The stability condition therefore implies that the value of the slope of the *IS*-curve plus the value of the slope of the *LM*-curve with its sign changed must be negative.

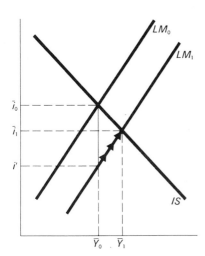

13|2|3
Stability of the Keynesian system: case I.

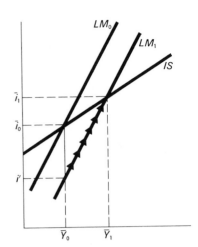

13|2|4
Stability of the Keynesian
System: case II.

We are now in a position to examine, via diagrammatic analysis, what the stability condition implies for comparative statics. In Fig. 13.2.3, the *IS*-curve has a negative slope and the *LM*-curve has a positive slope. Call this case I. The initial *LM*-curve is LM_0 and the initial equilibrium values of income and the rate of interest are at $\bar{Y}_0$ and $\bar{i}_0$, respectively. If an increase in the money supply causes *LM* to shift to LM_1, comparative-static analysis would predict that income would rise to $\bar{Y}_1$ and that the rate of interest would fall to $\bar{i}_1$. Dynamic analysis confirms this result. Via the dynamic assumption that money-market adjustments are instantaneous, the shift in the *LM*-curve implies that the rate of interest must immediately fall to i'. But at this rate of interest and income level $\bar{Y}_0$, intended investment exceeds saving and income therefore begins to rise. Since monetary adjustments are instantaneous, the system follows an upward path along the LM_1-curve until the new equilibrium is reached at $\bar{Y}_1$ and $\bar{i}_1$. This case obviously meets the stability condition, since the value of the slope of the negative *IS*-curve plus the value of the slope of the *LM*-curve with its sign changed must be negative.

Next consider case II, which is depicted in Fig. 13.2.4. Here it is assumed that the marginal propensity to invest exceeds the marginal propensity to save and the *IS*-curve is therefore positively sloped. The shift in the *LM*-curve to LM_1 causes an immediate drop in the rate of interest to i'. At income level $\bar{Y}_0$ this fall in the rate of interest implies that intended investment will be in excess of saving and that income will therefore rise. The path of the system follows the arrows along the LM_1-curve and reaches equilibrium as predicted by comparative statics at $\bar{Y}_1$ and $\bar{i}_1$. A rise in income would induce additional spending in excess of the rise in income if the interest rate remains constant. However, in this case the rate of interest that maintains monetary equilibrium rises faster as income expands than does the rate of interest that would maintain equilibrium in the product

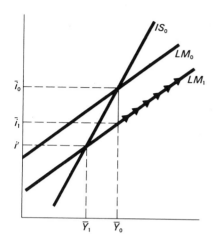

13|2|5
Stability of the Keynesian
system: case III.

market, and a stable equilibrium is therefore attained. Since the slope of the *LM*-curve is greater than the slope of the *IS*-curve, it is apparent that when we add the value of the slope of *IS* to the value of the slope of *LM* with its sign changed, the resultant sum is negative and the stability condition is therefore met.

Finally, consider Case III, which is depicted in Figure 13.2.5. The *IS*-curve is again positively sloped, but unlike case II, the *IS*-curve now has a steeper slope than the *LM*-curve and we therefore expect this to be an unstable case. Beginning at the initial equilibrium of $\bar{Y}_0$ and $\bar{i}_0$, comparative-static analysis predicts that the increase in the money supply which shifts the *LM*-curve to LM_1 will lower the level of income to $\bar{Y}_1$.

This result does not make sense. However, we require some knowledge of the dynamics of the situation to show us where the trouble lies. The increase in the money supply lowers the rate of interest to i' and this means that intended investment will exceed saving. Income now must rise and, via our assumption of instantaneous monetary adjustment, the path of the system will be along the LM_1-curve. As income rises, the rise in the rate of interest that provides monetary equilibrium is always less than the rise in the rate of interest that would be needed to equate intended investment with saving. Income therefore continues to expand indefinitely.

In this case we see that the comparative-static equilibrium solutions, $\bar{Y}_0$, $\bar{i}_0$, and $\bar{Y}_1$, $\bar{i}_i$, respectively, are erroneous since any deviation from these equilibrium points will lead to progressively larger deviations as time goes on. Thus the comparative-static result—that the shift of *LM* to LM_1 will cause income to fall to Y_1—is incorrect. Note that since the slope of the *IS*-curve exceeds the slope of the *LM*-curve, the value of the slope of *IS* added to the value of the slope of *LM* with its sign changed yields a positive value and the formal stability condition is violated.

What we have attempted to illustrate here is a fundamental proposition which is due to Samuelson,* and which he calls the *correspondence principle*. The principle states that it is sometimes impossible to determine the effect of shifts in certain parameters—for example, a change in the money supply—by means of comparative-static analysis. However, when dynamic assumptions are introduced and the model is tested for stability, those comparative-static results that are incompatible with the stability condition may be ruled out as erroneous. Thus the correspondence principle would rule out the comparative-static result of Case III above and this means that if an increase in the money supply changes income at all, the change in income must be positive.†

13.3 SOME EXTENSIONS OF THE CORRESPONDENCE PRINCIPLE

In the last section we saw that comparative-static solutions are erroneous if equilibrium is unstable, and we therefore found that stability analysis helps to distinguish correct from incorrect comparative-static results. It is possible to extend the correspondence principle to cover some additional territory.

First, it can be argued that any policy that narrows the stability range is, other things being equal, a bad policy. As an example of such a policy, it has been said that the Federal Reserve System has frequently followed a policy that is directed primarily toward the maintenance of stable interest rates rather than a stable level of income. Under an extreme form of such a policy, the money supply would always be changed in such a way as to maintain the interest rate constant and the LM-curve would therefore become a horizontal line. The effect of the policy therefore is to produce a situation that is identical to what would occur if the speculative demand for money were infinitely elastic with respect to the rate of interest. However, when $L_i \to \infty$, the stability condition reduces to

$$q = 1 - C_y - I_y < 0,$$

which means that the IS-curve can no longer be positively sloped if the system is to be dynamically stable. If the marginal propensity to spend, $C_y + I_y$, is greater than unity, an increase in income would induce additional spending in excess of

---

* Samuelson, *Foundations, op. cit.*, Chapter 9.

† This analysis confirms that an increase in the money supply can never lower the level of income. Note, however, that no similar statement can be made about the rate of interest, which may either rise or fall. Thus the correspondence principle does not guarantee that we will always be able to tell the direction of change of all the variables of the model.

As an exercise the reader may wish to analyze the effect of an increase in government purchases or of any other autonomous change that shifts the IS-schedule so that he may show that an increase in government purchases can never lower the level of income. The student may then wish to extend the analysis to see if definite statements can be made about the direction of change of any or all of the individual variables—income, the rate of interest, investment, consumption—following an autonomous change in any of the parameters of the system.

the increase in income unless the rate of interest rises and inhibits the increase in investment. However, if the monetary authority acts always to prevent any change in the rate of interest, this brake on expansion is lost, and the system, which otherwise might have been stable, becomes unstable. Looked at in terms of the three cases depicted in Figs. 13.2.3, 13.2.4, and 13.2.5, the adoption of the fixed-interest-rate policy would leave Case I as the only stable situation.

Of course, the fact that some policy raises the value of the characteristic root does not mean that the policy renders the system unstable unless the policy causes the root to become positive. However, going back to Eq. 13.2.13,

$$\frac{dY}{dt} = q(Y - \bar{Y}),$$

we see that the speed of adjustment depends upon the size of the initial displacement, $Y - \bar{Y}$, and upon the value of the root. Thus the smaller the root (the greater its absolute value), the quicker a stable system adjusts to disequilibrium. Thus the fixed-interest-rate monetary policy which raises the value of the root to

$$q = 1 - C_y - I_y$$

is an inferior policy not only because it increases the likelihood of instability, but also because it slows down the speed at which the system recovers from shocks.

A second possible application of the correspondence principle is that the stability conditions might provide some clues as to the actual values of certain parameters about which we know nothing either from empirical research, from *a priori* reasoning, or from intuitive guesses. However, in order to take such a step, we also have to add the assumption that our model is an adequate representation of the real world.

To illustrate, consider again the Keynesian model of the last section. Empirical research has disclosed considerable information about the value of the marginal propensity to consume, about the association between the demand for money balances and the volume of transactions, and about the interest responsiveness of investment to changes in the rate of interest. However, the parameter about which we know very little is the marginal propensity to invest, I_y. Suppose, in fact, that we know nothing at all about the value of I_y, but that we do have good estimates of the values of the other parameters of the system. We might then utilize these other known values together with the stability condition in order to determine the range within which I_y must lie. The stability condition may be arranged as

$$I_y < 1 - C_y + \frac{I_i L_y}{L_i},$$

and this puts an upper bound on the value of the marginal propensity to invest. In this manner we might be able to ascertain the range of values within which I_y must lie, even though we have no other knowledge about its actual value.

It must be emphasized that we are treading on very flimsy ground when we try to use a simple model of the present sort to make statements about the probable value of some unknown parameter. First of all, we have to assume that the system is actually stable. And second, we have to have a great deal of confidence in the ability of our model to describe the real world. In an economic system where most magnitudes are growing all the time, it is certain that equilibrium, even if it is stable, is of a dynamic rather than a stationary sort. Since the present model is constructed on the presumption of the existence of stationary equilibrium, and is vastly over-simplified as well, we cannot have very much confidence in its ability to tell us much about the value of the marginal propensity to invest. Of course, these considerations do not rule out the possibility that a more elaborate or "realistic" model could serve this purpose.

Third, since there are certain comparative-static results that can be ruled out as erroneous, stability analysis can serve as a very powerful error detection device. For example, it has been argued within the framework of a static linear national-income model, that an increase in government purchases, or a reduction in tax rates, might so raise the level of income that the induced increase in tax yield equals or overcomes the effect of the initial change, and that government purchases could therefore be raised or tax rates reduced without these changes causing any permanent deficit.

Consider again the static linear model of Chapter 2. The equations of the model are

$$Y = C + I + G,$$
$$C = a + b(Y - T), \tag{13.3.1}$$
$$T = u + vY, \tag{13.3.2}$$

and the equilibrium level of income is

$$\bar{Y} = \frac{I + G + a - bu}{1 - b(1 - v)}. \tag{13.3.3}$$

An increase in government purchases raises the equilibrium level of income by

$$d\bar{Y} = \frac{dG}{1 - b(1 - v)},$$

and it therefore induces a change in tax collections of

$$dT = v(d\bar{Y}) = \frac{v(dG)}{1 - b(1 - v)}.$$

It follows that if $dT \geq dG$,

$$1 \leq \frac{v}{1 - b(1 - v)},$$

and this implies that

$$(1 - b)(1 - v) \leq 0. \tag{13.3.4}$$

Consequently, if the marginal propensity to consume disposable income or the marginal tax rate exceed unity, the rise in G will generate more than enough additional revenue to offset itself. Neither assumption is likely to be valid, and this should be enough to defeat the proposition. Nevertheless, let us go on with the dynamics of the case.

The usual dynamic hypothesis is that

$$\frac{dY}{dt} = (I + G) - (S + T).$$

Using 13.3.1 and 13.3.2 to substitute for saving and taxes yields the differential equation

$$\frac{dY}{dt} = (G + I + a - bu) - [1 - b(1 - v)]Y,$$

which we may write as

$$\frac{dY}{dt} = -[1 - b(1 - v)](Y - \bar{Y}), \tag{13.3.5}$$

when Y is replaced by its displacement from equilibrium plus its equilibrium value.

Since the root of the differential equation is $-[1 - b(1 - v)]$, stability of equilibrium requires that the product of the marginal propensity to consume disposable income and one minus the marginal tax rate, $b(1 - v)$, must not exceed unity. If this marginal propensity to consume national product, as $b(1 - v)$ is often called, exceeds unity, an increase in income of a dollar would raise consumption spending by more than a dollar and this would mean that output could never catch up to demand.

We have seen that the stability condition is

$$1 - b(1 - v) > 0, \tag{13.3.6}$$

and that the condition under which a rise in G would generate at least an equivalent amount of induced tax yield is

$$(1 - b)(1 - v) \leq 0. \tag{13.3.4}$$

Suppose now that income taxation is absent. In this case the stability condition reduces to $1 - b > 0$, while 13.3.4 reduces to $1 - b \leq 0$, and the two conditions therefore plainly contradict each other.

Evidently, the proposition at issue implies that the model would be unstable in the absence of income taxation and that the only thing that saves the system from blowing up (or down) is the presence of income taxation. Thus, bearing in

mind that the model is excessively simple and that the idea of stationary equilibrium in a dynamic world is an analytical artifact, it nevertheless seems probable
that anyone who tries to tell us that a rise in G will generate additional tax collections in an amount equal to or greater than the change in G, is excessively
optimistic.

Finally, and this may be the most important application of all, stability
analysis plays a central role in the theory of economic policy. In examining the
static theory we saw that a set of n targets generally implied a unique simultaneous
solution for n policy instruments. In practice the exact form of the equations of
the system and their equilibrium solutions are rarely known. The question then
is whether some rule of thumb can be devised that will permit policy to move the
system toward the attainment of its targets, even though the information needed
to solve the simultaneous equations is insufficient.

To illustrate the problem as well as its solution, we consider Professor
Mundell's discussion of the problem of reconciling full employment with balance-
of-payments equilibrium under fixed exchange rates.* In Fig. 13.3.1 we measure
the governmental budgetary surplus vertically and the rate of interest horizontally.
We assume that fiscal policy has control over the budget while monetary policy
controls the rate of interest. The curve XX' is described by Mundell as the "internal balance" function, and it represents the combinations of interest rates and
associated budgetary surpluses that provide full employment. Evidently, XX'
must have a negative slope because a smaller budgetary surplus (greater deficit)
would be inflationary, unless this were offset by a higher rate of interest. For the
same reason, it is evident that any point to the left of XX' represents an inflationary situation, while any point to the right implies recession.

Consider next the "external balance" FF' curve. This curve traces out the
combination of budgetary surpluses and interest rates that yield equilibrium in
the balance of payments. This curve, too, must have a negative slope. A smaller
budgetary surplus would be associated with a higher level of income. Since this
would imply a higher level of imports, a balance-of-payments deficit would result
unless foreigners could be induced to purchase domestic securities in response to
a higher rate of interest; i.e., unless there is an offsetting capital inflow. Because,
with a given budget, a higher rate of interest would increase capital inflows, any
point to the right of FF' implies a balance of payments surplus while any point
to the left implies a deficit.

Point E is the equilibrium point at which the economy attains both full
employment and balance-of-payments equilibrium. This situation is associated
with values of $\bar{B}$ and $\bar{i}$ for the values of the respective policy instruments. The
difficulty is that the exact shape or location of the XX' and FF' curves is not
known. Consequently, the magnitude of the appropriate changes in the instru-

---

* Robert A. Mundell, "The Appropriate Use of Monetary and Fiscal Policy for Internal and
External Stability," *International Monetary Fund Staff Papers*, March, 1962.

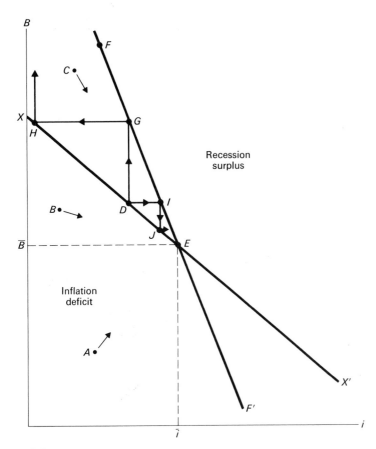

13|3|1
Assigning instruments to targets.

ment variables is not known. And in some cases, the direction in which some policy variable should be changed is not even clear.

Usually, the information available to the policy maker is of such a sort that it discloses only the general range in which the economy lies. We may know that there is a balance of payments deficit combined with inflation, or a deficit combined with a recession, and so on, but that is often the extent of our information. In 1961 the economy suffered from unemployment and a balance-of-payments deficit and was therefore at a point such as C. Here the direction in which the instruments must be changed is clear: the interest rate must be raised and the budget must be eased, although by how much remains unknown. Since 1966 the policy problem has been even more complicated. The balance-of-payments deficit has persisted and the economy has been beset by inflation. Thus during this period we must have been at a point such as A or B. But at which point? If at A, the interest rate should be raised and the budget tightened; but if we are at B, the budget should be eased despite the presence of inflation. Is there, then, a rule of thumb that permits the appropriate policy response to be made given the presence only of qualitative information that places us in one of the four ranges but that does not delineate the four *quadrants* that have point E as their origin?

Imagine that the economy is at point D. It enjoys full employment but suffers from a balance-of-payments deficit. Now imagine that fiscal policy is used to eliminate the deficit and the budget is tightened so that point G is reached. At this point the deficit is eliminated because the fall in income reduces the demand for imports. However, if we now desire to utilize monetary policy to eliminate unemployment, the interest rate will have to be lowered to reach XX' at point H. But this lower interest rate produces a capital outflow, and the net result is that the new payments deficit is larger than the original deficit, while the level of employment is the same as it was at the outset.

Clearly, this set of policy responses produces a divergence away from E, and if continued, will bring about successive deficits and recessions, each of which will be greater than the one that preceded it.

Starting again at D, let us now assume that monetary policy is employed to eliminate the deficit. This will move the economy to I and create unemployment. The budget must now be eased to attain full employment at J. Although this creates a payments deficit, it is obvious that the deficit is smaller than initially and that, if this sequence of responses is continued, full employment and balance-of-payments equilibrium will soon be reached.

Evidently, the solution to our problem of insufficient information is to ignore the simultaneous relation between all instruments and targets, and instead to assign specific responsibility for a single target to a single instrument. Moreover, the criterion by which this assignment must be made is a stability criterion. Incorrect assignment produces ever wider divergences of the variables from their target values, while correct assignment produces an orderly progression toward the target values.

In the present case a stable solution is reached if fiscal policy is assigned responsibility for full employment while monetary policy is assigned responsibility for the balance of payments. The reason for this, of course, is that fiscal policy has a relatively greater effect on internal balance than it does on the balance of payments, while the opposite is the case for monetary policy. In other words, correct assignment depends upon the fact that the slope of the FF' curve is steeper than the slope of XX'. How do we know this is the case?

Consider point D again. The economy is at full employment and the level of income is the same as at E. If imports are a function of the level of income while exports depends on foreign income, it must be the case that the trade balance (exports minus imports) is the same at D as at E. However, at D the interest rate is lower than at E. Consequently, if the balance of payments is in equilibrium at E, there must be a deficit at D, and this must mean that external balance could be attained only with a higher interest rate. It follows that the FF' curve must have a steeper slope than the XX' curve.

To conclude: We have seen that the correct assignment of instruments to targets helps to solve the problem of missing information. But note also that the problem of policy coordination has been simplified. As long as each instrument pursues its single target, the desired overall result will be attained without any explicit coordination.

13.4 REVIEW AND PREVIEW

The importance of stability analysis should require little further comment. Stability analysis permits the economist to distinguish correct from erroneous comparative-static results; it assists him to detect analytical error; it facilitates his efforts to distinguish between good and bad policies; and it may even serve to provide him with hints about the values of unknown parameters.

In order to test a simultaneous equation system for stability of equilibrium, the analyst first puts the model into dynamic form by introducing dynamic assumptions that describe the rates of reaction of the several variables of the model to disequilibrium. He then usually attempts to simplify his problem by transforming the model into linear form. If the linear approximations represent the respective partial derivates at equilibrium multiplied by the displacements from equilibrium, the result is to produce not only a set of simultaneous linear equations, but a set of homogeneous ones as well.

Stability of equilibrium in a differential equation system is obtained if the real parts of all the characteristic roots are negative. In a difference equation model stability of equilibrium requires the moduli of all the roots to lie within the unit circle of the complex plane. In the example of this chapter, the problem of stability analysis was simplified because the model was constructed in such a way that the simultaneous differential equations could, by means of simple substitution, be reduced into a first-order differential equation in one variable. Since it is a simple matter to find the characteristic root of such an equation, the analysis was straightforward and required little technical knowledge beyond what we learned in Chapter 7.

However, complications do set in as soon as there are several compartments to the model and where (unlike the example of this chapter) it cannot be assumed that adjustment to disequilibrium is instantaneous in all but one of the compartments. In the next chapter we shall attempt to eliminate the need for such simplification by setting forth the general principles of stability analysis in simultaneous differential and difference equation models.

A selected bibliography relating to the material of Part III is provided at the end of Chapter 15.

Appendix to Chapter 13

LINEAR APPROXIMATION OF A FUNCTION

Consider a general polynomial equation such as

$$f(x) = a_0 + a_1(x - b) + a_2(x - b)^2 + a_3(x - b)^3 + \cdots + a_n(x - b)^n,$$
$$(13.A.1)$$

where b is some arbitrary value. When we take the successive derivatives of this function with respect to x, we obtain the set of equations,

$$f'(x) = a_1 + 2a_2(x - b) + 3a_3(x - b)^2 + \cdots + na_n(x - b)^{n-1},$$
$$f''(x) = 2a_2 + 6a_3(x - b) + \cdots + n(n - 1)a_n(x - b)^{n-2},$$
$$f'''(x) = 6a_3 + \cdots + n(n - 1)(n - 2)a_n(x - b)^{n-3},$$
$$f^n(x) = n!\,a_n.$$

If we evaluate these equations at $x = b$ and solve for the coefficients, we obtain

$$a_0 = f(b),$$
$$a_1 = f'(b),$$
$$a_2 = \frac{f''(b)}{2},$$
$$a_3 = \frac{f'''(b)}{3!},$$
$$\vdots$$
$$a_n = \frac{f^n(b)}{n!}.$$

These results imply that the value of the function at any point x may be expressed in terms of the value of the function and its derivatives at any arbitrary point b. In other words, Eq. 13.A.1 may be written

$$f(x) = f(b) + f'(b)(x - b)$$
$$+ \frac{f''(b)}{2}(x - b)^2 + \frac{f'''(b)}{3!}(x - b)^3 + \cdots + \frac{f^n(b)}{n!}(x - b)^n.$$

When we return to our original problem of approximating the value of the function at some point, we see that the linear approximation merely consists of the first two terms of the general equation, namely $f(b) + f'(b)(x - b)$, and that if we wish to improve the approximation, we may add the second term,

$$\frac{f''(b)}{2}(x - b)^2,$$

and if that is not good enough, we may go on to the fourth, fifth, and nth terms.

CHAPTER 14

General Principles of Stability
Analysis in Simultaneous Equation Models

14.1 SIMULTANEOUS DIFFERENTIAL EQUATIONS

In the last chapter we saw that one step in the analysis of the stability of equilibrium is the transformation of the dynamic equations of the model into linear approximations. Inasmuch as we are now familiar with this step we shall permit ourselves to bypass it in the present discussion. Moreover, we shall begin with the simplest kind of two-equation model in order to obtain a firm grasp of the principles involved. Once we understand the essentials of this simple model we can readily move on to more complicated cases and, indeed, speak in perfectly general terms.

The most important thing to be understood in attempting to analyze the stability of equilibrium of a system of simultaneous differential or difference equations is that a dynamic system of simultaneous equations has a single characteristic equation. Once this equation is derived, stability analysis proceeds exactly as though the original model had consisted of a single differential equation in one variable and its time derivatives, or as a single difference equation in one variable and its own lagged values.

To illustrate this most important point, we attempt to show that a simultaneous equation system such as

$$\frac{dx_1}{dt} = a_{11}x_1 + a_{12}x_2,$$

$$\frac{dx_2}{dt} = a_{21}x_1 + a_{22}x_2$$

can be rearranged to yield equations of the form

$$\frac{d^2x_1}{dt^2} + c_1 \frac{dx_1}{dt} + c_2x_1 = 0,$$

$$\frac{d^2x_2}{dt^2} + c_1 \frac{dx_2}{dt} + c_2x_2 = 0,$$

where the coefficients are the same in both equations. If this is the case, both equations have the same characteristic equation and we may therefore say that the entire simultaneous equation system has a single characteristic equation.

Throughout this chapter we take the simple Leontief open model as a prototype of the kind of model with which economists are frequently concerned. We shall begin with a two-sector model in order to illustrate the basic principles, and we then move on to general cases.

In the simplest static two-industry Leontief model we have

$$\begin{aligned} x_1 &= a_{11}x_1 + a_{12}x_2 + y_1, \\ x_2 &= a_{21}x_1 + a_{22}x_2 + y_2, \end{aligned} \tag{14.1.1}$$

where the x_j's are gross output levels, the y_j's are the final demands, and the a_{ij}'s are the interindustry input coefficients. Typically, the dynamic assumption regarding the behavior of production when supply and demand are not in equilibrium is that output in each industry changes at a rate which is equal to the difference between the level of sales and the level of production. Consequently, we specify the dynamic model,*

$$\frac{dx_1}{dt} = [a_{11}x_1 + a_{12}x_2 + y_1] - x_1 = (a_{11} - 1)x_1 + a_{12}x_2 + y_1,$$

$$\frac{dx_2}{dt} = [a_{21}x_1 + a_{22}x_2 + y_2] - x_2 = a_{21}x_1 + (a_{22} - 1)x_2 + y_2.$$

Our model consists of two simultaneous linear first-order nonhomogeneous differential equations in two variables. Our problem is to see if these equations can be expressed as homogeneous differential equation in only one variable and its time derivatives. This can be accomplished by use of a most important concept known as the differential operator, D.

---

* To generalize the analysis, system 14.1.2 is frequently written

$$\frac{dx_1}{dt} = k_1[a_{11}x_1 + a_{12}x_2 + y_1 - x_1],$$

$$\frac{dx_2}{dt} = k_2[a_{21}x_1 + a_{22}x_2 + y_2 - x_2],$$

where k_1 and k_2 are positive "reaction coefficients" that allow for differences in the speed of adjustment. For present purposes it is best to ignore differences in adjustment speeds. However, the effect of such differences will be discussed in the next chapter.

It is possible to write the derivative dy/dt as Dy, where the operator D conveys the instruction to take the first derivative with respect to time of y. The important thing about D is that it can be treated as an algebraic quantity and can be manipulated as such just as though it were a coefficient or a variable. Similarly, d^2y/dt^2 can be written D^2y, where the notation conveys the instruction to take the second derivative with respect to time of variable y. Until the time arrives when it is desirable to follow the instruction to differentiate with respect to time, D^2 may also be treated as an algebraic quantity that has a value equal to D times D.*

Using operator notation, we may write Eq. 14.1.2 as

$$Dx_1 = (a_{11} - 1)x_1 + a_{12}x_2 + y_1,$$
$$Dx_2 = a_{21}x_1 + (a_{22} - 1)x_2 + y_2, \tag{14.1.3}$$

or as

$$(1 - a_{11} + D)x_1 - a_{12}x_2 = y_1,$$
$$-a_{21}x_1 + (1 - a_{22} + D)x_2 = y_2. \tag{14.1.4}$$

To solve for x_1 and x_2, we apply Cramer's Rule and obtain

$$x_1 = \frac{\begin{vmatrix} y_1 & -a_{12} \\ y_2 & (1 - a_{22} + D) \end{vmatrix}}{\begin{vmatrix} (1 - a_{11} + D) & -a_{12} \\ -a_{21} & (1 - a_{22} + D) \end{vmatrix}}, \qquad x_2 = \frac{\begin{vmatrix} (1 - a_{11} + D) & y_1 \\ -a_{21} & y_2 \end{vmatrix}}{\begin{vmatrix} (1 - a_{11} + D) & -a_{12} \\ -a_{21} & (1 - a_{22} + D) \end{vmatrix}}$$

$$\tag{14.1.5}$$

where, it should carefully be noted, the denominator determinants are the same in both cases. Evaluating these determinants, we obtain

$$\{D^2 + [(1 - a_{11}) + (1 - a_{22})]D + (1 - a_{11})(1 - a_{22}) - a_{12}a_{21}\}x_1$$
$$= (1 - a_{22} + D)y_1 + a_{12}y_2,$$

$$\{D^2 + [(1 - a_{11}) + (1 - a_{22})]D + (1 - a_{11})(1 - a_{22}) - a_{12}a_{21}\}x_2$$
$$= a_{21}y_1 + (1 - a_{11} + D)y_2. \tag{14.1.6}$$

---

* Note that if all the operators D, D^2, and so on can be treated as algebraic quantities, a differential equation such as

$$a_0 \frac{d^ny}{dt^n} + a_1 \frac{d^{n-1}y}{dt^{n-1}} + \cdots + a_n y = 0,$$

could be written as

$$a_0 D^n y + a_1 D^{n-1} y + \cdots + a_n y = 0,$$

or as

$$(a_0 D^n + a_1 D^{n-1} + \cdots + a_n)y = 0,$$

and the characteristic equation can therefore immediately be identified.

The next step is to multiply through by x_1 and x_2 in the respective equations and to follow the operator instruction to differentiate. Since the derivative of a constant is zero, the terms Dy_1 and Dy_2 are zero, and we are therefore left with the set of second-order nonhomogeneous differential equations,

$$\frac{d^2x_1}{dt^2} + [(1 - a_{11}) + (1 - a_{22})]\frac{dx_1}{dt} + [(1 - a_{11})(1 - a_{22}) - a_{12}a_{21}]x_1$$
$$= (1 - a_{22})y_1 + a_{12}y_2,$$

$$\frac{d^2x_2}{dt^2} + [(1 - a_{11}) + (1 - a_{22})]\frac{dx_2}{dt} + [(1 - a_{11})(1 - a_{22}) - a_{12}a_{21}]x_2$$
$$= a_{21}y_1 + (1 - a_{11})y_2.$$
$$(14.1.7)$$

The time has now arrived when it is useful to take a summary look at what has happened:

1. The original two simultaneous first-order differential equations in two variables have been expressed as two second-order differential equations in a single variable and its own time derivatives. As a general rule it is the case that if we have a system of n simultaneous first-order differential equations in n variables, the system may be rearranged so as to yield n differential equations of order n, each one of which has as its variables x_i and its own time derivatives, and each one of which has identical coefficients on the left-hand side.

2. Since the respective coefficients on the left-hand side of the equations are identical, it follows that both equations have the same characteristic equation, and thus the entire simultaneous equation system has a single characteristic equation. Thus, if x_1 is stable, x_2 must also be stable, and the entire system is then dynamically stable. The solutions will be of the form

$$x_1 = \bar{x}_1 + m_{11}e^{q_1t} + m_{12}e^{q_2t},$$
$$x_2 = \bar{x}_2 + m_{21}e^{q_1t} + m_{22}e^{q_2t},$$

and the entire system will be dynamically stable if it can be ascertained that the real parts of the characteristic roots, q_1 and q_2, are both negative.

3. Inspection of Eqs. 14.1.7 shows immediately that the characteristic equation is

$$q^2 + [(1 - a_{11}) + (1 - a_{22})]q + [(1 - a_{11})(1 - a_{22}) - a_{12}a_{21}] = 0.$$
$$(14.1.8)$$

Going back to 14.1.5, we see that the characteristic equation is merely the expanded form of the determinant in the denominators with the roots q replacing the operator D, and with the determinant set equal to zero. We therefore define

$$\begin{vmatrix} (1 - a_{11} + q) & -a_{12} \\ -a_{21} & (1 - a_{22} + q) \end{vmatrix} = |I - A + qI| = 0 \qquad (14.1.9)$$

as the *characteristic determinant*, where $|I - A|$ is the determinant of the Leontief matrix, namely

$$|I - A| = \begin{vmatrix} 1 - a_{11} & -a_{12} \\ -a_{21} & 1 - a_{22} \end{vmatrix}, \tag{14.1.10}$$

and, as a general matter, is designated as the *determinant of coefficients*.

4. The equilibrium solutions are, as expected, the same as in the static model. At equilibrium the time derivatives in Eqs. 14.1.6 and 14.1.7 are zero so that the system reduces to the result of Chapter 4,

$$\bar{x}_1 = \frac{(1 - a_{22})}{|I - A|} y_1 + \frac{a_{12}}{|I - A|} y_2,$$

$$\bar{x}_2 = \frac{a_{21}}{|I - A|} y_1 + \frac{(1 - a_{11})}{|I - A|} y_2, \tag{14.1.11}$$

We have seen that the original set of two simultaneous first-order differential equations could be reduced to a set of second-order equations of the form

$$\frac{d^2 x_1}{dt^2} + c_1 \frac{dx_1}{dt} + c_2 x_1 = k_1,$$

$$\frac{d^2 x_2}{dt^2} + c_1 \frac{dx_1}{dt} + c_2 x_2 = k_2, \tag{14.1.12}$$

where the c's and k's are shorthand notation for the respective coefficients and right-hand-side constants of Eqs. 14.1.7. If we now follow the conventional procedure for obtaining a solution, we replace x_i by $\bar{x}_i + u_i$, where u_i is the displacement of x_i from its equilibrium value, and this has the effect of reducing the equations to the homogeneous form,

$$\frac{d^2 x_1}{dt^2} + c_1 \frac{dx_1}{dt} + c_2(x_1 - \bar{x}_1) = 0,$$

$$\frac{d^2 x_2}{dt^2} + c_1 \frac{dx_2}{dt} + c_2(x_2 - \bar{x}_2) = 0. \tag{14.1.13}$$

Proceeding with the conventional means of obtaining a solution, we attempt the trial values,

$$x_i = \bar{x}_i + m_i e^{qt}, \tag{14.1.14}$$

which imply that

$$\frac{dx_i}{dt} = qm_i e^{qt} = q(x_i - \bar{x}_i) \tag{14.1.15}$$

and

$$\frac{d^2 x_i}{dt^2} = q^2(x_i - \bar{x}_i).$$

Substituting these trial values into 14.1.13, we obtain

$$[q^2 + c_1 q + c_2](x_1 - \bar{x}_1) = 0,$$
$$[q^2 + c_1 q + c_2](x_2 - \bar{x}_2) = 0. \qquad (14.1.16)$$

If these equations are to be valid regardless of the values of the displacements, it must be the case that

$$q^2 + c_1 q + c_2 = 0, \qquad (14.1.17)$$

and this, then, is the characteristic equation.

Our procedure thus far has been unnecessarily involved because it has been our purpose to demonstrate that a set of simultaneous differential equations has a single characteristic equation. It is now time to simplify matters. Note that Eq. 14.1.17 is exactly the same as the expression

$$D^2 + [(1 - a_{11}) + (1 - a_{22})]D + [(1 - a_{11})(1 - a_{22}) - a_{12}a_{21}]$$

of the left-hand side of Eqs. 14.1.6 with the root q replacing the differential operator D. This suggests that a less involved way of deriving the characteristic equation is available.

Suppose we begin by taking the initial set of simultaneous differential equations (14.1.2), that we calculate the equilibrium values of the variables (14.1.11), and that we replace each variable by its equilibrium value plus its displacement. This would cause the constant terms to drop out and we could then write the system in the homogeneous form,

$$\frac{dx_1}{dt} = (a_{11} - 1)(x_1 - \bar{x}_1) + a_{12}(x_2 - \bar{x}_2),$$
$$\frac{dx_2}{dt} = a_{21}(x_1 - \bar{x}_1) + (a_{22} - 1)(x_2 - \bar{x}_2). \qquad (14.1.18)$$

Next, if we use the trial solution obtained from 14.1.15 to replace the left-hand terms with $q(x_1 - \bar{x}_1)$ and $q(x_2 - \bar{x}_2)$, and rearrange the expressions, we get

$$[q + (1 - a_{11})](x_1 - \bar{x}_1) - a_{12}(x_2 - \bar{x}_2) = 0,$$
$$-a_{21}(x_1 - \bar{x}_1) + [q + (1 - a_{22})](x_2 - \bar{x}_2) = 0. \qquad (14.1.19)$$

If these equations are to hold regardless of whether or not the displacements equal zero, the determinant formed by the coefficients must be zero. Consequently, we must have

$$\begin{vmatrix} q + (1 - a_{11}) & -a_{12} \\ -a_{21} & q + (1 - a_{22}) \end{vmatrix} = 0.$$

When this characteristic determinant is evaluated, we get the characteristic equation,

$$q^2 + [(1 - a_{11}) + (1 - a_{22})]q + [(1 - a_{11})(1 - a_{22}) - a_{12}a_{21}] = 0,$$
$$(14.1.8)$$

which, via our shorthand notation, we write as

$$q^2 + c_1 q + c_2 = 0. \qquad (14.1.17)$$

In summary: This discussion shows that it is necessary merely to put the model into linear homogeneous form; then to substitute the trial solution and to form the characteristic determinant; and finally to evaluate this determinant to obtain the characteristic equation.

Analysis of the model for stability of equilibrium is facilitated if we recall that the characteristic determinant is

$$|qI + (I - A)| = \begin{vmatrix} q + (1 - a_{11}) & -a_{12} \\ -a_{21} & q + (1 - a_{22}) \end{vmatrix} = 0, \qquad (14.1.9)$$

and that the determinant of coefficients is

$$|I - A| = \begin{vmatrix} (1 - a_{11}) & -a_{12} \\ -a_{21} & (1 - a_{22}) \end{vmatrix}. \qquad (14.1.10)$$

As can readily be seen from inspection of the determinant of coefficients, the coefficient c_1 of the characteristic equation is the sum of the elements of the principal diagonal of $|I - A|$, and it therefore follows from our earlier discussion of the rule of signs that the sum of the elements of the principal diagonal of $|I - A|$ is the sum of the characteristic roots with the sign of this sum reversed. Observe also that the elements $1 - a_{11}$ and $1 - a_{22}$ are the first-order principal minors* of the determinant of coefficients and that c_1 is the sum of these first-order minors.

The coefficient c_2 is the product of the characteristic roots. Since $c_2 = (1 - a_{11})(1 - a_{22}) - a_{12}a_{21} = |I - A|$, it follows that the value of the determinant of coefficients equals the product of the roots.

---

* For those who bypassed the Appendix to Chapter 4, a principal minor is a minor of an element of the principal diagonal of a determinant. If we have the determinant

$$\begin{vmatrix} b_{11} & b_{12} & b_{13} \\ b_{21} & b_{22} & b_{23} \\ b_{31} & b_{32} & b_{33} \end{vmatrix},$$

the first-order principal minors are the elements b_{11}, b_{22}, and b_{33}, while the second-order principal minors are the determinants

$$\begin{vmatrix} b_{11} & b_{12} \\ b_{21} & b_{22} \end{vmatrix}, \quad \begin{vmatrix} b_{11} & b_{13} \\ b_{31} & b_{33} \end{vmatrix}, \quad \begin{vmatrix} b_{22} & b_{23} \\ b_{32} & b_{33} \end{vmatrix}.$$

Stability of equilibrium requires the real parts of the roots to be negative. Assuming, for the moment, that all roots are real, it is evident that since $c_2 = |I - A|$ is the product of the roots and $c_1 = [(1 - a_{11}) + (1 - a_{22})]$ is the sum of the roots with its sign changed, the system will be stable if c_1 and c_2 are both positive. This condition is satisfied if the determinant of coefficients $|I - A|$ is positive, and if the first-order principal minors, $(1 - a_{11})$ and $(1 - a_{22})$, are positive.

Before moving on to the three-industry case, it should be observed that the characteristic determinant can be expressed either as

$$|qI + (I - A)| = \begin{vmatrix} q + (1 - a_{11}) & -a_{12} \\ -a_{21} & q + (1 - a_{22}) \end{vmatrix} = 0,$$

or as

$$|(A - I) - qI| = \begin{vmatrix} (a_{11} - 1) - q & a_{12} \\ a_{21} & (a_{22} - 1) - q \end{vmatrix} = 0.$$

The characteristic equation in either case is the same. However, the determinant of coefficients now has the signs of its elements reversed. Thus while

$$|I - A| = \begin{vmatrix} 1 - a_{11} & -a_{12} \\ -a_{21} & 1 - a_{22} \end{vmatrix} = |A - I| = \begin{vmatrix} a_{11} - 1 & a_{12} \\ a_{21} & a_{22} - 1 \end{vmatrix},$$

the signs of the first-order principal minors are reversed.

The rule of signs requires that all coefficients of the characteristic equation be positive. When the characteristic equation is expressed as $|qI + (I - A)| = 0$, this condition implies that the principal minors be positive and that the determinant $|I - A|$ be positive. On the other hand, when the characteristic determinant is expressed as $|(A - I) - qI| = 0$, we see that the principal minors of $|A - I|$ are $a_{11} - 1$ and $a_{22} - 1$, which will be negative if $1 - a_{11}$ and $1 - a_{22}$ are positive, and it therefore follows that the first-order principal minors must now be negative. Since $|A - I| = |I - A|$, the value of the determinant remains positive. This implies that when a characteristic determinant is expressed as

$$|qI + (I - A)| = 0,$$

the rule of signs requires that the determinant and its principal minors be positive, but when the characteristic equation is expressed as

$$|(A - I) - qI| = 0,$$

the determinant and its principal minors must have the opposite sign. Much confusion can be avoided if it is later recalled that apparent differences in stability conditions are sometimes solely attributable to the fact that the way the characteristic equation is expressed is sometimes reversed.

Let us now move to the three-industry case. The model is

$$\frac{dx_1}{dt} = a_{11}x_1 + a_{12}x_2 + a_{13}x_3 + y_1 - x_1,$$

$$\frac{dx_2}{dt} = a_{21}x_1 + a_{22}x_2 + a_{23}x_3 + y_2 - x_2,$$

$$\frac{dx_3}{dt} = a_{31}x_1 + a_{32}x_2 + a_{33}x_3 + y_3 - x_3.$$

When each x_i is replaced by its equilibrium value plus its displacement from equilibrium, and when the trial solution

$$\frac{dx_i}{dt} = q(x_i - \bar{x}_i)$$

is substituted on the left-hand side, it becomes possible immediately to form the characteristic determinant

$$|qI + (I - A)| = \begin{vmatrix} q + (1 - a_{11}) & -a_{12} & -a_{13} \\ -a_{21} & q + (1 - a_{22}) & -a_{23} \\ -a_{31} & -a_{32} & q + (1 - a_{33}) \end{vmatrix} = 0.$$

When the determinant is evaluated, we get a characteristic polynomial of the form

$$q^3 + c_1 q^2 + c_2 q + c_3 = 0,$$

where

$$c_1 = [(1 - a_{11}) + (1 - a_{22}) + (1 - a_{33})],$$

$$c_2 = \begin{vmatrix} 1 - a_{11} & -a_{12} \\ -a_{21} & 1 - a_{22} \end{vmatrix} + \begin{vmatrix} 1 - a_{11} & -a_{13} \\ -a_{31} & 1 - a_{33} \end{vmatrix} + \begin{vmatrix} 1 - a_{22} & -a_{23} \\ -a_{32} & 1 - a_{33} \end{vmatrix},$$

$$c_3 = |I - A|.$$

Observe that c_1 is the sum of the first-order principal minors of $|I - A|$, while c_2 is the sum of the second-order principal minors.

From the analysis of Chapter 12 we know that c_1 is the sum of the roots with the sign of this sum changed. Consequently, the rule of signs will be satisfied if the first-order principal minors are positive. The coefficient c_2 is the sum of the product of the roots taken two at a time. This coefficient will be positive if the second-order principal minors of $|I - A|$ are positive. Finally, c_3 is the product of the roots with its sign changed, and this coefficient will be positive if $|I - A|$ is positive. Thus it again appears that the rule of signs will be satisfied if the determinant of coefficients and its first- and second-order principal minors are all positive.

Once again it is important to note that if the characteristic equation had been expressed as $|(A - I) - qI| = 0$, we would have had

$$c_1 = [(a_{11} - 1) + (a_{22} - 1) + (a_{33} - 1)],$$

$$c_2 = \begin{vmatrix} a_{11} - 1 & a_{12} \\ a_{21} & a_{22} - 1 \end{vmatrix} + \begin{vmatrix} a_{11} - 1 & a_{13} \\ a_{31} & a_{33} - 1 \end{vmatrix} + \begin{vmatrix} a_{22} - 1 & a_{23} \\ a_{32} & a_{33} - 1 \end{vmatrix},$$

and

$$c_3 = |A - I| = -|I - A|.$$

The first-order minors now reverse in sign; the second-order minors are the same; and the determinant of $|A - I|$ equals $-|I - A|$. Consequently, when the characteristic equation is expressed as

$$|(A - I) - qI| = 0,$$

the rule of signs implies that any odd-ordered principal minor will be negative and any even-ordered minor will be positive.

These sign changes come about because the multiplication of a determinant by -1 is equivalent to changing all the signs of the elements of the determinant. Thus to change the signs in a determinant whose rows and columns are even numbered does not change the value of the determinant. However, in the case of a determinant with an odd number of rows and columns the effect is to change the sign of the determinant.

The general case can now be examined. Given the set of simultaneous differential equations,

$$\frac{dx_1}{dt} = a_{11}x_1 + a_{12}x_2 + \cdots + a_{1n}x_n + y_1 - x_1,$$

$$\frac{dx_2}{dt} = a_{21}x_1 + a_{22}x_2 + \cdots + a_{2n}x_n + y_2 - x_2,$$

$$\vdots$$

$$\frac{dx_n}{dt} = a_{n1}x_1 + a_{n2}x_2 + \cdots + a_{nn}x_n + y_n - x_n,$$

we can immediately write the characteristic determinant,

$$|qI + (I - A)| = \begin{vmatrix} q + (1 - a_{11}) & -a_{12} & \cdots & -a_{1n} \\ -a_{21} & q + (1 - a_{22}) & \cdots & -a_{2n} \\ \vdots & & & \vdots \\ -a_{n1} & -a_{n2} & \cdots & q + (1 - a_{nn}) \end{vmatrix} = 0,$$

and the characteristic equation,

$$q^n + c_1 q^{n-1} + c_2 q^{n-2} + \cdots + c_k q^{n-k} + \cdots + c_n = 0,$$

where

$$c_1 = \sum_1^n (1 - a_{ii}),$$

$$c_2 = \sum \begin{vmatrix} 1 - a_{ii} & -a_{ij} \\ -a_{ji} & 1 - a_{jj} \end{vmatrix},$$

$$c_3 = \sum \begin{vmatrix} 1 - a_{ii} & -a_{ij} & -a_{ik} \\ -a_{ji} & 1 - a_{jj} & -a_{jk} \\ -a_{ki} & -a_{kj} & 1 - a_{kk} \end{vmatrix},$$

$$\vdots$$

$$c_k = \sum_k |I - A|_{ii},^*$$

$$\vdots$$

$$c_n = |I - A|.$$

The properties of the general case conform to the expectation of symmetry suggested by the 2×2 and 3×3 cases. Any coefficient c_k represents the sum of the principal minors of order k of the determinant $|I - A|$. Since c_k also represents the sum of the product of the roots taken k at a time, with the sign of this sum reversed if k is odd, it follows that each c_k will be positive, and the rule of signs will be satisfied if all principal minors of whatever order are positive. We may therefore write that the rule of signs is satisfied when all the successive principal minors,

$$|1 - a_{ii}|, \quad \begin{vmatrix} 1 - a_{ii} & -a_{ij} \\ -a_{ji} & 1 - a_{jj} \end{vmatrix}, \quad \begin{vmatrix} 1 - a_{ii} & -a_{ij} & -a_{ik} \\ -a_{ji} & 1 - a_{jj} & -a_{jk} \\ -a_{ki} & -a_{kj} & 1 - a_{kk} \end{vmatrix}, \quad \cdots, \quad |I - A|,$$

are positive. Alternatively, if the characteristic equation is expressed as

$$|(A - I) - qI| = 0,$$

the successive principal minors are

$$|a_{ii} - 1|, \quad \begin{vmatrix} a_{ii} - 1 & a_{ij} \\ a_{ji} & a_{jj} - 1 \end{vmatrix}, \quad \begin{vmatrix} a_{ii} - 1 & a_{ij} & a_{ik} \\ a_{ji} & a_{jj} - 1 & a_{jk} \\ a_{ki} & a_{kj} & a_{kk} - 1 \end{vmatrix}, \quad \cdots, \quad |A - I|.$$

Since the odd-ordered minors change in sign while even-ordered minors remain the same, the condition now is that the successive principal minors alternate in sign with the sign of $|A - I|$ given by the sign of $(-1)^n$.

---

* Coefficient c_k is the sum of the principal minors of order k.

The conditions set forth above are known as the Hicks conditions for perfect stability. They are not sufficient to establish dynamic stability because it is possible for some of the roots to be complex with positive real parts even though the Hicks conditions are met. Consequently, unless we know beforehand that there are no complex roots, or that if there are complex roots, their real parts are less than the value of a larger real root, then the Hicks conditions will not be sufficient to ensure dynamic stability.

Unless we have established that our matrix of coefficients is of a particular class such that the Hicks conditions are sufficient to ensure dynamic stability, and unless we have already found a real positive or zero root and declared the system unstable, we have no alternative but to take the final laborious step and to form the Routh determinants and attempt to ascertain if all these determinants are positive. Recalling the discussion of Chapter 12, we take the characteristic equation

$$q^n + c_1 q^{n-1} + c_2 q^{n-2} + \cdots + c_k q^{n-k} + \cdots + c_n = 0,$$

and use the coefficients of this equation to form the successive Routh determinants,

$$|c_1|, \quad \begin{vmatrix} c_1 & c_3 \\ 1 & c_2 \end{vmatrix}, \quad \begin{vmatrix} c_1 & c_3 & c_5 \\ 1 & c_2 & c_4 \\ 0 & c_1 & c_3 \end{vmatrix}, \quad \begin{vmatrix} c_1 & c_3 & c_5 & c_7 \\ 1 & c_2 & c_4 & c_6 \\ 0 & c_1 & c_3 & c_5 \\ 0 & 1 & c_2 & c_4 \end{vmatrix}, \quad \cdots ;$$

and if all n of these determinants are positive, we can conclude that the system is dynamically stable. Otherwise it is unstable.

This completes the main outlines of stability analysis in simultaneous differential equation models. To summarize: First, we take the comparative-static model and put it into dynamic form. Second, we put the model into linear and homogeneous form by defining the variables as deviations from their equilibrium values and by taking linear approximations in the neighborhood of equilibrium. Third, we form the characteristic determinant. Fourth, we evaluate the characteristic determinant, thereby obtaining the characteristic equation. If there are any sign changes between the coefficients of the characteristic equation, we know immediately that there is at least one root with a positive real part and that the system is therefore unstable. Fifth, if all of the coefficients of the characteristic equation are positive and if there is nothing in the nature of the model that permits us to exclude the presence of complex roots, we take the final step and use the coefficients of the characteristic equation to form the Routh determinants. If all these determinants are positive, we may conclude that the system is stable. On the other hand, if any of the Routh determinants is negative, the system is unstable.

14.2 MATRIX METHODS AND SIMULTANEOUS DIFFERENTIAL EQUATIONS

By sticking to scalar algebra in the last section, we hoped to make clear the principles of stability analysis. However, it would be poor policy to bypass a powerful and highly efficient tool with which we are already familiar and which economists use extensively in the analysis of multisectoral models. Consequently, let us quickly translate the foregoing into matrix algebra form.

Using operator notation, we write the general model with which we have been dealing as

$$Dx_1 = a_{11}x_1 + a_{12}x_2 + \cdots + a_{1n}x_n + y_1 - x_1,$$
$$Dx_2 = a_{21}x_1 + a_{22}x_2 + \cdots + a_{2n}x_n + y_2 - x_2,$$
$$\vdots$$
$$Dx_n = a_{n1}x_1 + a_{n2}x_2 + \cdots + a_{nn}x_n + y_n - x_n,$$

or as

$$DX = AX + Y - X, \tag{14.2.1}$$

where,

$$DX = \begin{bmatrix} D & 0 & \cdots & 0 \\ 0 & D & \cdots & 0 \\ \vdots & & & \vdots \\ 0 & 0 & \cdots & D \end{bmatrix} \begin{bmatrix} x_1 \\ x_2 \\ \vdots \\ x_n \end{bmatrix},$$

A is the matrix of production coefficients, X is the column vector of gross outputs, and Y is the column vector of final demands.

We begin by writing 14.2.1 as

$$DX = (A - I)X + Y, \tag{14.2.2}$$

and proceed by attempting to calculate the vector of equilibrium gross output levels, $\bar{X}$. At equilibrium $DX = 0$, so that

$$Y = (I - A)\bar{X}, \tag{14.2.3}$$

and, as in Chapter 4,

$$\bar{X} = (I - A)^{-1}Y.$$

Using 14.2.3 to replace Y by $(I - A)\bar{X}$ in Eq. 14.2.2, we get

$$DX = (A - I)(X - \bar{X}), \tag{14.2.4}$$

which is the homogeneous form of the differential equations.

We can now proceed to a solution. As usual, we attempt the trial solution, $x_i = m_i e^{qt}$, from which it follows that

$$\frac{dx}{dt} = Dx_i = qm_i e^{qt} = q(x_i - \bar{x}_i),$$

so that in matrix form we try

$$DX = q(X - \bar{X}). \qquad (14.2.5)$$

Substituting this expression into 14.2.4 yields

$$q(X - \bar{X}) = (A - I)(X - \bar{X})$$

or

$$[qI + (I - A)](X - \bar{X}) = 0, \qquad (14.2.6)$$

where $[qI + (I - A)]$ is known as the characteristic matrix and $(X - \bar{X})$ is the characteristic vector.

If the characteristic matrix has an inverse, it would follow that

$$[qI + (I - A)][qI + (I - A)]^{-1}(X - \bar{X}) = 0,$$

and it would therefore have to be the case that $(X - \bar{X}) = 0$. Thus the only solution in this case would be that the characteristic vector

$$(X - \bar{X}) = \begin{bmatrix} x_1 & -\bar{x}_1 \\ x_2 & -\bar{x}_2 \\ \vdots & \vdots \\ x_n & -\bar{x}_n \end{bmatrix} = 0.$$

If this alternative is rejected as trivial, and if 14.2.6 is to hold for all values of $X - \bar{X}$, it must be assumed that the characteristic matrix is singular, and that the value of its determinant is therefore zero. Consequently, we arrive at the all-important result that

$$|qI + (I - A)| = 0. \qquad (14.2.7)$$

Equation 14.2.7 is the familiar characteristic equation which can be solved for the characteristic roots. Once this is accomplished the solution will be of the form $X = Me^{q_i t} + \bar{X}$, where M is an $n \times n$ matrix of constants that depend upon the initial conditions, and $e^{q_i t}$ is the vector

$$\begin{bmatrix} e^{q_1 t} \\ e^{q_2 t} \\ \vdots \\ e^{q_n t} \end{bmatrix}.$$

14.3 SIMULTANEOUS DIFFERENCE EQUATIONS

The difference equation counterpart of the simultaneous two-industry differential equation system is

$$\begin{aligned} x_1(t + 1) - x_1(t) &= [a_{11}x_1(t) + a_{12}x_2(t) + y_1] - x_1(t), \\ x_2(t + 1) - x_2(t) &= [a_{21}x_1(t) + a_{22}x_2(t) + y_2] - x_2(t), \end{aligned} \qquad (14.3.1)$$

which states that the change in output between period t and $t + 1$ is equal to the difference between the level of sales and the level of gross output in period t. Inspection of these equations immediately confirms that $x_i(t)$ can be canceled from each side. We then have

$$x_1(t + 1) = a_{11}x_1(t) + a_{12}x_2(t) + y_1,$$
$$x_2(t + 1) = a_{21}x_1(t) + a_{22}x_2(t) + y_2. \tag{14.3.2}$$

To solve for the equilibrium gross-output levels, we let $x_i(t + 1) = x_i(t) = \bar{x}_i$, so that as usual,

$$(1 - a_{11})\bar{x}_1 - \qquad a_{12}\bar{x}_2 = y_1,$$
$$-a_{21}\bar{x}_1 + (1 - a_{22})\bar{x}_2 = y_2$$

or

$$(I - A)\bar{X} = Y \quad \text{and} \quad \bar{X} = (I - A)^{-1}Y.$$

Substitution of the equilibrium values of the variables plus their displacements into Eqs. 14.3.2 yields the set of homogeneous equations,

$$x_1(t + 1) - \bar{x}_1 = a_{11}[x_1(t) - \bar{x}_1] + a_{12}[x_2(t) - \bar{x}_2],$$
$$x_2(t + 1) - \bar{x}_2 = a_{21}[x_1(t) - \bar{x}_1] + a_{22}[x_2(t) - \bar{x}_2]. \tag{14.3.3}$$

To get a solution, we try a trial solution just as in the single-equation case. There we expected a solution of the form $x(t) - \bar{x} = m\lambda^t$. Consequently,

$$x(t + 1) - \bar{x} = m\lambda^{t+1},$$

and it therefore follows that

$$x(t + 1) - \bar{x} = \lambda[x(t) - \bar{x}]. \tag{14.3.4}$$

Using 14.3.4 to substitute in 14.3.3, we get

$$\lambda[x_1(t) - \bar{x}_1] = a_{11}[x_1(t) - \bar{x}_1] + a_{12}[x_2(t) - \bar{x}_2],$$
$$\lambda[x_2(t) - \bar{x}_2] = a_{21}[x_1(t) - \bar{x}_1] + a_{22}[x_2(t) - \bar{x}_2]. \tag{14.3.5}$$

By the rules of matrix multiplication, Eq. 14.3.5 may be written

$$\begin{bmatrix} \lambda - a_{11} & -a_{12} \\ -a_{21} & \lambda - a_{22} \end{bmatrix} \begin{bmatrix} x_1(t) & -\bar{x}_1 \\ x_2(t) & -\bar{x}_2 \end{bmatrix} = (\lambda I - A)(X_t - \bar{X}) = 0. \tag{14.3.6}$$

If 14.3.6 is to hold for all values of the characteristic vector, the characteristic matrix

$$\begin{bmatrix} \lambda - a_{11} & -a_{12} \\ -a_{21} & \lambda - a_{22} \end{bmatrix} = (\lambda I - A) \tag{14.3.7}$$

cannot have an inverse, and it therefore follows that its determinant must equal zero. Accordingly, the characteristic determinant is

$$\begin{vmatrix} \lambda - a_{11} & -a_{12} \\ -a_{21} & \lambda - a_{22} \end{vmatrix} = 0, \tag{14.3.8}$$

and the characteristic equation is*

$$\lambda^2 - (a_{11} + a_{22})\lambda + (a_{11}a_{22} - a_{12}a_{21}) = 0. \qquad (14.3.9)$$

Analysis of the stability of equilibrium in the difference equation model is slightly complicated by the fact that, while in a differential equation system (with all roots known to be real) the roots must be negative, in a difference equation system they must lie between -1 and $+1$. Thus the rule of signs appears, at first, to offer no assistance, since the rule of signs merely distinguishes positive from negative roots.

The rule of signs may be resurrected by the following procedure. Take the characteristic determinant and subtract -1 from each root in such a way as to leave the value of the determinant unchanged. Thus write 14.3.8 as

$$\begin{vmatrix} (\lambda - 1) + (1 - a_{11}) & -a_{12} \\ -a_{21} & (\lambda - 1) + (1 - a_{22}) \end{vmatrix} = 0.$$

Evaluating the determinant, we get the characteristic equation,

$$(\lambda - 1)^2 + [(1 - a_{11}) + (1 - a_{22})](\lambda - 1) + |I - A| = 0,$$

which, of course, is identical to 14.3.9. However, in the present form, if the coefficients are all positive, it follows from the rule of signs that no $(\lambda - 1)$ can be positive and therefore no λ can be greater than $+1$. Consequently, if all the coefficients of the characteristic equation, when put in the present form, are positive, instability cannot be due to the presence of roots that are greater than $+1$.

Of course, instability could occur if one or more of the roots is less than -1. To check for this contingency, we reverse the foregoing procedure and now add $+1$ to each λ in such a way as to leave the value of the characteristic determinant unchanged. The result is

$$\begin{vmatrix} (\lambda + 1) - a_{11} - 1 & -a_{12} \\ -a_{21} & (\lambda + 1) - a_{22} - 1 \end{vmatrix} = 0,$$

and the characteristic equation may therefore be written as

$$(\lambda + 1)^2 - [(1 + a_{11}) + (1 + a_{22})](\lambda + 1) + [(1 + a_{11})(1 + a_{22}) - a_{12}a_{21}] = 0. \qquad (14.3.10)$$

Via the rule of signs, if all coefficients of this equation are positive, all $\lambda + 1$ terms would be negative and all λ's would therefore be less than minus one. Since the opposite is required for stability, we require that there be as many sign changes in Eq. 14.3.10 as there are roots. Thus, if the respective coefficients are alternately

---

* Note that, as in the case of a differential equation system, this result implies that a set of n first-order simultaneous difference equations can be converted into a set of n, nth-order difference equations in one variable and its own lagged values. The coefficients of each equation are the same, and the entire system therefore has a single characteristic equation.

negative and positive, each $(\lambda + 1)$ must be positive, and this means that no λ can be less than -1.

The rule of signs is not sufficient to establish stability of equilibrium unless we know that complex roots are absent or that the root with the largest modulus is real. The necessary and sufficient condition is that all the n successive Schurr determinants, already discussed in Chapter 12, be positive. If all the determinants are positive, we can conclude that no root has a modulus equal to or greater than $+1$, and that the system is therefore dynamically stable.

To complete the outline of the general principles of stability analysis, we put the simultaneous difference equation system into matrix form. The general inter-industry model may be written

$$
\begin{aligned}
x_1(t + 1) &= a_{11}x_1(t) + a_{12}x_2(t) + \cdots + a_{1n}x_n(t) + y_1. \\
x_2(t + 1) &= a_{21}x_1(t) + a_{22}x_2(t) + \cdots + a_{2n}x_n(t) + y_2, \\
&\vdots \\
x_n(t + 1) &= a_{n1}x_1(t) + a_{n2}x_2(t) + \cdots + a_{nn}x_n(t) + y_n.
\end{aligned}
\tag{14.3.11}
$$

By use of a device which is very similar to the differential operator, D, we can write these equations as

$$
\begin{aligned}
Ex_1 &= a_{11}x_1 + a_{12}x_2 + \cdots + a_{1n}x_n + y_1, \\
Ex_2 &= a_{21}x_1 + a_{22}x_2 + \cdots + a_{2n}x_n + y_2, \\
&\vdots \\
Ex_n &= a_{n1}x_1 + a_{n2}x_2 + \cdots + a_{nn}x_n + y_n,
\end{aligned}
\tag{14.3.12}
$$

where E is known as a shift operator. The operator E conveys the instruction to shift the time period by one. Thus $Ex = x(t + 1)$, $E^2x = x(t + 2)$, $E^{-1}x = x(t - 1)$, and so forth. Like the differential operator, E may be regarded as an algebraic quantity and manipulated as such.

Using the shift operator E, we may now write the system of equations expressed in 14.3.10 in matrix form. The result is

$$
EX = AX + Y,
\tag{14.3.13}
$$

where

$$
EX =
\begin{bmatrix}
E & 0 & \cdots & 0 \\
0 & E & \cdots & 0 \\
\vdots & & & \vdots \\
0 & 0 & \cdots & E
\end{bmatrix}
\begin{bmatrix}
x_1 \\
x_2 \\
\vdots \\
x_n
\end{bmatrix}.
$$

At equilibrium $EX = X = \bar{X}$, so that $\bar{X} = A\bar{X} + Y$, and, as before, $\bar{X} = (I - A)^{-1}Y$.

Following the usual procedure for obtaining a solution, we attempt to reduce the difference equation to homogeneous form by defining $X = \bar{X} + U$, where U is the column vector of displacements from equilibrium. Using this definition to make substitutions in 14.3.12, we obtain

$$E(U + \bar{X}) = A(U + \bar{X}) + Y.$$

However, since $E\bar{X} = \bar{X}$ and $\bar{X} = (I - A)^{-1}Y$, we have $EU = AU$, or

$$E(X - \bar{X}) = A(X - \bar{X}). \qquad (14.3.14)$$

In the case of difference equations we should try a solution of the form $X - \bar{X} = M\lambda^t$. Since this implies that $EX - \bar{X} = M\lambda^{t+1}$, it follows that

$$EX - \bar{X} = \lambda(X - \bar{X}).$$

Using this result, we see that Eq. 14.3.14 becomes

$$(\lambda I - A)(X - \bar{X}) = 0. \qquad (14.3.15)$$

If Eq. 14.3.15 is to hold for all values of the characteristic vector, the characteristic matrix $(\lambda I - A)$ cannot have an inverse, and its determinant must therefore equal zero. Consequently,

$$|\lambda I - A| = \begin{vmatrix} \lambda - a_{11} & -a_{12} & \cdots & -a_{1n} \\ -a_{21} & \lambda - a_{22} & \cdots & -a_{2n} \\ \vdots & & & \vdots \\ -a_{n1} & -a_{n2} & \cdots & \lambda - a_{nn} \end{vmatrix} = 0$$

is the characteristic determinant which represents a generalization of the 2×2 case previously derived and shown as Eq. 14.3.7.

14.4 SUMMARY

We have seen in this chapter that a first-order simultaneous difference or differential equation system in n variables may be reduced to an nth order system in one variable and its own time derivatives or its own lagged values. The characteristic equation for each variable is the same and the entire simultaneous equation system therefore has the same characteristic equation. Once the characteristic equation has been derived, the rule of signs may be used to establish the presence or absence (in differential equation models) of positive real roots, and (in difference equation models) of roots lying outside the range -1 to $+1$. However, the rule of signs is not sufficient if complex roots are a possibility. In this event it is necessary to use the coefficients of the characteristic equation to form the Routh determinants (differential equations), and the Schurr determinants (difference equations) in order to test the models for dynamic stability.

In order to form the Routh determinants, it is first necessary to calculate the coefficients of the characteristic equation. Thus all principal minors of the determinant of coefficients must first be evaluated as must the value of the determinant itself. Once the coefficients of the characteristic equation are known, they can then be used to calculate the Routh determinants. The labor involved in such computations is formidable and attempts have therefore been made to see if simpler tests for stability could be devised for particular classes of models that are of interest to the economist. A review of some of these attempts, together with a discussion of some of the more well-known multicompartment economic models, is the subject of the next chapter.

CHAPTER 15

The Comparative Statics and Dynamics of Multiple Markets, Multi-Regional Trade, and Interindustry Relations

15.1 THE STABILITY OF MULTIPLE MARKETS, METZLER MATRICES, AND THE HICKS CONDITIONS

Of the books in economics that were published during the 1930's J. M. Keynes's *General Theory of Employment, Interest, and Money* was undoubtedly the most important. However, J. R. Hicks's, *Value and Capital* * ran a strong second and it continues to be among the most important theoretical works of modern economics. Among Hicks's many contributions in this book was an attempt to derive stability conditions for a system of multiple markets. These conditions, which we already set forth in Chapter 14, are essentially conditions that cause the coefficients of the characteristic equation of a simultaneous differential equation system to obey the Descartes rule of signs. Hicks's results have been criticized on the grounds that they were derived without benefit of an explicit dynamic model and on the grounds that the conditions are not sufficient to ensure stability because complex roots with positive real parts may be present even when the rule of signs is satisfied.†

The problem of the stability of multiple markets has been analyzed by a number of economists and it continues to be a source of lively interest. An early analysis is that of Metzler,‡ which will be followed closely here because of its importance for subsequent progress in the analysis of dynamic interindustry models, models of international trade, and models of multisectoral income flows.

---

* J. R. Hicks, *Value and Capital* (London: Oxford University Press, 1939).
† Samuelson, *Foundations, op. cit.*, Chapter 9, has shown, by an ingeniously constructed example, that the Hicks conditions not only are not sufficient conditions for stability but under certain circumstances may not even be necessary.
‡ L. A. Metzler, "Stability of Multiple Markets: The Hicks Conditions," *Econometrica*, XII October, 1945).

Metzler's conclusions may be stated at the outset, namely, when all commodities are "gross substitutes" for each other, the Hicks conditions are both necessary and sufficient conditions for the stability of equilibrium in a system of n inter-related markets.

If all commodities are gross substitutes, a rise in the price of commodity j will reduce excess supply of commodity i. In addition, a rise in the price of j increases the excess supply of j. To take a simple example, if apples and oranges are substitute commodities, a rise in the price of apples causes consumers to substitute oranges in place of apples. This will be reflected as an upward shift in the demand for oranges and would therefore reduce the excess supply associated with any price in the market for oranges. Similarly, the rise in the price of apples reduces the quantity of apples demanded and increases excess supply of apples.

If apples and oranges are complementary commodities—imagine in the extreme that they are jointly consumed in fixed proportions in a fruit salad—the foregoing market characteristics would be altered. If the price of apples rises, the demand for oranges would decline, and the excess supply of oranges associated with any orange price would increase. As the reader can easily imagine, such fruit-salad cases create problems of instability. If both markets are initially characterized by excess supply, the equilibrating tendency that results from falling prices in the individual markets tend to be offset by induced demand shifts that act to increase excess supply.

Economists have not made much headway with the complications introduced by complimentarity. However, the gross substitutes case is straightforward and is the one discussed below. We have seen that if all commodities are gross substitutes, a rise in the price of commodity j reduces the excess supply of commodity i. On the other hand, a rise in the price of j increases the excess supply of j. As a consequence of this circumstance, the diagonal coefficients of the matrix of coefficients of a multiple-market model have the characteristic that they all have the same sign, while the off-diagonal coefficients will all have the opposite signs. Since markets of multiple-region trade, multisector multipliers, and interindustry product flows conform to the gross substitutes case, Metzler's proofs are of great significance to the economist. By deriving the stability conditions, and ruling out unstable cases, fruitful comparative-static results can be worked out for cases involving n markets, sectors, industries, or countries.

To proceed with Metzler's analysis, let the excess supply in the market for commodity i be a function of the prices in all n markets of the system. Thus excess supply* for good i might be written

$$x_i = x_i(p_1, p_2, \ldots, p_i, \ldots, p_n). \tag{15.1.1}$$

---

* Hicks and Metzler both work with excess demand rather than excess supply functions. The results are the same whichever way we proceed, and we choose to deal with excess supply functions because the character of the resulting model is more in keeping with the kind of models that we dealt with in the preceding chapter and with the models of international trade and interindustry relations that we shall take up in this chapter.

Metzler's dynamic hypothesis is that the rate at which price falls in each market is proportional to the level of excess supply which prevails in that market. Accordingly, let the dynamic system be written

$$Dp_1 = -k_1[x_1(p_1, p_2, \ldots, p_n)],$$
$$Dp_2 = -k_2[x_2(p_1, p_2, \ldots, p_n)],$$
$$\vdots \qquad\qquad\qquad\qquad\qquad (15.1.2)$$
$$Dp_n = -k_n[x_n(p_1, p_2, \ldots, p_n)],$$

where the k_i's are positive "reaction coefficients" that allow for differences in the speed of adjustment to disequilibrium in the various markets.

As we know from previous experience, this system of equations may be approximated in linear-homogeneous form by the equations

$$Dp_1 = -k_1[a_{11}(p_1 - \bar{p}_1) + a_{12}(p_2 - \bar{p}_2) + \cdots + a_{1n}(p_n - \bar{p}_n)],$$
$$DP_2 = -k_2[a_{21}(p_1 - \bar{p}_1) + a_{22}(p_2 - \bar{p}_2) + \cdots + a_{2n}(p_n - \bar{p}_n)],$$
$$\vdots \qquad\qquad\qquad\qquad\qquad\qquad\qquad\qquad (15.1.3)$$
$$Dp_n = -k_n[a_{n1}(p_1 - \bar{p}_1) + a_{n2}(p_2 - \bar{p}_2) + \cdots + a_{nn}(p_n - \bar{p}_n)],$$

where the coefficient $a_{ij} = \partial x_i/\partial p_j$ is the change in the excess supply of good i that accompanies an increase in the price of good j, all other prices held constant.

The characteristic determinant implied by this model is

$$\begin{vmatrix} q + k_1 a_{11} & k_1 a_{12} & \cdots & k_1 a_{1n} \\ k_2 a_{21} & q + k_2^j a_{22} & \cdots & k_2 a_{2n} \\ \vdots & & & \\ k_n a_{n1} & k_n a_{n2} & \cdots & q + k_n a_{nn} \end{vmatrix} = 0. \qquad (15.1.4)$$

This characteristic determinant does not look much different than the models of the last chapter except for the presence of the reaction coefficients which allow for differences in adjustment speed in the several markets. However, by the assumption that all commodities are gross substitutes, it must be the case that each a_{ij} $(i \neq j)$ coefficient will be negative, and that each a_{ii}-coefficient will be positive. Therefore the determinant of coefficients,

$$\begin{vmatrix} k_1 a_{11} & k_1 a_{12} & \cdots & k_1 a_{1n} \\ k_2 a_{21} & k_2 a_{22} & \cdots & k_2 a_{2n} \\ \vdots & & & \\ k_n a_{n1} & k_n a_{n2} & \cdots & k_n a_{nn} \end{vmatrix} = k_1 k_2 \cdots k_n |A|, \qquad (15.1.5)$$

will be characterized by the fact that all principal diagonal elements are positive and all off-diagonal elements are negative. This circumstance (or its exact opposite) is a common occurrence in economic models, and it is therefore hardly surprising that determinants and matrices that possess this characteristic are often referred to by economists as Metzler matrices.

It is for this type of model that the Hicks conditions can be shown to be necessary and sufficient conditions. Metzler's proof, which we follow here, begins with an examination of the corresponding set of difference equations. In difference equation form we could say that the fall in the price of commodity i is proportional to the level of excess supply which prevails at time $t - 1$. Write $u_i(t) = p_i(t) - \bar{p}_i$ as the displacement of price in market i from its equilibrium value. The difference equation counterpart of the differential equation for market i would then be

$$u_i(t) - u_i(t - 1) = -k_i[a_{i1}u_1(t - 1) + a_{i2}u_2(t - 1) + \cdots + a_{in}u_n(t - 1)].$$

Transferring $u_i(t - 1)$ to the right-hand side of the equation and writing out the complete model for n markets, we get

$$u_1(t) = (1 - k_1a_{11})u_1(t - 1) - \quad k_1a_{12}u_2(t - 1) - \cdots - \quad k_1a_{1n}u_n(t - 1),$$
$$u_2(t) = \quad -k_2a_{21}u_1(t - 1) + (1 - k_2a_{22})u_2(t - 1) - \cdots - \quad k_2a_{2n}u_n(t - 1),$$
$$\vdots$$
$$u_n(t) = \quad -k_na_{n1}u_1(t - 1) - \quad k_na_{n2}u_2(t - 1) - \cdots + (1 - k_na_{nn})u_n(t - 1).$$

$$(15.1.6)$$

The characteristic determinant in this case is

$$\begin{vmatrix} (\lambda - 1) + k_1a_{11} & k_1a_{12} & \cdots & k_1a_{1n} \\ k_2a_{21} & (\lambda - 1) + k_2a_{22} & \cdots & k_2a_{2n} \\ \vdots & & & \vdots \\ k_na_{n1} & k_na_{n2} & \cdots & (\lambda - 1) + k_na_{nn} \end{vmatrix} = 0,$$

$$(15.1.7)$$

where the λ's represent the characteristic roots of the difference equations. Comparison of this characteristic determinant with the characteristic determinant of the differential equations (15.1.4) shows that the determinants are identical except that each of the characteristic roots of the difference equations exceeds the roots of the differential equations by exactly $+1$.

In the case of difference equations, stability of equilibrium necessitates that none of the roots have a modulus equal to or in excess of unity. Consequently, if there are no roots with a modulus of $+1$ or more, there can be no roots of the differential equation system with real parts in excess of zero because of the fact that $q = \lambda - 1$. Stability of the difference equations therefore is sufficient to establish stability of the differential equations.

However, the opposite need not be the case. Even though there may be no positive or zero real parts of the roots of the differential equations, it is possible for the roots of the difference equations to have moduli in excess of $+1$. For example, suppose we have the complex conjugate difference equation roots, $\lambda_1 = 0 + \beta i$. Since the corresponding roots of the differential equations are,

$$q_1 = -1 + \beta i,$$
$$q_2 = -1 - \beta i,$$

the real parts are negative, and the differential equation is stable. However, the modulus of the roots of the difference equations is

$$M = \sqrt{0^2 + \beta^2} = \beta,$$

and if $\beta > 1$, then $M > 1$, and the difference equation is unstable. Thus while stability of the difference equations ensures stability of the differential equations, the reverse may not be the case.

Metzler's analysis continues with a demonstration that, for the present class of models, the differential equations cannot be stable unless the difference equations are also stable. The solution to the difference equations for market 1 may be written

$$\begin{aligned}
u_1(t) = {} & M_1^t(v_{11} \cos \theta_1 t + v_{12} \sin \theta_1 t) \\
& + M_2^t(v_{21} \cos \theta_2 t + v_{22} \sin \theta_2 t) \\
& + \cdots \\
& + M_i^t(v_{i1} \cos \theta_i t + v_{i2} \sin \theta_i t),
\end{aligned} \qquad (15.1.8)$$

where M_i is the modulus of the ith distinct pair of complex roots,* θ_i is its angle, and the v_{ij}'s are constants that depend upon the initial conditions. Now assume that the largest modulus is M_1 and rewrite the solution as

$$\begin{aligned}
u_1(t) = {} & M_1^t[v_{11} \cos \theta_1 t + v_{12} \sin \theta_1 t \\
& + (M_2/M_1)^t(v_{21} \cos \theta_2 t + v_{22} \sin \theta_2 t) \\
& + \cdots \\
& + (M_i/M_1)^t(v_{i1} \cos \theta_i t + v_{i2} \sin \theta_i t)].
\end{aligned} \qquad (15.1.9)$$

From this arrangement of the solution we see that when t gets very large and when M_1 is the root with the largest modulus, all the ratios $(M_j/M_1)^t$ $(j = 2, \ldots, i)$ approach zero as $t \to \infty$, and the system then behaves in accordance with the dominant term,

$$M_1^t(v_{11} \cos \theta_1 t + v_{12} \sin \theta_1 t). \qquad (15.1.10)$$

If the dominant root is complex, Eq. 15.1.10 must at some time take on negative values. However, this can be shown to be impossible. To see this we need to go back to the original set of difference equations (15.1.6). The choice of

---

* Metzler's analysis is more general than our representation of it. He allows for the possibility of identical pairs of complex roots while we bypass this generalization and assume that each pair of complex root is distinct.

a time unit in the difference equation model is arbitrary. However, as the time period is narrowed, the degree to which prices fall in response to a given level of excess supply during the period diminishes, and this means that a shortening of the time unit reduces the value of the reaction coefficients. Consequently, the time unit can be chosen in such a way as to make the reaction coefficients small enough to make any term such as $1 - k_i a_{ii}$ positive. If this is the case, all terms on the right-hand side of Eqs. 15.1.6 are positive, provided all the displacements $u_i(t - 1)$ are positive. But if all the $u_i(t - 1)$ terms are positive, it must be the case that all $u_i(t)$ terms on the left-hand side of the equations will also be positive. It follows that if all prices were initially in excess of their equilibrium levels, they will remain that way throughout subsequent periods. And from this it follows, further, that the dominant root of the difference equations must be real. The angle θ_1 must be zero because that is the only way in which Eq. 15.1.10 could never generate negative values. The root of the difference equations with the largest modulus must therefore be a real root.

The fact that the root with the largest modulus must be real proves that stability of the difference equations is a necessary condition for stability of the differential equations. If the dominant root of the difference equations exceeds unity, the largest root of the differential equations will be positive and both systems are unstable. If the differential equation root with the largest real part is negative, the real part of the root of the difference equation must be less than unity, and since this root is real, its modulus is less than unity. Finally, since this modulus is the largest modulus of any root of the difference equations, there can be no roots with a modulus greater than or equal to one. Thus, to repeat, stability of the difference equations is both a necessary and a sufficient condition for stability of the differential equation system.

Since we now know that the possible presence of complex roots will have no bearing on the outcome in the gross substitutes case, it follows that a sufficient condition for stability is that the rule of signs be satisfied. From the characteristic determinant (15.1.4) it is evident that the characteristic equation of the differential equations is

$$q^n + [\textstyle\sum k_i a_{ii}]q^{n-1} + \left[\textstyle\sum k_i k_j \begin{vmatrix} a_{ii} & a_{ij} \\ a_{ji} & a_{jj} \end{vmatrix}\right]q^{n-2} + \cdots + k_1 k_2 \cdots k_n |A| = 0,$$
$$(15.1.11)$$

where $|A|$ is the determinant of coefficients. The positive-reaction coefficients can be factored out of the respective principal minors, and they have no effect on the signs of the coefficients of the characteristic equation. Consequently, the signs of the coefficients depend only upon the successive determinants,

$$|a_{ii}|, \quad \begin{vmatrix} a_{ii} & a_{ij} \\ a_{ji} & a_{jj} \end{vmatrix}, \quad \begin{vmatrix} a_{ii} & a_{ij} & a_{ik} \\ a_{ji} & a_{jj} & a_{jk} \\ a_{ki} & a_{kj} & a_{kk} \end{vmatrix}, \quad \cdots, \quad |A|, \quad (15.1.12)$$

and a sufficient condition for stability therefore is that all such determinants be positive for all i, j, and k. Further, since the signs of the coefficients are unaffected by the presence of the reaction coefficients, stability, in the gross substitutes case, is unaffected by the speed of adjustment. Thus a system that satisfies the Hicks conditions for one set of adjustment speeds will do so for all sets of adjustment speeds.

The condition that the determinants in 15.1.12 all be positive for any i, j, and k is known to economists as the Hicks conditions for perfect stability for a set of multiple markets. The lower-order determinants are all principal minors of $|A|$, while $|A|$ itself would be a principal minor of a system of $n + 1$ markets. From now on, any principal minor that is positive will be called a Hicksian determinant.

We have established that the Hicks conditions are sufficient to ensure stability in the gross substitutes case. However, are they also necessary? Suppose the complete system of difference equations is the three-market model,

$$u_1(t) = [1 - k_1 a_{11}]u_1(t - 1) - \qquad k_1 a_{12} u_2(t - 1) - \qquad k_1 a_{13} u_3(t - 1),$$

$$u_2(t) = \qquad -k_2 a_{21} u_1(t - 1) + [1 - k_2 a_{22}]u_2(t - 1) - \qquad k_2 a_{23} u_3(t - 1),$$

$$u_3(t) = \qquad -k_3 a_{31} u_1(t - 1) - \qquad k_3 a_{32} u_2(t - 1) + [1 - k_3 a_{33}]u_3(t - 1),$$

and recall that if all $u_1(t - 1)$, $u_2(t - 1)$, and $u_3(t - 1)$ are positive, then all $u_1(t)$, $u_2(t)$, and $u_3(t)$ must be positive, provided that the time period is chosen in such a way as to make all diagonal elements, $[1 - k_i a_{ii}]$ positive.

Next, suppose that price in market 3 is held constant so that the system reduces to the subset

$$\hat{u}_1(t) = [1 - k_1 a_{11}]\hat{u}_1(t - 1) - \qquad k_1 a_{12}\hat{u}_2(t - 1),$$

$$\hat{u}_2(t) = \qquad -k_2 a_{21}\hat{u}_1(t - 1) + [1 - k_2 a_{22}]\hat{u}_2(t - 1).$$

Finally, suppose that initially all of the $u_i(t - 1)$ terms are greater than each $\hat{u}_i(t - 1)$ term, and that both displacements are positive. Since the terms $-k_1 a_{13}u_1(t - 1)$ and $-k_2 a_{23}u_3(t - 1)$ are positive, it follows that $u_i(t)$ must always be greater than $\hat{u}_i(t)$. Consequently, if $\hat{u}_i(t)$ does not approach zero as to increases, then neither can the larger term $u_i(t)$. The complete system cannot therefore be stable unless each arbitrary subset is stable. This means, finally, that the Hicks conditions are not only sufficient conditions for stability but necessary conditions as well. Each combination of subgroups of markets represents a Hicksian minor and each such subgroup must be stable. Consequently, all the principal minors of $|A|$ must be positive.

To complete this review of Metzler's analysis, we note again that in the present gross substitutes case, stability of the system is independent of the adjustment speeds. This should not be taken to mean, however, that relative speeds of adjustment are not important determinants of stability in other types of models. A simple differential equation illustration, again borrowed from Metzler, can be used to show this. Let the characteristic equation be*

$$q^2 + (k_1 - k_2)q + k_1 k_2 = 0.$$

The characteristic roots,

$$(q_1, q_2) = \frac{k_2 - k_1 \pm \sqrt{(k_1 - k_2)^2 - 4k_1 k_2}}{2},$$

will have positive or negative real parts depending upon whether k_2 is greater than k_1 in absolute value. Here, clearly, stability depends upon relative speeds of adjustment and it cannot therefore be generally stated that adjustment speeds have no bearing on the stability of a simultaneous equation model.

In summary, we have obtained the following results in the gross substitutes case:

1   Because the roots of the differential equations in a system of multiple markets have values exactly $+1$ less than the respective roots of the corresponding difference equations, stability of the difference equations is a sufficient condition to establish stability of the differential equations, since stability of the difference equations means that the roots of the differential equations must all have negative real parts.

2   The dominant root of the difference equations is a real root. If this root is less than one, all other roots must have moduli of less than one, and instability cannot therefore be caused by complex roots. Consequently, stability of the difference equations is not only a sufficient condition for stability of the differential equations, it is a necessary condition as well.

3   Since the system cannot be rendered unstable by the presence of complex roots, the Hicks conditions are sufficient conditions for the establishment of stability of equilibrium.

4   Since the Hicks conditions are unaffected by the values of the positive reaction coefficients, a system that is stable for one set of adjustment speeds will be stable for all sets.

5   Since a system of three markets cannot be stable unless each subset of two markets is also stable, the Hicks conditions are not only sufficient conditions for stability, but are necessary ones as well.

---

* The characteristic determinant in this case might be

$$\begin{vmatrix} q + k_1 & -k_1 \\ 2k_2 & q - k_2 \end{vmatrix} \quad \text{or} \quad \begin{vmatrix} q + k_1 & 2k_1 \\ -k_2 & q - k_2 \end{vmatrix},$$

and thus cannot belong to the gross substitutes class of models.

15.2 STABILITY OF EQUILIBRIUM AND THE EXISTENCE OF POSITIVE GROSS OUTPUTS IN THE LEONTIEF MODEL

In shorthand form, the static Leontief interindustry system may be written

$$Y = (I - A)X$$

or

$$X = (I - A)^{-1}Y, \tag{15.2.1}$$

where A is the matrix of production coefficients, X is the vector of gross outputs, and Y is the vector of final demands. Some of the questions which were not answered in Chapter 4 are the following: (1) What are the conditions for dynamic stability of the interindustry model; (2) Given some vector of positive final demands, will the vector of gross outputs be positive, and what are the conditions that must be met if this is to be the case; (3) Can the stability conditions for an interindustry model be simplified so as to avoid having to compute Routhian and Hicksian determinants?

To test the model for stability, we form the dynamic hypothesis that the rate of change in output is proportional to the excess of sales over output. Accordingly,

$$
\begin{aligned}
Dx_1 &= -k_1[(1 - a_{11})x_1 - & a_{12}x_2 - \cdots - & a_{1n}x_n - y_1], \\
Dx_2 &= -k_2[& -a_{21}x_1 + (1 - a_{22})x_2 - \cdots - & a_{21}x_n - y_2], \\
&\ \ \vdots \\
Dx_n &= -k_n[& -a_{n1}x_1 - \quad a_{n2}x_2 - \cdots + (1 - a_{nn})x_n - y_n].
\end{aligned}
\tag{15.2.2}
$$

Putting this set of equations into matrix form, we have

$$DX = -KI[(I - A)X - Y], \tag{15.2.3}$$

where

$$
KI = \begin{bmatrix}
k_1 & 0 & \cdots & 0 \\
0 & k_2 & \cdots & 0 \\
\vdots & & & \vdots \\
0 & 0 & \cdots & k_n
\end{bmatrix}.
$$

From inspection of 15.2.3 it is immediately apparent that the characteristic determinant is

$$
\begin{vmatrix}
q + k_1(1 - a_{11}) & -k_1 a_{12} & \cdots & -k_1 a_{1n} \\
-k_2 a_{21} & q + k_2(1 - a_{22}) & \cdots & -k_2 a_{2n} \\
\vdots & & & \vdots \\
-k_n a_{n1} & -k_n a_{n2} & \cdots & q + k_n(1 - a_{nn})
\end{vmatrix} = 0,
\tag{15.2.4}
$$

and the determinant of coefficients is

$$
k_1 k_2 \cdots k_n
\begin{vmatrix}
1 - a_{11} & -a_{12} & \cdots & -a_{1n} \\
-a_{21} & 1 - a_{22} & \cdots & -a_{2n} \\
\vdots & & & \vdots \\
-a_{n1} & -a_{n2} & \cdots & 1 - a_{nn}
\end{vmatrix}
= k_1 k_2 \cdots k_n |I - A|.
$$

$$(15.2.5)$$

From the assumption that each industry uses less of its own input than it produces, all $1 - a_{ii}$ terms must be positive, and from the assumption that an increase in output in industry j cannot reduce the demand for good i, all $a_{ij} \geq 0$. The determinant of coefficients therefore has positive diagonal elements and negative (or zero) off-diagonal elements. It therefore is a Metzler model of the gross-substitutes class. Consequently, we can conclude immediately that whether the model is expressed in difference or in differential equation form, the necessary and sufficient conditions for stability are that all the successive principal minors,

$$
|1 - a_{ii}|, \qquad
\begin{vmatrix}
1 - a_{ii} & -a_{ij} \\
-a_{ji} & 1 - a_{jj}
\end{vmatrix}, \qquad \ldots, \qquad
|I - A|,
$$

be positive. Thus the Hicks conditions apply to the Leontief case, and such a system, if it is initially stable, cannot be rendered unstable by changes in the rate at which different industries adjust production to an excess of sales over output, nor can an initially unstable system be rendered stable by such a change.

The next question to be dealt with is the question of whether all the elements of the static solution for the vector of gross outputs, X, will be positive if all elements of the vector of final demands, Y, are positive. This problem has been analyzed by Hawkins and Simon,[*] and the conditions for ensuring such a positive solution are known as the Hawkins-Simon conditions. Since $\bar{X} = (I - A)^{-1} Y$, it is obvious that a sufficient condition for all elements of the vector X to be positive when all elements of Y are positive is that all elements of the inverse of the Leontief matrix be positive. The Hawkins-Simon conditions, which ensure that this will be the case, can be derived by use of a theorem of great importance, known as Mosak's theorem,[†] which we must pause to digress on.

Mosak's theorem states that if a determinant is Hicksian, i.e., all of its principal minors and the determinant itself are positive, and if all off-diagonal elements are negative while all diagonal elements are positive, the cofactor of any element of the determinant will be positive. Since the inverse of the Leontief matrix is formed by transposing the matrix of cofactors and dividing each element

---

[*] D. Hawkins and H. Simon, "Note: Some Conditions of Macroeconomic Stability," *Econometrica*, XVII (July–October, 1949).

[†] Jacob Mosak, *General Equilibrium Theory in International Trade*, Cowles Commission Monograph No. 7 (Evanston, Ill.: The Principia Press, 1944), pp. 49–51.

of the resulting matrix by the positive determinant $|I - A|$, it is obvious that if the system is Hicksian (stable), Mosak's theorem will ensure that all elements of the $\bar{X}$-vector will be positive if the vector of final demands is positive.

Mosak's theorem can be understood by resort to an example. Consider the 4×4 determinant

$$
B = \begin{vmatrix} b_{11} & b_{12} & b_{13} & b_{14} \\ b_{21} & b_{22} & b_{23} & b_{24} \\ b_{31} & b_{32} & b_{33} & b_{34} \\ b_{41} & b_{42} & b_{43} & b_{44} \end{vmatrix}
$$

which we assume to be of the gross-substitutes class so that all off-diagonal elements are negative and all diagonal elements are positive. Next, consider the cofactor of the element b_{31}, namely

$$
B_{31} = \begin{vmatrix} b_{12} & b_{13} & b_{14} \\ b_{22} & b_{23} & b_{24} \\ b_{42} & b_{43} & b_{44} \end{vmatrix}, \tag{15.2.6}
$$

and let us expand this determinant about its first row. This yields

$$
B_{31} = b_{12} \begin{vmatrix} b_{23} & b_{24} \\ b_{43} & b_{44} \end{vmatrix} + b_{13} \left(- \begin{vmatrix} b_{22} & b_{24} \\ b_{42} & b_{44} \end{vmatrix} \right) + b_{14} \begin{vmatrix} b_{22} & b_{23} \\ b_{42} & b_{43} \end{vmatrix}. \tag{15.2.7}
$$

When these determinants are evaluated, and we recall the assumption about the signs of the elements, it becomes apparent that the first and the third determinant are both negative. Moreover, the determinant

$$
- \begin{vmatrix} b_{22} & b_{24} \\ b_{42} & b_{44} \end{vmatrix},
$$

is a Hicksian second-order minor with its sign changed and it must therefore be negative. As a consequence, it is obvious from inspection of 15.2.7 that B_{31} cannot be anything other than positive provided the Hicks conditions hold. And it is therefore plainly the case that in a gross-substitutes model satisfaction of the Hicks conditions implies that all the cofactors of B be positive.

To generalize further, let us write B_{31} as

$$
B_{31} = b_{12} B_{31,12} + b_{13} B_{31,13} + b_{14} B_{31,14}, \tag{15.2.8}
$$

where, for example, the term $B_{31,13}$ is a shorthand way of writing the cofactor of the element b_{13} in the determinant B_{31}, namely

$$
B_{31,13} = - \begin{vmatrix} b_{22} & b_{24} \\ b_{42} & b_{44} \end{vmatrix}.
$$

Next, consider a principal minor of B such as

$$B_{11} = \begin{vmatrix} b_{22} & b_{23} & b_{24} \\ b_{32} & b_{33} & b_{34} \\ b_{42} & b_{43} & b_{44} \end{vmatrix},$$

and expand this about its second row. This gives

$$B_{11} = b_{32}\left(-\begin{vmatrix} b_{23} & b_{24} \\ b_{43} & b_{44} \end{vmatrix}\right) + b_{33}\begin{vmatrix} b_{22} & b_{24} \\ b_{42} & b_{44} \end{vmatrix} + b_{34}\left(-\begin{vmatrix} b_{22} & b_{23} \\ b_{42} & b_{43} \end{vmatrix}\right)$$

$$(15.2.9)$$

or, in terms of the shorthand notation adopted above,

$$B_{11} = b_{32}B_{11,32} + b_{33}B_{11,33} + b_{34}B_{11,34}. \qquad (15.2.10)$$

Now by comparing the determinants in 15.2.7 with those of 15.2.9, and using the notation of 15.2.8 and 15.2.10, it is clear that

$$B_{31,12} = -B_{11,32},$$
$$B_{31,13} = -B_{11,33},$$
$$B_{31,14} = -B_{11,34}.$$

This result suggests that we may quite generally write for any determinant B,

$$B_{ij,jk} = -B_{jj,ik}, \qquad (15.2.11)$$

and it means that in a cofactor such as $B_{31,12}$, we need merely place the first subscript in the third position, change the sign, and obtain $-B_{11,32}$.

By referring to the determinant B, the reader can easily verify that

$$B_{ij,kl} = B_{kl,ij}, \qquad (15.2.12)$$

so that, for example,

$$B_{12,34} = B_{34,12},$$
$$B_{11,22} = B_{22,11},$$

and

$$B_{13,31} = B_{31,13}.$$

Before we go on, be sure to observe the sign changes; $B_{11,22} = B_{22,11}$, and $B_{13,31} = B_{31,13}$, however, $B_{12,21} = -B_{22,11}$. Thus whenever the first-position-to-third-position rule is invoked, the sign of the result changes. However, it does not change otherwise.

Via the rules expressed in 15.2.11 and 15.2.12, it is evident that the determinant B_{31}, as expressed in 15.2.8, may be written

$$B_{31} = b_{12}[-B_{11,32}] + b_{13}[-B_{11,33}] + b_{14}[-B_{11,34}]. \qquad (15.2.13)$$

Consequently, B_{31} may be expressed as a linear function of the cofactors of the principal minor B_{11}. As the reader may easily verify, a similar result could be obtained for any cofactor B_{ij} of B.

Mosak's theorem now follows without difficulty. If the theorem holds for the cofactors of B_{11}, the determinant B_{31} must, via 15.2.13, be positive. Consequently, all of the cofactors of B are positive provided that all the cofactors of $B_{11}, B_{22}, \ldots$, and so on are positive. Now, B_{11} and B_{22} are Hicksian determinants. Consequently, whatever holds as between B and B_{11} must hold for B_{11} and one of its principal minors, such as $B_{11,22}$, and so on down the line. To complete the proof of Mosak's theorem, it is therefore only necessary to show that the second-order principal minors have positive cofactors. The minor

$$B_{11,22} = \begin{vmatrix} b_{33} & b_{34} \\ b_{43} & b_{44} \end{vmatrix}$$

has the cofactors $b_{44}, -b_{43}, -b_{34}, b_{33}$, all of which are positive.

Mosak's theorem implies that all elements of the determinant of a Leontief matrix will have positive cofactors if the Hicks conditions for stability are met. This means that all the successive principal minors,

$$|1 - a_{ii}|, \quad \begin{vmatrix} 1 - a_{ii} & -a_{ij} \\ -a_{ji} & 1 - a_{jj} \end{vmatrix}, \quad \begin{vmatrix} 1 - a_{ii} & -a_{ij} & -a_{ik} \\ -a_{ji} & 1 - a_{jj} & -a_{jk} \\ -a_{ki} & -a_{kj} & 1 - a_{kk} \end{vmatrix}, \quad \ldots, \quad |I - A|,$$

must be positive. If this is the case, the transposed matrix of cofactors will have all positive elements, and since $|I - A|$ is positive, all elements of $(I - A)^{-1}$ will be positive. It follows that if the vector of final demands is positive, the vector of gross outputs must also be positive. This result, that all principal minors of the Leontief matrix must be positive, is known to economists as the Hawkins-Simon conditions. These conditions are nothing other than the Hicks conditions in a slightly different setting.

Conceivably, some elements of the inverse matrix might be negative and the X-vector might yet be positive. To prove that this is impossible, and that the Hawkins-Simon conditions are therefore necessary as well as sufficient, it is necessary only to consider any arbitrary two-industry subset.

Any principal minor of $|I - A|$ represents a subgroup of industries. The condition that all the principal minors be positive implies that each group of industries, regardless of how they are grouped or how many industries comprise the group, must be capable of supplying its own demands upon itself. If the minor involving the subgroup 1 and 2 is negative, the quantity of good 2 required to produce one unit of good 1 is greater than the quantity of 2 that can be produced with an input of one unit of commodity 1, and it would therefore be impossible to produce one unit of final demand for either commodity. If such a group of industries tried to continue to operate, they would resemble the fanatic who redoubles his efforts as he sees his target receding.

To make this clear, consider the minor for the subgroup consisting of industries 1 and 2,

$$\begin{vmatrix} 1 - a_{11} & -a_{12} \\ -a_{21} & 1 - a_{22} \end{vmatrix}.$$

An increase in production in industry 1 of $1.00 requires added inputs from itself of a_{11}. To produce these added inputs, its own inputs must rise by $(a_{11})^2$, and to produce this by $(a_{11})^3$, and so on. Consequently, if no inputs from industry 2 were required, the increase in output in industry 1 would be

$$dx_1 = 1 + a_{11} + (a_{11})^2 + \cdots + (a_{11})^{n-1} = \frac{1}{1 - a_{11}},$$

provided that $0 \leq a_{11} \leq 1$, so that $(a_{11})^n \to 0$.

However, the change in output in industry 1 raises purchases from industry 2 by $a_{21}\, dx_1$, and this implies that output in industry 2 must rise by

$$dx_2 = \frac{a_{21}}{1 - a_{11}} [1 + a_{22} + (a_{22})^2 + \cdots + (a_{22})^{n-1}] = \frac{a_{21}}{(1 - a_{11})(1 - a_{22})}.$$

The increase in output in industry 2 requires added inputs from industry 1 of $a_{12}\, dx_2$, so that the induced increase in output in industry 1 is

$$dx_{1.2} = \frac{a_{12}a_{21}}{(1 - a_{11})(1 - a_{22})} [1 + a_{11} + (a_{11})^2 + \cdots + (a_{11})^{n-1}]$$

or

$$dx_{1.2} = \frac{a_{12}a_{21}}{(1 - a_{11})^2(1 - a_{22})}.$$

If the original increase in output, dx_1, is greater than the induced increase, then $dx_1 > dx_{1.2}$, and it follows that

$$\frac{1}{1 - a_{11}} > \frac{a_{12}a_{21}}{(1 - a_{11})^2(1 - a_{22})},$$

which implies that

$$(1 - a_{11})(1 - a_{22}) > a_{12}a_{21}$$

and, in turn, that

$$\begin{vmatrix} 1 - a_{11} & -a_{12} \\ -a_{21} & 1 - a_{22} \end{vmatrix} > 0.$$

We can now conclude that if the minor corresponding to industries 1 and 2 is negative, the industry group is incapable of supplying sufficient inputs to itself to produce a positive level of output, that is, dx_1 would be less than $dx_{1.2}$, which in turn would be less than $dx_{1.3}$ and so on. Under such circumstances, "the production of these two commodities could not be continued, for they would exhaust each other in their joint production."* Presumably then, it is necessary that all two-industry groupings exhibit positive minors. Similarly, since a two-industry group that cannot satisfy its own demands upon itself certainly cannot satisfy the demands placed upon it by the purchases of a third or a fourth industry, it must be the case that *all* principal minors (all industry groupings) must be positive.

To conclude: The correspondence between the Hicks conditions for perfect stability and the Hawkins-Simon conditions is complete. If the Hicks conditions are met, the system will be dynamically stable; all elements of the inverse of the Leontief matrix will be nonnegative, and all elements of the vector of equilibrium gross outputs must then be positive.

The Hicks conditions are necessary and sufficient conditions for stability and for the existence of a positive solution for the vector of gross outputs. The fact that the Routh determinants need not therefore be calculated already marks considerable progress. However, is there a simpler sufficient test for stability which, if it is met, will eliminate the need to calculate all the principal minors of the Leontief matrix?

The column sums of the matrix of coefficients represent the value of inter-industry purchases per unit of gross output for the respective industries. Consequently, the column sums in the Leontief matrix, $I - A$, represent the industry's value added per unit of gross output. Since each industry can generally be assumed to produce positive value added, the column sums are expected to be positive.† It is our purpose, in what follows, to show that the existence of positive column sums in the Leontief matrix is sufficient to guarantee that the system meets the Hicks conditions.

Suppose we have the determinant

$$
B = \begin{vmatrix}
b_{11} & b_{12} & b_{13} & b_{14} \\
b_{21} & b_{22} & b_{23} & b_{24} \\
b_{31} & b_{32} & b_{33} & b_{34} \\
b_{41} & b_{42} & b_{43} & b_{44}
\end{vmatrix},
$$

where each $b_{ij} \leq 0$, if $i \neq j$, and $0 < b_{ii} \leq 1$. This determinant could, for example, represent the determinant of a four-industry Leontief model where, for purposes of notational simplicity, b_{ii} replaces $1 - a_{ii}$ and b_{ij} replaces $-a_{ij}$.

The value of a determinant is unchanged if a constant multiple of the elements of one row is added to the corresponding elements of another row. We can therefore add the elements of rows 2, 3, 4, ..., n to row 1 without changing

* Hawkins and Simon, *op. cit.*, p. 248.

† Value added should not be confused with profits. Profits might easily be negative, while value added is positive. Value added will be positive provided that the value of the industry's gross output exceeds the value of its interindustry inputs, including inputs from itself.

the value of the determinant. Accordingly, we could write

$$B = \begin{vmatrix} Sb_{i1} & Sb_{i2} & Sb_{i3} & Sb_{i4} \\ b_{21} & b_{22} & b_{23} & b_{24} \\ b_{31} & b_{32} & b_{33} & b_{34} \\ b_{41} & b_{42} & b_{43} & b_{44} \end{vmatrix}, \tag{15.2.14}$$

where, for example, the notation Sb_{i2} means the sum, over all rows, of the elements in the second column. When we expand this determinant about the elements of its first row, we obtain

$$B = Sb_{i1}B_{11} + Sb_{i2}B_{12} + Sb_{i3}B_{13} + Sb_{i4}B_{14}, \tag{15.2.15}$$

where B_{12} is the cofactor of the element b_{12} of B. Now consider the term $Sb_{i2}B_{12}$. Explicitly, we have

$$Sb_{i2}B_{12} = Sb_{i2}\left(-\begin{vmatrix} b_{21} & b_{23} & b_{24} \\ b_{31} & b_{33} & b_{34} \\ b_{41} & b_{43} & b_{44} \end{vmatrix} \right).$$

Expanding B_{12} about its first column yields

$$Sb_{i2}B_{12} = Sb_{i2}\left[-b_{21}\begin{vmatrix} b_{33} & b_{34} \\ b_{43} & b_{44} \end{vmatrix} - b_{31}\left(-\begin{vmatrix} b_{23} & b_{24} \\ b_{43} & b_{44} \end{vmatrix} \right) - b_{41}\begin{vmatrix} b_{23} & b_{24} \\ b_{33} & b_{34} \end{vmatrix} \right],$$

or, in shorthand form,

$$Sb_{i2}[b_{21}B_{12,21} + b_{31}B_{12,31} + b_{41}B_{12,41}].$$

However, we know from 15.2.11 that $B_{12,21} = -B_{11,22}$, $B_{12,31} = -B_{11,32}$, and $B_{12,41} = -B_{11,42}$; and we can therefore write

$$Sb_{i2}B_{12} = -Sb_{i2}[b_{21}B_{11,22} + b_{31}B_{11,32} + b_{41}B_{11,42}].$$

Similar procedures could be applied to the cofactors B_{13} and B_{14}, and when we do this, we can write the determinant B as

$$\begin{aligned} B = Sb_{i1}B_{11} &- Sb_{i2}[b_{21}B_{11,22} + b_{31}B_{11,32} + b_{41}B_{11,42}] \\ &- Sb_{i3}[b_{21}B_{11,23} + b_{31}B_{11,33} + b_{41}B_{11,43}] \tag{15.2.16} \\ &- Sb_{i4}[b_{21}B_{11,24} + b_{31}B_{11,34} + b_{41}B_{11,44}]. \end{aligned}$$

To digress for a moment: This way of expressing the determinant B shows that if we first divide the determinant into

$$B = b_{11}B_{11} + \begin{vmatrix} 0 & b_{12} & b_{13} & b_{14} \\ b_{21} & b_{22} & b_{23} & b_{24} \\ b_{31} & b_{32} & b_{33} & b_{34} \\ b_{41} & b_{42} & b_{43} & b_{44} \end{vmatrix},$$

and then expand the "bordered" determinant on the right first by its top row and then by its left-hand column, the result is to express the determinant as a linear function of the cofactors of one of its principal minors. With this result, which is known as a Cauchy expansion, along with Mosak's theorem, it can now be easily shown that the Hicks conditions will be satisfied if the column sums of the Leontief matrix are positive.

Consider the expression 15.2.16 and suppose that B_{11} is Hicksian. According to Mosak's theorem, all of the cofactors of B_{11} that enter into 15.2.16 must then be positive. Since the b_{ij} coefficients are negative, it follows that B must be positive if all the column sums Sb_{ij} are positive. Consequently, if B_{11} is Hicksian, the presence of positive column sums in B implies that B must also be Hicksian.

If we were to consider the column sums of B_{11}, these would have to be positive if the column sums of B were all positive, since the column sums of B_{11} are the same as the sums of columns 2, 3, and 4 of B with the negative terms b_{12}, b_{13}, and b_{14} deleted from the respective sums. Thus, if B has positive column sums, it must be the case that all lower-ordered principal minors also have positive column sums. Consequently, what holds between B and B_{11} must hold between any lower-ordered principal minor and its own minors of the next lower order. Therefore, to complete the proof of the column sum rule, it is necessary only to show that the second-order principal minors are positive. Consider the minor

$$\begin{vmatrix} b_{11} & b_{12} \\ b_{21} & b_{22} \end{vmatrix} = b_{11}b_{22} - b_{12}b_{21},$$

which could be negative with positive b_{ii} and negative b_{ij}. However, adding the elements of each row to the elements of the first row, we get

$$\begin{vmatrix} b_{11} + b_{21} & b_{12} + b_{22} \\ b_{21} & b_{22} \end{vmatrix} = (b_{11} + b_{21})b_{22} - (b_{12} + b_{22})b_{21},$$

which must have positive column sums if B does so, and since $b_{22} > 0$, while $b_{21} \le 0$, the determinant must be positive. We conclude that in a gross-substitutes model (positive diagonal and negative off-diagonal elements) a sufficient condition for stability is that all column sums be positive.

This stability condition is sufficient although it is by no means necessary. Consider the determinant

$$\begin{vmatrix} 1 & -\frac{1}{2} & -\frac{1}{4} \\ 0 & \frac{1}{4} & 0 \\ 0 & 0 & \frac{1}{2} \end{vmatrix} = \frac{1}{8}.$$

The characteristic roots of the model are, respectively, -1, $-\frac{1}{4}$, and $-\frac{1}{2}$, and the system is therefore stable. The determinant itself and all its second-order principal minors are positive. However, the sum of the elements in column two is $-\frac{1}{4}$. Consequently, the condition that all column sums be positive is a sufficient condition for stability but by no means a necessary one.

15.3 MULTICOUNTRY TRADE AND THE MULTICOUNTRY MULTIPLIER

The various tools of analysis that we have forged permit us to move directly into an examination of multisectoral multiplier models. Problems involving multisectoral income flows have been extensively analyzed by Metzler* within an international trade context and by Chipman† and Goodwin‡ within a multiregional context. The models are quite similar and we will, in the main, restrict ourselves to a review of Metzler's model of multicountry trade.

Define b_1 as the marginal propensity to spend of country 1, where this concept represents the combined increase in spending on consumption, investment, and imports that is induced by a change in income in country 1 of \$1.00. Next, let m_{j1} be the marginal propensity of country 1 to import from country j, and let $m_1 = m_{21} + m_{31} + \cdots + m_{n1}$ be the *total* marginal propensity of country 1 to import. The marginal propensity of country 1 to spend internally is therefore given by $b_1 - m_1$ which, in Chipman's terminology, is 1's marginal propensity to intraspend.

In equilibrium the level of spending in each country equals its level of income, and we may therefore write the set of static equations

$$
\begin{aligned}
y_1 &= (b_1 - m_1)y_1 + & m_{12}y_2 + \cdots + & m_{1n}y_n + a_1, \\
y_2 &= & m_{21}y_1 + (b_2 - m_2)y_2 + \cdots + & m_{2n}y_n + a_2, \quad (15.3.1) \\
&\ \ \vdots \\
y_n &= & m_{n1}y_1 + & m_{n2}y_2 + \cdots + (b_n - m_n)y_n + a_n.
\end{aligned}
$$

The term b_1y_1 is the total level of induced spending by country 1. When the level of imports m_1y_1 is deducted, we get $(b_1 - m_1)y_1$, which therefore is the level of induced domestic spending by the economic units of country 1. To this must be added the level of exports from country 1 to countries 2 through n, namely $m_{12}y_2 + \cdots + m_{1n}y_n$, and the level of autonomous spending, a_1. The combined total equals the level of spending in country 1 which, in equilibrium, equals the level of income.

By the usual dynamic assumptions that the rate of income change is proportional to the difference between expenditures and income, we can write

$$
\begin{aligned}
Dy_1 &= k_1[(b_1 - m_1 - 1)y_1 + & m_{12}y_2 + \cdots + & m_{1n}y_n + a_1], \\
Dy_2 &= k_2[& m_{21}y_1 + (b_2 - m_2 - 1)y_2 + \cdots + & m_{2n}y_n + a_2], \\
&\ \ \vdots \\
Dy_n &= k_n[& m_{n1}y_1 + & m_{n2}y_2 + \cdots + (b_n - m_n - 1)y_n + a_n]. \\
& & & (15.3.2)
\end{aligned}
$$

---

* L. A. Metzler, "Underemployment Equilibrium in International Trade," *Econometrica*, **X** (April, 1942); and "A Multiple-Region Theory of Income and Trade," *Econometrica*, **XVII** (October, 1950).

† J. S. Chipman, "The Multi-Sector Multiplier," *Econometrica*, **XVII** (October, 1950).

‡ R. M. Goodwin, "The Multiplier as Matrix," *Economic Journal*, **LIX** (December, 1949).

In matrix form this set of simultaneous differential equations may be written

$$DY = KI[(M - I)Y + A], \qquad (15.3.3)$$

where

$$KI = \begin{bmatrix} k_1 & 0 & \cdots & 0 \\ 0 & k_2 & \cdots & 0 \\ \vdots & & & \vdots \\ 0 & 0 & \cdots & k_n \end{bmatrix}$$

and

$$(M - I) = \begin{bmatrix} b_1 - m_1 - 1 & m_{12} & \cdots & m_{1n} \\ m_{21} & b_2 - m_2 - 1 & \cdots & m_{2n} \\ \vdots & & & \vdots \\ m_{n1} & m_{n2} & \cdots & b_n - m_n - 1 \end{bmatrix}. \qquad (15.3.4)$$

In equilibrium $DY = 0$ and 15.3.3 becomes $(M - I)Y + A = 0$, so that the vector of equilibrium income levels, $\bar{Y}$, is

$$\bar{Y} = (I - M)^{-1}A. \qquad (15.3.5)$$

Replacing DY by the trial solution, $q(Y - \bar{Y})$, and A by $(I - M)\bar{Y}$ in Eq. 15.3.3, we get

$$[qI + KI(I - M)](Y - \bar{Y}) = 0, \qquad (15.3.6)$$

where $[qI + KI(I - M)]$ is the characteristic matrix and $(Y - \bar{Y})$ is the characteristic vector. If the equation is to hold for all values of the characteristic vector, the characteristic matrix must be singular and its determinant must therefore be zero. Accordingly,

$$|qI + KI(I - M)|$$

$$= \begin{vmatrix} q + k_1(1 - b_1 + m_1) & -k_1 m_{12} & \cdots & -k_1 m_{1n} \\ -k_2 m_{21} & q + k_2(1 - b_2 + m_2) & \cdots & -k_2 m_{2n} \\ \vdots & & & \vdots \\ -k_n m_{n1} & -k_n m_{n2} & \cdots & q + k_n(1 - b_n + m_n) \end{vmatrix} = 0$$

$$(15.3.7)$$

is the characteristic determinant.

If all marginal propensities to import are nonnegative, that is, $m_{ij} \geq 0$, while the marginal propensity to spend minus the total marginal propensity to import is less than $+1$ for each country, the model fits into the gross-substitutes class where all diagonal elements of the determinant of coefficients are positive and all off-diagonal elements are negative or zero. When this is the case, the Hicks conditions are necessary and sufficient conditions for stability of equilibrium, and the values of the reaction coefficients have no bearing on stability. Consequently, the system is stable when

$$|I - M| = \begin{vmatrix} 1 - b_1 + m_1 & -m_{12} & \cdots & -m_{1n} \\ -m_{21} & 1 - b_2 + m_2 & \cdots & -m_{2n} \\ \vdots & & & \vdots \\ -m_{n1} & -m_{n2} & \cdots & 1 - b_n + m_n \end{vmatrix}$$

$$(15.3.8)$$

and all its lower-ordered principal minors are positive.

In a simple one-country multiplier model stability would require that the marginal propensity to spend must be less than unity. However, in the multi-country trade model it appears that the diagonal elements $1 - b_i + m_i$ could be positive while yet all terms such as $1 - b_i$ are negative. The dampening effect of imports serves as a brake on expansion much as does the dampening effect of saving.

Let us replace the notation $|I - M|$ by the more compact notation, V. Adding the elements of each column of V (15.3.8) to the corresponding elements of the first row, we get

$$V = \begin{vmatrix} 1 - b_1 & 1 - b_2 & 1 - b_3 & \cdots & 1 - b_n \\ -m_{21} & 1 - b_2 + m_2 & -m_{23} & \cdots & -m_{2n} \\ -m_{31} & -m_{32} & 1 - b_3 + m_3 & \cdots & -m_{3n} \\ \vdots & & & & \vdots \\ -m_{n1} & -m_{n2} & -m_{n3} & \cdots & 1 - b_n + m_n \end{vmatrix}. \quad (15.3.9)$$

Inspection of this determinant shows that it is of the gross substitute class and that its column sums are positive provided that each country's marginal propensity to spend is less than one. It follows, via our analysis of the last section, that if all countries' marginal propensities to spend are less than one, the system is necessarily Hicksian and stable. Conversely, via the Cauchy expansion of the last section (Eq. 15.2.16), it follows that if all marginal propensities to spend are greater than one, V would be negative if V_{11} is positive, and V therefore could not be Hicksian, so the system would be unstable. Thus, a stable system requires that at least some countries have marginal propensities to spend that are less than unity. Since the positive-column sum condition is a sufficient condition for stability, but not a necessary one, one economy may be dynamically unstable in isolation. If trade is opened up, a rise in income may raise imports more rapidly than exports and the two-country combination could then become stable. However, if both countries have marginal propensities to spend in excess of unity, any increase in income in either country would raise spending in the combined countries by more than the combined increase in income, and the entire system would be unstable.

With the assumption that all marginal propensities to import are non-negative and that all marginal propensities to spend are less than unity, we can go on to the derivation of some comparative-static results, confident that these results will be correct because they ensure stability of equilibrium.

Total differentiation of the static equations (15.3.1) yields

$$
\begin{aligned}
dy_1 &= (b_1 - m_1)dy_1 + & m_{12}dy_2 + \cdots + & m_{1n}dy_n + da_1, \\
dy_2 &= & m_{21}dy_1 + (b_2 - m_2)dy_2 + \cdots + & m_{2n}dy_n + da_2, \\
&\;\vdots \\
dy_n &= & m_{n1}dy_1 + & m_{n2}dy_2 + \cdots + (b_n - m_n)dy_n + da_n,
\end{aligned}
$$

$$(15.3.10)$$

which we may rewrite as

$$
\begin{aligned}
(1 - b_1 + m_1)dy_1 & & -m_{12}dy_2 \cdots & & -m_{1n}dy_n &= da_1, \\
-m_{21}dy_1 + (1 - b_2 + m_2)dy_2 \cdots & & -m_{2n}dy_n &= da_2, \\
\;\vdots \\
-m_{n1}dy_1 & & -m_{n2}dy_2 \cdots (1 - b_n + m_n)dy_n &= da_n,
\end{aligned}
$$

$$(15.3.11)$$

and in matrix form as

$$(I - M)dY = VdY = dA. \tag{15.3.12}$$

Premultiplying the matrix equation by V^{-1} gives the static multiplier

$$dY = V^{-1}dA. \tag{15.3.13}$$

From the stability condition and Mosak's theorem it follows that all elements of V^{-1} are positive. Consequently, our first comparative-static result is that no country can suffer a decline in income as the result of an increase in autonomous spending somewhere in the system.

Consider next the special case of an increase in autonomous spending in country 1 alone. The vector dA now becomes

$$
dA = \begin{bmatrix} da_1 \\ 0 \\ \vdots \\ 0 \end{bmatrix},
$$

and Eq. 15.3.11 becomes

$$
\begin{aligned}
(1 - b_1 + m_1)dy_1 & & -m_{12}dy_2 \cdots & & -m_{1n}dy_n &= da_1, \\
-m_{21}dy_1 + (1 - b_2 + m_2)dy_2 \cdots & & -m_{2n}dy_n &= 0, \\
\;\vdots \\
-m_{n1}dy_1 & & -m_{n2}dy_2 \cdots + (1 - b_n + m_n)dy_n &= 0.
\end{aligned}
$$

$$(15.3.14)$$

Using Cramer's rule to solve for the change in income in country 1, we get

$$dy_1 = (V_{11}/V)da_1 \tag{15.3.15}$$

or

$$\frac{dy_1}{da_1} = \frac{V_{11}}{V} \tag{15.3.16}$$

as the multiplier of country 1 with respect to an increase in its own level of autonomous spending.

Via the stability condition, we know that both V and V_{11} are positive and dy_1/da_1 is therefore positive. An increase in autonomous expenditure in a country must therefore raise its own level of income.

Similarly,

$$\frac{dy_2}{da_1} = \frac{V_{12}}{V}, \tag{15.3.17}$$

and this, too, must be positive, provided that not all the marginal propensities to import of other countries from country 2 are equal to zero. We conclude that an increase in autonomous spending in country 1 tends to raise income throughout the world economy and that it cannot lower income anywhere.

If all economies were isolated from each other, all marginal propensities to import would equal zero, and it would then be the case that

$$V = \begin{vmatrix} 1 - b_1 & 0 & \cdots & 0 \\ 0 & 1 - b_2 & \cdots & 0 \\ \vdots & & & \vdots \\ 0 & 0 & \cdots & 1 - b_n \end{vmatrix} = (1 - b_1)(1 - b_2) \cdots (1 - b_n).$$

Similarly, V_{11} would reduce to $(1 - b_2)(1 - b_3) \cdots (1 - b_n)$ and V_{12} would equal zero. Consequently, the multipliers given in 15.3.16 and 15.3.17 reduce to

$$\frac{dy_1}{da_1} = \frac{1}{1 - b_1} \quad \text{and} \quad \frac{dy_2}{da_1} = 0,$$

respectively. In an isolated economy the multiplier with respect to an internal increase in autonomous spending reduces to the conventional multiplier, equal to the reciprocal of one minus the marginal propensity to spend. The multiplier with respect to an external increase in autonomous spending, of course, is zero.

If country 1 is so small that a change in its income level produces no change in spending elsewhere, all dy_j $(j = 2, \ldots, n)$ terms equal zero and Eqs. 15.3.11 reduce to

$$(1 - b_1 + m_1)dy_1 = da_1,$$

from which we obtain the well-known "small-country" multiplier,

$$\frac{dy_1}{da_1} = \frac{1}{1 - b_1 + m_1}.$$

The general multiplier for economy 1 given by Eq. 15.3.16 can be shown to lie between the isolation and the small-country extremes. Since

$$\frac{dy_1}{da_1} = \frac{V_{11}}{V} = \frac{V_{11}}{(1 - b_1 + m_1)V_{11} - m_{12}V_{12} - \cdots - m_{1n}V_{1n}},$$

it follows that

$$\frac{dy_1}{da_1} = \frac{1}{(1 - b_1 + m_1) - m_{12}(V_{12}/V_{11}) - m_{13}(V_{13}/V_{11}) - \cdots - m_{1n}(V_{1n}/V_{11})}.$$

Since all terms such as (V_{1j}/V_{11}) are positive via Mosak's theorem and since all m_{ij} propensities to import are positive, it follows that

$$\frac{dy_1}{da_1} > \frac{1}{1 - b_1 + m_1},$$

and the general multiplier is therefore greater than the small-country extreme.

Similarly, since V is unchanged when all elements of a column are added to the corresponding elements of its first row, we have

$$V = \begin{vmatrix} 1 - b_1 & 1 - b_2 & \cdots & 1 - b_n \\ -m_{21} & 1 - b_2 + m_2 & \cdots & -m_{2n} \\ \vdots & & & \vdots \\ -m_{n1} & -m_{n2} & \cdots & 1 - b_n + m_n \end{vmatrix}. \qquad (15.3.18)$$

It follows that the multiplier V_{11}/V may be written

$$\frac{dy_1}{da_1} = \frac{1}{(1 - b_1) + (1 - b_2)(V_{12}/V_{11}) + \cdots + (1 - b_n)(V_{1n}/V_{11})}.$$

Mosak's theorem ensures that all ratios V_{1j}/V_{11} are positive. Therefore if all $1 - b_j$ terms are positive, the multiplier must be less than the conventional multiplier $1/(1 - b_1)$. We may therefore conclude that if all the marginal propensities to spend are less than unity,

$$\frac{1}{1 - b_1} > \frac{dy_1}{da_1} > \frac{1}{1 - b_1 + m_1}.$$

It follows from 15.3.18 that

$$V = (1 - b_1)V_{11} + (1 - b_2)V_{12} + \cdots + (1 - b_n)V_{1n},$$

and from 15.3.11 that

$$V = (1 - b_1 + m_1)V_{11} - m_{12}V_{12} - \cdots - m_{1n}V_{1n}.$$

These two expressions may be rearranged as

$$\frac{V_{11}}{V} = \frac{1}{1 - b_1} - \frac{(1 - b_2)V_{12}}{(1 - b_1)V} - \cdots - \frac{(1 - b_n)V_{1n}}{(1 - b_1)V}$$

or, by substitution,

$$\frac{V_{11}}{V} = \frac{1}{1 - b_1 + m_1} + \frac{m_{12}V_{12}}{(1 - b_1 + m_1)V} + \cdots + \frac{m_{1n}V_{1n}}{(1 - b_1 + m_1)V},$$

and it is therefore evident that dy_1/da_1 may be expressed as a function of the other country multipliers, either as a deduction from the conventional multiplier, or as an addition to the small-country multiplier. Finally, note that since the maximum value of m_1 is b_1, the minimum value that the multiplier can have is $+1$.

The third comparative-static problem we wish to consider is the effect of the changes in autonomous spending in country 1 on all countries combined. The total income change in the world economy is the sum of the individual country income changes. The total world multiplier is therefore

$$\sum_1^n \frac{dy_j}{da_1} = \frac{V_{11} + V_{12} + \cdots + V_{1n}}{V} = \frac{\sum V_{1j}}{V}. \tag{15.3.19}$$

If all marginal propensities to spend are equal, it would follow from 15.3.18 that

$$V = (1 - b) \begin{vmatrix} 1 & 1 & \cdots & 1 \\ -m_{21} & 1 - b_2 + m_2 & \cdots & -m_{2n} \\ \vdots & & & \vdots \\ -m_{n1} & -m_{n2} & \cdots & 1 - b_n + m_n \end{vmatrix} = (1 - b) \sum V_{1j}.$$

Consequently,

$$\frac{\sum dy_j}{da_1} = \frac{\sum V_{1j}}{(1 - b) \sum V_{1j}} = \frac{1}{1 - b},$$

and we therefore conclude that the multicountry multiplier reduces to the conventional multiplier if all marginal propensities to spend are equal.*

Our fourth comparative-static problem is to consider the effect of a redistribution of the level of autonomous spending between countries with the overall level of autonomous spending remaining fixed. If consumer tastes change in such a way that citizens of country 2 suddenly decide that they prefer to purchase automobiles from 1 rather than from their own car makers, the vector dA becomes

$$dA = \begin{bmatrix} da \\ -da \\ 0 \\ \vdots \\ 0 \end{bmatrix},$$

---

* Chipman, *op. cit.*, proves this for both the dynamic and the static multipliers.

and Eqs. 15.3.11 become

$$(1 - b_1 + m_1)dy_1 \qquad -m_{12}dy_2 \qquad -m_{13}dy_3 \cdots -m_{1n}dy_n = da$$
$$-m_{21}dy_1 + (1 - b_2 + m_2)dy_2 \qquad -m_{23}dy_3 \cdots -m_{2n}dy_n = -da$$
$$-m_{31}dy_1 \qquad -m_{32}dy_2 + (1 - b_3 + m_3)dy_3 \cdots -m_{3n}dy_n = 0$$
$$\vdots$$
$$-m_{n1}dy_1 \qquad -m_{n2}dy_2 \qquad -m_{n3}dy_3 \cdots$$
$$+ (1 - b_n + m_n)dy_n = 0.$$

$$(15.3.20)$$

Using Cramer's rule to solve for dy_1, we get

$$V dy_1 = \begin{vmatrix} da & -m_{12} & -m_{13} & \cdots & -m_{1n} \\ -da & 1 - b_2 + m_2 & -m_{23} & \cdots & -m_{2n} \\ 0 & -m_{32} & 1 - b_3 + m_3 & \cdots & -m_{3n} \\ \vdots & & & & \vdots \\ 0 & -m_{n2} & -m_{n3} & \cdots & 1 - b_n + m_n \end{vmatrix}.$$

Adding all elements of each column to the corresponding elements of the second row, we see that this becomes

$$V dy_1 = \begin{vmatrix} da & -m_{12} & -m_{13} & \cdots & -m_{1n} \\ 0 & 1 - b_2 & 1 - b_3 & \cdots & 1 - b_n \\ 0 & -m_{32} & 1 - b_3 + m_3 & \cdots & -m_{3n} \\ \vdots & & & & \vdots \\ 0 & -m_{n2} & -m_{n3} & \cdots & 1 - b_n + m_n \end{vmatrix},$$

and when we expand the determinant about the second row and divide by V, we get the multiplier

$$\frac{dy_1}{da} = \frac{(1 - b_2)V_{11,22} + (1 - b_3)V_{11,23} + \cdots + (1 - b_n)V_{11,2n}}{V}.$$

$$(15.3.21)$$

All of the terms $V_{11,2i}$ are cofactors of the Hicksian determinant V_{11}. Via Mosak's theorem, it follows that they are positive and that (dy_1/da) is positive. We conclude that a redistribution of autonomous expenditures from country 2 to country 1 must raise income in country 1. Thus even though the reduction in autonomous spending in country 2 may tend to reduce income in 2, and therefore imports from 1, the increase in autonomous spending in 1 will overcome this effect.

Any country that receives an autonomous increase in spending will enjoy an income increase. It follows that any country that loses autonomous spending will suffer a decline in income. Consequently, income in country 2 must drop.

Formally, we can use Cramer's rule to solve for dy_2 in Eqs. 15.3.20 to obtain

$$\frac{dy_2}{da} = \frac{-[(1 - b_1)V_{22,11} + (1 - b_2)V_{22,13} + \cdots + (1 - b_n)V_{22,1n}]}{V},$$

which is negative.

Incomes in third countries may rise or fall when autonomous spending is transferred from country 2 to country 1. If the marginal propensity of country 3 to export to country 1 (m_{31}) is greater than its marginal propensity to export to country 2, and/or if the income increase in 1 is greater than the fall in country 2, there will be the strong presumption that income in country 3 will rise, provided the net induced expansion of exports to 1 and 2 is not offset by an induced reduction in exports to third countries.

To summarize: Provided that all marginal propensities to import are non-negative, a sufficient condition for stability is that all marginal propensities to spend be less than unity. If this condition is obtained, the following comparative-static results will be obtained:

1 An increase in autonomous spending tends to raise the level of income in all countries, and cannot reduce income in any country.

2 An increase in autonomous spending in country 1 will raise income in country 1 and tend to raise income in other countries. It cannot reduce income anywhere.

3 The multiplier in country 1 with respect to an increase in internal exogenous spending will be at least as large as the small country multiplier, and no greater than the conventional (isolation) multiplier, and it can have a value no less than $+1$.

    a) It follows as a corollary of 2 and 3 that an increase in autonomous spending must raise the level of world income by at least as much as the increase in autonomous spending.

4 If all marginal propensities to spend are equal, the world multiplier (the ratio of the total change in world income to the change in autonomous spending) will equal the conventional multiplier equal to the reciprocal of 1 minus the marginal propensity to spend.

5 Given a constant level of autonomous spending, a transfer of autonomous spending from economy 2 to 1 will raise income in 1, lower income in 2, and it may either raise or lower income in third countries. The total effect on world income of such a redistribution is ambiguous.

15.4 CONCLUSIONS

The discussion of the last section illustrates, as clearly as any of our other examples, the principle with which this book has been concerned. We cannot tell from a system of equations such as 15.3.11 very much about the effect of a change in the pattern of autonomous spending upon the income levels of the respective economies. However, stability conditions impose restrictions upon the values of parameters and, together with assumptions about their signs, it becomes possible to derive fruitful comparative-static theorems.

We have only scratched the surface in this book. However, we hope that a reasonable (necessary but not sufficient) set of tools has been provided so that the additional questions which economists ask can be approached intelligently. Among these are the following: What are the conditions for stability in a multiple-market system where some commodities are complimentary and where the convenient gross substitutes assumption is therefore abandoned? Similarly, what are the conditions for stability, and therefore for the validity of comparative-static results, in intersectoral income transmission models where the possibility that some sectors produce inferior goods is admitted? Finally, is it possible to derive stability conditions when only the signs of the coefficients of a matrix are known? This is the body of analysis which is known as "qualitative economics," and it represents the vanguard of the sort of work for which this volume has hoped to serve as an introduction.

REFERENCES

J. S. Chipman, "The Multi-Sector Multiplier," *Econometrica* (October, 1950).

T. F. Dernburg and D. M. McDougall, *Macro-Economics* (New York: McGraw-Hill, 1963), Chapter 15 and Appendix.

R. M. Goodwin, "The Multiplier as Matrix," *Economic Journal* (December, 1949).

D. Hawkins and H. Simon, "Note: Some Conditions of Macroeconomic Stability," *Econometrica* (July–October, 1949).

J. R. Hicks, *Value and Capital* (London: Oxford University Press, 1939), Chapter 5.

L. A. Metzler, "Stability of Multiple Markets: the Hicks Conditions," *Econometrica*, **XII** (October, 1945).

L. A. Metzler, "Underemployment Equilibrium in International Trade," *Econometrica* (October, 1950).

L. A. Metzler, "A Multiple-Region Theory of Income and Trade," *Econometrica* (October, 1950).

J. Mosak, General Equilibrium Theory in International Trade, *Cowles Commission Monograph No. 7* (Evanston, Ill.: The Principia Press, 1944), pp. 49–51.

R. A. Mundell, "The Appropriate Use of Monetary and Fiscal Policy for Internal and External Stability," *International Monetary Fund Staff Papers* (March, 1962).

P. A. Samuelson, *Foundations of Economic Analysis* (Cambridge, Mass.: Harvard University Press, 1947), Chapters 9 and 10.

P. A. Samuelson, "The Stability of Equilibrium: Comparative Statics and Dynamics," *Econometrica* (April, 1941).

P. A. Samuelson, "The Stability of Equilibrium: Linear and Nonlinear Systems," *Econometrica* (January, 1942).

INDEX

Acceleration principle, 90, 136. *See also* Accelerator, Multiplier-accelerator interaction
Accelerator, assymetry of, 162
 general form of, 169
 Goodwin's nonlinear, 166–168
Adaptive expectations. *See* Cobweb theorem
Aggregate demand, 11
Arithmetic series, summation of, 125 n
Automatic stabilizers, 9, 18

Balanced budget, as inappropriate target, 26
Balanced budget multiplier, and income taxation, 17–20
 and lump-sum taxation, 17
Behavioral relations, comparative static, 4
 dynamic, 4
Bernoulli equation, 186, 199
 solution to, 186–188
Bonds, demand for, 31
 value in relation to interest rate, 31
Brown, E. C., 21 n
Buchanan, J. M., 123 n
Business Cycles, 3. *See also* Cycle models, Nonlinear models of the cycle

Calculus of finite differences, 94
Capital accumulation in the Goodwin model, 166. *See also* Nonlinear models of the cycle: Goodwin model
Capital Coefficient, 120. *See also* Growth models: Harrod-Domar
Capital consumption allowance, 10. *See also* Depreciation
Cauchy expansion, 277, 280
"Ceiling." *See* Output ceiling
Chenery, H. B., 78
Chipman, J. S., 278
Clark, P. G., 78
Cobb-Douglas function. *See* Production function

Cobweb theorem, 5–8, 100–102
 adaptive expectations, and derivation of normal price, 103–104
 as learning, 103
 and market stability, 102–106
 and "normal" price, 103–104
 stability range of, 105–106
 as first-order difference equation, 100
 and public prediction, 108–109
 stability of, 108–109
 stability of solution, 102
 use in public forecasting models, 100
Cofactor, defined, 49
 alien cofactors, expansion of determinant in terms of, 59–60
Comparative statics, defined, 3
 erroneous solutions in, 46
Complementary commodities, 262
Complex roots, imaginary numbers and, 143
 modulus of, 144
 properties of, 143
 as trigonometric functions, 144
Compound interest, as difference equation, 95–96
Consumption, defined, 10
 function, 10
Correspondence principle, 8, 232
 and values of parameters, 233
Cramer's rule, 40 n, 48, 50
Cycles. *See also* Nonlinear models of the cycle
 cobweb, 7
 multiplier-accelerator, 7
 nonlinear, 155–173

Deflationary gap, 13
Delay multipliers, 88
Demand, change in price and quantity, 5
 equilibrium, 4
De Moivre's theorem, 144

288